FILIPINOS IN CANADA

Disturbing Invisibility

Edited by Roland Sintos Coloma, Bonnie McElhinny, Ethel Tungohan, John Paul C. Catungal, and Lisa M. Davidson

By 2010, the Philippines had become Canada's largest source of short- and long-term migrants, surpassing China and India, both of whose populations vastly exceed that of the Philippines. The fourth-largest visible minority group in the country, the Filipino community is frequently associated with such figures as the victimized nanny, the selfless nurse, and the gangster youth. On one hand, these narratives concentrate attention, although in narrow and stereotypical ways, on critical issues. On the other, they render invisible other serious matters facing Filipino communities.

This groundbreaking work, the first wide-ranging edited collection on Filipinos in Canada, explores gender, migration and labour, youth, and the politics of identity. Looking at these from the vantage points of anthropology, cultural studies, education, geography, history, information science, literature, political science, sociology, and women and gender studies, *Filipinos in Canada* provides a strong foundation for further research.

ROLAND SINTOS COLOMA is an assistant professor in the Department of Sociology and Equity Studies in Education at the Ontario Institute for Studies in Education, University of Toronto.

BONNIE McELHINNY is an associate professor in the Department of Anthropology and director of the Women and Gender Studies Institute at the University of Toronto.

ETHEL TUNGOHAN is a PhD candidate in the Department of Political Science and the Women and Gender Studies Institute at the University of Toronto.

JOHN PAUL C. CATUNGAL is a PhD candidate in the Department of Geography and Program in Planning at the University of Toronto.

LISA M. DAVIDSON is a PhD candidate in the Department of Anthropology at the University of Toronto.

Filipinos in Canada

Disturbing Invisibility

Edited by Roland Sintos Coloma,
Bonnie McElhinny, Ethel Tungohan,
John Paul C. Catungal, and
Lisa M. Davidson

UNIVERSITY OF TORONTO PRESS
Toronto Buffalo London

© University of Toronto Press 2012
Toronto Buffalo London
www.utppublishing.com
Printed in the U.S.A.

Reprinted 2013

ISBN: 978-1-4426-4540-0 (cloth)
ISBN: 978-1-4426-1349-2 (paper)

Printed on acid-free paper

Library and Archives Canada Cataloguing in Publication

Filipinos in Canada : disturbing invisibility / edited by Roland
Sintos Coloma . . . [et al.].

Includes bibliographical references and index.

ISBN 978-1-4426-4540-0 (bound)   ISBN 978-1-4426-1349-2 (pbk.)

1. Filipino Canadians – History.   2. Filipino Canadians – Social
conditions.   3. Filipino Canadians – Economic conditions.   I. Coloma,
Roland Sintos

FC106.F4F54 2012   305.89′921071   C2012-902656-5

University of Toronto Press acknowledges the financial assistance to its
publishing program of the Canada Council for the Arts and the Ontario
Arts Council.

University of Toronto Press acknowledges the financial support for its
publishing activities of the Government of Canada through the Canada
Book Fund.

 Canada Council   Conseil des Arts
for the Arts   du Canada

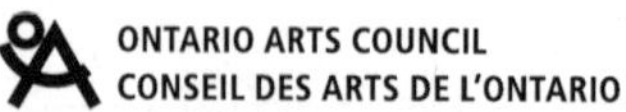 ONTARIO ARTS COUNCIL
CONSEIL DES ARTS DE L'ONTARIO

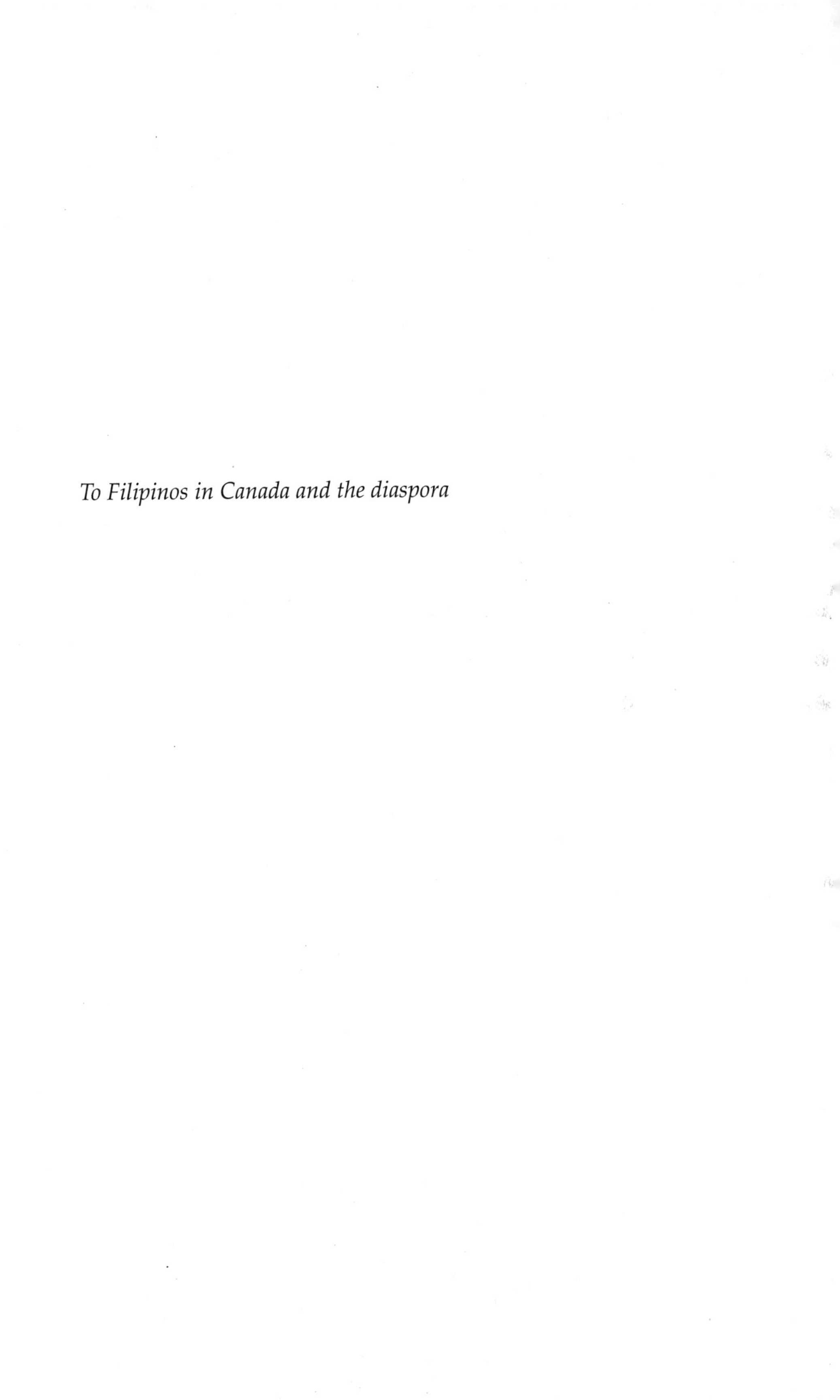

To Filipinos in Canada and the diaspora

Contents

Part Two: Gender, Migration, and Labour

Part Three: Representation and Its Discontents

Illustrations

Tables

Acknowledgments

'Ang hindi lumingon sa pinangagalingan ay hindi makakarating sa parooroonan' is an old Filipino adage that can be roughly translated as 'those who do not look at their origins will not reach their destination.' In that spirit, we would like to look back and thank everyone who has been involved in our journey to make this book a reality.

First and foremost, we truly appreciate the trust, patience, and intellectual and creative engagement of all of the contributors to this book. We could not have done this without you.

We thank the Social Sciences and Humanities Research Council (SSHRC) for providing us with a research workshop grant to convene the 'Spectres of Invisibility: Filipino/a Lives in Canada' national symposium in October 2009 and to help subsidize the publication of this edited volume. For the symposium, we also acknowledge the generous financial support of our University of Toronto co-sponsors, including the Ontario Institute for Studies in Education–Office of the Associate Dean of Research and Graduate Studies; Faculty of Arts and Science–Dean's Office; Faculty of Information–Dean's Office; Women and Gender Studies Institute; Asian Institute–Munk Centre; Centre for Southeast Asian Studies–Munk Centre; Department of Geography and Program in Planning; Department of Adult Education and Counseling Psychology; and Department of Sociology and Equity Studies in Education.

To the wonderful scholars and colleagues who visited University of Toronto over the past few years and shared their insights and enthusiasm for this project–Delia Aguilar, Leonora Angeles, Yen Le Espiritu, Lisa Lowe, Martin Manalansan, Geraldine Pratt, Vicente Rafael, Rhacel Salazar Parreñas, and Neferti Tadiar–we appreciate your generous intellectual and professional support.

We extend our gratitude to our editors and the staff at the University of Toronto Press: thank you to Virgil Duff for his patience, good humour, and enthusiasm in guiding us through the first stages of the publication process and to Doug Hildebrand for his insights and initiative in ensuring the success of our manuscript. We also want to thank Judy Williams and Anne Laughlin, who respectively copyedited and facilitated the production of the manuscript.

We acknowledge Kim Abis for her good-humoured and excellent organizational skills. Thanks to Sheena Resplandor for her cheerful and efficient assistance, to Yuko Bessho, Catherine Febria, and Laura Kwak for their logistical and technical support during the symposium, to Joy Sioson and the Philippine Women's Centre of Ontario for their delicious catering at the symposium, and to Meghan Sbrocchi for helping with assorted tasks related to our manuscript. Thanks to Eric Tigley for the book cover artwork and the symposium poster, to Ron Philipps Aberin for the symposium website, to Wayne Chu for helping to draft press releases, and to Alistair T. Giffin for assisting us with manuscript formatting. We also thank Paul Tsang and Mary Macri of OISE/UT Sociology and Equity Studies in Education for handling many of the financial details for the SSHRC grant, the national symposium, and this book.

There are numerous individuals whom we thank for their involvement in our project. These include those who participated in the first set of 'Kritikal Kolektibo' meetings where we began conversations on what 'Filipina/o Canadian Studies' as a field would look like, those who attended and participated in the 'Spectres of Invisibility' symposium in 2009, and those who helped us turn the presented papers into a collective manuscript. Special thanks go to Rose Ann Torres and Jo SiMalaya Alcampo for their participation at the symposium, and to Patrick Alcedo, Carolina S. Austria, Jenilee Austria, Yuko Bessho, Celia Correa, Catherine Febria, Lynne Milgram, Paul Pabello, Mykelle Pacquing, Rommel Salvador, Maita Sayo, Toshiko Tsujimoto, and Teodosia Villarino for taking part in our ongoing Kritikal Kolektibo discussions.

Finally, we express our appreciation to our families and friends, whose love and support were invaluable in giving us the strength over the past two years to see this project to completion.

FILIPINOS IN CANADA

Disturbing Invisibility

PART ONE

Difference and Recognition

Chapter 1

Spectres of (In)visibility: Filipina/o Labour, Culture, and Youth in Canada

BONNIE McELHINNY, LISA M. DAVIDSON,
JOHN PAUL C. CATUNGAL, ETHEL TUNGOHAN,
AND ROLAND SINTOS COLOMA

Haunted by Hypervisibility and Invisibility

Prevalent conversations in Canadian media, academic, and politicized public spheres tend to represent and account for Filipina/os living in Canada within the tropes of victimized nanny, selfless nurse, and problematic gangster youth. These images render hypervisible in social and academic spaces certain problems facing Filipina/o communities, which are then calcified as Filipina/o stereotypes. These spectral figures on the one hand enable the visibility of Filipina/o lives in Canada within a narrow purview and on the other hand contribute to the misrecognition and alienation of the diverse experiences and histories of Filipina/os in Canada. Filipina/o communities are therefore put into the paradoxical position of being invisible *and* hypervisible: invisible because numerous kinds of people, problems, and achievements are ignored, and hypervisible because only the stereotypes are deemed relevant and significant for public circulation. In this landmark volume, the first wide-ranging edited collection of academic writings on Filipina/os in Canada, we ask how the contours of Canadian political, academic, and social institutions, both historical and contemporary, shape the politics of Filipina/o invisibility, visibility, and hypervisibility, how Filipina/o spectral figures 'haunt' processes, representations, and agentive experiences of being and becoming Filipina/o Canadians, and how we can disrupt and intervene in the prevailing themes of the spectral figures that have come to define the lives of Filipina/os in Canada.

Although the contributors to this volume recognize the productive value of academic and community-based knowledge projects in rendering Filipina/o communities more visible, they nonetheless critically interrogate the value of 'visibility' as a response to invisibility. The phrase 'spectre of invisibility' is drawn from Oscar Campomanes (1992), and is central to a recent collection on emerging areas of inquiry for Filipina/o studies in the United States (Tiongson, Gutierrez, and Gutierrez 2006). Campomanes reflects on the ways that the specificities of Filipina/o experiences challenge the boundaries in traditional and emergent disciplines, and asks scholars to consider the particular sets of social relations and historical circumstances that define the terms of their intelligibility (see also Pisares 2006). 'Visibility' is not just a metaphor in Canada, however, but a legal and census category. According to the Canadian *Employment Equity Act*, 'visible minorities' are defined as 'persons, other than Aboriginal persons, who are non-Caucasian in race or non-white in colour.' The language of 'visibility' is widely contested by activists and critical theorists for the ways that it naturalizes white hegemony (see, e.g., contributions in Dua and Robertson 1999, especially Das Gupta 1999), as it hypervisibilizes and homogenizes people of colour. Ideologically, 'visible minority' status is often collapsed into immigrant status, which renders racialized groups as outside of the nation. Sunera Thobani (2007) argues that 'the racialized category immigrant paradoxically helps sustain the myth of the nation as homogeneous by constructing as perpetual strangers those to whom the category is assigned, even when they are second and third generation Canadians' (76).

This has been evident most recently, and chillingly, in the *Maclean's* magazine article entitled '"Too Asian"?' published in November 2010 in its widely read annual issue ranking universities in Canada. The article quoted White students saying that they would not attend the University of Toronto because it was 'too Asian,' which in their view meant it was so academically focused that White students could not have fun and might have a difficult time competing. The term 'Asian' was used in the article to designate both Asian Canadians and international students from Asia.[1] A related article in the *Toronto Star* recycled some of the quotations from the *Maclean's* article, arguing that 'the growing profile of students of Asian heritage on many campuses is fuelling resentment among some non-Asian students and even concerns among some university administrators about the demographic make-up of their student bodies.' Numerous commentators have critiqued these two articles for the role they play in fuelling racist and anti-immigrant sentiments, constructing a normative White standard for citizenship, education, and success, perpetuating stereotypes, and erasing the political and economic challenges that many racialized students face in gaining access to higher education.

These articles flag some of the limitations of the hegemonic notions of multiculturalism, which are also taken up in the first section of this volume. The racialized and cultural classification system of Canadian census data is an institutionalized mode of liberal democratic governmentality, which, in its ideal form, highlights state interest in promoting plurality and tolerance. The census categorization of Canadian 'ethnic' groups is oddly parsed and mixed, allocating population differences in terms of ethnic, racial, national, and regional groupings. The Canadian census specifies the following groups as 'visible minorities': Chinese, South Asians, Blacks, Arabs, West Asians, Filipinos, Southeast Asians, Latin Americans, Japanese, Koreans, and Pacific Islanders. Some categories lump ('Blacks' includes Black Canadians whose families have been in Canada for generations, as well as certain first-generation immigrants from, e.g., Nigeria)[2] and some split (note the separation of Filipinos from other Southeast Asians).

Understanding the categories as problematic, we can nonetheless use census statistics carefully and critically to give approximate numbers of some groups as well as a picture of how racialization works in Canada. The numbers are perhaps more useful for Filipina/os than for other groups, given that Filipina/os are designated as a separate category. In 2006, the census found 5,068,100 individuals who identified as visible minorities (Statistics Canada 2006). Visible minorities made up 16.2 per cent of the total population in Canada; however, visible minorities are 22.8 per cent of the provincial population of Ontario (where 54.2 per cent of visible minorities live), and 42.9 per cent of the 5.1 million residents of metropolitan Toronto. The largest visible minority groups in Canada are South Asians (24.9 per cent of visible minorities), Chinese (24.0 per cent of visible minorities), Blacks (15.5 per cent of visible minorities), Filipina/os (8.1 per cent of visible minorities), Latin Americans (6.0 per cent of visible minorities), Arabs (5.2 per cent of visible minorities), Southeast Asians (4.7 per cent of visible minorities), West Asians (3.1 per cent of visible minorities), Koreans (2.8 per cent of visible minorities), and Japanese (1.6 per cent of visible minorities). In Toronto, the four largest visible minority groups are South Asians (684,100), Chinese (486,300), Blacks (352,200), and Filipina/os (172,000). Filipina/os are thus the fourth largest visible minority group in Canada, and in Toronto, the site of many of the studies in this volume. The top three source countries for migration to Canada in recent years are all Asian (China, India, and the Philippines). In 2010, the Philippines was the largest source of migrants to Canada (Citizenship and Immigration Canada 2010).

Given the problematic ways that 'visibility' is linked to racialization in Canada, the solution to invisibility is probably not helpfully framed as visibility, or even as recognition, which still implies the centrality of White recognition. Following the work of Elizabeth Povinelli (2002) on Australian multiculturalism, the political practice of recognition entails a 'méconnaissance' or misrecognition by which a subject is known through correlations and negations. 'Visibility' could also be seen as simply integrating Filipina/os into disciplinary and national formations in ways that do not fully question the ways those disciplines and nations are currently defined. Campomanes (1995), paraphrasing Frantz Fanon, notes that recognition can lead to representation, but there can be representation without recognition. In a recent analysis of the way Muslim practices are being adapted to life in France, and French law and practices to Muslims in France, anthropologist John Bowen (2010) notes that the integration of any marginalized or new group into a national political tradition requires the national tradition to come to terms with its own contradictions. One of the Canadian contradictions is a celebration of multiculturalism in a context of continuing privilege for White people. Thobani (2007) notes that the official form of Canadian multiculturalism 'facilitated both a material inclusion of increased numbers of immigrants within the population *and* their simultaneous exclusion from the nation, primarily through their reification as cultural outsiders' (147). Ultimately, the solution is not fetishizing either difference or similarity in the way that the metaphor of visibility does; instead, the focus should be on substantive equality, not only in formal and legal realms, but also in what Thobani calls the 'social customs and conventional acts' of empowered citizenship in daily encounters (78). A review of Filipina/o histories in Canada suggests some of the challenges to be overcome before such equality is achieved as well as some of the ongoing forms of activism addressing those challenges.

The migration of Filipina/os to Canada has followed a pattern different from that of other immigrant groups. Filipina/os in Canada are predominantly recent immigrants (Kelly 2006). Less than 5 per cent of the population arrived prior to 1970, and in 2001 over half of all Filipina/os in Canada had arrived in the previous ten years. Overwhelmingly Filipina/os have tended to settle in Canada's urban centres (Kelly 2006). Toronto and Vancouver, alone, account for nearly two-thirds of all Filipina/o (immigrant and non-immigrant) residents; nearly 80 per cent

Table 1.1. Geography of Filipina/os in Canada

City	% of Filipina/os
Toronto	43
Vancouver	18
Winnipeg	10
Montreal	8
Calgary	5
Edmonton	5
Other	13

Source: adapted from Kelly 2006, 14

of those identifying as Filipina/o live in four cities: Toronto, Vancouver, Winnipeg, and Montreal (see table 1.1).

Toronto has 133,675 Filipino residents, comprising 43.3 per cent of Filipina/os in Canada (Kelly 2006, 13). This volume concentrates largely on Toronto, with a few chapters also addressing Montreal and Vancouver, because Toronto has been such a significant site for Filipina/o migration. We recognize, however, the importance of studies of Filipina/os in other locations in Canada, for the ways that this will contribute, as Lusis (n.d.) argues, towards understanding the experiences of migrants and racialized minorities when there may be less extensive community-based resources to draw upon and for a fuller understanding of the relationship between so-called 'gateway' cities and others.[3]

The recent increase in Filipina/o migration has three key explanations: (1) changes in Canadian immigration regulations in the 1960s that stressed educational qualifications and skills as the main conditions of admission regardless of country of origin (Aranas 1983); (2) conditions of underdevelopment and poverty in the Philippines, which are experienced by worker-citizens as unemployment, underemployment, lack of educational and occupational opportunities, and low standards of living (Briones 1984; Eviota 1992); and (3) the role United States imperialism has played in constructing North America as an attractive destination goal for Filipina/os (Choy 2003; Espiritu 2003).

In the 1950s and 1960s, Filipina/os who migrated to Canada were mostly professionals, including nurses, doctors, laboratory technicians, and office workers recruited to overcome the labour shortages in those fields (see Aranas 1983; Chen 1998; Cusipag and Buenafe 1993; Kelly 2006; Laquian 1973; see also Damasco in this volume). These workers entered Canada as landed immigrants (i.e., permanent residents); many originally worked in the United States under various exchange programs, and migrated north when their two-year visas expired (Cusipag and Buenafe 1993). This first wave of immigrants peaked in 1974.

In the late 1970s, the age, gender, and occupational profile of the Filipina/o community changed. There was a higher proportion of clerical, manufacturing, and service workers, and the number of Filipina/o professionals declined, reaching its lowest point in the mid-1980s (Laquian 1973). With the addition of the family reunification category in 1978, many family members of the first wave of immigrants were sponsored, leading to a dramatic increase in the number of Filipina/o senior citizens (Aranas 1983; Bustamante 1984; Chen 1998). The Philippine government's labour export policy that took effect during the Marcos regime (Bakan and Stasiulis 1997b, Stasiulis and Bakan 2005) and the Canadian government's efforts to recruit Filipina/os to work in Canada through migrant worker schemes like the Foreign Domestic Workers Program, the Live-In Caregiver Program, and the Temporary Foreign Worker Program explain the concentration of Filipina/os in 'non-professional' fields.

During the 1980s, many Filipinas entered Canada through the Foreign Domestic Movement (FDM), a program in which domestic workers were eligible to apply for landed immigrant status after two years of live-in service with a designated employer. Programs earlier in the twentieth century had recruited European domestics, but these domestics were given landed immigrant status upon arrival. As recruitment turned to the Caribbean in the mid-1950s and the Philippines in the 1980s, access to citizenship rights was more sharply curtailed. In 1992, the FDM was replaced by the Live-In Caregiver Program (LCP), a program in which the eligibility criteria for entry to Canada became more restrictive than in the FDM, partly in the name of improving the quality of childcare in Canada (Bakan and Stasiulis 1997a; Arat-Koç 1999). Close to 12 per cent of all Philippine-born arrivals came under the LCP category between 1980 and 2001, and Filipinas overwhelmingly accounted for those recruited (25,846 out of 32,474 or 79.6 per cent of arrivals) (Kelly 2006). Filipina/o migration to Canada has thus taken on a distinctive gendered skew, with almost 60 per cent of immigrants from the Philippines during this period being women (ibid.). Many professionals – nurses, midwives, graduate students in linguistics, office workers – now come to Canada through the LCP, hoping to find work in their own careers afterward, though these hopes are often dashed (see Harris-Galia 2011 for an account of a Filipina who was hired as a live-in caregiver in the Arctic and then became a nurse).[4] The different political and economic realities and policies shaping Filipina/o migration in different periods have also created socio-economic class distinctions and bifurcations among Filipina/os in Canada, with earlier migrants in predominantly white-collar employment and middle-class positions, and later migrants in primarily working-class jobs (see Eric in this volume).

Despite the differences in employment patterns among earlier and later waves of Filipina/o immigrants, what has always remained constant is the dominance of women in Filipina/o migration flows (see Chen 1998). In 2006, 57.5 per cent of all Filipina/os in Canada were women (Statistics Canada 2006). Hence, for the Filipina/o community, immigration and migration inevitably bring to the fore gender concerns, specifically those of women.[5] Gender concerns are linked to the forms that youth concerns take as well; for example, youth problems stemming from family separation and family reunification when women act as the primary wage earners but are kept apart and then reunited with their families (Pratt with UKPC 2003; Pratt with PWC 2009; Pratt 2012; de Leon 2009). Several rich documentary films exist on these topics (Ami 2002; Bautista and Boti 1999; Boti 1997; Boti and Bautista 1992). For these reasons, this volume has two sections focusing on gender and labour as well as youth issues.

Whereas Filipina/o Canadian studies participates in and engages with critical race studies in Canada, it also extends diaspora studies in relation to Philippine studies. The transnational experiences of Filipina/os in Canada cannot be completely divorced from the politics and economy of the Philippines. The vast majority of Filipina/os in Canada were born in the Philippines, although the numbers of those who are second- and third-generation Filipina/o Canadians are growing. Therefore, the beliefs and outlook in life for most Filipina/os in Canada are both derived from Canada and the Philippines. If one were to read the various Filipina/o Canadian newspaper publications or listen to different conversations in Filipina/o Canadian homes, businesses, and gatherings, one could see and hear ardent interest in what is taking place in both nations. For instance, community events feature services and discussions on the Live-In Caregiver Program, fundraising efforts for the Mayon Volcano eruption in 2006 and for Typhoon Ondoy in 2009, and report backs on the Philippine national elections in 2010. Meanwhile, the Internet blogs talk about the victories of boxer Manny

Pacquiao as well as Filipina/o Canadians in beauty pageants like the *Binibining Pilipinas* (Miss Philippines) competition and in television shows like 'Canadian Idol' and 'Pinoy Big Brother.' Consequently, as we examine how Filipina/o Canadians imagine their community, feel their sense of belonging, and indicate their reference points, it would be difficult and indeed inappropriate to clearly demarcate which aspects are identifiably Canadian and which ones are indelibly Filipina/o. Neither Canadian studies nor Philippine studies fully acknowledges these transnational dynamics yet. This volume thus aims to contribute to re-imagining both.

Genealogies of Filipina/o Canadian Scholarship

The analytic dilemmas of developing Filipina/o Canadian studies are like and unlike those faced by Filipina/o American studies. Compared to the literature on Filipina/o American studies, scholarship on Filipina/os in the Canadian context is decidedly more recent and more limited in scope.[6] A shorter immigration history has meant a shorter incubation period for both cultural and academic production. There is also a generational difference between Filipina/o American studies and Filipina/o Canadian studies. In Canada, it is possible to see a rather bimodal distribution of Filipina/o academic labour that reflects the two generations of migration that are flagged elsewhere in this volume (see chapters by Damasco and Eric; see also Chen 1998), in that early professionals worked in their fields, while later arrivals were de-skilled. A very small number of full professors, many now emeritus and Philippine-born, came at the time when a larger number of professionally trained Filipina/os were being hired as professionals;[7] however, the largest number of Filipina/o scholars are much younger (graduate students and assistant or junior associate professors), and many are Canadian-born (see Coloma in this volume). By contrast, a number of distinguished Filipina/o scholars in the United States (e.g., Rick Bonus, Catherine Ceniza Choy, Martin Manalansan, Rhacel Salazar Parreñas, Vicente Rafael, Dylan Rodriguez, Sarita See, and Neferti Tadiar) have become important figures not only in Filipina/o American studies, but also in the broader fields of anthropology, ethnic studies, Asian American studies, women's studies, history, cultural studies, and sociology.

Moreover, the geopolitical relationship between the Philippines and the United States has conditioned the contours of Filipina/o American studies. Spanish colonial interests in the Philippines began in 1521, with the arrival of Ferdinand Magellan. In 1898, while the United States was at war with Spain over Cuba, Filipina/o revolutionaries renewed an armed campaign against the Spanish colonizers that had begun some years earlier, and with help from Americans whom they understood as allies, declared independence from Spain, and established the first Republic of the Philippines. However, Spain, rather than surrendering to Filipina/o revolutionaries, ceded the Philippines to the United States for twenty million dollars. The United States retained formal sovereignty until the end of the Second World War. U.S. colonization led to an extensive and intertwined, but not necessarily mutually beneficial, network of trade interests, labour migration, cultural and educational exchanges, and military experiences and structures. The spectre of U.S. imperialism in the Philippines continues to haunt Filipina/o lives and livelihoods in the United States as well as the diaspora's relationship to the Philippines itself. Because of the historical and contemporary U.S. imperial interest in the Philippines, Orientalist research on Filipina/os has been ongoing since (and perhaps even before) Frederick Jackson Turner declared the U.S. frontier to be abroad. Anthropologists, for example, displayed Filipina/os to Americans in Chicago and St Louis during their respective World's Fairs (1893 and 1904) (see McElhinny in this volume); and the *National Geographic* has had a sustained history of publishing about the Philippines and Filipina/os since 1898 (Tuason 1999). As a consequence, in much of the work on the Philippines or Filipina/o American issues from the United States, the central and most extended disciplinary approach has, arguably, been history which fosters continuing discussions about the impact of U.S. imperialism on the Philippines and on the metropolitan United States (Anderson 2006; Go 2008; Hoganson 1998; Kramer 2006; Rafael 1995, 2000; Salman 2001). The respective research of this volume's editorial team members Roland Sintos Coloma, as a U.S.-trained scholar, and Bonnie McElhinny, as an American and now also Canadian scholar, both working in Canada, also contributes to these historical perspectives (Coloma 2012, 2011, 2009, 2006; McElhinny 2009, 2007a, 2007b, 2005).

Canadian scholarship on Filipina/os and the Philippines has not been as sustained, in large part because the imperialist drive to 'know' the Filipina/o 'Other' at home and abroad has not existed quite as formally as it has in the U.S. context. Moreover, compared to Canada, the U.S. socio-political climate of civil rights and Third World activism that gave rise to the institutionalization of 'ethnic studies' did not exist in quite the same way in Canada. One can argue that the governmental construction of a benevolent Canadian multiculturalism, a federal policy and national 'brand' (Mackey 2002; Thobani 2007), has contributed to the de-fanging of an agonistic racial politics that names government-sanctioned social exclusion of certain ethnic groups, including Filipina/os (Goonewardena and Kipfer 2005). Given that one major *raison d'être* for ethnic studies is precisely an anti-racist politics that names state violence, the absence of such a scholarly field in Canada (though see the work of Researchers and Academics of Colour for Equality/Equity [RACE] in elaborating a network of scholars engaged in critical studies of race in Canada) – which might include Filipina/o Canadian studies – has meant that such academic engagement has not occurred in quite the same way in the Canadian academy. To date, no institutionalized national academic network of scholars of Filipina/o Canadian issues exists, and when national gatherings on such issues do occur, they tend to be organized by community groups that focus on particular themes. In contrast, the U.S. academy boasts regular meetings of scholars of Filipina/o American issues, as well as Asian American studies more broadly. Asian American studies has two journals, *Amerasia* and the *Journal of Asian American Studies*, and faculty at the University of the Illinois at Urbana-Champaign organized a 'state of the field' national conference on Filipino Studies in March 2008. The rich possibilities of Filipina/o Canadian studies are hence yet to be fully realized.

This is not to say that there hasn't been knowledge production on Filipina/o lives in Canada. In 1989, Anita Beltran Chen, the founding chair of the department of sociology and anthropology at Lakehead University, published a review article on information available on Filipina/o Canadians to date in *Canadian Ethnic Studies* (later reprinted in Chen 1998). She reported forty-three publications (books, conference proceedings, pamphlets, articles, MA theses, and government publications). Many of these, however, were not devoted exclusively or even largely to Filipina/os; some focused on immigrants or on Asian Canadians. (Indeed, Chen serves as one of the earliest analysts of Asian Canadian experience, as she advocates for the distinction of Filipina/o Canadian experiences from others.) Documents which included information on Filipina/os were, for instance, documents produced by the Canadian Department of Manpower and Immigration and by the Canadian Department of State, Multicultural Directorate, or Nagata's (1987) article on Southeast Asian Christians in Toronto. The overwhelming majority of the publications were, Chen (1998) notes, 'descriptive and exploratory in nature, if not purely impressionistic' (50). Many, like Chen, drew on data from government publications to offer demographic descriptions of Filipina/os in Canada: sex ratios, age profiles, work profiles, province of residence, etc. Others focused on the question of Filipina/o 'adjustment' in Canada. Chen concluded that these early studies on 'adaptation and adjustment of Filipino Canadians provide evidence that they do not seem to have encountered serious difficulties in integrating themselves into the mainstream of Canadian society' (53). It is difficult to assess the nature of this claim. It could be that the early immigration policies which recruited professionals and permitted Filipina/os to work in jobs reasonably similar to those for which they were trained meant that many reported more positive experiences compared to those in more recent studies. It could also, however, be that studies tended to survey precisely those most likely to report satisfactory experiences. Or, it could be that the analysts or respondents themselves under-emphasized reports of discrimination, in an attempt to stress what Filipina/os could contribute to Canadian society. Studies on adjustment often focus on 'integration' into society and whether new immigrants 'fit' into Canada, in ways that lead to an emphasis on Western cultural influences in the Philippines and fluent command of English, rather than instances of racism.

Looking closely at Laquian (1973), the earliest extended study done on Filipina/os, allows us to illuminate these points in more detail. Laquian's meticulous account is based on a survey of Filipina/os whose names were generated with the help of the Filipina/o labour attaché and taken from rosters of Filipina/o associations. Although Laquian's study is often cited as a demographic portrait of the Filipina/o community in the early 1970s, it is important to flag the ways in which her methodological approach would have been skewed towards reaching professionals. As she notes, surveys tend to be returned generally by respondents with higher levels of education. Furthermore, Filipina/o associations of the time tended to be civic and social, and thus also likely to be the domain of professional participants (see also the critiques offered by the working-class respondents in Budohan's (1972) study in Winnipeg, who noted the ways in which putatively social and civic organizations tended to work for the benefit of professionals). Finally, and most crucially, martial law was declared in the Philippines on September 22, 1972. Lacquian had intended to administer her survey in October 1972 and waited until January 1973, because of concerns that people would be wary or fearful of responding to the survey. It is difficult to believe that this brief wait would have made much of a difference; in addition, the survey was accompanied by a letter of endorsement from the Office of the Labour Attaché, Embassy of the Philippines, so there was an explicit link to the government. The document was published by the United Council of Filipino Associations in Canada, an organization that Cusipag and Buenafe (1993, 33) argue had, until the mid-1980s at least, a relatively conservative profile in the community in no small part because it sanctioned the imposition of martial law. Laquian's respondents were mostly middle-level professionals (e.g., nurses, teachers, medical technologists, and clerks) who were highly mobile (22 per cent had resided in the United States before residing in Canada, many likely as part of the exchange visitor program which had a two-year limit on stay). Most reported that their initial adjustment was easy and that they were not pushed from the Philippines, but pulled to Canada. Once again, it is difficult to assess the nature of this claim, one which seems to avoid direct critique of the political or economic challenges in the Philippines, since 65 per cent of the respondents also noted that they felt they would have better opportunities in Canada. Strikingly, the problem most commonly reported in adjusting to Canada was climate, followed by the non-recognition of work experience and education in the Philippines and the employers' requirement of Canadian experience. Nonetheless, and somewhat oddly, the majority report no experiences with discrimination. This suggests that further probing is necessary to understand what respondents meant by the notion of 'discrimination.' Another striking point of concern was the critique of a recent tax system implemented by the Philippine government, which many experienced as onerous and unfair, leading them to consider abandoning their Philippine citizenship for Canadian citizenship. Laquian produced a list of recommendations at the end of the document, all of which were focused on what 'Philippine authorities' could do better to manage these transnational flows. She did not advise restricting or harshly controlling emigration, noting that 'it may become a source of unrest and discontent if potential migrants are denied the right to seek "better opportunities"' (27). Instead, her recommendations would serve to draw nets of governmentality more closely around Filipina/os abroad, in ways that would be inattentive to the concerns that Filipina/os were likely to have about government surveillance after the declaration of martial law. The call for increased data-gathering and monitoring anticipates, and may even have shaped, policies later implemented in the Philippines (e.g., the monitoring of overseas Filipina/os and their income by the Philippine

Overseas Employment Administration). Her recommended policies include maintaining closer liaisons with the Canadian government and closer ties to individuals and organizations, expanding consular assistance, re-examining existing taxation laws, arranging accreditation agreements, and regulating recruiters, travel agents, and fly-now-pay-later promotions. The report does not focus on changes that Canadian government or organizations need to undertake, unlike many later studies which focus on what Canadian institutions need to do to change policy in order to redress racist assumptions and practices.

Cusipag and Buenafe (1993) display more attentiveness to the political conditions of knowledge production and to a wider range of political and economic activities in Windsor, Ottawa, and Toronto. Their account, drawing significantly on community newspapers, offers a rich set of chapters on topics such as the histories of various civic and social organizations, the rise and fall of various newspapers, radio programs, and television shows, the role of churches in community-building and politics, the significance of sports and dance, and participation in formal politics and labour activism. It contains the longest history of anti-Marcos activism by Filipina/o Canadians (Cusipag is a former Manila newspaperman jailed by Marcos in the first months of the dictatorship) (see also Ordonez and Sayo 1980). It also contains glimpses of the ways activists involved in the anti-martial law movement later moved on to other causes which now feature centrally in Filipina/o and other social justice circles (for instance, Fely Villasin later played a prominent role in Intercede, an organization which advocates on behalf of domestic workers). This engagingly written account still tends to highlight professional experiences and activism rather than working-class ones; however, it flags a number of topics which deserve extensive further research. Indeed, the breadth of topics addressed is in contrast with a deeper, but more narrow, focus over the past twenty years, a focus provoked by the increasing centrality of Filipinas who work as live-in caregivers to community dynamics.

Over the past two decades, the overwhelming focus in Filipina/o Canadian studies has been an issue which is treated briefly at the end of Cusipag and Buenafe's (1993) narrative of the 1960s to the 1990s, and that is the issue of live-in caregivers. This research has documented the abysmal conditions for Filipina/o caregivers, citing deplorable labour conditions, the constraints of the live-in requirement, and the de facto lack of legal protections (Arat-Koç 2001; Bakan and Stasiulis 1997a; Elvir 1997; England and Stiell 1997; Macklin 1994; Pratt 1999; Stasiulis and

Bakan 2005; Velasco 1997; see chapters in part 2 of this volume). Similarly, many scholars have critiqued the policy contexts that enable the entry of live-in caregivers in Canada. Geraldine Pratt (1999), for example, has critiqued the racialization of gendered care work in Canada, as well as the Philippine state's labour export policy and the Canadian state's prioritization of this form of social reproduction. In so doing, scholars have made more visible the injustices perpetrated by labour migration policies. Whether or not this work has led to the reconsideration of Canadian state benevolence is, of course, another issue; indeed, Roland Sintos Coloma (in this volume) suggests that Canadian national pedagogy has learned precious little from this literature.

Much of this recent work has been conducted by academics, often in collaboration with community organizations. In Canada, the sites from which most work on Filipina/o Canadian issues have been generated are anthropology, geography, political science, and women's studies because of the ways that these disciplines are often closely articulated with policy discussions and grassroots political discussions. In some cases, White anthropologists and geographers based in Canada whose research careers began with work in the Philippines find themselves compelled to follow migratory trajectories, commodity chains, development practices, or corporate investments, which lead back to Canada (Barber 2000, 2008; Kelly 2006; Kelly, Astorga-Garcia, Esguerra, and CASJ 2009). The significant impact of the Live-In Caregiver Program on the form of Filipina/o migration explains the centrality of these issues to the discipline of women's studies; indeed, an overwhelming proportion of the academic scholars working on Filipina/o Canadian issues have appointments or cross-appointments in women's studies, which itself has, not without controversy or discussion, taken on a social scientific shape in many universities. At the University of Toronto, documentary films, such as *Brown Women, Blonde Babies* (Boti and Bautista 1992), are widely used in undergraduate classes; two of the winners of the University of Toronto undergraduate paper prize in women's studies in the past five years have written about the Live-In Caregiver Program. In all these disciplines, transnational analytics have been mobilized which question the ways concepts such as migration and racialization are bounded by a national rubric when the focus is on settlement or assimilation.

Filipina/o Canadian studies has a strong community-based focus: community organizations in general conduct research on the communities they serve in order to document the challenges that their target communities face and to support their advocacy efforts in the areas of policymaking and social service provision. Filipina/o community organizations are no different in this regard. In addition, rather than re-creating the wheel, early and recent academic scholarship on Filipina/os has strategically tapped into this community-based expertise to benefit from the sophisticated scholarly labour that community organizations already have as well as the established history of scholarship that already exists through these organizations. This is particularly true of scholars who are not of the community, whose access to the community might not be as easy, and who, for ethical and political reasons, require community buy-in to make their research feasible. An early example of an organization drawing on community expertise was Bustamente's work with the Multicultural Historical Society, which employed members of various communities to do oral histories with community members; some findings from this research were published in a popular history magazine (e.g., Bustamente 1982, 1983, 1984, 1986). Other books have been self-published or published in small local presses by indefatigable researchers and journalists involved in community organizations (cf. Cusipag and Buenafe 1993). Pratt's work with the Philippine Women's Centre (PWC) and other Filipina/o migrant groups in Vancouver and elsewhere has been going on since the mid-1990s (Pratt in collaboration with PWC and UKPC/FCYA 2007; Pratt 2012); Habiba Zaman has also closely worked with the PWC (Zaman 2003; Zaman with Diocson and Scott 2007). Similarly, Philip Kelly's work with Toronto's Community Alliance for Social Justice (CASJ) has been going on for a few years (Kelly, Astorga-Garcia, Esguerra and CASJ 2009), while Sedef Arat-Koç (2001) engaged in a participatory action research project under the auspices of Intercede with live-in caregivers to produce *Caregivers Break the Silence*.

Given the centrality of community organizations in knowledge production about Filipina/os in Canada, it is perhaps not surprising that the political priorities of community-based organizations are mirrored in the focus on labour, political economy, gender equality, and, increasingly, police violence and racial profiling also evident in this volume. Collaborative work with community organizations also occurs not just to facilitate academic access to communities or to tap into the relatively recent acceptance of community-based work as valid academic work. Benefits also accrue to community organizations. This can happen in several ways. Collaboration can serve to strengthen relationships between academics and the communities they study. Collaboration can also enable the application and use of academic research in community-based political advocacy, and can strategically tap into the social capital of 'academic expertise.' Scholars of Filipina/o Canadian lives sometimes act as advocates, speaking to governments and the media about their work in order to rally public and government support towards policy changes.

This notion of scholars as 'advocates for' suggests scholars are outside the communities they represent, and in recent years, researching as an 'outsider' or 'ally' is a common scenario in Filipina/o Canadian studies, with several White scholars successfully forming long-term research relationships with Filipina/o community organizations (see Pratt in collaboration with PWC and UKPC/FCYA 2007 for a description of certain kinds of research rejected by Filipina/o activists in Vancouver). This is evidence, in part, of the process of racialization and de-skilling evident elsewhere; those with scholarly expertise are working in other areas. Increasingly, however, as is evident in this edited collection, there are scholars of Filipino descent who do research in the broad field of Filipina/o Canadian studies. Being an insider poses its own set of restrictions. As Chen (2010) notes, 'those who live and work "in the local" are often mired in complex networks of relations that erode critical distance' (227). In addition, given the diversity of both political opinions around solutions to issues facing Filipina/os and the very definition of what it means to be Filipina/o, one potential issue is whether access to Filipina/o community organizations will get policed along notions of 'fit,' both in terms of normative political ideas and definitions of identity. Simply put, if scholars of Filipina/o descent refuse to frame their work and politics around an already calcified political project and understanding of Filipina/o-ness, is there room for critique elsewhere? And should these problems arise and Filipina/o Canadian scholars choose to work independently instead of forcing 'fit,' critiques might be levelled at scholars for separating themselves from 'community' in its singularized iteration. Striking a fine balance between these two scenarios is a difficult task indeed, and the question of what it means to do 'insider' research itself calls up what being an 'insider' really means. In this case, identifying as Filipina/o Canadian might not be enough to claim a place in community-based research. Filipino/a Canadian scholars may be required to prove their adherence to 'authentic' Filipino/a-ness through their familiarity with cultural norms, their political beliefs and political actions, and their willingness to promote certain defined Filipino community interests. As members of the so-called academic elite, Filipino/a Canadian scholars may be placed under an obligation not to let community organizations down by doing research that enhances the well being of Filipinos in Canada. The problem, of course, is that there is no consensus on how this can be done.

How scholarship on Filipina/o Canadians is to take place is, therefore, an important terrain for potential conflict and contestation. Like other forms of academic knowledge production, this scholarship is beset with issues that have been and continue to be discussed internally. One particularly salient issue for the project of Filipina/o Canadian studies is the usefulness of imagining a singular, unitary 'Filipina/o' as an object of scholarly inquiry and political advocacy. Forming political and academic identities around the category 'Filipina/o' can be limiting insofar as it calcifies a unitary object that, in reality, is differentiated by regional, linguistic, cultural, political, and religious affiliations. It takes for granted Canadian census practices of constructing singularized communities around ethno-racial categories. The federal policy of multiculturalism, with its cultural mosaic approach, treats the census category 'Filipino' as a single tile that contributes to this mosaic, thereby enabling the lumping of Filipina/o bodies into a complex category that naturalizes sameness along particular ethno-national logics (compare Thobani 2007 on the communalizing logic of multiculturalism and the challenges it poses for certain forms of alliance and activism).

Perhaps for strategic reasons, some community organizations have also taken up the nation-state's practice of classifying Filipina/os into one unitary whole. It is not surprising that community organizations and scholars who take the nation-state as the target of political advocacy might need to strategically use the bio-political discourse of ethno-racial classification to further their aims. However, one of the dangers of this practice of lumping is that it could potentially become a way to hail not just a unitary whole, but a normative form of Filipina/o-ness. This is problematic insofar as it replaces one set of ethno-racial norms and forms of knowledge with other problematic forms of identity. Such practice poses an epistemological problem for scholars of Filipina/o Canadian studies. How can one study issues of relevance to Filipina/o Canadians without necessarily calcifying a normative Filipina/o identity? To this, there may be three potential solutions. The first is to refuse the naturalness of an imagined 'Filipina/o' subject by emphasizing *social construction* as the beginning of analysis (see Aguinaldo in this volume). On this, one might seek to understand how Filipina/o identities are constructed through legal/policy mechanisms, cultural production, and popular discourse. One might investigate the conditions of possibility through which the figure of the Filipina nanny emerged through the complex collision of racialization, gendering, and political economy. Implicit in this attention to the *genealogy* of Filipina/o issues is a refusal to take as given common understandings of Filipina/o.

A second approach is to frame politics around issues as opposed to identities. Along with refusing the identitarian commitment to a structuralist idea of identity, a focus on the politics of issues enables the formation of alliances across different identifications in multiple locations. For Filipina/o Canadians, for example, advocacy and research around Filipina live-in caregivers has called up transnational, national, and regional alliances with diverse women's, ethno-racial, migrant, and labour groups around the issue of gendered and racialized labour. Intercede, an organization supporting domestic workers based in Toronto, linked the concerns of women workers from the Philippines and the Caribbean (Arat-Koç 2001), while Stasiulis and Bakan (2005) compare the challenges faced by Filipina and Caribbean nurses in addressing racism in Canadian medical institutions. Moreover, organizations such as Gabriela in Toronto and Pinay in Montreal are part of national and transnational grassroots networks like Women United against Imperialism and the International Women's Alliance in order to establish joint campaigns on migration reform, trafficking, domestic work, and other issues with national and community women's organizations. Similarly, in developing strategies for addressing police violence and racial profiling, the Filipina/o community has collaborated with Black activists with long histories of addressing such concerns (Astorga-Garcia 2007). There are also political linkages between various groups of migrant workers. Domestic workers, seasonal agricultural workers, and temporary labour migrants under the Temporary Foreign Workers Program from the Philippines and from other countries face adverse living and working conditions, with some being denied access to permanent Canadian residency (see master's research undertaken by Monina Febria). Such commonalities lead to the formation of grassroots alliances between migrant workers to combat common problems (see PhD research being undertaken by Ethel Tungohan). Churches in Canada shape a multi-ethnic, faith-based approach to multiculturalism (see PhD research currently being undertaken by Lisa Davidson). In the case of Filipina/o Canadian studies, locating this nascent field of study *within* broader scholarly communities and networks (e.g., ethnic studies and women's studies) might also facilitate political alliances around issues of common importance.

A final approach is to emphasize how transnational and postcolonial politics and theories complicate how we might understand 'Filipina/o,' which is no longer legible only in the context of a sovereign Philippine state. Spanish and U.S. colonialism in the Philippines as well as the movements of Filipina/o populations all over the world render a simplistic understanding of Filipina/o-ness obsolete. For scholars of Filipina/o Canadian studies, it is difficult – and indeed irresponsible – to create a normative Filipina/o identity that neglects on-the-ground contestations of what it means to identify and be identified as part of Filipina/o Canadian studies.

Cultural Interventions: Academic, Artistic, and Other Workplaces

Anthropologist and playwright Dorinne Kondo (1995) argues that like many marginalized people, Asian Americans are often erased from, or stereotyped in, realms of cultural representation. The significance of cultural production, then, 'for those of us "on the margins" is a process of representing our emergent, always historically mediated identities, creating a space for us to "write our faces," to paraphrase the playwright/performance artist/novelist Han Ong' (49). In many emergent fields of inquiry, a variety of forms of cultural production (essays, poems, novels, paintings, songs, etc.) become the first articulation of key social, political, and cultural themes, perhaps in part because they may require less capital or formal training than academic scholarship often does. A longer history of presence, including settlement, has meant that Filipina/os in the U.S. context have had much more time to cultivate a cultural, particularly artistic, presence that lends itself to humanistic analysis (de Jesus 2005). In the Canadian case, cultural production by Filipina/os has a much shorter history. Where present, their impact has not been documented robustly by academic analysis (though see Ty in this volume). The archive of cultural products and the opportunity to engage these in cultural analyses are also expanding. Our volume thus includes a selection of cultural works presented at the national symposium from which this volume is derived – a poem by Carlo Sayo and Jean Marc Daga, and images by Celia Correa, Eric Tigley, Reuben Sarumugam, and Bryan Taguba. Other presenters at the conference have made comparable contributions – Jo SiMalaya Alcampo (an interdisciplinary artist born in Manila and raised in the eastern suburbs of Toronto) and R. Patrick Alcedo (a specialist in Southeast Asian dance). As an important first step, Ty (in this volume) sets an example for future cultural analytical work by engaging with community-based theatrical productions and what they say about gender, belonging, immigration, and nation. Groups such as the Toronto-based Asian Arts Freedom School offer opportunities for intercultural programming with other Asian groups, and the Kapisanan Arts and Cultural Centre, also in Toronto, offers a space for 'empowering artists and entrepreneurs through positive and critical cultural identification' (also see chapters by Balmes, Largo, and Pratt in this volume). The Magkaisa Centre organized the Maleta (Suitcase) project in 2010 in Toronto, an art exhibit focused on portraying Filipina/o Canadian women's resilience and on enhancing women's equality and human rights.

Critical and Comparative Studies of Race and Ethnicity in Canada

An academic volume on Filipina/o Canadian studies throws into sharp relief the state of 'minority studies' in multicultural Canada. Filipina/o Canadian studies is by no means minor in Canadian academic studies if the term denotes an inferior or inconsequential position. Although a nascent academic field, its status as part of minority studies, in actuality, reveals more about the rationalities, operations, and effects of mainstream intellectual and institutional discourses and structures in Canada. It also illuminates the possibilities and limits of various ontologies, epistemologies, and methodologies that are utilized and available for empirical work. Consequently, it shares a similar position with other interdisciplinary fields like women's studies, area studies programs like Caribbean studies and Middle Eastern studies, as well as race/ethnic studies programs like Black Canadian studies and Asian Canadian studies, whose intellectual currency, symbolic standing, and material allocation in scholarly and institutional venues continue to remain disputed and uncertain.

Admittedly, Filipina/o Canadian studies as a formal institutional enterprise does not exist in any Canadian institution of higher education. Research institutes, programmatic centres, and undergraduate and graduate courses that focus on Asia are numerous and well supported in the universities. For instance, University of Toronto has the Asian Institute at the Munk School for Global Affairs, and the Asian Institute houses the Centre for Southeast Asian Studies where two of this book's co-editors, Bonnie McElhinny and Roland Sintos Coloma, are affiliated as faculty specialists on the Philippines. Even Southeast Asian studies, however, is a relatively marginalized area for study (Rafael 1995), and the extent to which Southeast Asian studies programs articulate with Southeast Asian Canadians remains uneven. The biennial conference of the Canadian Council of Southeast Asian Studies has not featured a scholar of Philippine and Filipina/o Diaspora studies as a keynote speaker. Tellingly, at one colloquium planning session for Southeast Asian studies at the University of Toronto when Catherine Ceniza Choy was suggested as a possible speaker, one interlocutor suggested that the Centre for Diaspora and Transnational Studies was a more appropriate site for such a talk. Choy is author of *Empire of Care* (2003), a book on U.S. colonial influences on nursing education, programs for fostering Filipina/o nurses' employment in the United States, and the kinds of structural inequity and racism such nurses experienced. Moreover, no Canadian university yet offers, to our knowledge, regular instruction of any Filipina/o language. York University teaches regularly a studio course on Philippine dance cultures, and University of Winnipeg offered a summer institute on 'Migration and Development in the Philippines, 1960–2010.' Much less attention and resources, however, have been provided to the development and teaching related to Asians and particularly Filipina/os in Canada. Faculty members with scholarly and teaching interests in Filipina/o Canadian studies either include relevant readings in their general courses or, in very rare cases, offer specialized courses on Filipina/o Canadian studies. Bonnie McElhinny taught in 2006 what was probably one of the earliest university courses in Canada that exclusively focused on Filipina/os in Canada; she taught 'Gender and the Filipina/o Diaspora' in Women and Gender Studies. The students in that class undertook a life history assignment as a way of contributing to the growing body of research on Filipina/os in Canada, and then continued to conduct and analyse life histories for several years after (McElhinny, Yeung, Damasco, DeOcampo, Febria, Salonga 2009; McElhinny, Collantes, Yeung, Febria, Damasco, Salonga, DeOcampo ms). A number of these students are now undertaking their own research on Filipina/o issues as graduate students in U.S. and Canadian universities. Consequently, since Canada's academic gaze has been primarily directed externally to the west across the Pacific, this edited volume aims to shift the gaze and focus internally in order to enact a key objective of Filipina/o Canadian studies: to document and analyse the lived experiences and representations of Filipina/os in Canada.

The lack of formal institutional structures for Filipina/o Canadian studies has by no means limited its development as a scholarly endeavour. This volume grew from conversations between and among Canadian academics concerned with the intellectual enterprise of developing and introducing Filipina/o Canadian studies as a scholarly, political, and pedagogical project. As evinced in the bibliographies of the various chapters in this book, numerous journal articles, government and community reports, books, and graduate theses address the experiences and representations of Filipina/os in Canada. 'Spectres of Invisibility: Filipina/o Lives in Canada,' the first national symposium on Filipina/o Canadian studies, held in October 2009 at University of Toronto, served as the foundation for this book. The symposium featured a keynote address by Eleanor Ty and three panels, which became the organizing framework for this book. Attended by more than 130 people, the symposium was organized by Kritikal Kolektibo, a group of professors and students mostly from University of Toronto who are interested in Filipina/o studies, and supported generously by internal funding from various faculties, institutes, departments, and programs at University of Toronto as well as a workshop grant from the Social Sciences and Humanities Research Council. The Kolektibo was organized by Roland Sintos Coloma and began meeting in September 2008. Despite having only six members in its first meeting, the Kolektibo expanded gradually through word of mouth and today has over thirty regular members. The Kolektibo did this by disseminating news and advertising events that were relevant to the membership's interests through an internal listserv, by advertising lectures by visiting academics who have done work on Filipina/o issues (in recent years, this has included Yen Le Espiritu, Martin Manalansan, Rhacel Salazar Parreñas, Geraldine Pratt, Vicente Rafael, and Neferti Tadiar), and by holding monthly meetings where Kolektibo members discussed articles and book chapters that allowed the group to better understand Critical Filipina/o studies. The decision to convene Kritikal Kolektibo at the University of Toronto was no accident: not only are there more Filipina/os in Toronto than in any other part of Canada, but also the significant bulge in Filipina/o migration in the last two decades means that there is now a sizeable number of second-generation graduate and undergraduate students and a few faculty members interested in Filipina/o Canadian issues. It will be important to consider in the future how the Great Lakes' focus in Filipina/o Canadian scholarship might throw up questions and perspectives that are different from the West Coast–centred perspective evident in Filipina/o American studies.

Discussions at the 'Spectres of Invisibility' national symposium were often spirited and occasionally difficult, highlighting some key questions for continued academic and activist work as well as alliance construction. After the screening of *SCRAP*, a documentary film produced by Reuben Sarumugam and Bryan Taguba arguing for the elimination of the Live-In Caregiver Program (LCP), some audience members called instead for the review and reform of the LCP, arguing that even though many program participants see the program as flawed, they nonetheless also view it as an important gateway for immigration which, if closed, might make it more difficult to migrate to Canada. Others argued that no reform was possible for a form of labour that is best understood, in their view, as modern-day slavery. According to them, the LCP not only 'enslaves' live-in caregivers by making them live and work under oppressive conditions but also 'enslaves' poor countries like the Philippines by forcing them to continually export labour to rich countries like Canada, leading to their continued dependency. The conference was widely covered in community- and university-based newspapers. The Kolektibo's hope for what the conference might do was eloquently captured in commentary on the conference reported in the *McGill Daily*. Reporter Braden Goyette (2009) quoted Alex Felipe, who works with the Kapisanan Centre for Philippine Arts and Culture, as well as Migrante and Migrante Youth. Felipe lauded the conference, as he called for continuing work on the involvement of the community: 'Academia, when it's done well, speaks for the people. It compiles the voices of the people in a manner that's suitable for academics and scholars, but it's still the voice of the people.'

This volume thus arises out of, and contributes to, diasporic Philippine studies, Canadian studies, critical studies of race and multiculturalism in Canada, a nascent Asian Canadian studies, and transnational feminist studies. As editors and contributors, we pursue our inquiries from the academic vantage points of the social sciences, the humanities, and the arts, including anthropology, cultural studies, education, geography, history, information science, literature, political science, sociology, and women's studies. We attend to the historical and contemporary conditions that shape and impact the experiences and representations of Filipina/os in Canada.

In this book, various iterations of identity terms are used, signalling diverse and differently political ways of (self-) identifying with or against categorizations. For example, the title of the volume refers to 'Filipinos in Canada,' reproducing the most common way of designating people of Philippine ancestry in Canada. This designation mirrors governmental understandings of the population as seen in the Statistics Canada publication 'The Filipino Community in Canada' and other similar demographic profiles (Lindsay 2007). For the purpose of the book title, the term 'Filipino' was chosen at the strong suggestion of the University of Toronto Press, our publisher, because it is less clunky and more searchable in online and library databases.

The marketing logic of this choice, of course, has its limits, and we remain quite uneasy and ambivalent about it. As editors, we are actually more partial to 'Filipina/o,' the term that we proposed at the beginning of the publication process. It is also the term that we use in the title of this introduction, and the term of choice for some chapters in this volume. To us, 'Filipina/o' is an important political term because its dually gendered morphology signals the centrality of gender for Filipina/o lives in the Canadian context, a theme that is central to the theoretical contributions of several subsequent chapters and indeed to Filipina/o community organizing and activism in Canada. Moreover, following de Jesus (2005), we believe that the erasure of women in the term 'Filipino' maintains the invisibility of women's lives in academic analysis, rendering a nascent field constituted as simply 'Filipino studies' really androcentric. We also use the term in keeping with the political spirit of ensuring the importance of gender and its intersectionalities for Chicana/o (Elenes 1997) and Latina/o studies (Hernandez-Truyol 1997), fields that emerged in the 1960s and 1970s in the context of Third World and civil rights activisms in the United States.

As editors, we encouraged contributors to think about the feasibility of the term 'Filipina/o' for their own chapters. Some in fact did adopt this term, but not everyone did. The volume retains the diversity of terms out of respect for different people's political orientations and choices. It also does so to signal that there is no consensus among scholars of this nascent field about which term is best, or indeed among Filipina/o activists themselves.

The four sections in the book address the central themes that are germane to our inquiries: 'Difference and Recognition'; 'Gender, Migration, and Labour'; 'Representation and Its Discontents'; and 'Youth Spaces and Subjectivities.' The final chapters in the second, third, and fourth sections provide detailed responses to the chapters in that section. Two scholars from critical social sciences and public health, Nora Angeles and Jeffrey Aguinaldo, who served as discussants at the symposium on panels on labour and youth, have contributed revised versions of their comments to this volume, in ways which further describe, and much more extensively contextualize, each of these chapters; geographer Geraldine Pratt comments on the politics of cultural representation of Filipina/os, as she adds insights from her collaborative work with the Philippine Women's Centre in Vancouver on *Nanay*, a documentary play (Pratt and Johnson 2009).

The first section, 'Difference and Recognition,' considers how racial differentiation is – or is not – recognized in Canada, a country whose official state ideology is multiculturalism and which relies significantly upon immigration to sustain economic growth. In addition to the editorial team's introduction, this section includes chapters by literary scholar Eleanor Ty and by geographer Philip Kelly with the collaboration of activists Mila Astorga-Garcia and Enrico Esguerra from the Community Alliance for Social Justice. Ty's chapter engages critically with Charles Taylor's thoughts on multiculturalism as a solution to the problem and politics of recognition by looking at how negative and positive stereotypes of Filipina/os have been produced within inequitable political and economic conditions in Canada and globally. She pays particular attention to the growing market for affect in which Filipina/os, especially in the roles of nurse and domestic worker, are imbricated, in ways which shape individual interactions, interactions within states, interactions between individuals and states, and of course academic research. She turns to the role that cultural production can play in challenging certain problematic forms of 'recognition' by analysing *Miss Orient(ed)*, a play about three young women who are contestants in the 'Miss Pearl of the Orient' beauty pageant which highlights and satirizes some of the idealizations, misconceptions, and stereotypes of being a Filipina in Canada. Kelly, Astorga-Garcia, and Esguerra take up the questions of recognition using a different theoretical and methodological approach. They are interested in the question of why and how Filipinos are deprofessionalized and de-skilled in the Canadian labour market, overrepresented in some jobs and underrepresented in others. Using quantitative and survey data, they consider the impact of the Philippines as the sending country, of the relatively high use of family reunification and the Live-In Caregiver Program for migration, of the ways that Philippine credentials and education are understood, and the impact of culture and racialization. The issues of differentiation, recognition, and erasure also become the themes around which the remaining sections pivot.

The second section focuses on the intertwined realities of 'Gender, Migration, and Labour,' which have been central since the 1960s in shaping the conditions of Filipina/o Canadian lives and livelihood. Four chapters continue to focus significant attention on nurses and live-in caregivers, but from different angles than previous scholarship, while a fifth chapter investigates entrepreneurs, a topic which has received little attention from researchers thus far. Valerie Damasco, drawing on the experience of her aunt and other nurses, tells the little-told story of the recruitment of Filipinas to serve as healthcare professionals in Canada in the early 1960s, before the wide-scale liberalization of the Canadian immigration system removed national and racial quotas. Josephine Eric, a former live-in caregiver who is now a community activist and researcher with two graduate degrees, notes that she has been told by some Filipina/os that to mention her work as a nanny is an embarrassment, to herself and the community. To try to understand this sentiment, she compares the experiences of early cohorts of Filipinas in Canada (like those described by Damasco) with later cohorts, as a way of examining the import of different forms of Canadian immigration policy for Filipina/os and their families in a variety of domains: for career trajectories, for a sense of belonging, for social relations and class sentiment within the community, and for perceptions of Filipina/os by others. Lisa Davidson notes that many activists and analysts have challenged the notion that live-in caregivers are 'just like one of the family' for the paid labour and the sexual and economic exploitation that this metaphor obscures. She notes that live-in caregivers are, however, sometimes actual family members; she investigates the hopes and experiences of Filipinas who have worked for other family members as caregivers. She notes that, though some are using the LCP as a creative way to effect family reunification and challenge the notion of family embodied in Canadian immigration policy, many women find themselves subject to the same exploitative practices familiar to domestic workers in non-Filipina/o families. She parses how these women explain these challenges by seeing their family members as relating to them as *domestic helpers*, with practices appropriate in the Philippines, but inappropriate in Canada where they are *domestic workers*, with different rights, duties, and privileges. Ethel Tungohan, noting that many discussions of live-in caregivers focus on economic arguments, considers how to use receiving states' rhetoric about what a liberal democracy means to build an argument for political integration. She extends her theoretical account by examining the forms of political agency and engagement manifested by and on behalf of Filipinas working as live-in caregivers in a range of political organizations with different, and sometimes opposed, strategies for effecting change. Noting that most of the work on labour and Filipina/os in Canada has focused on nurses and live-in caregivers, Cesar Polvorosa investigates the role of entrepreneurs in Toronto, considering the kinds of workplaces, sites of consumption, and projects of Filipino-place-making that small businesses constitute.

The third section, 'Representation and Its Discontents,' showcases the ways in which Filipina/os and the Philippines are represented and imagined both by mainstream technologies, such as museums, textbooks, and public libraries, and by Filipina/o artists themselves. Chapters in this section build on Ty's insight that the labour conditions in which Filipina/os regularly find themselves create certain stereotypes of Filipina/os, as they look at other sites where forms of hypervisibility, erasure, and misrepresentation are circulated. Chapters in this section also consider how representations function not only as a way to construct and circulate certain ideas and identities, but also as a source of advocacy and empowerment. Bonnie McElhinny's chapter examines the cultural politics of the re-exhibition of colonial artifacts, by looking at a recent exhibit mounted at the Royal Ontario Museum in Ontario which recirculates Filipina/o artifacts originally displayed at the 1904 St Louis World's Fair, a fair meant to celebrate the benevolence of U.S. empire. She scrutinizes when exhibitions on colonial history serve to challenge racialized hierarchies and when and how they might ratify them. Marissa Largo describes a collaborative art project she undertook with Kabataang Montreal, an organization for Filipina/o youth in that city. She analyses the ways that two different projects, the development of a mural project which helped youth name problems in the community and hopes for the future, and a video on the project, represent different ways for a community artist to work in collaboration with others. She considers the kinds of social and political consciousness that participants developed while working on the project, and thus what such projects can contribute to community organizing. Vernon Totanes examines the kinds of Tagalog materials available in public libraries in Toronto, the second busiest public library system in the world, and documents the ways these materials are underrepresented in comparison with collections that serve other ethno-linguistic communities. He also considers the spatial politics of the distribution of the materials, noting that concentrations of Tagalog materials and Tagalog speakers are oddly mismatched, and offers some recommendations for transformations in library policy. Situating his work within critical studies of race in Canada, Roland Sintos Coloma examines the politics of representation in another key site, books and textbooks which offer general accounts of Canadian history to secondary school students, university students, and general audiences. He notes the significant erasure of Filipina/o, and other Asian Canadian, histories in Canada from these accounts, and offers three recommendations for redressing invisibility in historical narrations.

The fourth section, 'Youth Spaces and Subjectivities,' highlights the experiences of Filipina/o and Filipina/o Canadian youth. Virtually all of the scholarship on Filipina/os in Canada has focused on adults – their labour conditions, their community organizations, their activism, their experiences of racism. However, the long periods of separation enforced upon Filipinas working as live-in caregivers and their families has drawn attention to what happens when families reunify. A number of activist organizations in Canada are youth-run, and have begun to draw attention to the ways racism affects youth in schools, peer groups, and elsewhere. John Paul Catungal analyses public discourses on the murders of four Filipino youth, in part for what they reveal about discourses of race, violence, and immigration. In particular he attends to how the idea of 'inter-ethnic violence' circulated to describe some of these murders and to construct youth of colour as threats to, and outsiders in, successful multicultural cities. Challenging media representations which individualize crime and downplay institutional and political contexts, Catungal examines these representations for what they reveal about how discussions of individual bodies, and policies that address them, also construct ideologies and practices of exclusion and inclusion in families, communities, and Canada. Christine Balmes, drawing on her participation in an artistic collective at the Kapisanan Philippine Centre for Arts and Culture in Toronto, documents the emergence of a Filipina/o Canadian cultural movement, and how artworks, music, and performance contribute towards the decolonization of Filipina/o youth (see also Largo above). Maureen Mendoza adopts a case study approach to investigate the experiences of eleven Filipina/o students, half Canadian-born and half Philippine-born, at the University of British Columbia. While she finds that these students are relatively privileged in terms of economic position and educational background when compared with many other Filipina/o students, she also documents the forms of isolation they experience, in part because of the significant underrepresentation of Filipina/o students at UBC and their underrepresentation in the curriculum (see also Coloma above). Significantly, this lack of visibility is assessed with respect to both White Canadian and other Asian Canadian students. She documents a largely incipient attempt to understand their own experiences within the context of class stratification in the Filipina/o community, and racial and class stratification in Canada, and considers the economic and political explanations for why these students remain rather inarticulate about these questions. Conely de Leon also explores differentiation within the Filipina/o community, in this case linked to self- and other-identification as dark-skinned or lighter-skinned. She considers how these attributions of skin colour are linked to spatial politics in the western and eastern suburbs of Toronto, which are also often ideologically understood as distinguished by class (middle-class vs working class) and degree of racialization (largely White vs largely racialized groups). She embeds discussions of intraracial colourism within a thoughtful history of colonialism and the bodily hierarchies it has established, their continuing meaning, and what it might take to transcend these forms of differentiation.

Future Directions of Filipina/o Canadian Studies

At the conclusion of Chen's (1999) survey article, she suggests a number of directions for future research on Filipina/o Canadians. In addition to the need to focus on Filipina/o Canadians as a distinct ethno-cultural group (a goal on which there has been considerable progress), she calls for attention to specific topics that she, as a sociologist, thinks deserve more attention. These topics include attention to diversity among Filipina/os, the rise of new institutions, internal migration within Canada, family dynamics and marriage (including 'mixed' marriages, intergenerational relationships, forms of contact with family in the Philippines), and retirement plans. Although this volume engages with some central themes pertinent to Filipina/o Canadian studies, the editors are keenly aware that there are further areas that are undeveloped. We have flagged some of these above. In this final section, we also point to the role of religion, regional identity, and Canadian intervention projects as research sites requiring further consideration. One key theme that continues to be omitted in Asian Canadian studies, as in Asian American studies, is the intersection of religion and ethnic identity (Bramadat and Seljak 2008; Yoo 1999, 11). Indeed, the contributors to this volume acknowledge the reproduction of the invisibility of religious and Filipina/o identity; we remain conscious that contemporary academic and community-based research does not fully address the link between Filipina/o religious affiliation, community socialization, and political networking. Religious-based participation and para-church organizations are central venues for newly arrived Filipina/os to access broader and established Filipina/o Canadian publics, specifically Filipina/o communities oriented towards issues on family, generation, class, gender, and sexuality (Busto 1999; San Buenaventura 1999). We suggest that further work is required in considering how Filipina/os experience and make sense of migration and settlement into Canada given their participation in religious networks (though see Eric 2011). Through church organizations, we can consider the strategies of Filipina/os in acquiring social and legal-oriented service networks and in gaining necessary information to navigate the structures of various Canadian institutions, such as hospitals and schools, and the processes of Canadian policies, such as labour, immigration, and citizenship. Work on religion also provides fertile ground for investigating inter-ethnic relations between Filipina/os and other 'visible minority' Christian groups, such as Chinese Canadians, Korean Canadians, Tamil Canadians, and Vietnamese Canadians, in ways which allow us to consider what a faith-based perspective on Canadian multiculturalism and social practices might be. Following this, we point to the flows of Catholic charismatic movements developed in the Philippines and disseminated in Canada, such as *Cursilo*, Marriage and Engaged Encounter, Singles for Christ, Couples for Christ, Families for Christ, The Christian Life Program, and El Shaddai (McGowan 2008; Wiegele 2007), as vehicles in which Filipina/o identity is socially reproduced.

Another research direction to explore is the influence and significance of Filipina/o regional identities from the Philippines within the contours of Filipina/o communities in Canada. Often, after two Filipina/os meet for the first time, the question that follows is *taga saan ka sa atin?* (where are you from in the Philippines?), a query that cues the interlocutors towards the determination of familial, national, and class identification. In understanding and making sense of the intricacies of community-building efforts among Filipina/os, we require further consideration of the relationship between region, nation, family, and class in the formation of social and political alliances among Filipina/os in Canada. How have divergent regional and national histories and class formations in the Philippines been transplanted, cultivated, challenged, or reaffirmed within the terrain of Filipina/o Canadian communities? Why are some regions in the Philippines more politically active than others, and how does this play out within the multiple practices of Filipina/o activism in Canada? How do indigenous Filipina/os in Canada affirm their communities' struggles for self-determination in the Philippines while also supporting Aboriginal people's struggles in Canada (see Mahtani and Roberts in this volume)? How do they foster transnational linkages that would simultaneously allow them to bolster indigenous nationalist efforts in the Philippines and to fight against the activities of the Canadian state and Canadian mining companies in their communities? We are thus conscious of the ways in which an overarching Filipina/o identity obscures a regional and national identity, one that tells a more nuanced story of the micropolitics of belonging, unity, and diversity vis-à-vis family, ethnicity, nation, and class.

In the dialogical and dialectical spirit of the conference from which this volume was derived, Parts II, III, and IV have comments from the original discussants which, as they contextualize the papers in the section within ongoing research in Philippine studies, Canadian studies, feminist studies, and transnational studies, offer some directions for future research on each of the key topics flagged in these sections. Much as they did for the panels in the 'Spectres of Invisibility' symposium, these discussant responses provide a crucial framework from which to analyse each section. Along with showing the connections between the various chapters in each section, the discussants critically reflect on each theme from their vantage points as scholars with a long history of engagement with the Filipino/a community in Canada. By including Angeles', Aguinaldo's, and Pratt's thought-provoking pieces, we endeavour to show the divergent ways in which senior scholars have responded to the issues raised by the contributors, thus showing the diverse directions the nascent field of Filipino/a Canadian studies can take. Finally, this volume also features an afterword by scholars well versed in the field of Canadian Studies, Minelle Mahtani and David Roberts, whose comments help contextualize these papers over against, and place them in dialogue with, this wider field of inquiry. With the introductory chapter by the editors and Ty foregrounding transnational approaches, the book is thus bracketed by two intertwined approaches to the future development of Filipina/o studies in Canada.

As much as we have highlighted the significance and role of Filipina/os in Canada, it is crucial to continue to investigate the role of Canadians and Canadian government and non-governmental organizations in the Philippines. McCoy (1991), for instance, describes the complicity of the Canadian International Development Agency in indirectly funding Filipina/o militia groups with resources distributed for the implementation of democracy and 'fair' election practices during the political transition period from Marcos to Aquino (127). Framed as 'good intentions' and humanitarian aid, Canadian interventions in the Philippines have consequences for the social, political, and economic mobility, both local and transnational, of various indigenous groups (see Angeles 2003). How has the implementation of humanitarian-based projects and dispersal of small grants shaped class and gendered politics? It is important to consider how Canadian projects, agencies, and personnel contribute to the politics of Filipina/os in Canada. This rapid overview, however, provides only a sampling of the exciting and timely forms of research we hope this volume provokes, as it show-cases some of the most important research initiatives that are currently underway.

NOTES

1 *Maclean's* has since changed the title of the online article to read 'The Enrollment Controversy: Worries That Efforts in the US to Limit Enrollment of Asian Students in Top Universities May Migrate to Canada.' See http://www2.macleans.ca/2010/11/10/too-asian/, accessed December 2, 2010. 'Educators Encourage Parents of Asian Background to Let Their Children Study Trades and Arts,' *Toronto Star*, November 10, 2010, http://www.thestar.com/article/888368–asian-students-being-forced-into-university-maclean-s.

2 See Rinaldo Walcott (2003) for a critique of essentialist understandings of Black Canadian identity and a set of questions about whether 'African Canadian' can have the same utility or resonance in Canada as 'African American' does in the United States.

3 Some of the existing studies which focus on Filipina/os outside of Toronto and Vancouver in Canada include Bejar (2006) on nurses in rural Manitoba, Budohan (1972) on garment workers in Winnipeg, Manitoba; Budohan and Oandason (1981) on students in Manitoba schools; Chen (1981) on kinship networks in Thunder Bay, Ontario; Cusipag and Buenafe (1993) on communities in Ottawa and Windsor; Guidote and Baba (1980) on Montreal; Harris-Galia (2011) on a live-in caregiver in the Arctic, Holsteen (1988) on relationships between Filipina/o Canadians and European Canadians in Winnipeg; Magsino (1982) on Newfoundland; Ordonez and Sayo (1980) on the deteriorating economic position and anti-Marcos activism of Filipina/os in Quebec. Other studies include Filipina/os as part of larger research projects. See Stymeist with Salazar and Spafford

(1989) for a bibliography with detailed annotations; Chen (1999) provides a more recent overview.

4 The history in the preceding four paragraphs is adapted from McElhinny, Yeung, Damasco, DeOcampo, Febria, Collantes, and Salonga (2009, 96–97).

5 One might contrast this with the critical role that male agricultural labourers play in Filipina/o American studies.

6 For just a few influential works in Filipina/o American studies, see Bonus (2000), Bulosan (1973), Choy (2003), Espiritu (1995, 2003), Isaac (2006), Manalansan (2003), McCoy and Scarnao (2009), Okamura (1998), Root (1997), and Tiongson et al. (2006). See also Rafael (2008) for a helpful review.

7 These scholars include Eusebio Koh, Professor Emeritus (Mathematics, University of Regina), Romulo Magsino, Dean and Professor Emeritus (Education, University of Manitoba), and Aprodicio Laquian, Professor Emeritus (Community and Regional Planning, University of British Columbia). Our thanks to a helpful and knowledgeable reviewer for this list.

REFERENCES

Ami, Arlene. 2002. *Say I do*. Red Storm Productions.

Angeles, Leonora. 2003. Creating social spaces for transnational feminist advocacy: The Canadian International Development Agency, the National Commission on the Role of Filipino Women, and Philippine women's NGOs. *Canadian Geographer* 47 (3): 283–302.

Aranas, Marcial Q. 1983. *The dynamics of Filipino immigrants in Canada*. Edmonton: Coles.

Arat-Koç, Sedef. 1999. 'Good enough to work but not good enough to stay?': Foreign domestic workers and the law. In *Locating law: Race/gender/class connections*, ed. Elizabeth Comack, 129–52. Halifax: Fernwood.

– 2001. *Caregivers break the silence: A participatory action research on the abuse and violence, including the impact of family separation, experienced by women in the live-in caregiver program*. Toronto: Intercede.

Anderson, Warwick. 2006. *Colonial pathologies: American tropical medicine, race and hygiene in the Philippines*. Durham, NC: Duke University Press.

Astorga-Garcia, Mila. 2007. The road to empowerment in Toronto's Filipino community: From crisis to capacity-building. Joint Centre for Excellence on Research in Immigration and Settlement (CERIS) Working Paper No. 54. April 2007.

Bakan, Abigail, and Daiva Stasiulis. 1997a. Foreign domestic worker policy in Canada and the social boundaries of modern citizenship. In *Not one of the family: Foreign domestic workers in Canada*, ed. Abigail Bakan and Daiva Stasiulis, 29–52. Toronto: University of Toronto Press.

– 1997b. Introduction. In *Not one of the family: Foreign domestic workers in Canada*, ed. Abigail Bakan and Daiva Stasiulis, 3–28. Toronto: University of Toronto Press.

Barber, Pauline Gardiner. 2000. Agency in Philippine women's migration and provisional diaspora. *Women's Studies International Forum* 23 (4): 399–411.

– 2008. The ideal immigrant?: Gendered class subjects in Philippine-Canada migration. *Third World Quarterly* 29 (7): 1265–85.

Bautista, Fiorchita, and Marie Boti. 1999. *When strangers re-unite*. Productions Multi-Monde. 55 minutes, video.

Bejar, James. 2006. Transnational communities: Filipina nurses in rural Manitoba, 1965–1970. Master's thesis, Ryerson University, Toronto, Ontario.

Bonus, Rick. 2000. *Locating Filipino Americans: Ethnicity and the cultural politics of space*. Philadelphia: Temple University Press.

Boti, Marie (director). 1997. *Modern heroes, modern slaves*. Diffusion Multi-Monde. 44 minutes, video.

Boti, Marie, and Florchita Bautista (producers). 1992. *Brown women, blonde babies*. Diffusion Multi-Monde. 30 minutes, video.

Bowen, John. 2010. *Can Islam be French?: Pluralism and pragmatism in a secularist state*. Princeton: Princeton University Press.

Bramadat, Paul, and David Seljak. 2008. Charting the new terrain: Christianity and ethnicity in Canada. In *Christianity and ethnicity in Canada*, ed. Paul Bramadat and David Seljak, 3–48. Toronto: University of Toronto Press.

Briones, Leonor M. 1984. Roots of the present crisis and internal and external forces crucial in the crisis. In *Foreign capital and the Philippine crisis*, ed. Rosalinda Pineda-Ofreneo, 2–7, 25–9. Quezon City: University of the Philippines Press.

Budohan, Cleto. 1972. An urban village: The effect of migration on the Filipino garment workers in a Canadian city. MA thesis, Department of Anthropology, University of Manitoba, Winnipeg.

Budohan, Cleto, and Lolita Oandason. 1981. Filipino students in Manitoba schools. Winnipeg Curriculum Services, Manitoba Department of Education.

Bulosan, Carlos. 1973. *America is in the heart*. Seattle: University of Washington Press.

Bustamante, Rosalina E. 1982. Filipino ethnic newspapers in metropolitan Toronto. *Polyphony: The Bulletin of the Multicultural Historical Society of Ontario* 4: 74–6.

– 1983. Filipino traditions in music, dance and drama. *Polyphony: The Bulletin of the Multicultural Historical Society of Ontario* 5: 99–103.

– 1984. Filipino Canadians: A growing community. *Polyphony: The Bulletin of the Multicultural Historical Society of Ontario* 6: 168–71.

– 1986. Filipino women and equality. *Polyphony: The Bulletin of the Multicultural Historical Society of Ontario* 8: 77–9.

Busto, Rudy V. 1999. The gospel according to the model minority?: Hazarding an interpretation of Asian American evangelical college students. In *New Spiritual Homes: Religion and Asian Americans*, ed. David K. Yoo, 169–87. Honolulu: University of Hawai'i Press.

Campomanes, Oscar. 1992. Filipinos in the United States and their literature of exile. In *Reading the literatures of Asian America*, ed. Shirley Geok-lin Lim and Amy Ling. Philadelphia: Temple University Press.

– 1995. Afterword: The new empire's forgetful and forgotten citizens: Unrepresentability and unassimilability in Filipino American postcolonialities. *Critical Mass* 2 (2): 145–200.

Chen, Anita Beltran. 1981. Kinship system and chain migration: Filipinos in Thunder Bay. In *Asian Canadians: Regional perspectives: Selections from the proceedings, Asian Canadian Symposium V*, ed. K. Victor Ujimoto and Gordon Hirabayashi. Halifax: Mount Saint Vincent University.

– 1998. *From sunbelt to snowbelt: Filipinos in Canada*. Calgary: Canadian Ethnic Studies Association, University of Calgary.

– 1999. Filipinos. In *Encyclopedia of Canada's Peoples*, ed. Paul Robert Magocsi, 501–13. Toronto: University of Toronto Press.

Chen, Kuan-Hsing. 2010. *Asia as method: Toward deimperialization*. Durham, NC: Duke University Press.

Choy, Catherine Ceniza. 2003. *Empire of care: Nursing and migration in Filipino American history*. Durham, NC: Duke University Press.

Citizenship and Immigration Canada. 2010. *Canada facts and figures 2010: Immigration overview – permanent and temporary residents*. Ottawa: CIC.

Coloma, Roland Sintos. 2006. Putting queer to work: Examining empire and education. *International Journal of Qualitative Studies in Education* 19 (5): 639–57.

– 2009. 'Destiny has thrown the Negro and the Filipino under the tutelage of America': Race and curriculum in the age of empire. *Curriculum Inquiry* 39 (4): 495–519.

– 2011. Who's afraid of Foucault?: History, theory, and becoming subjects. *History of Education Quarterly* 51 (2): 184–210.

– 2012. White gazes, brown breasts: Imperial feminism and disciplining desires and bodies in colonial encounters. *Paedagogica Historica* 48 (2): 243–61.

Cusipag, Ruben J., and Maria Corazon Buenafe. 1993. *Portrait of Filipino Canadians in Ontario (1960–1990)*. Etobicoke: Kalayaan Media.

Das Gupta, Tania. 1999. The politics of multiculturalism: 'Immigrant women' and the Canadian state. In *Scratching the surface: Canadian anti-racist feminist thought*, ed. Enakshi Dua and Angela Robertson, 187–206. Toronto: Women's Press.

de Jesus, Melinda, ed. 2005. *Pinay power: Peminist critical theory: Theorizing the Filipina/American experience*. New York: Routledge.

de Leon, Coneley. 2009. Picking up the pieces. MA thesis, University of Toronto.

Dua, Enakshi, and Angela Robertson, eds. 1999. *Scratching the surface: Canadian anti-racist feminist thought*. Toronto: Women's Press.

Elenes, C.A. 1997. Reclaiming the borderlands: Chicana/o identity, difference and pedagogy. *Educational Theory* 47 (3): 359–76.

Elvir, Miriam. 1997. The work at home is not recognized: Organizing domestic workers in Montreal. In *Not one of the family: Foreign domestic workers in Canada*, ed. Abigail Bakan and Daiva Stasiulis, 147–56. Toronto: University of Toronto Press.

England, Kim, and Bernadette Stiell. 1997. 'They think you're as stupid as your English is': Constructing foreign domestic workers in Toronto. *Environment and Planning A* 29: 195–215.

Eric, Josephine. 2011. Religious experiences of Filipinos in southern Ontario. Master's research paper, Department of Anthropology, University of Toronto.

Espiritu, Yen Le. 1995. *Filipino American lives*. Philadelphia: Temple University Press.

– 2003. *Home bound: Filipino American lives across cultures, communities and countries*. Berkeley: University of California Press.

Eviota, Elizabeth Uy. 1992. *The political economy of gender: Women and the sexual division of labour in the Philippines*. London: Zed.

Go, Julian. 2008. *American empire and the politics of meaning: Elite political cultures in the Philippines and Puerto Rico during US colonialism*. Durham, NC: Duke University Press.

Goonewardena, Kanishka, and Stefan Kipfer. 2005. Spaces of difference: Reflections from Toronto on multiculturalism, bourgeois urbanism and the possibility of radical urban politics. *International Journal of Urban and Regional Research* 29 (3): 670–8.

Goyette, Braden. 2009. Against post-colonial invisibility: First Filipino Canadian symposium tries to bridge ivory tower and community activism. *McGill Daily*. Accessed October 20, 2010. http://www.mcgilldaily.com/articles/22203.

Guidote, Pedtro, and Vishwanath V. Baba. 1980. On the relationship between demographic factors and need fulfillment, participation in decision making, stress, alienation, and acculturation: An empirical study of the Filipino community in Montreal. In *Asian-Canadians and multiculturalism: Selections from the proceedings, Asian-Canadian symposium IV*, ed. K. Victor Ujimoto and Gordon Hirabayashi. Montreal: Université de Montréal.

Harris-Galia, Rhose. 2011. Arctic bayanihan. In *Cultivating Canada: Reconciliation through the lens of cultural diversity*, ed. Ashok Mathur, Jonathan Dewar, and Mike DeGagné, 193–202. Ottawa: Aboriginal Healing Foundation.

Hernandez-Truyol, B.E. 1997. Borders (en)gendered: normativities, Latinas and a LatCrit paradigm. *New York University Law Review* 72 (4): 882–927.

Hoganson, Kristine. 1998. *Fighting for American manhood: How gender politics provoked the Spanish-American and Philippine-American wars*. New Haven: Yale University Press.

Holsteen, Mel. 1988. Intercultural adjustments between Filipino-Canadians and European-Canadians in Winnipeg. Winnipeg, Unpublished preliminary report to the Manitoba Intercultural Council.

Isaac, Allan Punzalan. 2006. *American tropics: Articulating Filipino America*. Minneapolis: University of Minnesota Press.

Kelly, Philip. 2006. Filipinos in Canada: Economic dimensions of immigration and settlement. *Joint Centre of excellence for research on immigration and settlement – Toronto* 48: 1–37.

Kelly, Philip F., Mila Astorga-Garcia, Enrico F. Esguerra, and the Community Alliance for Social Justice, Toronto. 2009. *Explaining the deprofessionalized Filipino: Why Filipino immigrants get low-paying jobs in Toronto*. CERIS Working Paper Series, No. 75. October 2009.

Kondo, Dorinne. 1995. Bad girls: Theater, women of colour and the politics of representation. In *Women writing culture*, ed. Ruth Behar and Deborah Gordan, 49–65. Berkeley: University of California Press.

Kramer, Paul. 2006. *The blood of government: Race, empire, the United States and the Philippines*. Chapel Hill: University of North Carolina Press.

Laquian, Eleanor R. 1973. *A study of Filipino immigration to Canada, 1962–1972*. Ottawa: United Council of Filipino Associations in Canada.

Lindsay, C. 2007. *The Filipino community in Canada*. Ottawa: Social and Aboriginal Statistics Division, Statistics Canada.

Lusis, Tom. n.d. Filipino immigrants in Canada: A literature review and directions for further research on second-tier cities and rural areas. Accessed June 24, 2011. http://www.geography.ryerson.ca/hbauder/Immigrant%20 Labour/filipinoSettlement.pdf.

Mackey, Eva. 2002. *The house of difference: Cultural politics and national identity in Canada.* Toronto: University of Toronto Press.

Macklin, Audrey. 1994. On the inside looking in: Foreign domestic workers in Canada. In *Maid in the market: Women's paid domestic labour,* ed. Wenona Giles and Sedef Arat-Koç, 13–39. Halifax: Fernwood.

Magsino, Romulo F. 1982. Tropical islanders in the Atlantic: A study of Filipino experiences in Newfoundland. St John's: Memorial University of Newfoundland.

Manalansan, Martin. 2003. *Global divas: Filipino gay men in the diaspora.* Durham, NC: Duke University Press.

McCoy, Alfred. 1991. The restoration of planter power in La Carlota city. In *From Marcos to Aquino: Local perspectives on political transition in the Philippines,* ed. Benedict Kerkvliet and Resil Mojares, 105–42. Honolulu: University of Hawai'i Press.

McCoy, Alfred, and Francisco Scarnao, eds. 2009. *Colonial crucible: Empire in the making of the modern American state.* Madison: University of Wisconsin Press.

McElhinny, Bonnie. 2005. 'Kissing a baby is not at all good for him': Infant mortality, medicine and colonial modernity in the US-occupied Philippines' *American Anthropologist* 107 (2): 183–94.

– 2007a. Recontextualizing the American occupation of the Philippines: Erasure and ventriloquism in colonial discourse around men, medicine and infant mortality. In *Words, worlds, material girls: Language and gender in a global economy,* ed. Bonnie McElhinny, 205–36. Berlin: Mouton de Gruyter.

– 2007b. Prétextes de l'empire Américain aux Philippines: Recontextualisation des histoires de la médecine impériale [Pretexts of American empire in the Philippines: Recontextualizing histories of American medicine]. *Anthropologie et Sociétés* 31 (1): 75–95.

– 2009. Producing the A-1 baby: Puericulture centres and the birth of the clinic in the US occupied Philippines, 1906–1946. *Philippine Studies* 57 (2): 219–60.

McElhinny, Bonnie, Shirley Yeung, Valerie Damasco, Angela DeOcampo, Monina Febria, Christianne Collantes, and Jason Salonga. 2009. 'Talk about luck': Coherence, contingency, character and class in the life stories of Filipino Canadians in Toronto. In *Beyond yellow English: Toward a linguistic anthropology of Asian Pacific America,* ed. Angela Reyes and Adrienne Lo, 93–110. Oxford: Oxford University Press.

McElhinny, Bonnie, Christianne Collantes, Shirley Yeung, Monina Febria, Valerie Damasco, Jason Salonga, and Angela DeOcampo. Ms. 'So what's the Filipino thing to do?': Music, struggle and ideologies of identity among Filipino Canadian youth in Toronto. Submitted to *Journal of Asian American Studies.*

McGowan, Mark G. 2008. Roman Catholics (anglophone and allophone). In *Christianity and ethnicity in Canada,* ed. Paul Bramadat and David Seljak, 49–100. Toronto: University of Toronto Press.

Nagata, Judith. 1987. The role of Christian churches in the integration of Southeast Asian immigrants in Toronto. *Southeast Asian Ethnography* 6:39–59.

Okamura, Jonathan. 1998. *Imagining the Filipino American diaspora: Transnational relations, identities and communities.* New York: Garland.

Ordonez, E.A., and E.Y. Sayo. 1980. Filipinos in Quebec: A progressive view. In *Asian-Canadians and multiculturalism: Selections from the proceedings,* Asian-Canadian symposium IV, ed. K. Victor Ujimoto and Gordon Hirabayashi. Montreal: Université de Montréal.

Pisares, Elizabeth. 2006. Do you mis(recognize) me?: Filipina Americans in popular music and the problem of invisibility. In *Positively no Filipinos allowed: Building communities and discourse,* ed. Antonio T. Tiongson, Edgardo V. Gutierrez, and Ricardo V. Gutierrez, 172–98. Philadelphia: Temple University Press.

Povinelli, Elizabeth. 2002. *The cunning of recognition: Indigenous alterities and the making of Australian multiculturalism.* Durham, NC: Duke University Press.

Pratt, Geraldine. 1999. From registered nurse to registered nanny: Discursive geographies of Filipina domestic workers in Vancouver, B.C. *Economic Geography* 75: 215–36.

– 2012. *Families apart: Migrant mothers and the conflicts of labour and love.* Minneapolis: University of Minnesota Press.

Pratt, Geraldine, and Caleb Johnson. 2009. Translating research into theatre: *Nanay,* a testimonial play. *B.C. Studies* 163: 123–32.

Pratt, Geraldine, in collaboration with the Philippine Women Centre of BC. 2009. Circulating sadness: Witnessing Filipino mothers' stories of family separation. *Gender, Place and Culture* 16: 3–22.

Pratt, Geraldine, in collaboration with the Philippine Women Centre of BC and Ugnayan ng Kabataang Pilipino sa Canada / Filipino Canadian Youth Alliance. 2007. Working with migrant communities: Collaborating with the Kalayaan Centre in Vancouver, Canada. In *Participatory action research approaches and methods: Connecting people, participation and place,* ed. Sara Kindon, Rachel Pain, and Mike Kesby, 95–103. London: Routledge.

Pratt, Geraldine, in collaboration with Ugnayan ng Kabataang Pilipino sa Canada. 2003. Between homes: Displacement and belonging for second generation Filipino Canadian youths. *B.C. Studies* 139: 41–68.

Rafael, Vicente L. 2000. *White love and other events in Filipino history.* Durham, NC: Duke University Press.

– 2004. Southeast Asian studies in the age of Asian America. In *Southeast Asian studies for the twenty-first century*, ed. Anthony Reid. Tempe: Program for Southeast Asian Studies, Arizona State University.

– 2008. Orientations: Notes on the study of the Philippines in the United States. *Philippine Studies* 56 (4): 345–58.

Rafael, Vicente L., ed. 1995. *Discrepant histories: Translocal essays on Filipino cultures*. Philadelphia: Temple University Press.

Ronquillo, Charlene, Geertje Boschma, Sabrina T. Wong, and Linda Quiney. 2011. Beyond greener pastures: Exploring contexts surrounding Filipino nurse migration in Canada through oral history. *Nursing Inquiry* 18 (3): 262–75.

Root, Maria, ed. 1997. *Filipino Americans*. Thousand Oaks, CA: Sage.

Salman, Michael. 2001. *The embarrassment of slavery: Controversies over bondage and nationalism in the American colonial Philippines*. Berkeley: University of California Press.

San Buenaventura, Steffi. 1999. Filipino folk spirituality and immigration: From mutual aid to religion. In *New spiritual homes: Religion and Asian Americans*, ed. David K. Yoo, 52–86. Honolulu: University of Hawai'i Press.

Stasiulis, Daiva, and Abigail Bakan. 2005. *Negotiating citizenship: Migrant women in Canada and the global system*. Toronto: University of Toronto Press.

Statistics Canada 2006. Canada's ethnocultural mosaic, 2006 Census; Findings. Accessed December 2, 2010. http://www12.statcan.ca/census-recensement/2006/as-sa/97-562/index-eng.cfm.

Stymeist, David H., with Lilia Salazar and Graham Spafford. 1989. *A selected annotated bibliography on the Filipino immigrant community in Canada and the United States*. University of Manitoba Anthropology Papers No. 31. Department of Anthropology, University of Manitoba, Winnipeg, Manitoba.

Thobani, Sunera. 2007. *Exalted subjects: Studies in the making of race and nation in Canada*. Toronto: University of Toronto Press.

Tiongson, Antoni T., Edgardo V. Gutierrez, and Ricardo V. Gutierrez, eds. 2006. *Positively no Filipinos allowed: Building communities and discourse*. Philadelphia: Temple University Press.

Tuason, Julie A. 1999. The ideology of empire in *National Geographic* magazine's coverage of the Philippines, 1898–1908. *Geographical Review* 89 (1): 34–53.

Velasco, Pura. 1997. 'We can still fight back': Organizing domestic workers in Toronto. In *Not one of the family: Foreign domestic workers in Canada*, ed. Abigail Bakan and Daiva Stasiulis, 157–64. Toronto: University of Toronto Press.

Walcott, Rinaldo. 2003. *Black like who?: Writing Black Canada*. 2nd edition. London: Insomniac.

Wiegele, Katharine. 2007. *Investing in miracles: El Shaddai and the tranformation of popular Catholicism in the Philippines*. Manila: Ateneo de Manila University Press.

Yoo, David K. 1999. Introduction: Reframing the US religious landscape. In *New spiritual homes: Religion and Asian Americans*, ed. David K. Yoo, 1–18. Honolulu: University of Hawai'i Press.

Zaman, Habiba, with Cecilia Diocson and Rebecca Scott. 2007. *Workplace rights for immigrants in BC: The case of Filipina workers*. Vancouver: Canadian Centre for Policy Alternatives.

Zaman, Habiba. 2003. Migrant women workers and Filipino nurses in Canada: Looking at race, class, and gender dynamics of de-skilling. In *Advancing the rights and welfare of non-practicing Filipino and other foreign-trained nurses*, 35–9. Vancouver: Filipino Nurses Support Group.

Chapter 2

Filipino Canadians in the Twenty-First Century: The Politics of Recognition in a Transnational Affect Economy

ELEANOR TY

Two years ago, my elderly mother was rushed to the emergency ward of the Trillium Hospital in Mississauga because of dizziness and problems with balancing. It turned out that she was suffering from a condition called Ménière's disease, which lasted only a few days. However, in the crucial time between what looked like a very serious problem and the resolution of it, she was assigned a bed in the emergency ward, and had to undergo a number of tests. My siblings and I were naturally worried. When I went to visit her that night, I found to my surprise that, even though there was little privacy in the emergency ward, she was comfortable and well cared for. I discovered that the nurse in charge of my mother was a Filipina, who was very kind and attentive. When I was there, she brought my mother something to drink, addressed her by the very polite and endearing term '*Inay*' (mother). '*Inay*, do you want to sit here?' '*Inay*, would you like some apple juice?' She responded to my mother's questions with '*opo*' or '*hindi po*' (a polite form of yes and no). I was very touched by her obvious compassion, and thought how fortunate it was that my mother was under her care. It was a situation where being part of the Filipino diaspora worked to our advantage. To be 'recognized' and identified as Filipino, in my mother's case, had a practical, convenient, and fortuitous bonus.

About ten years earlier, I was watching my two young children: one was almost three and the other almost one then. Playing with them at the park near my home in suburban Mississauga one morning, I met a young Filipina with a little blond boy. Immediately I knew that she was a nanny on the Live-In Caregiver's Program.[1] My children were on the swings nearby – both had brown hair, and their father's Scottish Canadian colouring. After a friendly visual acknowledgment and the recognition that we were '*kababayan*' (folks from the same town/country), we exchanged the usual hellos and introductions. Daisy, who had just turned twenty, told me that she was working in her first domestic position. She had been in Canada for only about eight months.

'Oh,' I told her, with a smile. 'Me, I've been here for over twenty years now.'

She gave me a look of disbelief, mixed with scorn, and said, '*Ano*? [What?] You've been here over twenty years, and you are still a nanny?'

I had to explain somewhat embarrassingly that the two children I was watching were my own, and that I was not a nanny, but a 'teacher' at a university. We are both diasporic Asians, but our situations then were not similar. I have told this story to a few friends, and we laugh at Daisy's mistaking me for a 'nanny,' and especially at her assumption that I was so lazy or hopeless that I was stuck in that position for such a long time. Yet these two encounters reveal ways in which what I am calling 'recognition' and 'misrecognition' work in our globalized and multi-diverse country. What are the assumptions and preconceptions that come into play as we and others 'recognize' Filipino Canadians?

Filipinos are one of the largest growing immigrant groups in Canada. They are better educated than the rest of the population of Canada, but they have the second lowest average income among visible minority groups (see chapter 1 in this volume). As a group, Filipino Canadians have much to celebrate; at the same time there is still work to be done. In this chapter, I explore a number of pressing issues concerning Filipino Canadian subjectivities in the twenty-first century, using as a point of departure two theoretical concepts: the politics of recognition and the notion of an affect economy. In the last section of the chapter, I look at a stage production, *Miss Orient(ed),* as an example of how artistic representation also enters into discussions about subjectivity and addresses some of these issues (see chapters by Balmes, de Leon, and Largo in this volume on artistic endeavours). I use the term 'recognition' two ways: in the way that political philosophers use it, and also more loosely, in its everyday meaning of 'to know again, to identify from one's previous knowledge or experience' (Hawkins 1991). Feminist philosopher Nancy Fraser explains that the usual approach to the politics of recognition – called the 'identity model' – 'starts from the Hegelian idea that identity is constructed dialogically, through a process of mutual recognition' (Fraser 2000). According to Hegel, 'recognition designates an ideal reciprocal relation between subjects, in which each sees the other both as its equal and also as separate from it.

This relation is constitutive for subjectivity: one becomes an individual subject only by virtue of recognizing, and being recognized by, another subject. Recognition from others is thus essential to the development of a sense of self. To be denied recognition – or to be "misrecognized" – is to suffer both a distortion of one's relation to one's self and an injury to one's identity' (Fraser 2000).

In 'The Politics of Recognition,' Charles Taylor (1997) points out that recognition has become more crucial in the modern age, or around the eighteenth century. Before this period, identity depended on social categories, rather than on an inwardly generated sense of oneself. Following Rousseau and Hegel, Taylor stresses that recognition is important in both the private and social sphere: 'on an intimate plane, we are all aware of how identity can be formed or malformed through the course of our contact with significant others. On the social plane, we have a continuing politics of equal recognition' (104).[2] Demeaning images can be detrimental to an individual's psychic and social development and damaging to group affiliation. Frantz Fanon (1967) provides the most articulate expression of the way oppression can result in social and psychic damage in his often-quoted narrative of being hailed as a 'Negro' and feeling that his 'body was given back ... sprawled out, distorted, recolored, clad in mourning' (113).

Charles Taylor's solution is to espouse multiculturalism, which ensures the survival of different cultural communities living together by an official recognition of the 'equal value' of cultures other than English and French in Canada. Canada's multicultural policy, established by the government in 1971, has received its share of criticism from those who believe that it does not go far enough (Li 1999; Mackey 2002; Synnott and Howes 1996), but its supporters believe that it has facilitated the acceptance of cultural pluralism in the country (Kymlicka 1998). Kelly Oliver (2001) points out that Taylor's theory of multiculturalism does not 'take into account the effects of Western culture' on other groups: 'Indeed, his notion of intellectual judgment from the ethical presumption of worth resonates with the most insensitive operations of liberal multiculturalism, which begins from the benevolence of those in power without regard for the desires of those without power' (46). One philosopher who does see that struggles over worth are moral struggles is Axel Honneth, who describes 'three forms of recognition for proper independent individuality and democratic society' (Oliver 2001, 47): love in the form of primary relationships, such as parent-child or between lovers; legal recognition; and that of community or social group (Honneth 1996). Honneth's attention to the moral worth of the group, or the approval associated with solidarity, is important for my discussion. Of the third form of recognition, Honneth writes, 'Here, the individual knows himself or herself to be a member of a social group that can collectively accomplish things whose worth for society is recognized by all other members of society' (Honneth 1996, 128).

For Filipinos in Canada and the United States, early stereotypes included 'dogeaters' and brown-skinned 'savages' (Lee 1999, 111), while contemporary images, on the positive side, include Filipinos as hardworking, resilient, persevering people, beautiful, and sometimes seen as exotic women, good singers. On the negative, Filipinos are seen as servile, often late, lazy, deterministic or fatalistic (*bahala na*). Geraldine Pratt (1999), in her study of Filipina domestic workers in Vancouver, points out that Filipinas are 'discursively constructed as housekeepers, with inferior intellects and education' in comparison to European nannies (229). She says, 'the word "Filipina" is not only equated with "supplicant-preimmigrant"; the term also connotes "just-a-housekeeper" and "husband stealer"' (233). However, these stereotypes operate only within certain contexts. In Singapore, for example, as Beatriz Lorente (2010) points out, Filipino domestic workers, who are fluent in English, are seen to be 'competent, meticulous, and modern' compared to the Indonesian and Sri Lankan domestic workers, who are portrayed as more backward, traditional, and shy. In a rather self-deprecating and ironic article, writer Nick Joaquin (2008) has humorously associated Filipinos with a 'heritage of smallness,' citing the small rowboat, the barrio, the small sari-sari stall, the belief in the immediate: '*isang kahig, isang tuka.*' He points out that only in the Philippines can one buy and sell 'one stick of cigarette, half a head of garlic, a dab of pomade, part of the contents of a can or bottle, one single egg, one single banana.' After more than half a century of writing in English, Philippine literature is identified with the short story. He writes, 'We work more but make less. Why? Because we act on such a pygmy scale,' and he calls upon Filipinos to aspire to grander visions and bigger things.

Recognition and visibility of Filipinos in the public sphere, then, entail affirmation and strengthening of those values that we believe in and more vigilance in countering negative stereotypes, some of which may have arisen from specific circumstances or needs. Specific historical and cultural conditions have created some of these so-called tendencies. For example, the 'smallness' comes from having so few resources that every little bit becomes precious, every stick of Juicy Fruit gum becomes valuable. Another way of looking at the 'smallness' quality is to see its redeeming effects. Filipinos, compared to many people in the developed world, have less, and have become more resourceful and less wasteful. Every small piece of paper is used frugally, and every part of an animal, say a pig, is cooked and eaten.[3] But aside from the problem of cultural stereotypes, however, we have also been slotted into certain occupations in the world, partly as a result of colonialist and imperialist influences. The history of colonization of the Philippines, by the Spaniards and then by the United States, coupled with the teachings of the Catholic religion, has helped to create a nation of what Foucault (1979) calls 'docile' bodies, which may 'be subjected, used, transformed and improved' (136). We are now known in the transnational labour market as those Third World women with 'nimble fingers' (Elson and Pearson 1981), as a good source of migrant workers in 'both sea-based and land-based' jobs such as 'construction workers, domestic helpers, entertainers manufacturing and service workers, business people, [and] scholars' (Ofreneo and Samonte 2005, 4).

The growing number of Filipino migrant workers in Canada and in all parts of the world has made it seem as if Filipino bodies are particularly suited to certain kinds of labour, particularly cheap labour (see Kelly et al. in this volume). A number of scholars have noted that existing economic, social, and cultural conditions of the Filipino diaspora are linked to history, migration, globalization, and colonization. Daiva Stasiulis and Abigail Bakan (2005) point out, for example, that 'global realities, national state regulatory bodies, gatekeeping mechanisms and gatekeepers, families with all their various complexities in both the First World and the Third World, imperialism, sexism and racism, all figure into the analytical framework centred around the negotiation of citizenship' (4). They argue that 'the global, national and local contexts of capitalist and imperialist power relations intersect to produce particular life outcomes for women migrant workers' in Canada (ibid.). Similarly, Rhacel Parreñas (2001) notes that 'the contemporary outmigration of Filipinas and their entrance into domestic work is a product of globalization; it is patterned under the role of the Philippines as an export-based economy in globalization; and it is embedded in the specific historical phase of global restructuring' (11).[4] I would like to make some observations about the connection between the rise of migrant work and immigration in the last two decades and what has been called 'affect economy,' a term used by Patricia Clough (2007) and other sociologists.

In recent years, scholars have turned to theories of affect as a way to explain encounters that occur between people as well as between people and places that arouse feelings or a state of being. Sara Ahmed (2004) stresses that 'feelings are crucial to the forming of surfaces and borders ... what separates us from others also connects us to others' (25). She argues that feeling is 'shaped by contact with ... memory, and also involves an orientation towards what is remembered' (7). Eve Sedgwick (2003) notes that 'affects can be, and are, attached to things, people, ideas, sensations, relations, activities, ambitions, institutions, and any number of other things, including other affects. Thus, one can be excited by anger, disgusted by shame, or surprised by joy' (19). The terms 'affect labour' and 'affect economy' refer to work and economic interactions that do not involve the exchange of goods, but the exchange of something intangible, like the sense of pleasure or well-being. Michael Hardt (2007) notes that an affect 'forces us constantly to pose the problem of the relationship between mind and body with the assumption that their powers constantly correspond in some way' (x). In 'Affective Labor,' Hardt (1999) posits two kinds of labour that 'result in no material and durable good': those that produce a 'service, knowledge, or communication' and the kind of labour that is 'the affective labor of human contact and interaction' (94–5). He writes, 'Health services, for example, rely centrally on caring and affective labor, and the entertainment industry and the various culture industries are likewise focused on the creation and manipulation of affects. To one degree or another, this affective labor plays a certain role throughout the service industries, from fast-food servers to providers of financial services, embedded in the moments of human interaction and communication ... its products are intangible: a feeling of ease, well-being, satisfaction, excitement, passion, even a sense of connectedness or community' (95–6).

Feminist scholars have noted that this kind of labour is gendered and also often racialized. Drucilla Barker and Susan Feiner (2009) note that since the nineteenth century, 'caring labor – attending to the physical and emotional needs of others – has been considered the quintessential form of "women's work" ' (41) and that this kind of work has always posed a problem for feminist liberal economists or Marxist/socialist economists who do not agree on whether household labour should or should not be classified as (re)productive/caring labour or waged labour (45–6). Barker and Feiner point out that a further complication is that caring labour in the United States today is largely done by 'poor black, Latina, and Filipina women' who are paid and that this kind of 'paid care' is seen as 'inferior to unpaid care' (48–9). They write: 'The stigmatized social status of paid care workers affects the perception of the work they do; the fact that the service is being provided for money demeans the affective aspect of the work, which reinforces the low status and meager wages of those who do it' (49–50). Following these kinds of observations, Elizabeth Wissinger (2007) comments, an 'affect economy recognizes the insights gained from Marxist feminists' studies of women's unwaged domestic labor as a contribution to the family wage. But it also recognizes how social reproduction has been subsumed by capital, made a force of production, as socialization, therapeutic interaction, cooking, cleaning, child care, health care, and the like have been increasingly pulled into the domain of capital' (234). Today's 'affect economy developed out of the rise of the service sector and the shift to a consumer economy that has characterized postindustrial capitalism' (ibid.). Large numbers of Filipinos around the world work as affective labourers – in healthcare services, in child and elderly care, in service sectors, and in the entertainment industry.

The reasons for this phenomenon are complex. Carmelita Ericta and her colleagues (2003) argue that migration today is not simply due to the 'push-pull' theory, but due to many factors: 'Unwanted by the local economy, they are forced to seek employment abroad, unmindful of the onerous contract terms and risks, if only to escape poverty and unemployment at home' (1). They note, 'Filipino overseas workers create a growing middle class and contribute in building a more stable Philippine economy by investing their hard-earned money in industries, like transportation, housing, construction, education, and manufacturing' (ibid.). The Philippines has embarked on a labour export program for over twenty years now, meant initially to 'ease the country's high unemployment and foreign exchange problems' (ibid.). The government markets Filipinos as 'affect' labourers. For example, the Institute for Labor Studies (ILS) in the Philippines proclaims that 'the capacity of Filipinos to look after the sick can never be underestimated. In fact, this is the primary trait that makes other countries prefer Filipinos over other foreign caregivers. Filipinos are perceived to be humane, patient, and adaptable. Our workers' relatively good facility with the English language is also an edge' (ILS website). Similarly, the Philippine Overseas Employment Administration (2006) boasts that Filipinos are 'among the most sought-after workers in the world today. Since 1987, the Philippines has been the leading supplier of seafarers in the international market ... almost 20 percent of the total 1.23 million seafarers worldwide are Filipinos.' The POEA website proclaims that Filipinos are 'resilient. Adaptable. English-proficient. Loyal,' which are 'just among the reasons why Filipino seafarers are preferred by the world's best fleet.'

While one might not immediately think of affective qualities, such as caring and emoting, as requirements for seafaring, affective labour is precisely what is being marketed by a number of government agencies in the Philippines. Steven McKay (2007) observes that the Philippine Seafarers Promotion Council (PSPC) – a group of leading staffing agencies, labour unions, shipowners, and government agencies – projects a more 'feminine' character of Filipino seafarers, proclaiming, 'Filipinos go the extra mile and serve with a smile ... When you employ Filipinos, you have access to SKILL with a HEART. Filipinos are by nature a warm people who exude a high standard of customer service. They are also happy to work even under challenging conditions at sea' (71). According to McKay, 'in order to set Filipinos apart from their competitors, the state and the manning agencies also constructed an image of Filipino seafarers to better fit the requirements of the segmented labor market. This entails endowing the "natural" Filipino seafarers with the "innate" qualities of pliability' (70). The numbers of seafarers and remittances have grown dramatically since the late 1980s, but 'their positions on the occupational ladder have not substantially improved ... In 2003 only 8.5 percent had reached the senior officer level' (68). The Filipinos are mainly channelled into specific lower positions in the seafaring industry.

There is a link between recognition, identity politics, and the growing numbers of Filipinos in the affect economy. While as Filipino Canadians, we are far removed from the seafaring industry, we still are influenced by the propaganda and image of Filipinos in the world. Other people's perceptions of Filipinos in the larger diaspora shape and inevitably construct our subjectivities. We participate in this recognition, what Honneth calls 'group-pride or collective honour' (Honneth 1996, 128), even as diasporic subjects in Canada, in the sense that we consciously or unconsciously cultivate assumptions and react to these constructions in our daily interactions with other Filipinos. Think back to my opening personal anecdotes where I was relieved and happy that my mother was under the care of a Filipino nurse in the emergency ward. In addition to the comfort of a shared identity, I was pleased because I assumed the nurse would possess the qualities advertised in the promotional materials: that a Filipina would be caring, patient, and capable. And Daisy, the newly arrived caregiver, assumed that all Filipino women taking care of children were nannies. In Canada, most Filipinos continue to work in low-paying service sectors, because we serve 'with a smile,' as the seafarers' agency proclaims. As a people, we are 'feminized,' tagged with qualities of pliability, friendliness, willingness to please. To this day, we are still internalizing colonial assumptions of our ability and duty to serve and to please. Following Marx, feminist critic Neferti Tadiar uses the metaphor of prostitution in order to show the 'corporeal debasement of the worker under capitalism' (Tadiar 2009, 33). She writes of Filipinos in today's globalized economy, 'In this libidinal new world order, in which gendered sexualities are signifiers of the organizing principles of national economies and their political status in the international community, the Philippines functions as a hostess nation, catering to the demands and desires of her clients – multinational capital and the U.S. government and military' (25–6). Tadiar does not discuss the situation of Filipinos in Canada, but I am suggesting that by taking up these low-paying positions and becoming migrant workers in today's affect economy, many Filipino Canadians inadvertently continue, largely out of necessity, to maintain the kind of global inequities between nations described by Tadiar.

In the same way, our work as academics also plays a role in the shaping of the group identity and visibility of Filipino Canadians. When one does a search for 'Filipino Canadians' in scholarly journals and papers, one finds articles about a cluster of topics (Aitken 1987; England and Stiell 1997; chapters by Davidson and Tungohan in this volume). These include the problems faced by Filipino caregivers and domestics, transnational mothers and families, immigration patterns and employment statistics, ethnic acculturation and integration, especially of youths. The Philippine Women's Centre in BC and Ontario, the Kalayaan Filipino Community Centre in BC, and other community organizations have done very important grassroots works on behalf of Filipino overseas workers. But again and again the focus is on Filipinos as domestic workers. The proliferation of research on Filipino domestic workers shows that there is a strong network of feminist scholars, activists, and community workers who are striving to improve the conditions of what they see as a vulnerable group of migrant workers. Domestic workers tend to be very present and visible in everyday spaces, in parks, at the school, in shopping malls, or in nursing homes. For this reason, they have received more scholarly attention than Filipinos in other occupations and other circumstances, such as sailors or factory workers. In the news last year, we have topped the lists for immigrant and temporary workers in Canada (Jimenez 2008). However, what we do not find is also significant. We do not find many scholarly articles about Filipino Canadians topping the list as politicians, lawyers, entertainers, artists, engineers, doctors, dentists, architects, academics, even though we are there in those fields. Ideally, we would read stories of growing up, growing old, of love, of loss, of ambitions, of disappointments, of Filipino Canadians living full and complicated lives that mirror the daily beauty and messiness of our reality. My point is that journal articles, though empirical, also serve to construct a kind of collective identity for us. I am not suggesting that we stop working on and writing about problems of Filipino domestics and Filipino immigrants. It is imperative that work about and by Filipino Canadians continues to be done. However, I do want us to be aware of the ways in which these studies and our work help to create and shape the recognition and visibility of Filipino Canadians as a group. At the same time as we do research on Filipino domestics and immigration issues, we should also be doing research on other aspects of Filipino Canadian lives.

In 'Rethinking Recognition,' Nancy Fraser (2000) discusses the limitations of identity politics as it has been practised. She points out that while claims for the recognition of difference have risen in the last twenty years, there has been a 'relative decline in claims for egalitarian redistribution.' She argues that the politics of recognition needs to be linked to, and not displace, struggles for redistribution and struggles for economic equality.[5] In work done to date, the 'roots of injustice are located in demeaning representations, but these are not seen as socially grounded' (ibid.). We need to remember to connect the issues of identity politics to what Fraser calls the 'social-structural underpinnings' that cause misrecognition (ibid.). For example, there is a connection between work that has been devalued as 'feminine' and the low wages of the work performed by Filipinos in the diaspora who are perceived to be ideally suited to this kind of affect labour. The work that has been deemed suitable for Filipinos in North America has historically been the kind that is undervalued by our white androcentric culture. In the early part of the twentieth century, Filipinos were employed as houseboys, cooks, gardeners, similar to the Chinese who worked in restaurants and laundries. Today, Filipinos are domestics, caregivers for the young and the elderly. We work in hospitals as nurses, personal support workers, and orderlies; on ships as cleaners, busboys, wait staff, and kitchen help. The jobs are traditionally those that pay low wages and tend to be feminized. Yet, the economic situation in the Philippines has made these positions feasible because they represent a way to enter receiving countries such as Canada.

To complicate the problem, the recent influx of Filipino immigrants as domestic caregivers has contributed to the widespread perception of Filipinos in Canada as migrant domestic workers rather than professionals, entrepreneurs, or intellectuals. In contrast to earlier periods in Canadian history where Filipino immigrants came as nurses, doctors, technicians, and office workers, from the 1980s onward many Filipinos came as contract workers under the Live-In Caregiver Program (Damasco in this volume). Cecilia Diocson (2005) has noted that 'from 1998 to 2003, Filipino entrants made up an average of 92.6% of those entering Canada under the LCP' and has outlined a number of problematic issues of the program, including the potentially exploitative situations for employer and worker under the mandatory live-in requirement. The annual number of entrants under the LCP program has rapidly increased from about 2,000 in 1998 to approximately 4,000 in 2003. Diocson and others have written about the serious problems of immigrants who are admitted under the LCP program. Bakan and Stasiulis (1997) criticize the false benevolence behind Canada's policies forforeign domestic workers and argue that the compulsory live-in status for foreign domestics creates a situation where these workers gain none of the benefits and yet assume many of the costs of being 'one of the family.' As migrant workers, Filipinos are separated for a number of years from their families, causing emotional and familial disruption. In terms of Honneth's three forms of recognition, they and their families are prevented from obtaining the first form of recognition, which is 'love in the form of primary relationships' (Honneth 1996, 95) while they are away. Most community workers and scholars agree that the current policies for foreign domestics need to be revised. Some organizations, such as the Philippine Women's Centre, believe that the LCP should be eliminated altogether because the program results in long-term family separation and the de-skilling of workers (Philippine Women's Centre of Ontario 2009). Changes to immigration policies for foreign domestic workers and to the accreditation of education and work experience earned outside Canada would facilitate the transition from migrant worker to immigrant for Filipinos and other immigrants.

Inevitably, the subjectivity of the Filipino becomes shaped by the needs of global and transnational labour market. As Filipino Canadians, when we move from invisibility to recognition, what qualities are we solidifying, what images are we perpetuating about ourselves? Is there an economic and political consequence to being cast as 'pliable,' humane,' and 'co-operative'? Fraser (2000) warns against the model of recognition that 'tends also to reify identity.' She says, 'Stressing the need to elaborate and display an authentic, self-affirming and self-generated collective identity, it puts moral pressure on individual members to conform to a given group culture.' Instead of achieving recognition, she notes that 'the overall effect is to impose a single, drastically simplified group-identity which denies the complexity of people's lives, the multiplicity of their identifications and the cross-pulls of their various affiliations.' I am not suggesting that we suddenly become unfriendly, inhumane, or uncooperative in order to break the much-touted characteristics of good Filipinos. Rather, we ought to remember to represent ourselves not only as the Philippine Overseas Employment Administration wants Filipinos to be known, but also as ambitious leaders, courageous entrepreneurs, intelligent researchers, scientists, and visionary artists. We should encourage diversity within our cultural group whether in areas of professions and employment, our religious affiliations, sexual orientation, class and social status, age, or language.

In addition to research on Filipino Canadians as domestics, migrant workers, visible minorities, and immigrants, other areas of study might include inter-ethnic alliances, for example between Filipino and other Asian or black communities. We could examine the kinds of support and services provided by our religious affiliations – not just the Roman Catholic Church, but also an institution like the Iglesia ni Cristo, which has a rising and loyal following. What about the emergence of Filipino Canadian rap artists, or the consumer preferences and buying power of Filipino Canadians? Since we are becoming one of the largest groups among visible minorities in Canada, might we not press that more Southeast Asian history and culture to be included in elementary school curriculum? What about Tagalog as one of the languages to be included in more Saturday morning classes? How about Filipino shows on OMNI station in prime time? Another unexplored area of study is geography – the link between ethnic identity and space. Katherine McKittrick (2006), in her study of black women and geography, points out, 'social practices create landscapes and contribute to how we organize, build, and imagine our surroundings' (xiv). If we were urban planners designing living space for Filipino Canadians, would our streets and spaces look like the suburbs we have today?

Would shopping, eating, and socializing spaces be constructed differently? Would our houses be discrete single family homes separated by wooden fences? I know one thing I would definitely change. If I were an interior decorator, I would lower the mirrors hanging on the walls of public washrooms, because I can never see more than the top of my head. Public spaces in Canada and the United States are built for giants, in my view, and could be better designed to accommodate people who are non-Caucasian. The Filipino heritage of smallness could become a more appropriate model in our health- and environment-conscious culture, as a number of elements in our society have become oversized, wasteful, and over-indulgent in the last two decades: portions of food and drinks, excess packaging of merchandise, SUVs and other luxury cars.

Resisting Mis-Recognition: The Example of *Miss Orient(ed)*

In the last section of this chapter, I want to look at the artistic endeavours of talented Filipino Canadians in Toronto as an example of how some of these issues of recognition are handled. One group that has been featuring the work of Filipino Canadians since the 1980s is the Carlos Bulosan Theatre with its stated mandate: 'The Carlos Bulosan Theatre (CBT) aims to produce theatre that reflects on social and political issues affecting the Filipino and broader community. CBT is also committed to creating innovative work that reflects a vibrant, new generation of Filipino-Canadian artists' (Carlos Bulosan Theatre). The CBT encourages new play creation, showcases Filipino Canadian artists, and facilitates workshops on Philippine history. One of its most successful original productions to date is the play *Miss Orient(ed)*, written by Nina Lee Aquino and Nadine Villasin. First produced in 2003, the play highlights and satirizes some of the idealizations, misconceptions, and stereotypes of being a Filipina in Canada by juxtaposing the lives of three young women who are all contestants in the 'Miss Pearl of the Orient' beauty pageant.

Through comedy, parody, songs, and monologues, the play raises many of the issues of recognition and identity that I have been outlining in this chapter. The issues facing the three contestants are ones that have confronted other immigrant and ethnic groups: traditional old world values versus modern culture, the pleasures and dangers of assimilation into Western culture, and the negotiation of hybridized identities. For women, often the questions are linked to the performance of femininity, the exoticization and Orientalization of their bodies, and their sexuality. The play pokes fun at, but at the same time poignantly depicts, the aspirations and, often, misplaced hopes of two generations of Filipinas in Canada.

One of the contestants, Jennifer, expresses her confusion about her hyphenated cultural identity: 'What does being a Filipina mean to me. Being a Filipina means ... that I am from the Philippines ... means that I am a woman ... who is Filipino ... means that I am a good daughter to my mother ... means that I am an obedient daughter ...' (Aquino and Villasin 2009, scene 5). The passage raises important questions about recognition and belonging. Jennifer articulates issues that confront many Asian North Americans, particularly those second-generation youth whose parents engage in transnational practices. She reveals her confusion about the group identity of Filipino Canadians. Can one who does not speak Tagalog and who has never been to the Philippines be a 'Filipina'? Is the Filipina part of one's identity the residue that remains in one's blood, in one's physical appearance, or does it reside in cultural practice? Here Jennifer's definition of 'Filipina' slips from place of birth and origin to fulfilling one's familial responsibility. Part of her definition of the Filipina includes not only morally good behaviour, but filial obedience. The point is that second-generation youths are taught to see Filipino identity linked to an act of abnegation, which is contrary to Westernized notions of freedom and the pursuit of individual happiness.

Jennifer's feelings are similar to those expressed by second-generation Filipino Americans in California. Yen Le Espiritu (2003) notes that the identities of second-generation Filipino Americans are 'not fixed or singular, but multiple, overlapping, and simultaneous and that they reflect events both in the United States as well as in the "home country." Children of Filipino immigrants thus live with paradoxes. They feel strong symbolic loyalty to the Philippines, but they know very little about it and have little contact with their parents and other adults who might educate them about it. They feel pressured to become like "Americans," but their experiences as racialized subjects leave them with an uneasy relationship with both Filipino and U.S. culture' (204). In particular, the pressure for Jennifer to be an 'obedient daughter' reveals what Espiritu calls the 'paradox of immigrant resistance and accommodation' where 'Filipino families forge cultural resistance against racial oppression by stressing female chastity and sacrifice, and yet they reinforce patriarchal power and gender oppression by hinging ethnic and racial pride on the performance of female subordination' (216).

In another scene, Jennifer reveals her ambivalence about her ethnic and cultural identity. Remembering an old boyfriend named Andrew who was 'shiny and beautiful and perfect,' Jennifer says, 'There was something about being with him that made me feel ... dirty and crumpled ... I thought he should have been with someone tall and blonde and, you know ... the perfect Barbie and Ken couple. Me and Andrew? Well, we were more like ... Tonto and the Lone Ranger' (Aquino and Villasin 2009, scene 14). She explains that it was not anything that her white boyfriends did, but her own feelings of embarrassment when her 'mom brings the *lechon* to the table' or when her mom would get excited about the 'beautiful, fair babies' she would have. If she marries a white man, Jennifer wonders, 'are my kids going to look like me at all? ... when we walk down the street will people think, I'm their mommy or their nanny?' (Aquino and Villasin 2009, scene 14). Here, Jennifer expresses her anxieties about the social value of her race and ethnicity in comparison to white Canadians. The influence of Western (U.S.) popular media on her beliefs has been detrimental, as films, TV, toys, and cultural icons, such as Barbie and Ken, or Tonto and the Lone Ranger, do not provide adequate models for her. Up until very recently, U.S. pop culture has tended to reinforce racial whiteness as an ideal. Anne Cheng (2000) observes, 'There are still deep-seated, intangible, psychical complications for people living within a ruling episteme that privileges that which they can never be. This does *not* at all mean that the minority subject does not develop other relations to that injunctive ideal which can be self-affirming or sustaining but rather that a painful negotiation must be undertaken, at some point if not continually, with the demands of that social ideality, the reality of that always-insisted-on difference' (7). As Jennifer's comments illustrate, social policies and practices not only can have unintended and detrimental consequences for those directly involved, but can harm the social psyche of the whole community.

In the play, another character, Angie, whose husband owns the Macapanty Insurance, articulates the problems of assimilation and self-abnegation:

I have been living in Toronow since the nineties ... So how can you expect me to still speak fluent Tagalog? Or socialize with Filipinows? Oh, I don't mean I'm not proud to be Filipinow. I am but of course. I still eat adobo! ...

And let me tell you why. Well, first of all, they don't improve their English pro-nun-ci-a-shan! They don't improve their ed-u-ca-shan, for goodness sakes. Because they stick to each other and don't have a chance to practice speaking correct English with a Canadian accent, eh . . .

And this is a secret, but I'll tell you. That's why I had my nose fixed . . . It was a little flat and a little thick. I was starting to be really unhappy with it, because it was the only thing that was keeping me from being a true Canadian. (Aquino and Villasin 2009, scene 10)

Here Angie echoes right-wing conservative sentiment in her complaint about Filipinos not knowing how to 'integrate in Canadian society,' but this discourse is tinged with irony. Although she professes to be critical of Filipinos who are not assimilating well into Canadian society, through double-voiced discourse (Bakhtin 1981), her speech actually points out some of the ways Filipinos have been discriminated against, and what they have had to do in order to be perceived to be good citizens. As Angie notes, immigrants are not viewed as proper Canadians as long as they still speak with foreign accents. They have to work harder than others in order to be successful. This work ethic means competing against people in their own ethnic community sometimes, taking the shifts no one wants, seeing themselves as imperfect imitations of European Canadians. Angie even has to undergo surgery in order to make it as a Canadian. Regarding herself through the dominant white culture's gaze, she sees herself as inadequate. What she describes is the process of psychic disavowal and mimicry. Her nose job reveals her desire to be an 'authentic' Canadian through the process of what Homi Bhabha (1994) calls 'colonial mimicry.' Bhabha notes that mimicry produces a subject that is 'almost the same but not quite' the same as the white subject (88–9).

In addition, Angie reveals the degree in which she has abjected her own community in her effort to become integrated into society. She has internalized the demeaning images of Filipino Canadians and tries to distance herself from her own group. She tells us that her family saved money in order to move away from Toronto's Filipino town, as if it is only through ethnic disavowal that one is able to move up in the world. David Eng (2001) notes of this phenomenon, 'the untenable predicament of wanting to join a mainstream society that one knows clearly and systematically excludes oneself delineates the painful problem of becoming the instrument of one's own self-exclusion . . . In other words, the minority subject must, in the vein of the fetishist, simultaneously recognize and not recognize the material contradictions of institutionalized racism that claim his inclusion even as he is systemically excluded' (22). She reveals her insecurities about her ethnicity and has internalized cultural beliefs about her own people, leading to self-loathing. However, by re-enacting the problem on stage in a humorous way, *Miss Orient(ed)* changes the issue from an injury to an individual to a level of the social group and, in doing so, creates a kind of public awareness. Judith Butler (1997) notes that 'hate speech calls into question linguistic survival, that being called a name can be the site of injury,' yet she argues that 'this name-calling may be the initiating moment of counter-mobilization. The name one is called both subordinates and enables, producing a scene of agency from ambivalence, a set of effects that exceed the animating intentions of the call ... The word that wounds becomes an instrument of resistance in the redeployment that destroys the prior territory of its operation' (163).

Plays such as *Miss Orient(ed)* are important because they highlight a number of problems of recognition facing Filipino Canadians today. Through humour, exaggeration, and irony, the play repudiates common miscon/ceptions and mis-identifications about our contemporary lives as Filipinos in Canada. By showing some of ways we have been mis-orientated, it makes us more aware of assumptions about us made by others, and the conscious and unconscious ways we have been constructing ourselves. Artistic representations such as this play or spoken word performances may not be able to change policies directly, but they provide a forum for the articulation of problems and issues, and go a long way to validate and reinforce what Axel Honneth (1996) calls group 'solidarity.' As I have argued, while we should continue to study and examine pressing issues and inequalities that are experienced by our community members, we should also remember to highlight and celebrate the ways in which Filipino Canadians have been successful, the ways we have been participating in individual and collective resistance, in activism, invention, and leadership.[6] One of the challenges facing us, in our creative, academic, and professional endeavours as we go forward, is to find the best practices that will allow us to develop, experiment, affirm, recognize, and be recognized without falling into essentialist categories. In other words, ideally, we should be able to cultivate a healthy cultural group identity, take advantage of our strengths, while we welcome and allow for intragroup differences, and encourage and showcase the complexity and variety of our experience and desires as Filipino Canadians.

NOTES

1 In Canada, the Live-In Caregiver Program allows women from countries
   such as the Philippines to work as live-in domestics. After two years, they
   can apply to be permanent residents of Canada.
2 Taylor (1997) goes on to discuss the unresolved tension between equal
   recognition, which accords everyone with dignity and universal recognition, and the politics of difference, where we are asked to recognize the
   'unique identity of this individual or group, its distinctness from everyone
   else' (105).
3 I am thinking of ways of cooking a pig, where not only the *lechon* meat is
   considered a delicacy, but the ears, blood, liver, and guts are stewed, as in
   dinuguan or cooked in a *bopis*, which is made with pork lung, heart, and
   intestines.
4 E. San Juan, Jr (1996) traces the Philippines' neocolonial status back in
   history: 'Like other colonized formations, the Philippine precapitalist
   or tributary mode of production which evolved during three hundred
   years of Spanish rule was disarticulated and reworked by U.S. political-
   military power when it suppressed the Filipino revolutionary forces in the
   Filipino-American War of 1899–1903. This event harnessed the natural and
   human resources of the archipelago to the imperatives of accumulation of
   U.S. finance capital. But, while U.S. imperial diktat altered the economic-
   juridical mechanisms and adapted the feudal institutions to serve the
   paramount goal of extracting surplus value, the Philippines did not meta-
   morphose into a full-fledged industrial state' (55). Instead, Filipinos have
   become the 'transnational subaltern, virtually a new caste of "postcolonial"
   serfs – certainly not Goethe's world citizen but a wandering proletariat
   roaming the global village' (79).
5 In her article, Fraser does not cite any specific examples of those scholars
   who struggled for the 'recognition of difference' in the 1970s and 1980s,
   but what she stresses is that the politics of recognition affects not just one's
   social status, but also one's economic status. Taylor and Honneth, for example, do not discuss the economic repercussions when they discuss issues of
   recognition.
6 I am thinking of non-profit organizations, such as the Markham Association
   of Filipino Canadians, which gives a 'Distinguished Achievement' award
   every year to Filipino Canadians. The association mandate states, 'The
   Markham Federation of Filipino Canadians is a non-profit organization committed to the promotion and preservation of the Filipino culture and heritage

through dialogue, educational, social and cultural activities' (Markham Federation). In British Columbia, outstanding Filipino Canadians are similarly recognized by Dahong Pinoy (The Filipino Canadian Community and Business Directory), which recently celebrated its eighteenth anniversary (see Tobias 2011). By highlighting the leaders and successful individuals in the community, these associations contribute positively to what I have been calling the politics of recognition for Filipino Canadians.

REFERENCES

Ahmed, Sara. 2004. *The cultural politics of emotion*. New York: Routledge.

Aitken, Jenifer. 1987. A stranger in the family: The legal status of domestic workers in Ontario. *University of Toronto Law Review* 45: 394–415.

Aquino, Nina Lee, and Nadine Villasin. 2009. Miss orient(ed). In *Love +relasianships: A collection of contemporary Asian-Canadian drama*, vol. 2, ed. Nina Lee Aquino, 93–128. Toronto: Playwrights Canada Press.

Bakan, Abigail, and Daiva Stasiulis, eds. 1997. *Not one of the family: Foreign domestic workers in Canada*. Toronto: University of Toronto Press.

Bakhtin, Mikhail M. 1981. *The dialogic imagination: Four essays*, ed. Michael Holquist, trans. Caryl Emerson and Michael Holquist. Austin: University of Texas Press.

Barker, Drucilla K., and Susan F. Feiner. 2009. Affect, race, and class: An interpretive reading of caring labor. *Frontiers: A Journal of Women Studies* 30 (1): 41–54.

Bhabha, Homi. 1994. *The location of culture*. London: Routledge.

Butler, Judith. 1997. *Excitable speech: A politics of the performative*. New York: Routledge.

Carlos Bulosan Theatre. n.d. Mandate. Accessed September 12, 2009. www.carlosbulosan.com.

Cheng, Anne Anlin. 2000. *The melancholy of race*. New York: Oxford University Press.

Clough, Patricia Ticineto, ed. 2007. *The affective turn: Theorizing the social.* Durham, NC: Duke University Press.

Diocson, Cecilia. 2005. Filipino women in Canada, part 2. *Philreporter.com* February 28, 2005. http://www.philreporter.com/Issue04-1-15-05/Filipino%20Women%20in%20Canada.doc.

Elson, Diane, and Ruth Pearson. 1981. 'Nimble fingers make cheap workers': An analysis of women's employment in Third World export manufacturing. *Feminist Review* 7 (Spring): 87–107.

Eng, David L. 2001. *Racial castration: Managing masculinity in Asian America.* Durham, NC: Duke University Press.

England, Kim, and Bernadette Stiell. 1997. 'They think you're as stupid as your English is': Constructing foreign domestic workers in Toronto. *Environment and Planning A* 29: 195–215.

Ericta, Carmelita, et al. 2003. Profile of Filipino overseas workers: Results from the 2000 Census by population and housing, NSO. Paper presented to Statistical Research Centre (SRTC) annual conference. Quezon City, October. http://www.ancsdaap.org/cencon2003/Papers/Philippines/ Philippines.pdf.

Espiritu, Yen Le. 2003. *Home bound: Filipino American lives across cultures, communities, and countries.* Berkeley: University of California Press.

Fanon, Frantz. 1967. *Black skin, white masks,* trans. Charles Lam Markmann. New York: Grove.

Foucault, Michel. 1979. *Discipline and punish: The birth of the prison.* New York: Vintage.

Fraser, Nancy. 2000. Rethinking recognition. *New Left Review* 3 (May–June). http://www.newleftreview.org/?view=2248.

Hardt, Michael. 1999. Affective labor. *boundary 2* 26 (2): 89–100.

– 2007. Foreword: What affects are good for. In *The affective turn: Theorizing the social,* ed. Patricia Ticineto Clough with Jean Halley, ix–xiii. Durham, NC: Duke University Press.

Hawkins, Joyce, compiler. 1991. *Oxford paperback dictionary.* 3rd ed. Oxford: Oxford University Press.

Honneth, Axel. 1996. *Struggle for recognition: The moral grammar of social conflicts,* trans. Joel Anderson. Cambridge, MA: Massachusetts Institute of Technology Press.

Human Resources and Skills Development Canada. 2006. A profile of Filipinos in Canada. Accessed September 20, 2009. http://www.hrsdc.gc.ca/eng/lp/lo/ lswe/we/ee_tools/data/eedr/annual/2001/dgprofiles/filipinosprofile.shtml.

Institute for Labor Studies. 2004. Too many caregivers? (July – September). Accessed September 20, 2009. http://www.ilsdole.gov.ph/Publication/ NewsDigest/JSep2004/nDjs04_1.htm.

Jimenez, Marina. 2008. Filipinos top the immigrant and temporary-worker lists. *Globe and Mail,* December 17, 2008. http://kapisanancentre. com/2009/01/06/filipinos-top-the-immigrant-and-temporary-worker-lists/.

Joaquin, Nick. 2008. A heritage of smallness. In 'Nick Joaquin stereotypes the Filipino people and forgets to discuss their heritage of greatness' by Bobby Reyes. *Mabuhay Radio.* Tuesday, May 20. http://www.mabuhayradio.com/ content/view/2890/90/.

Kymlicka, Will. 1998. *Finding our way: Rethinking ethnocultural relations in Canada.* Toronto: Oxford University Press.

Lee, Robert G. 1999. *Orientals: Asian Americans in popular culture.* Philadelphia: Temple University Press.

Li, Peter S. 1999. The multiculturalism debate. In *Race and ethnic relations in Canada,* 2nd ed., ed. Peter S. Li, 148–77. Toronto: Oxford University Press.

Lorente, Beatriz P. 2010. Packaging English-speaking products: Maid agencies in Singapore. In *Language and the market,* ed. H. Kelly-Holmes and G. Mautner. New York: Palgrave-Macmillan.

Mackey, Eva. 2002. *The house of difference: Cultural politics and national identity in Canada.* Toronto: University of Toronto Press.

Markham Federation of Filipino Canadians. 2011. http://mffc.ca/m/.

McKay, Steven C. 2007. Filipino sea men: Identity and masculinity in a global labor niche. In *Asian diasporas: New formations, new conceptions,* ed. Rhacel S. Parreñas and Lok C.D. Siu, 63–83. Stanford: Stanford University Press.

McKittrick, Katherine. 2006. *Demonic grounds: Black women and the cartographies of struggle.* Minneapolis: University of Minnesota Press.

Ofreneo, Rene, and Isabelo Samonte. 2005. Empowering Filipino migrant workers: Policy issues and challenges. *International Migration Papers* 64. Geneva: International Labour Organization. http://www.ilo.org/public/english/protection/migrant/download/imp/imp64.pdf.

Oliver, Kelly. 2001. *Witnessing: Beyond recognition.* Minneapolis: University of Minnesota Press.

Parreñas, Rhacel Salazar. 2001. *Servants of globalization: Women, migration, and domestic work.* Stanford: Stanford University Press.

Philippine Overseas Employment Administration. 2006. Filipino workers moving the world today. Accessed July 9, 2009, http://www.poea.gov.ph/about/moving.htm.

Philippine Women's Centre of Ontario. 2009. Filipino women in Canada continue the struggle to scrap the LCP and for our genuine freedom. Accessed January 7, 2010, http://www.magkaisacentre.org/2009/03/09/filipino-women-in-canada-continue-the-struggle-to-scrap-the-lcp-and-for-our-genuine-freedom/.

Pratt, Geraldine. 1999. From registered nurse to registered nanny: Discursive geographies of Filipina domestic workers in Vancouver, B.C. *Economic Geography* 75: 215–36.

San Juan, Jr, E. 1996. *The Philippine temptation: Dialectics of Philippines – U.S. literary relations.* Philadelphia: Temple University Press.

Sedgwick, Eve Kosofsky. 2003. *Touching feeling: Affect, pedagogy, performativity.* Durham, NC: Duke University Press.

Stasiulis, Daiva K., and Abigail B. Bakan. 2005. *Negotiating citizenship: Migrant women in Canada and the global system.* Toronto: University of Toronto Press.

Statistics Canada. 2007. The Filipino community in Canada. Accessed July 20, 2009. http://www.statcan.gc.ca/pub/89-621-x/89-621-x2007005-eng.htm.

Synnott, Anthony, and David Howes. 1996. Canada's visible minorities: Identity and representation. In *Resituating identities: The politics of race, ethnicity, and culture,* ed. Vered Amit-Talai and Caroline Knowles, 137–60. Peterborough: Broadview.

Tadiar, Neferti X.M. 2009. *Things fall away: Philippine historical experience and the makings of globalization.* Durham, NC: Duke University Press.

Taylor, Charles. 1997. The politics of recognition. In *New contexts of Canadian criticism,* ed. Ajay Heble, Donna Palmateer Penne, and Tim Struthers, 98–131. Peterborough: Broadview.

Wissinger, Elizabeth. 2007. Always on display: Affective production in the modeling industry. In *The affective turn: Theorizing the social,* ed. Patricia Clough with Jean Halley, 231–60. Durham, NC: Duke University Press.

Chapter 3

Filipino Immigrants in the Toronto Labour Market: Towards an Understanding of Deprofessionalization

PHILIP F. KELLY, MILA ASTORGA-GARCIA,
ENRICO F. ESGUERRA, AND THE COMMUNITY
ALLIANCE FOR SOCIAL JUSTICE, TORONTO[1]

Introduction

Deprofessionalization, credential non-recognition, and concentration in certain kinds of jobs are all experiences that Filipinos share with many other immigrants to Canada. They are also processes that have received a great deal of popular and policy attention in recent years. In much of the discussion of these issues, however, labour market marginalization has been assumed to be a generic 'immigrant' issue, with newcomers finding difficulty breaking into Canadian professions because of regulatory barriers, differences in the cultures of professional practices, and employers' demands for 'Canadian experience.' These are all important and widely applicable issues, but assuming a universalized immigrant experience also masks a great deal that is specific to particular groups.

In this chapter, we argue first that there is a specific set of factors that shape the Filipino experience of integration into the Toronto labour market. While acknowledging that these factors taken in isolation are replicated in the experiences of other immigrant groups, and that there exists a great deal of diversity of experiences among the Filipino community, we believe that together they represent a distinctive set of circumstances that help us to understand the experiences of many Filipinos.

The first factor concerns the Philippines as a country of origin. Given the class structure of Philippine society, the class origins of most Filipino immigrants, and the place of the Philippines in the global economic order, Filipinos generally arrive in Canada with relatively modest financial assets, and this situation affects their integration into the labour market. The second factor concerns the distinctive profile of immigration programs used by Filipino immigrants, and particularly the implications of high usage of caregiver and family reunification categories. The third factor concerns credential assessment and access to professions. The final factor concerns the ways in which culturally 'being Filipino' is interpreted in Canadian workplaces and broader society. This relates to a certain culture of work brought to Canada from the Philippines, and the ways in which that is interpreted and valorized in Canadian workplaces. It also relates to how Filipino-ness is culturally 'read,' and often stereotyped, in Canadian society.

Understanding Filipino immigrant experiences in the labour market as shaped distinctively by these factors takes us beyond existing studies that have tended to focus on the conditions of work and citizenship imposed by the Live-In Caregiver Program (Bakan and Stasiulis 1997; McKay 2002; Pratt 2004; Spitzer and Torres 2008), or have provided more general accounts of the history of settlement (Laquian 1973; Cusipag and Buenafe 1993; Chen 1998; Laquian and Laquian 2008). Relatively few studies have examined the broader issue of labour market integration among Filipinos (although see Kelly 2006; Kelly and D'Addario 2008).

While establishing the context of Filipino settlement and labour market integration using quantitative data, this chapter develops its argument about the processes behind such patterns using qualitative material. This is an analytically important combination of methods and data types. While quantitative data provide important indications of aggregate patterns, and possibly some significant correlations, it is only through qualitative data that the social processes behind those patterns can be understood. It is also important to note that although we attempt to develop a picture of the distinctiveness of the Filipino experience, we do not engage in an explicit comparison with other immigrant groups. While this would be a fruitful avenue for inquiry, it was beyond the scope of the research described here.

This chapter is based upon a collaboration between university- and community-based researchers associated with the Community Alliance for Social Justice (CASJ), a Filipino advocacy organization in Toronto engaged in research, education, and community mobilization. In the first stage of the collaboration, in 2005–6, a survey of Philippine-educated immigrants in Toronto was undertaken, eliciting information on their immigration history, their educational and professional training, their experiences in the Canadian labour market, and their reflections on the barriers that prevent them from achieving their full potential. The survey was distributed by CASJ; 421 completed surveys were returned.

The survey was followed by two sets of focus groups. The first set was conducted in 2006–7 with groups of Filipino professionals (some were practising their professions, but most were unable to do so): engineers, accountants, physiotherapists, and nurses. These focus groups were designed to address the barriers that exist for Filipino professionals seeking access to specific licensed professions (selected to reflect the largest groups of professionals represented in Filipino immigration flows). The second set was conducted in 2007–8, and involved individuals working in occupations for which professional licensing is not a necessary pre-condition for upward mobility in the workplace: these participants worked in hotels, retail, manufacturing, clerical positions, and ancillary jobs in the healthcare system.

Filipino Immigration and Labour Market Integration

In recent years, the number of Filipino immigrant landings in Canada has grown dramatically. Between the late 1990s and 2010, Filipino landings almost quadrupled from 9,528 in 1999 to 36,578 in 2010. In 2010 the Philippines was Canada's largest single source country for new immigrants, constituting 13 per cent of all new arrivals. At the time of the May 2006 census, one-quarter of Filipino immigrants had arrived within the last five years. Almost two-thirds had arrived since the early 1990s. Thus although Filipino immigration began in significant numbers in the 1960s, the growing numbers arriving since the 1990s mean that the community as a whole is weighted towards recent immigrants. A second distinctive feature of the migration stream from the Philippines has been the importance of special immigration categories for domestic workers. In the 1990s, the Live-In Caregiver Program accounted for about one-quarter of all Filipinos who gained immigrant status in Canada (Kelly et al. 2009). By the late 2000s, this proportion was approaching 40 per cent. This program has had a major influence on the experiences of Filipinos in the Canadian labour market and on the gender composition of the Filipino community – overall, women composed 59 per cent of immigrants from the Philippines between 1980 and 2005.

In 2006, 41.3 per cent of all Filipino immigrants residing in Toronto aged twenty-five years and over had a university qualification at the bachelor's level or above, compared with 28.8 per cent for all immigrant groups, and 31.9 per cent for non-immigrant residents of the Toronto Census Metropolitan Area in the same age group. This relatively high level of education among Filipino immigrants is all the more striking given the high numbers arriving as sponsored family members or live-in caregivers – immigration programs that are not driven primarily by human capital considerations.

High levels of human capital have not, however, translated into an overall picture of labour market success for Filipino immigrants. Table 3.1 shows selected occupations where Filipinos are under- or overrepresented in the Toronto labour market. A striking overrepresentation in healthcare, clerical work, and manufacturing is evident, and a notable underrepresentation in managerial and supervisory roles as well as education and government. Within sectors, Filipinos are notably over-concentrated in lower-paid jobs, and underrepresented in better-paid, more secure positions.

This pattern of occupational segmentation translates into lower average wage levels overall (see table 3.2). Census figures show Filipino men in particular earning significantly less than the average for immigrants or for the population in general. A similar, although less pronounced disparity also exists for Filipina women. Clearly, however, Filipina women, and women in general, are disadvantaged in the labour market relative to their male counterparts – indeed gender accounts for a far greater degree of differentiation than immigrant status. Table 3.2 also shows the particular disadvantages faced by more recent immigrants.

We used our survey data to classify respondents into three groups: 'perfectly matched' implies that occupations before immigration, and currently, are roughly equivalent. That is, the individual is working in his or her professional field. The second category is 'different/flexible,' which implies that although the present job does not match previous experience in the Philippines, it did not necessarily represent a downward movement. Finally, the 'downward' category includes all of those cases where an individual has clearly been deprofessionalized.

Table 3.3 provides labour market outcome data broken down by gender, immigration category, and period of immigration. Overall, 53.9 per cent of respondents had experienced downward mobility, although it is notable that the incidence of downward mobility was substantially higher among men than women, and among live-in caregivers and recent immigrants.

A striking feature of table 3.4 is that the incidence of downward mobility was actually higher for those entering through the skilled worker

Table 3.1. Distribution across selected occupation of working population (by Filipino visible minority, and general population), Toronto Census Metropolitan Area, 2006

Occupation	Filipino* working population		Total working population		Over- or under-representation of Filipinos**	
	Male	Female	Male	Female	Male	Female
Senior management	120	135	35,540	11,265	0.1	0.3
Specialist managers	700	925	65,345	44,990	0.4	0.5
Managers in retail, food, and hotels	425	785	45,475	32,405	0.4	1.0
Professionals in business and finance	995	1,980	59,550	55,650	0.7	1
Finance and insurance administration	305	1,055	11,115	29,445	1	1.0
Secretaries		870	1,395	40,315		0.6
Administrative and regulatory	325	1,095	18,100	55,845	0.7	0.5
Clerical supervisors	265	395	9,495	10,710	1	1.0
Clerical	4,735	10,455	111,570	239,985	2	1
Professionals in natural and applied sciences	2,080	1,090	115,855	38,510	0.7	0.8
Technical jobs in natural and applied sciences	2,445	790	65,465	18,050	1	1
Professionals in health	115	360	17,005	18,295	0.3	0.5
Nurse supervisors and registered nurses	430	3,670	2,110	34,595	8	3
Technical and related occupations in health	505	1,595	7,840	20,805	3	2
Assisting jobs in support of health services	620	2,980	4,265	27,105	6	3
Judges, lawyers, psychologists, social workers, ministers of religion, and policy/program officers	315	460	33,450	42,300	0.4	0.3
Teachers and professors	175	590	37,505	78,185	0.2	0.2
Sales and service supervisors	360	615	10,490	11,540	1	1
Wholesale, technical, insurance, real estate sales specialists, and retail, wholesale, and grain buyers	665	595	48,345	33,105	1	0.5
Retail salespersons and sales clerks	1,025	2,250	59,690	81,430	0.7	0.7
Cashiers	260	1,880	10,815	45,590	0.9	1
Chefs and cooks	675	425	24,590	10,125	1	1
Occupations in food and beverage service	215	435	12,470	26,260	0.7	0.4

Occupation	Filipino* working population		Total working population		Over- or under-representation of Filipinos**	
	Male	Female	Male	Female	Male	Female
Occupations in protective services	540	140	29,350	7,485	0.7	0.5
Occupations in travel and accommodation, including attendants in recreation and sport	350	370	10,475	14,630	1	0.7
Childcare and home support workers	280	5,795	3,830	39,875	3	4
Sales and service occupations, n.e.c.	4,570	5,035	100,300	105,675	2	1
Supervisors in manufacturing	270	120	9,330	2,725	1	1
Machine operators in manufacturing	3,145	1,275	45,955	33,000	3	1
Assemblers in manufacturing	2,805	1,420	41,205	24,715	3	2
Labourers in processing, manufacturing, and utilities	1,435	1,505	24,475	32,365	2	1

* This refers to individuals who recorded their visible minority status as 'Filipino' in the 2006 Census. It therefore includes both immigrants and non-immigrants.

** The measure of over- or under-representation is calculated based on the proportion of Filipino men or women in an occupation relative to the proportion all men and women in an occupation. If Filipinos were found in a given job in exactly the same proportion as the general population, then the index would be 1.0. Lower than 1.0 indicates an under-representation. Hence 0.5 would imply that there are half as many Filipinos in a job as there 'should be.' An index of 2.0 implies that there are twice as many Filipinos as would be expected.

program (three-quarters of whom were the principal applicants) than the family reunification category. The more stringent selection criteria relating to human capital endowments associated with the skilled worker category would appear not to result in better labour market outcomes. This may reflect the fact that an overwhelming majority of our respondents were highly educated, regardless of the immigration category they used. Clearly, the discounting of this human capital is common across all immigrant categories.

This section has highlighted a general pattern of labour market integration for the Filipino community. High levels of human capital are clearly devalued, leading to distinctive patterns of occupational segmentation and a concentration in low-wage, non-professional

Table 3.2. Average employment income for those with full year, full-time employment, by gender, period of immigration, and selected places of birth, Toronto Census Metropolitan Area, 2005

	Average employment income (C$) for population aged 15 years and over with full-time, full-year employment income	Period of immigration			
		Before 1991	1991–5	1996–2000	2001–6
Female – born in philippines	39,315	45,595	35,547	36,689	30,504
ALL female immigrants	42,630	47,726	37,182	36,929	31,378
ALL female non-immigrants	55,302				
Total female population	48,881				
Male – born in Philippines	45,632	53,197	40,967	43,287	35,968
ALL male immigrants	58,318	67,937	47,738	48,246	40,629
ALL male non-immigrants	81,606				
Total male population	69,912				

Source: Calculated from Statistics Canada 2008

employment. In the next four sections of this chapter we address issues that arose in our qualitative research as we attempted to identify the processes behind these aggregate patterns.

Being from the Philippines: Financial Obligations and the 'Survival Job'

Immigrants are not simply newcomers to Canada, they are also arriving from *somewhere*. The features of the place of origin matter not only in terms of how racialized identities are ascribed (as we will discuss later), but also in terms of the types of individuals and families that migrate and the assets (both human capital and financial capital) that they bring with them.

Assets, relative wealth, and exchange rates matter because immigration is an expensive process. At the very least, immigration to Canada

Table 3.3. Occupational mobility between the Philippines and Canada for survey respondents, by gender

		Perfectly matched	Different / flexible	Downward	Total
Total	Count	59	41	117	217
	%	27.2	18.9	53.9	100.0
Sex					
Male	Count	21	16	67	104
	%	20.2	15.4	64.4	100.0
Female	Count	37	24	50	111
	%	33.3	21.6	45.0	100.0
Immigration category					
LCP / domestic	Count	5	10	29	44
	%	11.0	23.0	66.0	100.0
Family /	Count	21	18	29	68
reunification	%	30.9	26.5	42.6	100.0
Independent	Count	28	11	58	97
skilled worker	%	28.9	11.3	59.8	100.0
Period of immigration					
Immigrated	Count	26	23	17	66
before 1991	%	39.4	34.8	25.8	100.0
Immigrated 1991	Count	16	11	26	53
to 1995	%	30.2	20.8	49.1	100.0
Immigrated 1996	Count	4	4	20	28
to 2000	%	14.3	14.3	71.4	100.0
Immigrated 2001	Count	13	3	54	70
to 2006	%	18.6	4.3	77.1	100

Source: CASJ Survey, 2005

requires about $1,500 for immigration and landing fees, perhaps the same amount again for a single air ticket, and other expenses such as medical examinations, notarizing documents, obtaining passports, and so on. For many, the costs are further inflated by payments to immigration consultants and recruiters. In our survey, 25 per cent of respondents (n = 96) reported having used an immigration consultant or recruiter when they immigrated (two-thirds of that number had entered under the caregiver program). Costs vary, but one focus group participant estimated that consultants generally charged about $6,000 for a complete package of services.

Table 3.4. Levels of savings on arrival in Canada, and average month to find first job for immigrants from major source countries, by gender (for arrivals in 2000–1)

Top countries of origin	Total N (weighted)	Average savings on landing (in $2005)		Average months to 1st job	
		M	F	M	F
India	20,980	$20,300	$28,700	2.2	4.7
China	25,040	$31,800	$43,000	5.7	8.2
Philippines	11,040	$17,900	$18,400	2.3	4.3
Pakistan	6,170	$22,000	$28,800	2.3	5.2
Iran	3,620	$44,400	$48,000	9.6	16.6
Sri Lanka	3,040	$18,400	$21,600	3.5	12.8

Source: Longitudinal Survey of Immigrants to Canada

Filipino immigrants finance their immigration in various ways. Some sell or mortgage assets such as homes, businesses, or land. Others borrow from extended family networks in the Philippines, or from relatives working elsewhere overseas. Many immigrants have themselves worked overseas (for example in Singapore, Hong Kong, or the Middle East) before arriving in Canada. In our survey, almost one-third (130) of our respondents had worked in other countries before arriving in Canada.

For the most part, then, immigrants have access to financial resources to fund their applications, but these seldom provide sufficient capital to invest in property or to tide them over a period of job hunting, retraining, or educational upgrading. Upon arrival, they must pay for initial living expenses for food, accommodation, and transport. Even a family that has property to sell in the Philippines would be in a weak position to invest in Canada's expensive housing markets or to survive while a breadwinner undergoes retraining or credential evaluation. This situation represents an important difference between an immigrant arriving from a country such as the Philippines, and one arriving from a country such as Singapore, Japan, the United Kingdom, or the United States, where property prices and exchange rates allow for a soft landing in Canada.

The data in table 3.4 provide some striking indications of the savings that different groups of immigrants bring to Canada, and how these differences might be correlated with labour market outcomes. The data are derived from the Longitudinal Survey of Immigrants to Canada, which surveyed new immigrants who landed in 2000–1.

The data show that among the largest groups of immigrants (by country of origin) Filipinos arrive, on average, with the smallest amounts of savings. Not surprisingly, they are then among the quickest to find work, suggesting that having limited financial resources necessitates a rapid entry into the labour market. In some cases, the money that immigrants bring with them is a loan that must be repaid. The repayment of these debts incurred in the immigration process and the shortage of funds to support retraining or extended job hunting have important consequences for labour market integration, to which we will return shortly. Such financial imperatives are, however, exacerbated by the family circumstance of many Filipino immigrants.

Among Filipino immigrants, almost two-thirds arrive under the family reunification and caregiver categories, implying that the majority have experienced some form of separation from their immediate nuclear family – a period of separation that might include several years in a third country before arriving in Canada. In most cases, such individuals are trying to support family members back home, while saving to fund their immigration applications and travel expenses, so that the family can be reunited in Canada. The pressure to support family members in the Philippines creates a further strain on the personal finances of new immigrants.

In short, whether it is to pay off their own immigration and initial settlement costs, support family members back in the Philippines, or finance the reunification of their family in Canada, Filipino immigrants face an immediate need for income and for ongoing and stable employment. The fact that family separation is particularly common among Filipino immigrants, in combination with the class origins of Filipino immigrants, makes this an acute issue.

This finding has several consequences in the labour market. First, it means that immigrants must seek and accept survival jobs rather than waiting for an appropriate opening to come along. A participant in our focus group with Filipinos working in the manufacturing sector explained this process:

I came to Canada only last year, in September. Still fresh. My work in the Philippines was quite different from my work now. In the Philippines I worked for five years in an insurance company, so it was the typical office in Makati [Manila's financial district]. When I came to Canada, after a month, I was hired in my current workplace, first as a general labourer. So all the factories, the machines, it was quite shocking for me. But because of the urge of finding a job, for imme-diate survival in Canada, because I have a wife, I immediately grabbed it. (Male respondent, authors' focus group with manufacturing workers, 2007)

Second, financial distress means that the expense of studying or training to upgrade qualifications is often impossible to cover. In a focus group with hotel workers, a nurse trained in the Philippines noted this issue:

You have to upgrade. Even if you are a registered nurse back home or pharmacist you cannot practise here without a licence. You have to take the course. You go all over again. You have to spend a lot of money. When I took that nursing aide course – one course is … very expensive. Books. Not easy. When you are just earning a few dollars an hour … those are the things that lock you into this kind of job. And sometimes, even though you have the money, after working, if you are doing hard physical work, you can't study anymore. (Female respondent, authors' focus group with Filipino hotel workers, 2007)

Third, there is evidence that once in a workplace, Filipino immigrants may hold back from seeking advancement into higher-paid positions with supervisory or managerial responsibilities because of the require-ment for a steady and secure income. In some sectors, higher-paid jobs require employees to leave the safety of a unionized job for one from which they can be fired at any time. In focus groups, hotel cleaners and clerical workers described avoiding better-paid jobs, for example as front desk workers or clerical supervisors, because they were outside the union and had no job security.

Some do not apply for higher positions especially, because they perceive these as lacking in security. These positions are not unionized. So if one gets into a higher position that soon becomes redundant, or management decides to cut back and lay him off, that person will have no other option. (Male respondent, authors' focus group with clerical workers, 2007)

The combination of financial vulnerability, obligations to family back home, the need for a 'survival job,' the lack of time or money to undergo retraining or upgrading, and a desire to stay in secure unionized jobs rather than seek advancement might all be common to many immigrant groups as they integrate into the Toronto labour market. Two features, however, accentuate these processes in the Filipino community. The first is the class profile of immigrants coming from the Philippines and the wider question of the place of the Philippines in the global economic order, both of which mean that immigrants usually arrive with relatively few financial resources. The second is the widespread phenomenon of family separation which, in the case of the Live-In Caregiver Program, is actually enforced through conditions imposed by Canadian immigration regulations. Such separation means that Filipino immigrants, more than most, are working in Toronto with extensive obligations to support immediate family members back home.

Immigration Programs

All immigrant groups use a distinctive combination of immigration programs for their entry to Canada, although the majority of new immigrants still enter Canada as independent skilled migrants, with relatively fewer immigrants entering under the family reunification program. In 2010, 172,975 immigrants entered Canada as independent skilled migrants, whereas only 60,207 immigrants entered under the family reunification program (Statistics Canada 2011). Among Filipino immigrants, the especially high usage of family reunification and live-in caregiver categories implies that many migrations follow extended periods of family separation, with implications for the labour market integration of those seeking to support distant families and for family members after they reunite.

Of particular note in the Filipino case is the high number of arrivals under the Live-In Caregiver Program (LCP) and the specific rules and conditions that apply to this immigration category. In our survey, 133 respondents (125 females, 8 males) had entered Canada under the LCP. Of these, 73 had passed through the program requirements and acquired permanent resident status. No one in this group had less than a high school education, while 79 per cent had a college degree at the bachelor's level or higher. Despite this level of human capital, the survey revealed that two-thirds of caregivers for whom a comparison was possible had experienced downward mobility (see table 3.3). Most were either still working as caregivers, housekeepers, or personal support workers, or in clerical or customer-service roles, manufacturing employment, or aide/assistant positions in the healthcare sector. In only 5 out of 73 cases (11 per cent) were individuals employed in occupations that approximated their original occupational category in the Philippines – all had undergone further training in Canada.

This pattern of downward mobility is largely attributable to the regulatory requirements of the Live-In Caregiver Program. The program requires that the individual completes two years of work in the home of an employer within three years. Only then is the caregiver eligible to apply for permanent residency. The corollary of this requirement is that 'graduates' from the program have been removed from a professional working environment for at least two years. Since many arrive after completing contracts as domestic workers in Asia or the Middle East, the actual separation from professional employment is in fact much longer.

The institutionalized form of deprofessionalization imposed by the LCP clearly affects those enrolled in the program directly. The implications of the program are, however, felt more widely for two reasons. The first is that job search networks tend to operate through personal referrals and social networks. Thus, a large segment of the Filipino community is consigned to precarious and low-paid care work, since those who arrive under other immigration programs, but rely on relatives and friends who are already in Canada to find work, tend to be channelled into similarly precarious work. The prevalence of personal social networks in job search processes was also evident in survey data. Upon arrival, more than 44 per cent of our survey respondents were aided by friends or relatives in the process of finding work. Similarly, 47 per cent of all responses to the question indicated that Filipino family, friends, and networks had led individuals to their current job.

These figures are significant not because they are higher than in other groups (evidence suggests that a similar proportion of both immigrants and Canadian-born employees find work through family/friend networks – see Fang et al. 2010) but because the process of social network–based job searching can clearly lead to a self-perpetuating occupational segmentation. If Filipinos are relying heavily upon other Filipinos in their job searches, there will inevitably be a reproduction of existing occupational niches. An example of this process was provided by our focus group with hotel employees. For many, the hotel sector represented employment easily obtained through personal networks, but it seldom provided time or money to attend upgrading classes.

PHILIP: *So there are certain jobs in the hotel sector that are dominated by Filipinos. Why is that, do you think? Why are there so many Filipinos working as room attendants?*

RESPONDENT: *Maybe it's the easy job for them, I don't know. Because you know, we just came here, it's like, I don't know, so where was I gonna go. And they [fellow Filipinos] said, 'Come, I'm going to help you apply in the hotel.'*
PHILIP: *So you found it through a Filipino friend?*
RESPONDENT: *Yes, my brother. He was working in the hotel and he said, 'If you want to work right away, I'm going to help you.' I go to school also before, but I cannot handle [that] . . . because I still don't have money. So in that time, I go to that hotel.*
(Female respondent, authors' focus group with Filipino hotel workers, 2007)

The importance of the caregiver program thus extends not just to those who are enrolled in it, but also to larger numbers of new arrivals, whether or not they come under the LCP, who depend on their compatriots to find work. While the LCP directly accounts for just one-fifth of Filipino immigrant arrivals, it has multiplier effects on the wider Filipino immigrant community. Entry into 'survival jobs' is, so to speak, contagious.

The second implication of the caregiver program concerns the ways in which Filipinos are racialized and culturally represented in the labour market. A clear stereotype exists of 'what Filipinos do' and where their aptitudes lie. It is not uncommon to find that non-Filipinos believe that all Filipinos arrive in Canada as caregivers. Thus the types of work for which they are seen as culturally suited is highly circumscribed.

Regulatory Barriers: Credential Assessment and Cultures of Practice

The role of professional regulatory bodies as gatekeepers to licensed professions has been closely examined in the literature on immigrant integration (Boyd 2002; Girard and Bauder 2007; Turegan 2008). Upon arrival in Canada, licensed professionals are required to have their educational backgrounds assessed by provincially mandated professional bodies, which oversee the accreditation process. Successful completion of this process does not, of course, guarantee employment, but is the first step towards finding a job in a regulated profession.

In focus groups with Filipino professionals, specific problems were identified concerning the ways in which Philippine qualifications, in particular, were evaluated. The first was an ignorance on the part of evaluation bodies regarding the quality of specific Philippine educational institutions, the quality of their (North American–designed) curricula, and the rigour of the professional regulatory system in the Philippines. Focus group participants were especially critical of the ways in which Philippine institutions were judged. One noted that graduates of the Mapua Institute of Technology, the Philippines' foremost engineering college, would not fare well, as assessors tend to look down on 'institutes,' or anything not clearly identified as a university:

> *I would say that they [assessors] have little or no knowledge of what is happening. For example, the Institute of Technology … it doesn't say college, it doesn't say university. They would, say, take about a four- or six-month course. And they see University of Philippines, they see 'Philippines,' they would say 'Oh, that is nothing.' But one person came from National University [a minor university in the Philippines]. It's not 'Philippines,' it's 'National.' They gave him four subjects. But the same university, other curriculum, but same university, given eight subjects. So they are very inconsistent.* (Male respondent, authors' focus group with Philippine-educated engineers, 2005)

Another Philippine-trained accountant described the ignorance he felt existed among those assessing his education, training, and experience:

> *What I am saying here is that it's the level of knowledge of these people who evaluate the graduates and that's what causes the problem. I guess it is important for these people to be also educated to the kind of … They ask like 'Do you read English there?' Our books are American books! But they don't know that.* (Male respondent, authors' focus group with Philippine-trained accountants, 2006)

A second dimension of the accreditation process raised by focus group participants in certain professions was the role of the practical examination. For physiotherapists, for example, licensing in Ontario requires a 'hands-on' test of practical skills that includes communications with the patient. The Filipino physiotherapists in our focus group felt that assessing such practices was culturally specific and favoured candidates who conformed to the cultural expectations of the examiners.

RESPONDENT 1: *It is always an issue of subjectivity, because it is a person that is going to look at you, and I don't know if it is relevant to say that, but I've heard … because one of my colleagues, always working as a physical therapy assistant, he overheard a physical therapist here being an examiner and telling a colleague of his*

*that as soon as the examinee comes to the station, he already has the notion of what
to give.*
RESPONDENT 2: *I mean not only that, but how many stereotypes enter into that? It
becomes quite subjective.*
(Male respondents, authors' focus group with Philippine-educated physiotherapists, 2006)

Being Filipino: Cultures of Work and Racialization

More insidious ways in which being Filipino presents disadvantages in
the labour market derive from how Filipino-ness is represented, marked,
and understood. There are two ways in which being Filipino might be
construed as a disadvantage. The first concerns the cultural practices of
work that Filipino immigrants bring with them from their work experiences and socialization in the Philippines. Practices that in one cultural
context might be viewed as meritorious and virtuous may, in another,
hold an employee back from workplace advancement and upward
mobility. The second concerns discrimination and the racialization of
Filipinos, which involves the ascription of particular characteristics and
aptitudes on the basis of ethno-racial labelling. Racialization represents
a useful framework for understanding these processes as it implies the
insidious process of viewing groups as different and unequal through a
culturally invented racial framework (Galabuzi 2001).

Filipino Work Cultures and 'Promotability'

Focus group respondents repeatedly noted what they perceived to
be a specifically Filipino culture of work that they brought with them
from the Philippines. This set of cultural practices includes taking on
all tasks required of them, regardless of their job description, not being
assertive in relation to authority figures, and not being boastful of their
achievements and abilities. In focus group discussions, these cultural
traits were repeatedly identified, usually in comparison with white colleagues or other visible minorities.

In the Philippines, managerial hierarchies are more rigid than in
Canada, and superiors are addressed as 'Sir' or 'Ma'am.' Many respondents felt employers took advantage of this different, and deferential,
work culture. In some cases, focus group participants felt that employers had a clear interest in keeping capable and co-operative employees
in certain kinds of subordinate positions.

RESPONDENT 1: *But Filipinos are regarded well, right? We work hard, we are conscientious, we're caring. And so that works for us in a lot of ways, but then there is the limiting way that that also works 'cause then we may not be perceived in terms of a managerial role.*

RESPONDENT 2: *Because we are viewed, and perceived to be passive. That you don't speak up. You just keep on taking it and get it done, don't complain. So why would I move him if he is taking all of these responsibilities, same pay same everything, as opposed to I can give it to her, she complains all the time, for example. I see that in my workplace. And there are a lot of Filipinos in my area in data entry. And I have heard remarks. And even towards me, like if you don't speak up. So you really have to learn to speak up. And the data entry clerks, they were saying they don't speak up or complain, because everyone is scared, because they are a migrant here so you don't want to lose your job because you need that job. So you can't.*

(Female respondents, authors' focus group with Filipino retail workers, 2007)

Racialization of Filipinos

The second dimension of 'being Filipino' in a cultural sense in the labour market relates to racialization and stereotyping by broader Canadian society. In many instances, our respondents felt they were expected, in a sense, to occupy certain sorts of jobs in certain sectors. A respondent in our focus group with Philippine-educated manufacturing employees noted the specific assumptions he had observed being made about Filipino immigrants, even during a casual encounter in a bank:

> *It happened not directly to me in my job, but it was typical stereotyping of Filipino women. When I applied at a bank to open an account, the account manager talked to me about my stay here. She asked, 'How come you came to Canada?' I said, 'My wife petitioned me.' The second question was 'Was she a nanny?' And I said, 'Yes, she was.' And the third question 'Who is now your employer? Are you working at Tim Horton's?' I said, 'Oh, now I'm working in a manufacturing company.' For her, it was nothing. For me, stereotyping is degrading.* (Male respondent, authors' focus group with manufacturing workers, 2007)

Several respondents in different sectors noted that there was a racialized hierarchy in their workplaces, with lower-level jobs almost exclusively occupied by visible minorities, and managerial or supervisory jobs taken by white employees. This created a tendency for those in lower positions to perceive higher positions as being the preserve of white employees – thus in some cases, when promotions were available, Filipino employees did not apply, seeing higher positions as unattainable. In one focus group, a clerical employee of a large accounting firm in downtown Toronto described how the floors of an office tower occupied by the company got increasingly white with each additional storey. She described feeling out of place when having to visit the upper floors.

These examples suggest that it is not simply discrimination against visible minorities that Filipino immigrants experience. It is also a specific conception of the types of work in which Filipinos can (and should) 'normally' be found.

RESPONDENT: *No matter how hard your job is, how good you do your job or how fast you do it, they don't put you in higher positions. Only in the second level but not in the highest level.*
PHILIP: *What is your explanation for that?*
RESPONDENT: *Discrimination.*
(Male respondent, authors' focus group with Filipino retail workers, 2007)

Although we have addressed it explicitly in this section, it is also important to note that the racialization of Filipinos intersects with the other processes described in this chapter. The demand for Filipino caregivers, the treatment of Philippine credentials in assessment processes, and the practical assessment of job skills and 'promotability' are all clearly linked to the construction of a racialized Filipino identity.

Conclusion

The findings of this study suggest several conclusions. First, much analysis (both academic and policy-oriented) about immigrant labour market experiences tends to aggregate different groups into the category 'immigrant.' Our findings suggests that while there are certainly generic processes experienced by all immigrants, and by visible minority immigrants in particular, there is also a more nuanced account of labour market processes possible when specific groups are examined. The specificity of racialized identities, workplace cultures, and immigration programs that define the Filipino settlement process mean that there is a particular experience that needs to be understood. (Notwithstanding the fact that there are also, of course, important differences within the

Filipino community, according to gender and time of arrival for example, that further complicate the picture.)

Second, the policy debate on immigrant labour market integration has been concerned almost exclusively with foreign credential recognition. But many immigrant workers are in employment situations in which upward mobility and access to more secure or more favourable terms of employment are not necessarily impeded by formal professional licensing issues. Instead, it is everyday workplace 'micro-politics' that determine upward mobility and these often relate to systemic processes of racialization and cultural practices specific to particular ethno-linguistic groups.

Third, immigrant economic integration is often treated as a process that occurs within the bounded space of the labour market in which it happens. However, the lives of immigrants themselves – their obligations, commitments, calculations, etc. – are not bounded in this way, but made in a transnational space. The need to financially support family members in the Philippines is a responsibility felt by many respondents. While by no means a uniquely Filipino characteristic, the nature of Filipino migration (involving, for example, women arriving alone under the Live-In Caregiver Program) means that separation from immediate family members left behind is common, thereby intensifying such financial obligations. This situation translates into a need for job security that might make higher-level positions less appealing, especially if they are not unionized and are therefore more precarious.

NOTES

1 The research presented in this chapter would not have been possible without the participation of several individuals and groups. We would like to thank Rowena Jane Esguerra for co-ordinating the focus groups and reviewing the focus group transcriptions; Hermie Garcia for reviewing the manuscript and providing critical and insightful feedback; Mithi Esguerra for assisting in mobilizing participants for the survey and focus groups; the members of the CASJ Board, and the organizational and individual members of CASJ, who have provided various forms of support throughout this research project; and the professional associations, particularly the Association of Filipino Canadian Accountants and the Ontario Association of Filipino Engineers, that formally participated in the study. Finally, we

would like to thank the hundreds of survey and focus group participants, without whom this study would not have been possible. We also thank our university-based research assistants, Nel Coloma-Moya and Cesar Polvorosa at York University. Further research assistance was provided at various times by Sudarshana Bordoloi, Anne-Marie Debbane, Alex Lovell, Maryse Lemoine, and Junjia Ye. Funding was provided by SSHRC and by CERIS – The Ontario Metropolis Centre. An extended report on this research project is provided in Kelly et al. (2009).

REFERENCES

Bakan, Abigail, and Daiva Stasiulis, eds. 1997. *Not one of the family: Foreign domestic workers in Canada.* Toronto: University of Toronto Press.

Boyd, Monica. 2002. Skilled immigrant labour: Country of origin and the occupational locations of male engineers. *Canadian Studies in Population* 29: 71–99.

Chen, Anita Beltran. 1998. *From sunbelt to snowbelt: Filipinos in Canada.* Calgary: University of Calgary, Canadian Ethnic Studies Association.

Cusipag, Ruben, and Marites Buenafe. 1993. *Portrait of Filipino Canadians in Ontario (1960–1990).* Toronto: Kalayaan Media.

Fang, Tony, Nina Damsbaek, Philip Kelly, Maryse Lemoine, Lucia Lo, Valerie Preston, John Shields, and Steven Tufts. 2010. Are immigrant wages affected by the source of job search information? Toronto Immigrant Employment Data Initiative, Analytical Report No. 7. www.yorku.ca/tiedi.

Galabuzi, Grace-Edward. 2001. *Canada's economic apartheid: The social exclusion of racialized groups in the new century.* Toronto: Canadian Scholars' Press.

Girard, Eric, and Harald Bauder. 2007. Assimilation and exclusion of foreign trained engineers in Canada: Inside a professional regulatory organization. *Antipode* 39 (1): 35–53.

Kelly, Philip. 2006. Filipinos in Canada: Economic dimensions of immigration and settlement. Toronto: Joint Centre of Excellence for Research on Immigration and Settlement, CERIS Working Paper No. 48.

Kelly, Philip, and Silvia D'Addario. 2008. 'Filipinos are very strongly into medical stuff': Labour market segmentation in Toronto, Canada. In *The international migration of health workers,* ed. John Connell, 77–98. London: Routledge.

Kelly, Philip, Mila Garcia, Enrico Esguerra, and the Community Alliance for Social Justice. 2009. Explaining the deprofessionalized Filipino: Why Filipino immigrants get low-paying jobs in Toronto. CERIS Working Paper No. 75.

Laquian, Eleanor. 1973. *A study of Filipino immigration to Canada, 1962–1972,* 2nd ed. Ottawa: United Council of Filipino Associations in Canada.

Laquian, Eleanor, and Aprodicio Laquian. 2008. *Seeking a better life abroad: A study of Filipinos in Canada, 1957–2007.* Manila: Anvil.

McKay, Deirdre. 2002. *Filipina identities: Geographies of social integration/exclusion in the Canadian metropolis.* Vancouver: Centre of Excellence, Research on Immigration and Integration in the Metropolis, Working Paper Series, No. 02-18.

Pratt, Geraldine. 2004. *Working feminism.* Philadelphia: Temple University Press.

Spitzer, Denise, and Sara Torres. 2008. Gender-based barriers to settlement and integration for live-in caregivers: A review of the literature. Toronto: Joint Centre of Excellence for Research on Immigration and Settlement, CERIS Working Paper No. 48.

Statistics Canada 2008. Census of Canada, 2006. Ottawa: Statistics Canada, Cat. No. 97-564-X2006008.

Statistics Canada 2011. Permanent Residents by Category, 2006–2010. Ottawa: Statistics Canada. Accessed June 30, 2010. http://www.cic.gc.ca/english/resources/statistics/facts2010-preliminary/01.asp.

Turegan, Adnan. 2008. The politics of access to professions: Making Ontario's Fair Access to Regulated Professions Act, 2006. Toronto: Joint Centre of Excellence for Research on Immigration and Settlement, CERIS Working Paper No. 70.

MY FOLKS

Carlo Sayo and Jean Marc Daga

My folks are 7000 islands strong
Survivors of colonizers who defied white invaders
Haters who still claim they did no wrong

But they love to see us stuck in a state of war
Leaving my folks to wonder the why's and what for's
So my folks got no other options anymore
But to pack their bags and leave for foreign shores

See, my folks are in the ball courts
In the mall and corner stores
As you exiting the doors
They enter and begin their chores

On all fours scrubbing floors
Each night as daunting as before
Because that other job they got
It just ain't cutting it no more

Behind the counter, behind the scenes
Behind garbage carts cleaning latrines
Muffled pillow screams
Asking what it really means to be …

The most educated
But the least compensated
Disempowered and jaded
You hate it when they say it …

'Be grateful for your wages
Be happy that you made it to a country that's so gracious'
But that statement holds no basis
When you're a servant on a slave ship

Labour feminization watching our women be degraded

My folks are the live-in caregivers
Night time janitors, taxi drivers and fast food workers
My folks are the service sector

And these days even though we are dealt like commodities sold
My folks got high hopes of staying afloat
Working slave wages trying to earn them c-notes
While being held captive by bills and bank loans

My folks are living hand to mouth, check to rent
My folks are the brown skinned immigrants
The working proletarians
The silent opposition

Not because they can't speak
But because they been broken
They been made tokens of government policies
That silence the majority of visible minorities

My folks are the high school drop-outs
Berated and mis-educated
See, a myth was created to lead us to believe that my folks don't care

But that racism is systemic
See, educators just don't get it
And now it's a burden that my folks have to bear

My folks are the boys that are 17 years old
You've seen them on TV and news articles
Victims of beatings that got out of control
Shot in the back by a cop's pistol

What the folk, man

Meanwhile, I got folks with megaphones
Rocking the streets placards in hand
I'm one of those folks that rallies and chants

Out at the protest my folks got sore throats
We screaming and chanting and trying to invoke …
The spirit of our martyrs that gave us hope
We screaming and chanting while politicians gloat
Because Jason Kenney's recent changes to the LCP
They were all a hoax

So they ask why we militant
It's 'cause we provoked

My folks, stand up, take back what they stole
We've inherited an honorable struggle we hold
Close to our hearts is the culture of the brave and the bold

My folks ain't afraid to fight for rights that they know
That are owed to every human on the face of the globe

My folks are radicals and renegades
Heretics and hand grenades
On blocks we congregate
Sipping lemonade on better days

My folks communicate about finding a better way
That's why we organize, mobilize and educate

I learn from my folks
In turn, they learn from me
And we be causing a buzz like a bumblebee
We be ready to roll like a tumble weed
I never fought for a cause until they humbled me

Whatever obstacles we handle it
See, there ain't no handbook or manuscript
To tell us how to live in this labyrinth
So we take it as it come, and we manage it

See, god gave us the tools to be original
She gave us heart and mind to guide our principles
So keep the hating to a minimal
In times of crisis our unity is pivotal

C'mon ya'll, let's ride with the masses
We shaking our asses
To dance is miraculous
We fogging up glasses
It's hard to imagine
we rose from the ashes
Colonized but survived centuries of blasting

So when bullshit happens
It's time for the rapping, it's time for action
Live life with a passion
There's time for relaxing, there's time for laughing

So let's celebrate our resiliency
We brilliant, young people with ability
Intelligent so we marching to a different beat
Let's move our feet in unison like a millipede

The revolution is us, that meaning you and me
We hungry for justice starving for peace
We swing, bolos in the belly of the beast
My folks oppose foes and we never will cease

I say peace
Throw your fist in the sky
You got the right to resist
You're determined to rise

I say peace
Throw your fist in the sky
I got the right to resist
I'm determined to rise

I say peace
Throw your fist in the sky
We got the right to resist
We determined to rise

I say peace
Throw your fist in the sky
Scrap the LCP
We determined to rise

Artist Statement

Carlo Sayo and Jean Marc Daga

My Folks is a poem about the Filipino Canadian community. It encapsulates the struggles of Filipino youth, women, and workers, as they contend with racist and sexist Canadian institutions and policies. The poem is a call for Filipino Canadians to recognize their common struggles and collectively fight for their rights towards full entitlement and participation in Canadian society.

PART TWO

Gender, Migration, and Labour

SCRAP: The Struggle for Filipino Women's Liberation in Canada
Reuben Sarumugam and Bryan Taguba

Artist Statement

Reuben Sarumugam and Bryan Taguba

SCRAP is a story of resistance, following three Filipino community-based organizations' ongoing battle for the genuine liberation of Filipino women funnelled into systemic exploitation and oppression through the Canadian federal government's Live-In Caregiver Program (LCP). The film is an exposé giving us a closer look into the realities of women who have toiled under the program and whose experiences as nannies, caregivers, and domestic workers stand on the contrary to what has been claimed and promised by Canada's rosy immigration laws. Filipino women are clear targets, comprising 97 per cent of workers under the program and supplying the Canadian labour market's demand for cheap domestic workers. The demand is ever increasing as more Canadian women pursue a career, deeming the de facto universal childcare system as essential – the liberation of one group of women at the expense of another. In the international arena, Canada is propagated as a champion in advocating human rights and a leader of social justice with a gleaming immigration track record. What most Canadians do not know, let alone the world, is Canada's partaking in the exploitation and oppression of migrant workers from the Third World, ensuring their commodification by non-accreditation of foreign credentials and not readily issuing permanent resident status to the desperate multitude trying their luck at a better life in Canada. The systematic exclusion of foreign domestic workers from enjoying rights and freedoms equal to those of regular Canadian citizens, along with other bureaucratic hurdles attached to the LCP, has had a devastating effect on the lives of the women and their families. Since its implementation in 1992, circumstances leading into the present ultimately prove the LCP detrimental to the overall successful development and genuine settlement and integration of the Filipino community as a full participant in the broader Canadian society. As the breadwinners for families and entire chains of extended relatives in the Philippines, women under the LCP are looked upon as modern heroes but are treated as modern-day slaves by a country they help sustain. Yet, there is much to celebrate, as the Filipino community continues the fight for a fair treatment of foreign domestic workers and campaigns to completely scrap the program – a higher calling not bound by fear, desperation, or ignorance!

The principal objective of the project is to raise the social consciousness of the Canadian public on the issue of Filipino women entering Canada under the Live-In Caregiver Program as nannies, caregivers, and domestic workers, by exposing the program's exploitative and oppressive nature. Geared towards social change, the film will be used as an outreach and educational tool for the Filipino community and the Canadian public in general. In working closely with the Philippine Women's Centre of Ontario (PWC-ON), SIKLAB Ontario (a Filipino Canadian workers' advocacy group), and the Filipino Canadian Youth Alliance of Ontario (FCYA/UKPC-ON), the umbrella campaign of these organizations will also utilize the film to scrap the LCP and present resolutions in place of it. In so doing, the community members belonging to these contingents shed light on the shady world of domestic workers and their hidden experiences of emotional, psychological, physical, and economic trauma whether through sharing of personal experiences or through qualitative and quantitative studies of collected testimonies. Most importantly, it will offer analysis from these studies as being linked to the Filipino diaspora's history of forced migration leading into the current experience of systemic racism and will oppose the neoliberal agenda of the Canadian immigration system. In addition, the film will reveal the Filipino Canadian community's resilience in challenging the powers that be and promote an all too crucial message – the Filipino community must exhibit a culture of resistance for the future generation to inherit. Revolving around the intent to empower the Filipino community, *SCRAP* celebrates the fighting spirit of the Filipino woman and the community as a whole.

Chapter 4

The Recruitment of Filipino Healthcare Professionals to Canada in the 1960s

VALERIE G. DAMASCO

Beginning with Family Immigration

In 2006 I interviewed my Aunt Lourdes for my master's research. She was trained and employed as a midwife in the Philippines and in 1965 was recruited by Riverdale Hospital in Toronto[1] from the School of Midwifery, Maternity and Children's Hospital in Manila. She laid her briefcase on her dining table, opened it, and distributed old documents across the table. 'I have a few things to show you, Valerie,' she explained. I noticed several letter-sized documents with names and places that were familiar to me – *Lourdes Cultura* and *Lipa City, Philippines.* 'See, Valerie. These are all of my records from the 1960s and the years prior,' she explained.

I stood up and glanced at the documents. I recognized that they were her immigration and employment records. Scattered on the table was her record of employment with Riverdale Hospital, letters of affidavit of support from her former supervisors at the educational and healthcare institutions in the Philippines where she trained and worked, educational transcripts from the 1940s and 1950s from the elementary, secondary, and postsecondary educational institutions she attended, an airline ticket from Canadian Pacific Airlines, and a black and white photo of her in her early twenties wearing what looked like a nurse's cape (see figure 4.1).

One particular document caught my attention. It was a letter, dated October 7, 1965, that had been photocopied several times; it had a brownish-black background and the text in white font. On top, in bold block letters, *The Riverdale Hospital* with the logo of the hospital inscribed. A few inches below was my aunt's name – *Miss Lourdes*

Figure 4.1. Immigration and employment documents of Lourdes Cultura-Fazi

Cultura – and below it, the address to which the correspondence was sent – *21 Galo Reyes St.* – and underneath it – *Lipa City.*

'This is our home in the Philippines!' I blurted. 'What? Riverdale Hospital sent this to our house in the Philippines? A hospital in Toronto sent correspondence to the Philippines during the sixties?' *'Dear Miss Cultura,'* the letter began. I noticed that it was signed by an individual, *'George McCracken M.D., L.R.C.P., Medical Superintendent.'* Implications of place and time became important for me.

The house was my grandparents', which was built in the 1930s; it became my home when I visited the Philippines each summer from 1996 to 2001.

'This is fascinating,' I remarked. 'I never knew that this had happened.' I was confused. The context remained a mystery. 'Why was the correspondence sent to her in the Philippines during that year? What was it for? What instigated it? Why did they send it to her?' I asked myself.

I was oblivious to the history of my family's immigration to Canada. I was born in Toronto in 1981 and was raised by relatives who immigrated to Toronto during the 1970s and 1980s. Like many in society, I shared similar misconceptions pertaining to immigrant families. I had always assumed that my family immigrated to Canada to escape the growing political and economic crisis in the Philippines. How and why my Aunt Lourdes immigrated to Canada in the 1960s was a story that we never shared. Hence, I attempted to seek additional information from her.

'I was recruited from the Philippines by Riverdale Hospital from the school I attended to work here in the sixties, first as a nursing assistant and then as a registered nurse. They hired me. I was working as a midwife in the Philippines and then I came here,' she explained. I still did not understand what being 'recruited' from the Philippines meant.

'Look at this. They also confirmed the salary you would receive.' I read the details: *'starting salary of two hundred and thirty-five dollars per month with generous fringe benefits.'*

'Two hundred and thirty-five dollars a month was considered a sufficient income then,' she explained.

'Yes, I can imagine.' I continued reading, *'depending on experience and ability, you may qualify to start at a higher salary. On obtaining registration with the Ontario College of Nursing, higher salary levels will be implemented.'* I gazed at the name of a hospital at the bottom of the letter: *'Ortanez General Hospital.'* I asked, 'Why is there a name of a hospital in the letter?'

'That was the hospital I worked at in Manila when they were processing my application.'

In this chapter, I elucidate the institutional relations established between Canada and the Philippines in the realm of healthcare in the early 1960s. Although the liberalization in Canadian immigration policies leading to increased Filipino migration in 1967 has been relatively widely debated, this paper contributes a discussion of significant Filipino migration before these changes. I begin by reviewing the existing literature on Filipino migration to Canada, with particular attention to explanations for migration in the 1960s. I then turn to a description of the arrangements made for the recruitment of Filipino healthcare workers before the development of the Canadian 'points system.' Finally, I turn to a discussion of some of the marked differences between this earlier period and the challenge which currently face Filipino migrants, with a discussion of some of the implications of understanding this history.

In 2006, I interviewed participants who worked in Riverdale Hospital during the 1960s. The participants were chosen according to the following criteria: (1) They are/were Philippine-trained healthcare professionals (i.e., nurses, midwives, and nursing assistants); (2) They immigrated to Canada between 1960 and 1969; (3) They were recruited directly by Ontario hospitals from the Philippines (i.e., from hospitals, puericulture and maternity centres, or educational institutions that specialize in nursing) to provide healthcare services in Canada. The participants were from middle-class families in the Philippines who were trained in prominent nursing and midwifery educational institutions in the Philippines; for example, University of Santo Tomas College of Nursing.

Life history methodology was utilized to conduct the study. Primary data/materials (i.e., interviews) from the participants were obtained. In total, ten in-depth life history interviews were conducted. Moreover, secondary data/materials (i.e., immigration records, occupation-related documents, and photographs, etc.) were obtained from the Archives of Ontario to contextualize and accentuate the life history interviews. The interviews were complimentarily analysed with the secondary data/materials using life history research analysis to accentuate the historical phases that have substantiated the recruitment and deployment of Filipino healthcare professionals in Ontario.

The Growth of the Filipino Community in Canada

Chen (1998) argues that the migration of Filipinos to Canada is a recent phenomenon which has gained considerable attention during the latter half of the twentieth century. According to Kelly (2006), Filipino immigrants in Canada are predominantly recent immigrants. Less than 5 per cent arrived prior to 1970, more than three-quarters arrived since 1980, and in 2001 over half of all Filipinos in Canada had arrived in the previous ten years (1991–2001). Much of the existing academic literature focuses on this more recent migration (see chapter 1 and chapters by Eric and Tungohan in this volume for more detailed accounts). Scholars who have documented the history of Filipino immigration in Canada have described how many were Filipino healthcare professionals (i.e., those who were trained as nurses, nursing aides, and midwives in the Philippines coming to work as registered nurses and nursing assistants in Canada) during the 1960s (see Laquian 1973; Bustamante 1984; Cusipag and Buenafe 1993). They note that the migration of Filipino healthcare professionals in the 1960s was necessitated in part by the labour shortages in the nursing profession in Canada and the growth of healthcare institutions in Ontario. Moreover, they argue that the migration trajectory of those in the 'healthcare occupational group' was similar to that of Filipino professionals in other 'occupational categories' (e.g., physicians, engineers, clerical workers, laboratory technicians)[2] in that they immigrated to Canada as a result of the liberalization of Canadian immigration policies. They came to Canada to help combat the widespread labour shortages in the country, to escape the political and economic crisis in the Philippines, and to remain in the country permanently.

During the 1960s, Filipinos were able to practise in professions in Canada for which they were trained in the Philippines (e.g., nursing) (see Laquian 1973; Bustamante 1984; Cusipag and Buenafe 1993; Damasco 2009). They were employed as registered nurses and nursing assistants in Ontario hospitals. However, the immigration trends of Filipino healthcare professionals in Canada during the 1980s, 1990s, and 2000s present a different picture. Filipino healthcare professionals who immigrated to Canada in the 1980s through the Foreign Domestic Movement (FDM)[3] program migrated to work as domestic workers. Also, from the 1990s to the present, a considerable number have been migrating to Canada through the Live-In Caregiver Program (LCP) for employment as live-in caregivers. In both cases, it has been increasingly difficult for these women, almost often impossible, to work in Canada in the professions for which they were trained in the Philippines (i.e., nursing, midwifery).

One influential earlier study of Filipino migration in the 1960s (Laquian 1973) presents the immigration trends of all occupational categories in 'five-year increments.' Therefore, it is unclear what occurred

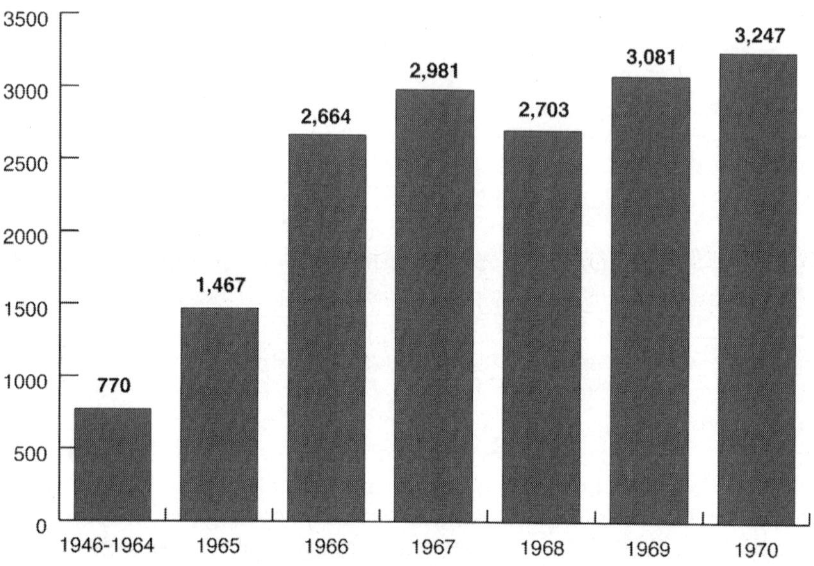

Figure 4.2. Filipino immigrant arrivals in Canada from 1946 to 1970

each year, from 1965 to 1970, pertaining to the immigration of Filipino healthcare professionals. However, it turns out this is a crucial period for understanding Filipino migration. To provide a more nuanced understanding of Filipino migration to Canada, I will present statistical figures provided by Laquian (1973), who notes that between 1946 and 1964, only 770 Filipinos were admitted to Canada. Prior to 1965, no separate figures were reported on Filipinos by the Department of Manpower and Immigration in its annual *Immigration Statistics Canada.* Instead, Filipinos were lumped with other groups in a category called 'other countries not British,' which included all nationalities with fewer than a thousand immigrants (see figure 4.2).[4] It is unclear why there was a sudden influx of Filipino immigrants in 1965. Some have argued that the influx was due in part to the documentation of Filipino immigrants as a 'separate ethnic category' in Statistics Canada (see Laquian 1973; Cusipag and Buenafe 1993; Chen 1998). Laquian (1973) notes that in 1965, Canadian immigration authorities began reporting Filipino immigrants as a separate entity. She observes, 'That year, for some curious reason, a total of 1,467 Filipino citizens entered Canada, nearly twice the number admitted in the past two decades [1945–65]' (1).

To understand in greater depth the migration trends of Filipino healthcare professionals, an analysis of the 'healthcare occupational group' is needed, independent from the analysis of other 'occupational categories.' Also, it is fruitful to understand the yearly migration trends of the healthcare occupational group, rather than seeing them in five-year increments. This may simply have been an accounting change, but even this requires an explanation. Why was the presence of Filipinos emerging as significant, in a way that led officials to count them separately? Striking, also, is the fact that though the Canadian immigration scheme was revised in 1967, we can see from figure 4.2 that the number of Filipino immigrants surged in 1965 and 1966, before this change, to numbers roughly comparable to those one would see for Filipinos in the five years after the major revision.

Critiquing Ideological Definitions of Immigration

The Liberalization of Canadian Immigration Policies

Many have argued that the immense growth of Filipino immigrants in 1967 was largely due to the 'liberalization of Canadian immigration policies' (see Laquian 1973; Cusipag and Buenafe 1993; Chen 1998; Kelly 2006). The Canadian Points System, which was enacted in October 1967, was designed to eliminate prejudice in the selection of independent immigrants. Immigration officers assigned points (up to a fixed maximum) to potential immigrants according to categories such as education, employment opportunities in Canada, age, personal characteristics, and degree of fluency in English or French. Other features of the policy included the elimination of discrimination based on nationality or race and the creation of a special provision that allowed visitors to apply for immigrant status while in Canada (Citizenship and Immigration Canada 2000).

Cusipag and Buenafe (1993) explain that during the mid-1960s and mid-1970s, immigration policies were further liberalized by forbidding discrimination against race and nationality. Chen (1998) also notes that the introduction of the Canadian Points System set the stage for arrivals from the Philippines, and elsewhere. She emphasizes that the occupational skills of Filipino professionals were in demand. A majority of the newcomers were healthcare professionals, particularly nurses. Nevertheless, it is not enough to conclude that the liberalizing trends in Canadian immigration policies facilitated the migration of Filipino healthcare professionals. From these studies, it is unclear how (e.g., which regulatory policies, practices, processes facilitated their migration) and why (e.g., economic conditions in sending and receiving nation, individual reasons, etc.) they immigrated.

It is important to note that the origins of Filipino nurse mass migration to the United States were largely a result of the U.S. Exchange Visitor Program of the 1950s and 1960s, when more than eleven thousand Filipino nurses entered the United States as exchange visitors. They worked and studied in the United States for two years, after which they were to return to the Philippines. However, many Filipino exchange nurses employed numerous strategies to remain abroad. For example, some migrated to Canada, others requested U.S. hospitals to extend their stay, and some even married U.S. citizens. In 1965, the passage of the U.S. Immigration Act created the new occupational immigrant visas which favoured the immigration of professionals with needed skills, for example, nurses. Hence, it facilitated the phenomenon of Filipino nurses working and residing in the United States on a more permanent basis (Hune and Nomura 2003, 336–7).

Combating the Canadian Nursing Labour Shortage in the 1960s

Many have argued that the immigration of Filipino healthcare professionals was necessitated in part by the nursing labour shortage in North America. According to Stasiulis and Bakan (2005), neoliberal restructuring policies limited the resources in the healthcare sector, and in particular nursing care in hospitals, across Canada. Furthermore, the province of Ontario has been a host to the greatest proportion of foreign nurses. For example, nurses from the Philippines and the West Indies were recruited to fill labour shortages in nursing (6–7). The majority of Filipino female immigrant professionals who arrived in Toronto during the mid-1960s were employed as nurses. Their enlistment in hospital units and other health services in Toronto was in demand because the local labour pool could not sufficiently provide for the employment needs in hospitals and health clinics. These were the positions Filipino nurses conveniently filled (Bustamante 1984). My analyses of archival documents like governmental records obtained from the Archives of Ontario reveal that the migration of Filipino healthcare professionals to Ontario during the late 1960s was instituted simultaneously by Canadian and Philippine governmental, healthcare, and educational institutions, Canadian nursing regulatory bodies, and Canadian travel agencies through a recruitment scheme (Damasco 2009). While it was an important tactic that was developed during the early to mid-1960s, it has not been discussed in the literature or in governmental and community deliberations.

The Political and Economic Crisis in the Philippines

Many have also attributed the immigration of Filipino healthcare professionals to bourgeoning political and economic crises in the Philippines (see Laquian 1973; Bustamante 1984; Cusipag and Buenafe 1993; Kelly 2006). Soon after the onset of the Marcos dictatorship in the Philippines, the outmigration of Filipino professionals from the late 1960s to the 1970s proliferated. Previous studies have veiled the agency of individuals. As such, personal reasons for immigration were rarely discussed and often absent from deliberations. While personal circumstances may have influenced individuals' decisions to migrate to industrialized nations, the analyses continue to frame this migration as a collective phenomenon shaped by national economic factors.

Hence, their reasons for migrating have constantly been framed in the context of global economies. The Philippines has continuously been represented as an 'underdeveloped nation' or 'Third World country' incessantly dependent on the economies of 'industrialized nations' or 'First World countries' such as Canada and the United States. Many have grounded their analyses using an economic logic (Choy 2003), arguing, for example, that Filipino healthcare professionals immigrate to industrialized nations in search of employment opportunities, work security, and to remain in the destination country to escape the detrimental and degenerating economic and political conditions in the Philippines.

On a similar note, many have argued that the Philippine government sends its citizens to industrialized nations because of limited professional and economic opportunities in the Philippines (see Ball 2004; Parreñas 2000, 2001). Their education, skills, and training, along with the professional and economic opportunities in industrialized nations, have produced professional migrant flows (see Ball 2004; Barber 2000; Kelly 2006; Laquian 1973; Pratt 1999; Zaman 2004). However, indepth life history interviews of Filipino healthcare professionals who were recruited to Ontario during the 1960s reveal that they had no knowledge of Canada prior to their recruitment. For example, my aunt stated:

> *And it was interesting because like I said, this was my first trip. It was my dream to go abroad but I never thought that it would happen. And at that time, I didn't even know about Canada. I knew a lot about the United States but Canada, you seldom hear about it. It was always about the United States and the Philippines. So for us, Canada is a country that we did not really know a lot about. I began to only learn about Canada when I started applying.*

Leticia, a nurse trained at the University of Santo Tomas College of Nursing, explained:

> *It was August 1966 when I came to Canada and I just graduated and at the schools they were talking about Canada. During that time I don't think they had a lot of professional nurses in Canada so they were going to different schools and were talking about these programs they had, enticing people to migrate and all that. Mind you, in the Philippines we don't study Canada. We know a lot about the United States! I had no information about Canada at all! Well actually, I thought it was part of the United States. I was rather surprised, this was a different country!*

Moreover, they had no overt intention of immigrating to Canada, and were to some degree satisfied with their employment and living circumstances in the Philippines. As my aunt stated in her interview:

> *I don't know, it was like a fluke. When I was young, I always wanted to go abroad but it really didn't occur to me that it would happen because I am a midwife, I am working as a midwife now. Then somebody told me to contact the school because they knew that they were recruiting midwives from the schools of midwifery in the Philippines to work in Canada because they needed them to work as nursing aides.*

Leticia explained:

> *In the beginning I wasn't really interested in coming to Canada. My parents would of course ask me and say, 'What are you going to do there? You don't know what's there.' They were so scared. So I promised them that I would only be away for one year to travel and after school, travel! To find out what's going on in the other side of the world! Before you know it, I never went back!*

According to Choy (2003), the complex links among nursing, nationalism, and educational and employment opportunities in the United

States for Filipino women had been established during the U.S. colonial period. These opportunities inspired some young Filipino women to study nursing and marked the beginning of their idealization of American work and academic experience (39). Filipino nurses who travelled to the United States to further their education settled there permanently and did not return to the Philippines. Even though U.S. colonial officials attempted to implement their agendas in the Philippines, colonial changes produced unintended consequences. For example, Filipino women had strong desires to travel to the United States and to stay there permanently and U.S. colonial officials were unable to control their mobility (40).

Other analyses seem to depict the migration of Filipino healthcare professionals as an inevitability. Their migration has incessantly been rendered as a typical process, an exchange of human labour between underdeveloped and developed nations which occurs as a result of the institutional tactics imposed by underdeveloped nations. Immigration trends have been depicted as a process 'that simply happens' because of political and economic turmoil in the sending nation and labour shortages in industrialized nations.

My research adds to this literature by showing that Canada was dependent on Filipino healthcare professionals' skills, educational training, and employment. Thus, Canada was proactively complicit in encouraging the migration of Filipino healthcare professionals. Healthcare professionals were recruited to help combat the nursing labour shortages in Ontario hospitals. Offer-of-employment letters were dispatched by Riverdale Hospital administrators to the Philippines during the mid-1960s to potential healthcare employees via the healthcare and educational institutions where they trained and/or worked as nurses, nursing aides, and midwives. Ontario hospitals sought healthcare professionals from the Philippines because they were educated through a North American nursing education system, and were trained and versed in North American nursing practices. Hence, they possessed the requisite healthcare training which enabled them to efficiently assimilate into the Canadian nursing work culture (Damasco 2009).

The Recruitment and Employment of Filipino Healthcare Professionals in the 1960s

According to the life and work accounts of the women, in 1964 and 1965, Canadian immigration and healthcare authorities visited numerous nursing and midwifery educational and healthcare institutions in the Philippines to promote immigration programs and benefits. In 1964 and 1965, the formal process of recruitment took place. However, prospective employees needed to meet compulsory requirements such as a high academic standing, the completion of particular nursing subjects, sound work experience, and training in their area(s) of specialization. When they met these criteria, Riverdale Hospital dispatched their offer-of-employment letter, which specified their professional appointment, starting salary, and benefits. Some were able to start at a higher salary depending on employment experience. It also stated that after they registered with the Ontario College of Nursing, they could attain higher salaries.

Along with the offer of employment, they were to provide the following to the Canadian Embassy in the Philippines: academic transcripts, nursing or midwifery certificates and licenses, and letters of affidavit from supervisors of the educational institutions they attended and previous workplaces. Upon receipt of these documents, the Canadian Embassy verified their credentials. Arrangements were then made between Canadian immigration authorities in the Philippines and Ontario hospitals. Ontario hospitals confirmed with the Canadian Embassy in the Philippines if they had received the requisite documentation from the healthcare professionals they *hired* from the Philippines.

Accordingly, Riverdale Hospital made necessary arrangements prior to the healthcare professionals' arrival. Hospital administrators communicated with airline industries like Canadian Pacific Airlines in Ontario and travel agencies in the Philippines to facilitate the travel arrangements for the recruited employees. When they arrived at Toronto International Airport, they were welcomed by a CPA representative who escorted them to a hotel in Toronto, where they stayed for one night, compliments of CPA. Then, they registered with hospital administrators at Riverdale Hospital. Prior to their arrival, Riverdale Hospital human resources personnel co-ordinated their living arrangements. They were grouped with other Filipino nurses who worked, for example, at Wellesley Hospital and Toronto General Hospital, and provided with accommodations until they established their own living arrangements. After a one-day orientation at Riverdale Hospital, they went to work in the departments they were assigned.

To contextualize their migration experiences, a nuanced understanding of the Canadian and Philippine historical context is required. Although they arrived in 1966 and 1967, it was unclear whether their recruitment had connections with the growth of Filipino immigrants in 1965, 1966, and 1967. The available statistics were too vague and problematic. Hence, I reviewed records from the Archives of Ontario in search of historical information that would provide some insight into the recruitment and employment of Filipino healthcare professionals in Ontario during the 1960s.

Moving beyond Academic Literature and Exploring Archival Records

I reviewed a handwritten report dated May 30, 1967, written by Mr A.M. de Swaaf, who researched the Filipino community in Toronto during the late 1960s. He was a field placement student from the School of Social Work, University of Toronto, and the Information and Referral Officer for the Ontario Human Rights Commission (OHRC). In 1967, the OHRC was in the planning stage of a small-scale study on the Filipino community in Toronto. Mr de Swaaf's report was a lengthy documentation of the interviews he conducted with contacts he made in the Filipino community in Toronto in 1967. The OHRC noted that the Filipino community expanded rapidly, from 4 individuals in 1962 to over 2,500 in 1967. The Commission deemed that it would be useful to get to know the community to determine if they had experienced discrimination, and to educate them about the OHRC's work and the Ontario Human Rights Code and the steps to be taken when discrimination was encountered.

On February 20, 1967, a newspaper clipping entitled 'Operation Nurses' was sent to Mr de Swaaf which discussed the personal tactics of an airline representative who developed a 'hobby for combating Ontario's nursing shortage.' Beginning in 1965, Barry F. Cunnings, a Canadian Pacific Airlines sales representative in Toronto, 'personally supervised the importation of approximately 500 nurses from the Philippines' and welcomed Philippine medical workers at Toronto International Airport. His personal interest in the importation of nurses from the Philippines began in 1965 when a Filipino friend asked him about the nursing situation in Canada. His friend noted that there was an excess of nurses in the Philippines during those years.[5]

Mr Cunnings considered what his friend had mentioned. He later dispatched letters to hospitals in Ontario inquiring about nursing shortages in the province and received an overwhelming response. He then contacted immigration authorities in Ottawa to determine the feasibility of importing nurses from the Philippines. He subsequently visited

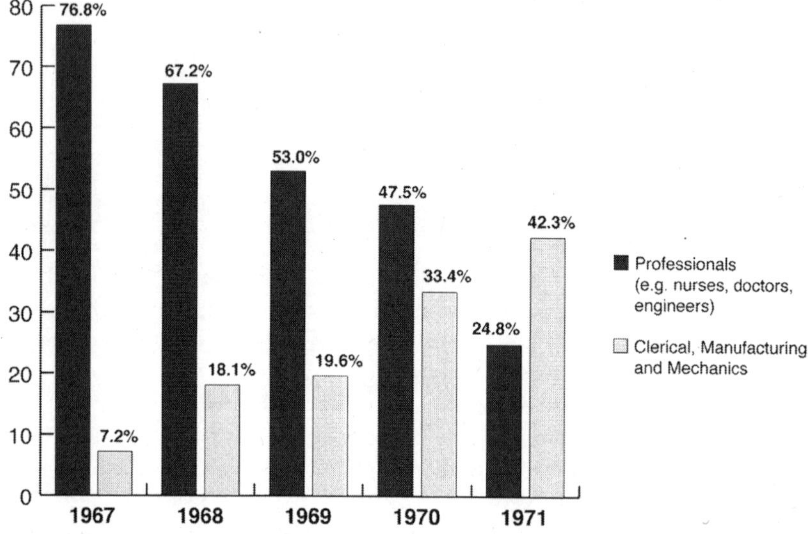

Figure 4.3. The declining proportion of Filipino immigrant professionals and their increase in clerical, manufacturing, and mechanics occupations, 1967 to 1971

former Ontario health minister Dr Matthew Dymond, who indicated that the province of Ontario would co-operate with the plan that he had developed for importing Filipino nurses.

In 1966, Mr Cunnings persuaded his employer, CPA, to co-operate. Ontario hospitals were to contact airline agents and provide them with information pertaining to the requirements they needed from prospective healthcare professionals in the Philippines, who were then asked to register with the CPA office in Manila. After their qualifications were verified and their employment in Ontario was arranged, they immigrated to Canada. The article highlighted that arrivals in the late 1960s included nurses, medical technicians, midwives, and three male nurses who were destined for hospitals in Kapuskasing, Kingston, Parry Sound, and New Liskeard. Three members of the group were destined for Riverdale Hospital. Mr Cunnings reported that everything seemed to be going well, but heard that nurses were becoming scarce in the Philippines.

Operation nurses

Barry Cunnings, a 31-year-old sales representative who claims he's no more civic-minded than the next man, has developed a hobby of combatting Ontario's nursing shortage.

In the past two years Mr. Cunnings has personally supervised the importation of about 500 nurses from the Philippines.

Last night he was at Toronto International Airport to welcome another 17 Philippine medical workers.

"It started in 1965 when a Philippine friend was visiting me," the Scarboro man said. "He happened to ask me how the nursing situation was in Canada because there was an excess of nurses in the Philippines.

"At that time I didn't even know whether we had a nursing shortage in Canada," he said with a smile.

M r. Cunnings began thinking about what his friend had said and a few days later sent out letters of inquiry to every hospital in Ontario.

"The response was overwhelming."

He contacted immigration authorities in Ottawa to find out the problems involved in importing nurses.

Next he visited Ontario health minister Matthew Dymond and was told the Province would co-operate with his plan.

"Before I realized what was happening I was in the nurse importing business," he laughs.

Last year Mr. Cunnings persuaded his employer, Canadian Pacific Airlines, to co-operate in the scheme.

Under the arrangement the hospitals contact agents in various parts of the Province and tell of their requirements.

The nurses register with the CPA office in Manila and after their qualifications have been checked and jobs have been arranged they fly to Canada.

They pay their own fare.

Last night's arrivals included nurses, medical technicians, mid-wives and three male nurses. They will go to hospitals in Kapuskasing, Kingston, Parry Sound and New Liskeard.

Three of the group will go to Riverdale Hospital.

"Everything seems to be going very well," Mr. Cunnings said. "But I've heard nurses are starting to become scarce in the Philippines."

Telegram, Feb. 20, '67

BARRY F. CUNNINGS

SALES REPRESENTATIVE
CANADIAN PACIFIC AIRLINES
ROOM 205, 69 YONGE STREET
TORONTO 1, ONTARIO
TELEPHONE: EM 2-5371

Figure 4.4. 'Operation Nurses' newspaper article in 'Project with the Toronto Filipino Community.' Received via telegram on February 20, 1967. Report by A.M. de Swaaf. Retrieved from Archives of Ontario

<u>REPORT</u>   March 14, 1967
                                                     Time: 12:00 nc

Re: Filipinos in Toronto

Meeting with Mr. Barry F. Cummings, Sales Representative,
<u>Canadian Pacific Airlines, 69 Yonge Street, Toronto1.</u>

<u>Notes of importance:</u>

Mr. Cummings feels that there is very little, if any at all,
discrimination experienced by the Filipinos.

Problems encountered center around their education which,
according to him, is of a higher caliber than here in
Canada, but nevertheless not recognized as such. (He called
them over-educated).

After initial problems, nurses are now accepted as qualified
upon entering Ontario (after the personal intervention of
Dr. Dymond, Minister of Health).

Medical doctors, architects and scientists are frustrated in
their attempts to get recognition. Many leave for the U.S.

Mr. Cummings organizes the "importation" of Filipinos partly
as business, partly as personal interest.

He has contactmen in the Phillipines and in major cities in
Ontario.

Literature will be distributed among these contactmen.

AMdeS/hm   A. M. de Swaaf,
                                       Information & Referral Officer.

Figure 4.5. Summary of interview with Mr Barry F. Cunnings, sales representative
of Canadian Pacific Airlines. March 14, 1967. 'Project with the Toronto Filipino
Community.' Report by A.M. de Swaaf. Retrieved from Archives of Ontario

On March 14, 1967, Mr de Swaaf interviewed Mr Cunnings and discussed the newspaper article, asking him about his role in importing Filipino nurses. According to Mr Cunnings, the recruitment occurred 'partly as a business enterprise and partly as personal interest.' After he received government approval, he contacted the College of Nurses of Ontario (CNO). He stated, 'If there is anything akin to discrimination, it is in this office.' Initially, the CNO refused to co-operate. The CNO was responsible for evaluating applicants' nursing education. Applications were received by contact men in Manila who were CPA employees. The CNO insisted on sending all correspondence by sea mail. Mr Cunnings had offered to provide complimentary airmail stamps and the services of CPA. However, the CNO refused. Hence, the application process was slow. Applicants had to wait up to a year to qualify.

Mr Cunnings enlisted the personal intervention of Dr Matthew Dymond. Within two weeks, everything was working smoothly. Dr Dymond commissioned two of his employees to Manila to interview prospective healthcare employees. All subsequent correspondence was then transmitted by airmail. Mr Cunnings became an expert in recruiting Filipino nurses and stated, 'Before I realized what was happening, I was in the nurse importing business.' He had contacts throughout Ontario who kept in touch with the nurses and reported, 'there is very little, if any at all, discrimination experienced by the Filipinos. Problems in employment are, as far as can be determined, nonexistent as the nurses have a job placement before coming to Canada. Also, in housing, there does not seem to be any problem.'

The newspaper article, the reports commissioned by the OHRC, my aunt's life and work accounts, and the narratives of the other women had significant connections. The way recruitment was organized was tied to the immigration application process my aunt had described when she was recruited to work in Toronto. The offer-of-employment letter she received from Riverdale Hospital in October 1965 that was sent to our house in the Philippines had roots in the institutional processes of the past, particularly with the recruitment scheme that was developed in 1965 and prompted by Mr Cunnings and Dr Dymond.

The OHRC report and newspaper article revealed that the migration of Filipino healthcare professionals was not initiated solely by governmental agendas. Their migration was made possible by individual interests that developed into a broader, institutional agenda which helped to develop the recruitment scheme that was utilized in the 1960s. Personal tactics developed into an institutional and international project between Canada and the Philippines, which organized the recruitment and employment of Filipino healthcare professionals to the province of Ontario in the late 1960s for the purposes of combating the nursing labour shortage.

Discovering the 'Disjuncture'

The historical complicity of the Canadian government, Canadian institutions, and Canadian individuals in encouraging the migration of Filipino healthcare professionals has since been forgotten. Such history, in fact, has effectively been erased. In May 2007, I made an unexpected visit to a nursing organization in Toronto. I was continuously searching for information that would provide insight into the recruitment of Filipino healthcare professionals to Ontario during the 1960s. I asked a staff member if they had any information pertaining to the history of nursing in Canada and the recruitment practices Ontario hospitals employed in the 1960s to enlist healthcare professionals from countries like the Philippines. I mentioned that, based on my preliminary findings, a large number of Filipino nurses, nursing aides, and midwives were recruited from educational and healthcare institutions in the Philippines during the 1960s to provide professional services in Ontario hospitals.

She looked at me with confusion, paused, smiled, and responded, 'I'm sorry, my dear, but we do not have such information. There weren't any Filipino nurses working in Ontario during that time. Filipino nurses did not arrive until the 1980s and 1990s. Instead, the majority were nurses who immigrated to Canada to work in Ontario healthcare institutions as personal support workers and domestic workers.' My cheeks were flushed with shock and anger. I had set out to find information, only to be told that there was no basis for my research. Our interaction shaped the moral purpose of my inquiry, which was to challenge the commonly held beliefs and misconceptions about Filipino immigration in Canada and the stereotypes that are continuously shaping the perceived identity and status of Filipino women.

Evidently, very little was known about the recruitment of Filipino healthcare professionals. I questioned why this history had been forgotten – whether this is a form of *collective amnesia* (Damasco 2009) – or intentionally hidden. I was disturbed by the ignorance of the past and how it has continued for so long. The staff member mentioned that the organization was releasing a publication that discussed the history of the nursing profession in Canada and asked if I wanted a copy.

I was sceptical about this book because it was being published by an organization that denied the early history of Filipino nursing in Canada. The organization, representing healthcare professionals in Ontario, dismissed the possibility of another reality in nursing history in Canada. It was difficult to believe that it did not know about the migration history of Filipino healthcare professionals. Again, the media and mainstream institutions promoted stereotypes and silencing. In such deliberations, it was important to question the sources of knowledge and their credibility and motivation.

Revisiting Current Issues in Society

The recruitment of Filipino healthcare professionals during 1960s is a history that was difficult to envision, since it was never discussed in the literature, the community, or the media. Memories of my observations and experiences growing up in the Thorncliffe Park neighbourhood in Toronto during the 1980s influenced how I conceived of their migration. Thorncliffe Park was densely populated with Filipino immigrants in the 1980s, a community that grew in subsequent decades. During the late 1980s, the number of Filipino domestic workers in Toronto increased. Much of the discussion in our family and in the community revolved around the 'sponsorship' of Filipino 'domestic workers' and 'nannies.'

The remarkable contrast between past and present trends sparked in me a profound need to understand and reconcile the two seemingly diverse eras – to interrogate how and why the migration of the healthcare occupational group shifted dramatically from the 1960s to the present decade from professionalization to deprofessionalization (see Eric and Tungohan, this volume). It was unclear *what* (e.g., immigration policies, accreditation practices, economic factors) necessitated the changes in immigration trends throughout the decades, how and why professionalization to deprofessionalization had occurred, and which individuals and institutions were responsible (see also Kelly et al. in this volume).

My research began from personal observations of women's lives and work accounts and not from, for example, the objective domain of sociological theory or ideological definitions of immigration. These kinds of 'problems of knowing,' of being told one thing but in fact knowing otherwise on the basis of personal experience, provided a starting point which pushed me to investigate and explicate how a regime works – in this case, how immigration and the recruitment of Filipino healthcare professionals was organized, which extends beyond the scope of local settings.

Aunt Lourdes immigrated to Canada as a skilled professional and was given landed immigrant status, a privilege which Filipino live-in caregivers are denied. The majority of the Filipino domestic workers and live-in caregivers in Toronto are educated and trained in the Philippines as, for example, nurses, midwives, and teachers. However, they are barred from practising in such professions even after obtaining landed immigrant status (see Kelly 2006; Pratt 1999). Several years of working as live-in caregivers channels them into the low-sector occupations of the Canadian economy. Moreover, scholars and activists have criticized the Foreign Domestic Movement and the Live-In Caregiver Program, arguing that it has promoted workplace abuses, the stigmatization and racialization of Filipina femininity, institutionalized de-skilling, and the psychological traumas of family separation, and has curtailed citizenship rights (Cohen 2000; Pratt 1997; England and Stiell 1997; Bakan and Stasiulis 1997; McKay and Philippine Women Centre 2002).

When the migration of Filipino healthcare professionals is discussed, the two eras are often represented independent of one another (see Eric in this volume). Current issues are merely seen as contemporary concerns unconnected with past trends. Tracing the history to determine how it has evolved is always absent from analyses. De-skilling, economic marginalization, family separation, and abuse are noted as the prevalent hardships Filipino live-in caregivers face as a result of immigrating through the LCP. Inevitably, the literature focuses largely on current immigration policies and temporary work programs and their consequences on the professional and personal lives of Filipino women and their families. The literature also discusses the economic and political situation in the Philippines, arguing that it has contributed to the exodus and saturation of Filipino women professionals in the international labour market – in industrialized nations in North America, Europe, and Asia – who incessantly take on roles as domestic workers or entertainment workers, or migrate as mail-order brides (see Parreñas 2000, 2001).

My approach differs in that I trace immigration history to show the similarities and variations between the two time periods, which allows for a more nuanced understanding of Canadian immigration policies and recruitment practices. Far from being constant, immigration policies actually shift to accommodate new racial and class hierarchies, and now Filipino professionals who would have qualified for entry under the skilled immigration program can only enter the country through the LCP. Undertaking a historical analysis of immigration policy and recruitment practices allows us to take into account shifts in structural context, showing that the shift from professionalization to deprofessionalization occurs not because the women entering Canada through both programs have drastically different qualifications but because of changing political-economic circumstances in Canada and the Philippines. This may also help us identify ways to bridge differences between these two groups.

Challenging the Historical Continuities

My goal is to bring the 'lost' history of Filipino healthcare professionals back into everyday discourse in the community. During the 1960s, the skills and expertise of Filipino healthcare professionals were, to some extent, recognized. However, it was hardly a clear-cut or a rosy process. The accreditation practices of the College of Nurses of Ontario during the 1960s were discriminatory and racist. Prior to 1965, the CNO refused the professional work of healthcare professionals from the Philippines. Instead, their priority was recruiting nurses from Europe. These practices were only altered when Dr Dymond intervened. Filipinos who arrived in Canada from the 1980s to the present as domestic workers and live-in caregivers are not aware of the migration process, trajectory, and experiences of Filipino healthcare professionals who immigrated during the 1960s. Conversely, those who arrived during the 1960s are removed from current struggles and are unaware of the issues Filipino live-in caregivers face.

There are ongoing debates pertaining to amendments to Canadian immigration policies and the abolition of temporary worker programs such as the LCP, which is perceived to curtail the career trajectories and personal lives of Filipino live-in caregivers. The majority were trained in the Philippines as healthcare professionals (e.g., nurses, nursing aides, and midwives). Scholars continue to examine the detrimental effects of such programs, which have contributed to the de-skilling, economic marginalization, and accreditation barriers Filipino domestic workers face. While such issues prevail and continue to escalate, the women are reluctant to challenge the oppressive structures of social control (Grandea and Kerr 1998). They continue to accept their circumstances and resign themselves to their realities as inevitable and simply 'the way things are.' Rather than being encouraged and equipped to know and respond to concrete circumstances, they are kept submerged in situations where critical awareness is practically impossible.

Citizenship status is crucial for the achievement of emancipatory change. However, not all individuals (e.g., live-in caregivers under the LCP) or community-based organizations are able to challenge existing social structures because of the (non)citizenship status that domestic workers and live-in caregivers possess. A community of citizens is often the nation-state and their rights and duties are codified in constitutions and laws. While citizens are supposed to benefit from equal rights, there are structures and dynamics of inclusion and exclusion that impede equality. Those who entered Canada through the LCP are classified as temporary visa workers and not under the immigrant category. As a result of their non-citizenship status, they are denied membership in communities and are deprived of civil, political, and social rights. Further, their autonomy is hindered and they lack the necessary rights to challenge oppressive forms of social control. While inclusive citizenship is fundamental for prosperity, those who are not (yet) full citizens are economically, politically, and socially disadvantaged (Schugurensky 2006).

The goal in the community is to help Filipino domestic workers come to a new awareness of selfhood so that they may begin to critically recognize their circumstances and take the initiative in acting to transform the society that has denied them opportunities of participation (see Eric and Tungohan, this volume). Structural and institutional barriers are often difficult to amend unless the issues are addressed directly by those who are affected by such oppressions. However, live-in caregivers are not able to independently challenge the existing social structures as a result of their non-citizenship status while in the LCP. In the present, there is great demand for community organizations and grassroots mobilization oriented towards social justice. There is also a great need for collectives to congregate to assist and protect the rights of those who are denied privileges to participate in community integration and political action.

In knowing more about each other's immigration histories, both groups will be able to see that there are still crucial similarities between their experiences, which will then help foster more interaction (and even less indifference) between the two groups. Filipino healthcare professionals who arrived in Canada during the 1960s feel that Filipinos coming through the LCP have lower skills and belong to lower classes, whereas those who came later, Filipino domestic workers who arrived in the 1980s, 1990s, and 2000s, are simply not aware that the earlier newcomers, too, faced hardships. Seeing their similarities may help close the divide between the two groups. Seeing such historical continuities (as well as differences) will allow us to have a better grasp of Filipino lives in Canada and may also open the doors for community mobilization on issues pertaining to the LCP. Highlighting an understanding of earlier and later histories for people in both eras will therefore lead to a more supportive community structure.

NOTES

1 Riverdale Hospital, currently known as Bridgepoint Health, is an institution that treats and manages complex chronic disease. Since its inception in 1860, it was a House of Refuge for 'incurables and the indigent poor.' It then became a Smallpox Hospital in 1872, followed by an Isolation Hospital (Riverdale Isolation Hospital) in 1891 to address communicable diseases, such as tuberculosis. In 1957, the hospital's name and mandate were changed and its focus shifted to helping those with chronic ailments and/or those needing rehabilitation. In 1963, it became known as Riverdale Hospital and opened with eight hundred beds to meet the growing need to support people with long-term illnesses in Toronto (Bridgepoint Health 2010).

2 The immigration trends of Filipino healthcare professionals have been analysed in juxtaposition with other occupational categories like physicians, engineers, and clerical workers. Hence, all occupational categories are homogenized into one 'professional group' to portray, in general, the growth of Filipino professionals in Canada, which includes the healthcare occupational group.

3 The Foreign Domestic Movement (FDM) program was implemented by the Canadian government in 1981, preceding the temporary visa system, Temporary Employment Authorization Program (TEAP), that was established in 1973. The FDM was a more regulated immigration program that marked the institutionalization of Canada's exploitation of women from developing countries for employment in domestic work. This policy of importing domestic workers was the direct result of women in Canada moving into the workforce. When women in industrialized countries leave the home to work, hiring a domestic worker becomes an affordable option for most middle- and upper-class families (Philippine Women Centre 2000).

4 Laquian (1973) argues that from 1967 to 1971 Filipino immigrants were predominantly female, in contrast to other nationalities, as a result of their professions (i.e., nursing, medical technology, secretarial, and clerical work). Such professions attracted more women. Moreover, Canada prioritized the recruitment of immigrants in these fields during these years. The professional group made up more than half of all Filipino immigrants, followed by the secretarial and clerical and the manufacturing and mechanical occupational groups. Among the professionals, nurses and medical technologists predominated.
5 For information regarding the excess of nurses in the Philippines during the 1960s, see Ball 2004; Choy 2003.

REFERENCES

Archives of Ontario. RG 76-3-0-593. Filipino association (Toronto, Ontario). 'Operation nurses' newspaper article, received February 20, 1967. Report by A.M. de Swaaf.

Archives of Ontario. RG 76-3-0-593. Filipino association (Toronto, Ontario). Summary of interview with Mr Barry F. Cunnings, March 14, 1967. Report by A.M. de Swaaf.

Bakan, Abigail, and Daiva Stasiulis, eds. 1997. *Not one of the family: Foreign domestic workers in Canada*. Toronto: University of Toronto Press.

Ball, Rochelle E. 2004. Divergent development, racialized rights: Globalised labour markets and the trade of nurses. The case of the Philippines. *Women's Studies International Forum* 27: 119–33.

Barber, Pauline Gardiner. 2000. Agency in Philippine women's labour migration and provisional diaspora. *Women's Studies International Forum* 23 (4): 399–411.

Bridgepoint Health. 2010. *Bridgepoint Health: About us*. Bridgepoint Health 2010 [cited July 11, 2011]. Available from www.bridgepointhealth.ca/aboutus.

Bustamante, Rosalina E. 1984. Filipino Canadians: A growing community. *Polyphony* 6: 168–71.

Citizenship and Immigration Canada. 2000. *Forging our legacy: Canadian citizenship and immigration, 1900–1977*. Available from http://www.cic.gc.ca/english/department/legacy/chap-6.html.

Chen, Anita Beltran. 1998. *From sunbelt to snowbelt: Filipinos in Canada*. Calgary: Canadian Ethnic Studies Association, University of Calgary.

Choy, Catherine Ceniza. 2003. *Empire of care: Nursing and migration in Filipino American history*. Durham, NC: Duke University Press.

Cohen, Rina. 2000. 'Mom is a stranger': The negative impact of immigration policies on the family life of Filipina domestic workers. *Canadian Ethnic Studies* 32 (3): 76–88.

Cusipag, Ruben J., and Maria Corazon Buenafe. 1993. *Portrait of Filipino Canadians in Ontario (1960–1990).* Toronto: Kalayaan Media.

Damasco, Valerie G. 2009. Philippine-trained nurses hired in Canada in the 1960s: Life histories of Philippine women. Master's thesis, Ontario Institute for Studies in Education, University of Toronto, Toronto.

England, Kim, and Bernadette Stiell. 1997. Domestic distinctions: Constructing difference among paid domestic workers in Toronto. *Gender, Place and Culture* 4 (3): 339–59.

Grandea, Nona, and Joanna Kerr. 1998. 'Frustrated and displaced': Filipina domestic workers in Canada. *Gender and Development* 6 (1): 7–12.

Hune, Shirley, and Gail M. Nomura, eds. 2003. *Asian/Pacific Islander American women: A historical anthology.* New York: New York University Press.

Kelly, Philip. 2006. Filipinos in Canada: Economic dimensions of immigration and settlement. Joint Centre of Excellence for Research on Immigration and Settlement – Toronto (CERIS – The Ontario Metropolis Centre). CERIS Working Paper No. 48: 1–37.

Laquian, Eleanor R. 1973. *A study of Filipino immigration to Canada, 1962–1972.* 2nd ed. Ottawa: United Council of Filipino Associations in Canada.

McKay, Deidre, and Philippine Women Centre. 2002. Filipina identities: Geographies of social integration/exclusion in the Canadian metropolis. Vancouver Centre of Excellence. Research on Immigration and Integration in the Metropolis. Working Paper Series, No. 02-18: 1–45.

Parreñas, Rhacel Salazar. 2000. Migrant Filipina domestic workers and the international division of reproductive labour. *Gender and Society* 14 (4): 560–81.

– 2001. Transgressing the nation-state: The partial citizenship and 'imagined (global) community' of migrant Filipina domestic workers. *Signs: Journal of Women in Culture and Society* 26 (4): 1129–54.

Philippine Women Centre of British Columbia. 2000. Canada: The new frontier for Filipino mail-order brides. http://dsp-psd.pwgsc.gc.ca/Collection/ SW21-62-2000E.pdf.

Pratt, Geraldine. 1997. Stereotypes and ambivalence: The construction of domestic workers in Vancouver, British Columbia. *Gender, Place and Culture* 4 (2): 159–77.

– 1999. From registered nurse to registered nanny: Discursive geographies of Filipina domestic workers in Vancouver B.C. *Economic Geography* 75 (3): 215–36.

Schugurensky, Daniel. 2006. Adult citizenship education: An overview of the field. In *Contexts of adult education: Canadian perspectives,* ed. Tara Fenwick, Tom Nesbit, and Bruce Spencer. Toronto: Thompson Educational Publishing.

Stasiulis, Daiva K., and Abigail B. Bakan. 2005. *Negotiating citizenship: Migrant women in Canada and the global system.* Toronto: University of Toronto Press.

Zaman, Habiba. 2004. Transnational migration and the commodification of im/migrant female labourers in Canada. *International Journal of Canadian Studies* 29: 41–62.

Chapter 5

The Rites of Passage of Filipinas in Canada: Two Migration Cohorts

JOSEPHINE ERIC

I was eighteen years old in 1988 when I left my hometown in the Philippines. I worked for two years in Belgium, and then in 1990 I came to Ontario as a nanny through the Live-In Caregiver Program. I found these overseas employment opportunities through my network of family and friends. As the oldest of nine children, I felt responsible for my family's well-being; therefore, I remitted money to the Philippines to pay for my parents' bank debts and to enable my younger siblings to pursue high school and university education. After working as a nanny and obtaining my landed immigrant status in Canada, I juggled three jobs: full time in a factory, in a grocery store after my regular day job, and in a twenty-four-hour convenience store on weekends. I got married in Calgary, Alberta, in 1997, and now have five children, ranging in age from five to eleven years old. After settling into married life, my family and I moved to Hamilton, Ontario, a city an hour away from Toronto. I was committed to continuing my education, which I had begun while living in Alberta, and in 2001 I received a bachelor's degree in anthropology with a minor in women's studies from the University of Calgary. Subsequently, I completed a master's degree in labour studies at McMaster University in 2007 and a second master's degree in anthropology at the University of Toronto in 2011. Twenty-three years after I left the Philippines, I look back at my journey of migration and realize that I am one of the lucky ones.

I started volunteering in a settlement organization in Hamilton in 1999 as an interpreter for Filipino, Bicol, and Sign and Oral languages to help Filipina/o newcomers adjust to their new lives in Canada. I could relate to their feelings of isolation and disorientation in a new country and their longing for their families and other loved ones in the Philippines. Interested in combining my academic and advocacy work, I was inspired by the work of Audrey Kobayashi, who stated that 'I do not use other people's struggles as the basis for my research; I use my research as a basis for struggles of which I am a part' (Kobayashi, in Chiu 2003, 6). Hence, for my master's thesis at McMaster University (Eric 2007), I examined the migration waves of Filipino women from the 1960s to the present. I wanted to find out which factors contribute to the different rites of passage in settlement and integration between the earlier and later cohorts of Filipino women to Canada.

Since my arrival in Canada, I have become relatively successful, in the eyes of some members of the community. My husband and I bought our own house in the more established west end of the city, and drove a van instead of taking the public transportation bus system. Since my husband's construction business was doing well, I did not need to go to work. We were able to sponsor my parents to Canada, and I attended university full time. As my research progressed, I became cognizant of my position between the two cohorts of Filipina migrants to Canada. My in-between position was made evident by comments from two fellow Filipinas from different cohorts. At the end of one of my research interviews, a participant from the later cohort asked, *'After you finish your schooling, what are you going to do with your research? Are you going to put it on the shelf like the rest of them? Or are you going to do something about the issue?'* Then, at a social gathering, a long-time community member whispered to me, after learning that I used to be a nanny, *'Don't let anyone else know about that. You're already successful. That is very shameful.'* I use this in-between position to delineate the generational conditions of these two cohorts, since, I contend, they have impacted considerably the rites of passage of these women's lives and career trajectories. These rites of passage include education and professional preparation achieved in the Philippines and prior overseas experience, as well as entry status and first employment in Canada. These rites also need to be contextualized within the political economic systems in the Philippines and Canada during these two time periods, since national and global dynamics are key factors in shaping migration and labour policies and experiences.

This chapter builds on my master's research and analyses the complex 'generational' similarities and differences between two cohorts of Filipina migrants in Canada – those who arrived in Canada between the 1960s and 1970s, and those who came since the late 1980s. The late

1980s was a pivotal moment for the history of Filipina/os in Canada, since that particular time period solidified the Live-In Caregiver Program (LCP), thus bringing the large waves of Filipinas to Canada (see Davidson and Tungohan in this volume).

Situating Filipina Migrants in the Philippines and Canada

Philippine Context

The Philippines gained independence from the United States in 1946. By the time the 1960s arrived, many changes were taking place. A strong foundation for the arts was established to enhance cultural work, the economy appeared to be gaining in strength, and the future was one of hope (Bresnan 1986). Although President Ferdinand Marcos declared martial law in the early 1970s, the economy remained robust, with trade, tourism, and budget surpluses. Against this backdrop of apparent success, the president and his wife led a life of corruption and excessive expenditure. By the end of the 1970s, corruption, nepotism, and civil unrest contributed to a serious decline in economic growth and development, and the country incurred enormous debt with the World Bank (Stasiulis and Bakan 2005). In order to maintain economic control, the Philippine government saw labour migration as a vital strategy and adopted a human export policy. As a result, many Filipina/os were encouraged to work in North America, Europe, the Middle East, and other parts of Asia.

Most of the early wave Filipina/o migrants who worked abroad following Marcos's adoption of the human export policy were men in the construction, oil, and agricultural industries (Guerrero 2001). Go (2002) argues that 'international labour migration is only a temporary, stop-gap measure to bolster the country's flagging economy. It does not promote overseas employment as a means to sustain economic growth and economic development' (4). The overthrow of the Marcos regime in 1986 led to a chain of events that furthered economic and political unrest in the Philippines. Subsequent government leaders did not make a substantial difference to the migration of Filipina/os out of the country, as structural adjustment programs from the World Bank and the International Monetary Fund made the Philippines more dependent on foreign remittances to meet its financial obligations. Such economic and political conditions led to the development of national policies, such as 'The Medium-Term Philippine Development Plan for 2001–2004,' which enabled the government to 'fully respect labour mobility, including the preference for overseas employment' (Go 2002, 5). Remittances from overseas workers account for a large source of revenue and foreign currency exchange. From 1990 to 1999, remittances to the Philippines contributed 20.3 per cent to the country's export earnings and 5.2 per cent of the gross national product. This accounts for the daily average of 2,748 Filipina/os leaving for work overseas (Go 2002).

Work migration as a labour strategy, which was originally meant as a temporary measure, has become a permanent economic policy. Moreover, the demographic composition of migrating workers has changed since the policy was enacted. In the 1970s, 36,035 Filipina/os were deployed overseas, a great majority of whom were men. By the 1990s, 866,590 Filipina/os left the Philippines to work abroad. The labour migration shifted from men to women: in 2001 a much higher percentage of those leaving the country were women (Go 2002, 13).

Despite the Philippine government's increased reliance on migrant workers' remittances, its labour and employment strategy does not include improving the condition of migrant workers abroad. Overseas workers are required to undergo additional training before leaving the country so that the government can increase their competitiveness in the labour market. I argue that the main issue for Filipina/o migrants is not their competitiveness as transnational workers, but rather their lack of political power in receiving countries like Canada when asserting their right to proper, humane treatment as workers. The responsibility for the exploitative conditions of Filipina/o workers is relegated to individual migrants, thus overshadowing the role of the state in both sending and receiving countries.

Canadian Context

When more White women in global north countries started working outside their homes, the need for domestic caregiving labour was filled by women of colour from Third World countries. Childcare provision is a major issue in Canada, especially with increased participation of women in the labour force (Prentice 2001; Tyyska 2001; Jenson and Sineau 2003). In the late 1960s, Britain was the main source of caregiver labour to Canada. However, when this favoured source did not generate enough to meet Canada's increasing demand, Canada turned to the West Indies to seek cheaper yet still English-speaking labour (Daenzer 1993). Because Canada does not have a national childcare provision, the government developed migrant labour initiatives such as the Foreign Domestic Movement (FDM) program. When Caribbean women rallied for systemic changes in the FDM program, the government sought out a new source of female workers (Stasiulis and Bakan 2005).

The Canadian government instituted the Live-In Caregiver Program (LCP) in the 1980s as a labour measure, and women from the Philippines who could not come to Canada under other immigration categories utilized this program to seek opportunities abroad. Since many Canadian women have access to the general labour market, they do not view domestic work as a desirable employment option. Caregiving work such as 'domestic work is undervalued, underpaid and stigmatized' (Arat-Koç 2005). Owing to the restrictions of live-in work under temporary legal status, Filipina workers under the LCP face limited opportunities to further their education and to pursue their professions as nurses or teachers. Unlike the early wave of Filipinas who came to Canada as professionals, Filipinas in the LCP took the place of Caribbean domestics in the racialized labour hierarchy. The early wave of Filipina migrants was composed mostly of nurses who filled the need for caring work in hospitals and medical facilities. During this period, Filipinas entered Canada as landed immigrants who were recruited and employed in the primary labour market (see Damasco in this volume).

In the FDM, there were bilateral agreements between Canada and the Caribbean which facilitated the employment of Caribbean domestic workers in Canada. However, in the Live-In Caregiver Program (LCP), there are no agreements between states, and the sending and receiving countries are not involved. Rather, private employment agencies mediate the flow of caregivers. Consequently, Canada saves costs as labour and migration gatekeeping move from the state to private agencies. Canada's shift in its gatekeeping role is in line with its alignment to neoliberal policies and its restructuring of the welfare state. Although private employment agencies charge both the employers and the employees for their services, the Canadian government does not have a monitoring mechanism to enforce labour laws. For example, one of my research participants said, *'I came to Canada through a recruitment agency. In 1990 I only paid $100 Canadian to an agency. That same agency is now charging anywhere from $3,000 to $6,000 Canadian for placement depending on destination countries.'* The high recruitment fees imposed by recruitment and employment agencies are a major source of hardship for Filipinas. Some caregivers stay with their abusive employers not only because they need to send money to their families, but also because they need to pay debts incurred from recruiters.

Research Methodology

This chapter draws from my master's thesis in labour studies, for which I undertook research in the spring and summer of 2007. Then, as now, I was heavily involved in various community activities and had strong social networks to distribute recruitment flyers throughout Southern Ontario. My research methods included individual interviews and participant observation, which I was able to undertake through my community involvement.

Although I interviewed sixteen women in my study, for this chapter I chose to focus on the narratives of three women from the earlier cohort and three women from the later cohort. I aimed to highlight the various ways that my participants entered Canada: as landed immigrants, through the FDM and the LCP, and through the skilled class category. The various categories of immigration entry to Canada illustrate the historical process of immigration changes in Canada after the 1960s (Daenzer 1993). At present, the categories of entry status include immigrants (including provincial nominee immigrants), skilled class, family class, refugee, visitor, or student.[1] The non-immigrant employment category encompasses temporary workers and includes the Live-In Caregiver Program. The Filipinas in the earlier cohort entered Canada as permanent residents and reported having successful integration experiences. However, even though those from the later cohort had similar educational and professional backgrounds to those from the earlier cohort, their entry status and experiences in Canada are radically different.

Philip Kelly (2006) highlights the cultural, political, and economic factors that influence the deprofessionalization of Filipina/os in Canada. Of these factors, economic marginalization arguably contributes to their deprofessionalization. Indeed, economic integration is a key that can unlock all the other spheres of newcomers' settlement and integration. After all, the non-recognition of foreign educational credentials and work experiences often affects immigrant earning (Satzewich and Liodakis 2007). Moreover, the existence of discrimination within labour unions disadvantages the influx of multicultural workers[2] trying to settle in the new country (Reitz and Verma 2003). By focusing on the intergenerational experiences of Filipinas in Canada, this chapter compares the migration waves of Filipinas to Canada with different categories of entry status, and shows how changes in political and economic policies directly affect the quality of life of newcomers and their families. This intergenerational comparison also highlights needed recommendations to better address the plight of caregivers in Canada and in the world.

Narrative Profiles of the Earlier Cohort

The experiences of Delila, Bella, and Jennifer (pseudonyms) represent the first cohort of Filipino women in Canada (also, see Damasco in this volume). Their narratives embody the following four characteristics: (1) they arrived with landed immigrant status; (2) their education and professional background were recognized and commensurate with their employment; (3) they enjoyed strong family relations, since many immigrated with their families or were able to immediately sponsor their families; and (4) they held strong feelings of belonging in Canada. Delila related,

> *I came in 1969. I came originally from the Bicol province, southern part of Luzon. I just finished nursing in one of the prestigious schools in the country. I did not find it hard to find a job when I arrived in Canada. I was offered a job on the spot after the interview. I passed the nursing exam the following year and got married afterwards. My husband was an electrical engineer in the Philippines. We bought our first house in 1972. We have brought over our families on both sides and now enjoy a lot of family get-togethers.*

Like Delila, Bella arrived as a landed immigrant from the Philippines and worked in a hospital as a nurse. Both women enjoyed working as nurses with stable financial benefits. Because of their earned economic capital, they were able to buy their homes. Through strong family support, they were also able to easily transition and settle in Canada. Consequently they have a sense of belonging in Canada, and have positive interactions with people of various racial backgrounds. Bella is very active in her community, which includes Filipina/o and non-Filipina/o friends. When I met her, she was preparing a publication for a nursing journal that contacted her the year before. Bella is married to an Egyptian man, has beautiful children, and enjoys ballroom dancing. In our phone interview, Bella shared, *'I came in 1982 from the Visayas region. I came as landed immigrant [and] was a nurse before coming to Canada . . . [My older sister and I] bought our first house on 1983. I am now working in the hospital and feel quite good working with other racial groups in the community.'*

Integration appeared to be easy for the earlier cohort of Filipino women in Canada. They seemed to be able to integrate and obtain secure jobs with benefits. Jennifer, like Delila and Bella, has a positive settlement and integration experience in Canada. She worked in the same hospital for thirty-five years, and retired as a hospital director. Her Filipino husband worked across the border in New York as a college professor teaching philosophy and science. Jennifer often travels, since most of her relatives are in the United States and the Philippines. She continues to correspond with colleagues from prestigious universities in the Philippines, and is seen as a role model by those who wish to follow her footsteps. Like Delila, she is well known with strong social networks inside and outside of the Filipina/o community. Jennifer explained,

> *I remember the first time I came; [the hospitals] were so desperate for registered nurses. They even provided for us [with] free board and lodging. We even have a maid and we have all the benefits that the hospital can provide to make us feel at home. We were even asked if we have other friends that might be interested to work with us. The director said that they needed more registered nurses so they can open the hospital. So, I told my friends in Chicago.*

Jennifer's arrival in Canada coincided with an important historical period when hospitals were being built and in need of nursing staff. During this period of nation building, Filipinas who worked as nurses were provided with material benefits, such as free board, lodging, and maid service, and became a vital part of the Canadian labour force (see Damasco this volume). Because of professional treatment and additional perks, Jennifer stayed with the same employer for thirty-five years, a direct contrast to those in the later cohort who wish to leave their employers after working for less than two years.

Narrative Profiles of the Later Cohort

For the later cohort, we could learn from the experiences of Madonna, Penelope, and Adelia (pseudonyms). In contrast to those in the earlier cohort who seem to have stable jobs and tend to spend quality time with their families, many newcomers in Canada have to work in several jobs to support their families in the Philippines. When their families reunite in Canada, they continue to work in several jobs to provide for them, making it difficult to spend time with their children, from whom they have been separated for years. These subsistence jobs are usually precarious and provide low wages (see Kelly et al. in this volume).

It was during my interview with Delila that I met Madonna, who came to Canada in 2003. Madonna lives with Delila's family on weekends. Delila called Madonna to tell her about my study, since Madonna was a nurse in the Philippines, a domestic worker in Hong Kong, and then a nanny in Canada. Madonna disclosed to me,

I graduated as a nurse. I worked almost two years in Hong Kong before coming here ... I am very frustrated and feel very discriminated. I always fight with my employer and I feel there is no difference between working in Hong Kong and working in Canada. I am not paid for overtime nor have a day off. I am taking courses as an RPN [registered practical nurse] which I feel is downgrading my degree as a registered nurse from the Philippines. I am currently looking for another employer and feel so upset [about] how the system does not allow me to fully meet my expectation.

Listening to Madonna, I noted that she did not have what Delila had: a home she could call her own, time to spend with family and friends, a secure daily living, and eventually a secure retirement life. Madonna's life as a caregiver in Canada was unstable and unsatisfactory, further compounded by Canada's non-recognition of her training and education from the Philippines. Madonna was in her productive working years; but how will her current living and working conditions influence her later years in Canada?

Contrasting the experiences of those in the earlier cohort with those in the later cohort reveals six factors that characterize the differences for the later cohort: (1) their international work experiences prior to coming to Canada; (2) the increasing role of private recruitment agencies as migration and labour gatekeepers; (3) their temporary entry status in Canada; (4) their employment in positions that are not commensurate with their educational and professional backgrounds; (5) the extended separation from their families in the Philippines for five years or longer; and (6) finally, their experiences of discrimination and feeling of non-belonging in Canada.

Penelope and I spoke about my research at a small coffee shop in downtown Hamilton. She was waiting for the College of Nurses' decision about accrediting the course that she was taking.[3] When internationally trained nurses arrive in Canada, their foreign academic credentials have to be assessed before they can take courses to gain their Canadian equivalence. Upon completion of these courses they can prepare for the licensing examination for nurses. Professional organizations like the College of Nurses of Ontario monitor the process of accreditation. Penelope related how the staff in the crediting office were not very helpful, and she felt that they were racist. These impressions stemmed from how they treated her when she went into the office and how they did not provide information that addressed her questions. When she tried to make herself clear to them, they simply looked at her with odd expressions on their faces. She confided, 'Wala man lang akong mapagtanungan kong ano pa ang dapat gawin ko (*I have nobody to ask about what else I need to do). I just work few hours in the retirement home and I am not able to be on my own yet.*' Then she said, '*I came in 1999 . . . I came and had been moving from different cities [Toronto, Hamilton, Niagara, Montreal] to find work and now almost ready to take my nursing examination. I came as a nanny and have been in Israel before coming here. I am still living in an apartment with other Filipina domestic workers.*'

Penelope has been struggling to settle in Canada for over ten years. Her life exemplifies the six characteristics of the later cohort. She has moved to different cities with the hope of getting a stable job to support her basic needs. Although she has undergone de-skilling because she worked outside her field of nursing for quite some time, she has tried to upgrade her employment situation from caregiver to nurse by taking additional coursework. Seeing that Canadian regulations mandate that nurses need to have worked in the field for the last two years, Penelope cannot get her nursing credentials recognized, nor does she qualify for the transfer of her Philippine nursing credentials to Canada. Penelope cannot work in places that require a recognized Canadian nursing licence.

Penelope and her best friend Adelia face the same dilemma. Both graduated as nurses in the Philippines and have been helping each other since they came to Canada. According to Adelia, '*I came as a domestic worker in 1999. I came from the northern province of Luzon. I am now upgrading in nursing and working as a nursing aide full-time plus a part-time job on the weekend. We are still renting and we are hoping to have a baby soon. I feel that with enough determination I can be successful in Canada.*' Adelia and Penelope came from the same region in the Philippines and have been friends since they came from Israel. It took Adelia eight years to sponsor her husband to Canada. She was separated from him for quite a while, and was experiencing de-skilling as a nanny (see Kelly et al. in this volume). In order to support her family and relatives in the Philippines, she decided to work full-time instead of upgrading her nursing education and skills after two years of live-in care work. Adelia was therefore earning less but working more hours. This affected her desire to have children, since she spent more time at work than with her husband. Adelia's precarious condition affected the type of family they would have in Canada. The last time I saw them, in 2009, she was suffering from a thyroid problem and there was no news of the baby she desired. She related that when she went to work in the morning, her husband came home from night shift work in a ceiling fan factory.

Analysis and Implications

To analyse the similarities and differences in the rites of passage between the two cohorts, I will focus on Delila's and Madonna's accounts. Although both women graduated as nurses from universities in the Philippines, they occupy opposite poles in the spectrum of newcomer experiences in Canada. Delila's account seems full of successful settlement experiences: she had a career as a nurse and her families are in Canada. From her perspective, life has been good in Canada. However, Madonna's account reflects a complex web of migration experiences that began prior to her arrival in Canada and was compounded by discrimination and exploitation. Their differences also manifested in their varying economic conditions and family relations.

I met Delila in 2007 through a friend in Niagara. Her home had a small garden and a wide grass area where her grandchildren played when they visited. The ability of those in the earlier cohort to provide for their families resulted in brighter prospects for the second generation, as evidenced in the university diplomas in Delila's living room. Delila and her husband had two sons who finished their university degrees: one was working in Citizenship and Immigration Canada and the other one was a police officer. Her husband and their children obtained gainful employment in their respective fields, and were able to enjoy a middle-class lifestyle with their families. Those in the later cohort were also able to provide for their families, but suffered from long separations with severe emotional and relationship implications. Delila was originally from Bicol, the same geographical region in the Philippines where I was born and raised. We spoke in our dialect, but when I started asking her research questions, she answered in English. She related her early years in Canada enthusiastically and fondly,

> *As soon as we arrived my friend from school took me to Toronto. She said there are a lot of Filipinos there (laughter).* May ipapakilala ako sa 'yo. *(I will introduce you to someone.) I just finish school so,* hindi naman ako nag-aapura na mag-anum ano, so, nagduman kami tapos nagkarakanan. Kunting parti tapos duman ko na bisto si Mister ko. *(I am not in a hurry to get married you know, so we went there and then we ate. A little bit of party and then, there I met my husband). Now [my husband and I] are both retired and we like to visit everywhere ...* mapuli ngani kami sa pasko *(we are going home [to the Philippines] this Christmas).*

Delila's account illustrates various opportunities for social activities with limited worries about work. Madonna also came to Canada as a young woman, yet her weekend activity was focused on scouting out a new nanny job. Delila enjoyed life outside of work, but Madonna's life centred on work. When I visited Delila, she was at home preparing for the arrival of her family. I arrived at 3 p.m., and she was preparing *adobo* for her husband, her two sons, and their families. She mentioned that her children lived several blocks away, so they visited often. She received many telephone calls during my visit and said, *'They [the callers] are my friends from the hospital where I used to work. They are inviting me for some party on the weekend.* Sana makabalik ka pa para makilala mo rin sila *(I wish you can come back so you can also meet them).'*

How many Filipinas in Canada are enjoying an afternoon and only worrying about what to serve for dinner? How many Filipinas are not burdened by worries of family members across the ocean? How many are not looking for jobs on weekends so they can make ends meet? Not many are enjoying a retired lifestyle like Delila. However, many who are still working or looking for work on weekends can relate to Madonna.

The different rites of passage between the two cohorts of Filipina migrants have three important effects and implications. First, these rites of passage impact their lived experiences, career trajectories, and sense of belonging in Canada. Second, these difficult experiences have lasting effects on their families, depending on the composition of the family, whether there are young children, teenagers, or young adults who are ready to leave home. Often these problems cause stress and place pressure on marital relationships. Third, they have consequences for social relations within the Filipina/o community and how the Filipina/o community is perceived as a group in Canada. In Geraldine Pratt's (1999) study in Vancouver, the earlier groups of Filipina/os who came to Canada as landed immigrants do not want to be associated with those who arrived as domestic workers or caregivers. There is a stigma associated with recent Filipinas who migrate as domestic workers. The class division between the earlier and later cohorts is a manifestation of the differences in their respective rites of passage. The rite of passage of registered nurses from the first cohort is important to highlight, especially since their ability to work with landed immigrant status enabled them to become professionally and personally successful. The rite of passage of nannies with temporary status puts them in precarious living and working conditions. Entry status is an important factor that contributes tremendously to the differences in their settlement and integration experiences.

The social position of Filipinas in the caring labour market in Canada and around the world brings advantages and disadvantages to the group. According to Daniel Hiebert (1997), the concentration of particular ethnic groups in certain types of economic activity becomes a significant point for group identification within and outside of those groups. For instance, Koreans are perceived as shop owners, Jews as lawyers, and Filipina/os as domestic workers and caregivers. The prevailing perception in Canada of Filipinas as domestic workers and nannies is not favoured by middle-class Filipina/os, especially when they get mistaken for domestic workers themselves. Like Pratt (1999), Rhacel Parreñas (2001) observed the social and class tensions between Filipina/o domestic workers and the established Filipina/os in Los Angeles. I was also cautioned by a prominent member of the Filipina/o community that I should not mention the fact that I was a nanny when I first came to Canada. This is an illustration of the detachment of established Filipina/os from the plight of newcomers within the Filipina/o community.

Ultimately the later cohort of Filipina migrants suffers from various challenges that are not present in the migration, living, and working conditions of the earlier cohort. Their entry status as temporary workers initiated their rite of passage to precarious employment and unstable living conditions. Filipina/os in the Live-In Caregiver Program feel overwhelmed by personal problems and end up enacting what Filipina/os consider 'kanya-kanya' – loosely translated as being individualistic – because of their often isolated and taxing jobs as live-in caregivers in private homes. An intergenerational analysis of Filipina migrants highlights the different conditions that shaped the opposite lived experiences of the earlier and later cohorts in Canada.

Research on other newcomer migrants highlights shared experiences of discrimination and other barriers to successful settlement in Canada. Racialized minorities continuously experience varying degrees of discrimination for several years as they attempt to integrate and struggle to find employment in Canada (Guo 2006). Women of colour in particular suffer from both overt and non-overt discrimination in work settings and interpersonal relations (Reitz and Verma 2003; Satzewich and Liodakis 2007). For example, Daiva Stasiulis and Abigail Bakan (2005) stress the negative stereotyping of Caribbean and Filipino women as domestic workers.

Recommendations and Conclusion

There is a burning need for the Filipina/o community to come together in order to address the injustices and situations arising in the lives of new Filipina/os entering Canada through the Live-In Caregiver Program. The differing point of view of established Filipina/o Canadians reflects differences in class status within the community and their sense of belonging in Canada. The difference in class status and sense of belonging between the established and newcomer Filipina/os is marked by their entry status category as landed immigrants and as temporary workers, respectively. The different entry status categories that were available for the earlier and later cohorts set the conditions for their rites of passage in Canada and consequently impacted their employment, family relations, social opportunities, and viewpoints of Canada. In other words, the ability of the earlier cohort to enter as landed immigrants offered greater possibilities for white-collar employment as nurses and engineers and for middle-class lives. I put forward several sets of recommendations in this chapter to address important key players that can transform the rites of passage of Filipina newcomers: recommendations for policymakers and, most importantly, for prospective newcomers.

Filipina/o lives in Canada do not correspond to the mythology of a global North with lots of money and happy lives. The challenges of migration and overseas employment need to be openly addressed. The political and economic policies of sending and receiving nation-states affect the lives of migrant workers. The Philippine government must take part in ensuring the safety and security of overseas workers. For the Canadian government, one of my research participants made the following plea:

> *The right of the nannies should be enforced by government bodies. Government should look after the rights of these workers. There has to be stricter regulations making employer accountable. Nannies should be allowed to know their rights. There should also be training for new workers such as orientation before they start working in Canada ... There is no resource in community to help migrant workers like Filipina domestic workers. There is nothing to help you upgrade yourself; well, what I mean is something that I like or Filipina women like, beside nursing aide or factory work.*

According to Patricia Daenzer (1993), 'changes in policy are based on improving the interpretation and status of Canadian citizens and not the domestic workers' (12). It is therefore necessary to create policy changes that also include the improvement of the status of workers under the Live-In Caregiver Program. Immigrant-serving agencies provide specific assistance and support to immigrants or refugees; however, they need to expand their mandate and scope so that they can be accessed by caregivers who are in Canada for temporary work. The Live-In Caregiver Program allows upper- and middle-class women to work and obtain gainful employment; however, the suffering of racialized minority women as caregivers reflects on all women. To move forward as a culturally diverse country, the Canadian government must provide equitable opportunities to all who come and live within its geopolitical space.

Dialogue within the Filipina/o community and with allies must also be sustained, not only during moments of crisis such as the murders of Filipino youth (see Catungal in this volume). Those in the earlier cohort represent crucial yet untapped resources for policy change and community action. They have established themselves in various social and professional spaces, and can serve as links between government agencies and the newcomers. It is important to merge both the structural and community struggles together. The macro- and micro-level changes must take place to have an emancipatory impact. A very important effort that captures the merging of the micro and macro levels in the community can be seen in the formation of the Community Alliance for Social Justice (CASJ) in response to the shooting of Jeffrey Reodica, a Filipino youth who was killed by police in 2004 (Astorga Garcia 2007). What is significant about CASJ is that Filipina/os and non-Filipina/os came together to address a crucial community issue. CASJ represents collaboration with other ethnic and community organizations that directly address racial discrimination and inequality. Establishing networks is vital in overcoming difficulties faced by racialized minorities and newcomers in Canada.

In addition, adequate information for prospective immigrants must be provided before they arrive in the country. For other Filipina/os who wish to come to Canada, Antonia – a former professor of English at the University of the Philippines and a research participant from the later cohort – expressed strong caution. At the time of my interview, Antonia was in the process of sponsoring her brother and his family to Canada. She came to Canada in 1995 and worked in a factory full-time. She was single and active in church activities. She always supported Filipina nannies in her area by referring them to new employers and helping them land new jobs, as in the factory where she worked. She remarked,

> *It is very unfortunate how such educated women waste their lives doing menial jobs when they are capable of doing more. As Filipinos we need to stop pretending everything is all right. Filipinos back home do not want to hear about the condition of domestic workers. The Philippine government does not want the influx of migration outside the country to stop. So, there are not a lot of options. For prospective nannies expectations are different from reality. I would say to them: prepare for the worst!*

Antonia's honesty shows the lack of communication between the earlier and later cohorts in the Filipina/o community. The limited information about hardships abroad can also be due to the Philippine government's support of workers abroad. Overseas Filipina/o workers have been idealized by the Philippine government as 'modern heroes,' which can blur and distract from the necessary focus on developing protective measures.

Finally, migrant workers themselves can contribute to making the world a better place for all. In 2007, after I defended my master's thesis at McMaster University, many of my research participants and I established a non-profit organization, the Migrant Workers Family Resource Centre, in Hamilton. With a mandate to provide dignity and rights to migrant workers and their families, this volunteer-run organization aimed to provide support for newcomers, especially the most vulnerable ones such as live-in caregivers and those under the Canadian government's temporary working programs. It also partners with other community groups, academics, and government entities for its annual conference to disseminate research findings about race, gender, labour, migration, and acculturation. Migrant workers have volunteered countless hours during their precious days. I have observed that, when migrant workers participate, they discover their strength from within. Through the Resource Centre, migrant women workers have become empowered and become agents of change. They have internalized and enacted the vision of working together to create a welcoming space and give voice to all.

NOTES

1 The ability of newcomers to enter Canada as immigrants depends on their capacity to satisfy requirements, which include financial savings, educational attainment, linguistic proficiency in English and/or French, and the professional and technical needs of Canada or a particular province. If newcomers are unable to satisfy these requirements, the skilled category option highlights work experience as a determining factor in the application. The family class category involves landed or permanent residents in Canada sponsoring their families overseas. Those applying for refugee as an entry status are individuals applying at the border or a Canadian embassy as a convention refugee or applying within Canada as asylum seekers. Visitor visa applicants must either have families to visit in Canada or demonstrate ability to travel with a guarantee to leave after visiting Canada. Finally those with student visas must show acceptance to an educational institution in Canada and capability to sustain themselves financially while studying in Canada (Wayland 2006).
2 The influx of migrants to Canada from non-European parts of the world has provided the country with a racially diverse labour force. The Philippines, China, and India are major sources of migrants to Canada (Kelly 2006).
3 The College of Nurses of Ontario has outlined several requirements, including written and spoken English proficiency, university academic transcripts, completion of particular courses or training, completion of licensing examination and practicum experience, and permanent residency papers. For more information, see http://www.cno.org.

REFERENCES

Arat-Koç, Sedef. 2005. Gender and race in non-discriminatory immigration policies in Canada: 1960 to the present. In *Scratching the surface: Canadian anti-racist feminist thought,* ed. Enakshi Dua and Angela Robertson, 207–36. Toronto: Women's Press.

Astorga Garcia, Mila. 2007. The road to empowerment in Toronto's Filipino community: Moving from crisis to community capacity-building. CERIS Working Paper No. 54. Toronto: CERIS–The Ontario Metropolis Centre.

Bresnan, John, ed. 1986. *Crisis in the Philippines: Marcos era and beyond.* Princeton: Princeton University Press.

Chiu, Shirley S. 2003. Ethnic identity formation: A case study of Caribbean and Indian Hakkas in Toronto. Master's thesis, York University, Toronto, Ontario.

Daenzer, Patricia. 1993. *Regulating class privilege: Immigrant servants in Canada, 1940's–1990's.* Toronto: Canadian Scholars' Press.

Eric, Josephine 2007. 'Prepare for the worst': Rite of passage of Filipino women's settlement and integration in Canada from 1960's to the present. Master's thesis, McMaster University, Hamilton, Ontario.

Go, Stella. 2002. Remittances and international labour migration: Impact on the Philippines' immigrants and homeland. Paper presented at Metropolis Inter-conference Seminar, Dubrovnik, Croatia, May 9–12.

Guerrero, Stella. 2001. *Women and gender in population and development.* Manila: University of the Philippines Press.

Guo, Shibao. 2006. Bridging the gap in social services for immigrants: A community-based holistic approach. CERIS Working Paper No. 06-04. Toronto: CERIS–The Ontario Metropolis Centre.

Hiebert, Daniel. 1997. The colour of work: Labour market segmentation in Montreal, Toronto and Vancouver, 1997. Research on Immigration and Integration in the Metropolis. Working Paper Series, No. 97-01. Accessed July 2007. http://www.sfu.ca/riim.

Jenson, Jane, and Mariete Sineau. 2003. *Who cares?: Women's work, childcare and welfare state redesign.* Toronto: University of Toronto Press.

Kelly, Philip. 2006. Filipinos in Canada: Economic dimension of immigration and settlement. CERIS Working Paper No. 48. Toronto: CERIS–The Ontario Metropolis Centre.

Parreñas, Rhacel Salazar. 2001. *Servants of globalization: Women, migration, and domestic work.* Stanford, CA: Stanford University Press.

Pratt, Geraldine. 1999. From registered nurse to registered nanny: Discursive geographies of Filipina domestic workers in Vancouver, B.C. *Economic Geography* 75 (3): 215–36.

Prentice, Susan. 2001. *Five decades of child care advocacy and policy in Canada.* Halifax: Fernwood.

Reitz, Jeffrey G., and Anil Verma. 2003. Immigration, race and labour: Unionization and wages in the Canadian labour market. *Industrial Relations* 43 (4): 835–54.

Satzewich, Vic, and Nick Liodakis. 2007. *Race and ethnicity in Canada: A critical introduction.* Don Mills, ON: Oxford University Press.
Stasiulis, Daiva K., and Abigail B. Bakan. 2005. *Negotiating citizenship: Migrant women in Canada and the global system.* Toronto: University of Toronto Press.
Tyyska, Vappu. 2001. *Women, citizenship and Canadian child care policy in the 1990's.* Toronto: University of Toronto, Childcare Resource and Research Unit.
Wayland, Sarah. 2006. *Unsettled: Legal and policy barriers to newcomers in Canada.* Ottawa: Community Foundations of Canada and the Law Commission of Canada.

Chapter 6

(Res)sentiment and Practices of Hope: The Labours of Filipina Live-In Caregivers in Filipino Canadian Families

LISA M. DAVIDSON

Implemented in 1992, Canada's Live-In Caregiver Program (LCP) is classified as a 'special' labour policy in the goal of targeting professionally trained, middle-class foreigners for employment as live-in domestic workers in Canadian households (see also Eric in this volume). For many transnational Filipino migrant workers seeking long-term settlement, the LCP makes Canada a destination of choice, as Canada is one of few migrant-receiving countries offering a promise of permanent residency for those who successfully complete two years of caregiving work within a three-year period[1] (Stasiulis and Bakan 2005, 47). Since its inception, the LCP has come under the scrutiny of Filipino and non-Filipino researchers and community-based activists calling for policy reforms or, more radically, for the abolition of the program. Their concerns have drawn attention to the biopolitical dimensions of the program that contribute to the perpetuation of feminized labour migration and the deprofessionalization of educated Filipinos. More specifically, debates have centred on (1) the live-in clause of the program in sustaining unregulated labour practices, (2) a potential for exploitative work conditions that are segmented within the household, and (3) the affective and social consequences of long-term parent-child separation within Filipino transnational families, all of which have enabled Canadian mothers and fathers to become economically productive citizens with increased freedom in navigating the domain of familial care (Parreñas 2008, 2005, 2001; Pratt 2008, 1999; Constable 2007; Stasiulis and Bakan 2005; Cohen 2000).

Scholarship on Filipino transnational families currently centres on the separation of the nuclear family, highlighting the emotional consequences of maternal absence and the rupture in mother-child relations (Cohen 2000; Pratt 2008; Parreñas 2005, 2001). Codified in the Philippine Constitution and articulated in the 1987 Family Code, the notion of 'good' motherhood is institutionalized, concretizing the moral obligation of the Filipina mother in maintaining the solidarity of the family (Parreñas 2008, 2005, 2001). As yet unstudied, however, is what happens when Filipinos employ family members through the LCP. This is another tactic in family reunification that implements a broader definition of family than that recognized by Canadian immigration policy. If, however, scholars and activists have argued that domestic workers should not be understood as 'one of the family' (Stasiulis and Bakan 2005) because of the ways this obscures work relations, should family members employed as live-in caregivers only be understood as family? How are work relations and family understood in such contexts?

In this chapter, I discuss the experiences of Filipinas who migrated to Canada in the late 1990s to work as caregivers within the homes of their Filipino Canadian family members. In particular, I describe how they perceive and understand their migration under the LCP as a form of hope for a better future – an opportunity to reunify with family while improving their middle-class standing. The task here, however, is to retain a critical framing of 'hope,' that is to say how hope emerges in everyday domestic practices and the ideological work of hope in familial relations and labour migration. My aim is to accomplish this in two parts. First, I will briefly discuss how some Filipino Canadian families navigate the institutional domain of the LCP in order to reunify with extended family members. In particular, I will focus on the experiences of Eliza, a Filipina who migrated to Vancouver under the Live-In Caregiver Program. Her narrative points out that migration and family reunification among adult migrants is an emotional hardship among diasporic siblings. Reunification thus entails family relations beyond the parent-child dyad. Second, I will consider the discursive practices of former live-in caregivers, such as Joy, who distinguish between *domestic worker* and *domestic helper* in making sense of the regulatory and, at times, exploitative conditions they experienced under the LCP. Here, I will examine the incommensurability of work and leisure within the domain of Filipino Canadian families as the conduct of live-in caregivers is limited and guided by family members who become representatives of Canadian governance in reconfiguring familial relations of care and work. Overall, I am concerned with the inventive practices and rationales of Filipinas in framing the Live-In Caregiver Program within a domain of hope – a strategy in realizing the desire for a better life in Canada.

Methodology

Interviews and ethnographic fieldwork were carried out in Vancouver, Canada and in Northern Luzon, Philippines between 2005 and 2006 for pilot studies researching the situation of Filipino women and children and the services provided by non-governmental organizations (NGOs). All interviews lasted approximately two hours at the residences of interview participants and were conducted in English. In Vancouver, I carried out interviews with five Filipino women who arrived in Canada as unmarried single women in the late 1990s via the Live-In Caregiver Program to work for family members. All interview participants had university education, having completed undergraduate degrees in engineering, nursing, psychology, computer science, and early child-hood development from various universities in the Philippines. At the time of the interviews, all participants were between twenty-seven and thirty-seven years of age. Four women had attained Canadian perma-nent residency and secured full-time employment in service-oriented sectors; whereas one Filipina, the youngest of the interview partici-pants, was unemployed, had not yet completed the two years of manda-tory live-in care work, and was negotiating a return to the Philippines. With these interview participants, questions focused on their decision to migrate to Canada as single women and their experiences under the Live-In Caregiver Program.

In the Philippines, I had several conversations with Tessy,[2] a thirty-one-year-old Filipina Canadian, whom I met while I was conducting research with elder members of her family in a rural area of Luzon. Tessy comes from a land-owning elite family and her aunt was in the process of forming a women's association to establish a community-based farming project on the family's land. Tessy was born in Canada, and her parents, aunts, and uncles had migrated to the United States and Canada in the early 1970s as nurses and doctors and had returned to the Philippines in the early 2000s for retirement. During our lively discussions, Tessy narrated her family's experience of sponsoring her cousin as a live-in caregiver. Specifically, our debates centred on the benefits and pitfalls of the LCP from the purview of both employers and employees – the labour conditions, family separation, the crisis of deprofessionalization, familial and gendered obligations in meeting the economic needs of the family, and political motivations in elevating the class status of her family.

Governmentality and Power: Where Is Hope?

In considering the politics and subject of hope, I look to Foucault's concept on governmentality as an exercise in power that opens up fields of possibilities, for it is within the domain of the potential that attention can be drawn to inventive strategies relative to an articulation of hope. Described as the 'conduct of conduct,' governmentality is an exercise in power through practices that guide, shape, direct, and manage the behaviour of individuals and segments of a population towards desired objectives and outcomes. 'To govern,' writes Foucault (1982), 'is to structure the possible field of action of others' (221). Foucault's (1991) essay on governmentality explains historical shifts in design and objects of rule; where the object of rule was once to secure territories, concerns refocused on population and economic knowledge to ensure the well-being of the populace. Population is thus the 'object of governmentality' and the 'point of intervention' managed through techniques and strategies of rule vis-à-vis sovereignty, discipline, and government (Foucault 1991, 102).

As a mode of regulation, governmentality is tied to a concept of freedom. Freedom does not signify unaccountable liberties; rather, freedom is understood as 'field of possibilities in which several ways of behaving, several reactions and diverse comportments may be realized' (Foucault 1982, 221). Freedom remains the basis in the art of governing by making certain choices possible, which shape subjective practices (Faubion 2001, 86). Indeed, these are constrained choices, regulated by those who are 'more' free as they control and guide the freedom of others (Foucault 1997, 300). Foucault's (1984) framing of freedom aligns with the notion of agency, as individuals exercise strategies, vocabularies, and forms of judgment to transform themselves for their own well-being–a process that Foucault describes as subjectivation. Mahmood clarifies this point as she encourages an understanding of agency 'not simply as a synonym for resistance to relations of domination, but as a capacity for action that specific relations of *subordination* create and enable' (Mahmood 2001, 210, emphasis in original). Fikes (2008) further elaborates on the tension among governmentality, subjectivation, and freedom through her analysis on self-management within diasporic communities. She contends that modes of surveillance, regulation, and control imply not only the presence of the state vis-à-vis the enforcement of state labour policies, but also state neglect of those policies. The self-formation of migrant and diasporic subjects occurs within a set of ethics and guidelines that are racialized, gendered, and class-related, all of which tends towards an experience of community. In this way, governmentality is a field for subject formation that is not simply reducible to domination, but considers the variety of tactics used to guide conduct and to transform individuals and populations (Foucault 1997, 300).

The domain of hope emerges within the spaces of freedom, the field of possibilities, through rationales that are reflective, creative, and practical. Recent scholarship on the subject of hope has questioned the negative framing of hope in political and intellectual discourse, looking to ways in which understandings, meanings, and narratives of hope broaden fields of possibilities. Hope is not simply about utopian visions and dreams 'where the future is seen as the end-point to all struggles' (Zournazi 2002, 18); rather, hope is a driving force that compels and motivates one to rationalize, strategize, and take action in the face of despair or hopelessness (Bloch 1998). In this way, hope is located in 'the realm of "not-yet," a place where entrance, and above all, final content are marked by an enduring indeterminacy' (Bloch 1998, 341), a domain where change and transformation remain possible, yet which also harbours opportunities for disappointment and despair attributed to the unfulfilment of hope. Perceptions and experiences come to alter the meaning of and strategies for hope as individuals seek to improve their future situation. As noted by Papastergiadis (2002), hope does not necessarily progress in a linear fashion towards satisfaction: 'it doesn't mean that you are aiming for one particular thing in this world and once you get that then everything else will be fine . . . that the struggle is over. But rather, one has to be constantly fighting to develop and push and make things the way you want them to be' (84). The cultivation of hope is thus situated as a process of change, multidimensional in its layers, as the measures of success are improved, (re)developed, and (re)formulated through experiences and interactions over time. Following this theoretical framing, the hope of one may curtail and delimit the hope of another. As such, an anthropology of hope inevitably entails an anthropology of power.

The Crisis of Reunification as Innovative Practice

For many Filipino migrant workers, the decision to migrate and work abroad creates a rupture in family relations. Indeed, the LCP is a program that contributes to family fragmentation. Prior to amendments made to the program in April 2010, live-in caregivers, such as those who participated in this study, were restricted from migrating with family members from the Philippines and remained ineligible to sponsor relatives until they had attained permanent residency status. With recent modifications, the potential for live-in caregivers in bringing family members to Canada is unclear and ambiguous. The current policy now states that live-in caregivers may request sponsorship of dependents, given 'a careful review' of their capacity to provide for family members. Without further information describing how such a review is assessed, implemented, or investigated, the live-in caregiver's capacity for care work is open to governmental scrutiny and regulation. The ability of caregivers in providing economic care and in cultivating a 'good' family while providing domestic and moral care for their employer's family is questioned, specifically given the governmental rationale that they are in Canada for the sole purpose 'to provide care for other persons.'[3] What is noted by immigration officials, moreover, is that, due to the live-in clause, the capacity 'to provide' falls within the domain of the employer in offering accommodation to the caregiver's family. Even with these recent modifications, the standpoint of Citizenship and Immigration Canada remains unchanged, as they state that it is 'not practical for live-in caregivers to bring their family members with them.'[4] 'From the perspective of the Canadian authorities,' writes Cohen (2000), 'the former life of a domestic worker is, at best, irrelevant' (82).

Despite the development of analyses focusing on the pain of family absence and separation, little consideration has been paid to the inventive practices of Filipinos who strive towards family reunification. This is especially relevant as changes in immigration policies in Canada and in the Philippines have rendered it more difficult for professionally trained Filipinos to enter, work, and settle in Canada (Stasiulis and Bakan 2005; Choy 2005; Barber 2000). As a result, analyses continue to focus on the subjection of Filipinos under the governance of Canadian immigration officials, effectively delimiting Filipino subjectivation and obscuring the ways in which Filipinos in Canada perceive their fields of possibility for ethical family formation.

With research focused on the separation of the nuclear family, the disruption of affective ties with kin who are external to the parent-child unit is predominantly characterized as an unintended consequence of labour migration (Parreñas 2008, 2005, 2001; Pratt 2008; Cohen 2000). Indeed, it is seen as a recent phenomenon, a problematic emergence, rather than an unaccounted variability in kinship formation that was in existence prior to overseas labour migration (Domingo 1977; Fox 1956; Guthrie 1966, 1961; Medina 1991; Stoodley 1957). Rendering extended family bonds problematic reifies family values and gendered ideologies for constituting the 'right kind of family' as defined by the Philippine state. The specificity in problematizing Filipino transnational mothering, however, connects with the Philippine state's propagation of a 'national crisis' in which feminized labour migration has contributed to the formation of 'broken homes.' This ossifies a legal interpretation on the heteronormative nuclear family structure. The 'good' family is one in which a strong sense of responsibility is inculcated by the mother; yet, if other family members take on the caregiving responsibilities connected with the maternal role, care work is described as a 'burden,' a moral obligation in the prevention of unethical formations of 'broken homes' (Parreñas 2005, 113, 117). In turn, this tends to obfuscate the relevance of affective ties between extended family members, obscuring aspects of familial variability in which an ethics of care unfolds, and acts to reaffirm the normative structure of the nuclear family as constitutive of familial solidarity. I thus look to the ways in which Filipina labour migration crystallizes alternative familial bonds that are sidelined from the normative family structure in the prioritizing of emotional and moral relations between parents and children (Borneman 2001). As most of my interview participants are younger members of large families, their affective relations and sense of familial solidarity lay with older siblings, cousins, and aunts as parents working overseas displaced care work onto these extended kin. As these family members migrated transnationally to Canada, their absence was experienced more painfully as they were remembered as significant family relations. One former live-in caregiver emphasized the affective rupture she experienced as her sister and brother migrated to Canada, stating 'It's not the mother and the father who have the problem, or the wife who has problems with family separation; it's also the siblings!'

For extended kin who migrated and received resident status in Canada, the Live-In Caregiver Program presents an opportunity to reunite with family members who are over the age of majority. According to

Citizenship and Immigration Canada, residents may sponsor extended kin, which the federal state defines as sisters, brothers, nephews, nieces, and orphaned grandchildren, only if they are under the age of eighteen years. As state regulations limit the possibilities for reunification with older family members, the LCP presents a creative mode in which to reunify with kin. This is exemplified through the narratives of Eliza, a thirty-seven-year-old Filipina from rural Luzon, who migrated to Canada under the LCP in 1997.

During our interview, Eliza at first explained to me that her parents forced her to migrate to Canada for the economic well-being of her family; yet with further reflection, she conceded that her father pressured her to migrate because of her political activism. Her father, a government official, curtailed her political inclinations through migration, delinking her from social relations that cultivated an ethic of leftist political activism. As the third youngest of eleven children, she was the seventh sibling to migrate abroad, with three siblings in the United States, two siblings in Canada, and one sibling in Saudi Arabia. Prior to migration, Eliza and her siblings in the Philippines worked in professional occupations and pooled significant portions of their income to help support and improve the household. However, their joint income remained insufficient to advance the family's middle-class status. Within the context of the Philippines, '"middle class" means that their family owns a vehicle, resides in a cement-structure house, and can afford private education for the children' (Parreñas 2005, 70).

In Eliza's case, sibling ties facilitated her migration process as her sister sponsored her as a caregiver for her nieces and nephews. Eliza's older sister migrated abroad when Eliza was thirteen years old, and eight years later, she sponsored Eliza's older brother, to whom Eliza was emotionally attached. For Eliza, migration thus presented a new beginning for self-formation that was reoriented towards the well-being of the family, an emergence supported by her father to regulate her radical ethics and stall her development as a political activist. Submission to her father's dictate was combined with emotional excitement and desire for reunification with her sister and brother in Vancouver. Eliza thus had a tendency to frame her decision to migrate through her commitment to improve the socio-economic welfare of her sister's family in Vancouver and the family household in the Philippines.

Eliza recalls reunification, a time in which hope is realized unsatisfactorily and experienced as a painful moment. In the following excerpt,

Eliza reflects on her memories of her brother in the Philippines and her experience in reunification:

ELIZA: *We were close actually, my brother and me, we were close. But now, we are not close anymore . . . yeah, it's no longer close. Because before, we hung out together in the Philippines. One day, he didn't see me; he asked my mom, 'Where is she? Where is she? I'm so bored.' It was like that. Not anymore, it's all gone! I think it's just because it's been a long time . . . We were apart for like eight years and my sister for another five years. It's sibling separation that affected us, it affected our relationship . . . Even my brothers in the United States, it's affected us. When I was in New York, my brother I saw him in tears, the first time!*

LISA: *When was this?*

ELIZA: *That was like three years ago [2002] . . . He was in tears when he saw me . . . He said, 'You're like a woman now, you're no longer a young girl!'* (laughs).

From this example, the absence of Eliza's sibling relationships was jarringly experienced despite the fulfilment of her hope for reunification. Hope for a better life and upward class mobility – a hope encouraged by capitalist endeavours – truncates a 'joyful hope' that compels a sense of happiness and elation in reunifying with transnational family members (cf. Hage in Zournazi 2002, 151–2). Reunification crystallizes a subjective and emotional crisis as different forms of hope converge and are affectively experienced through paradoxical emotions of pain and joy. Indeed, the hope for a better economic life comes together in a struggle for improving familial relations.

A hope for strengthened familial ties emerges in Eliza's narrative in her mobilization of a collective sense of belonging among siblings situated in a past where sibling interactions are void of tensions and contestations. Through memories, Eliza constructs a nostalgia of home – a locus of idealized sibling relationships. As the present is mediated by the past, memories are critical in framing how migrants make sense of their experiences and in adjusting their emotional and rational subjectivity (Chamberlain and Leydesdorff 2004). What is remembered becomes a strategy for mending familial ruptures, fragmentation, and alienation, and to make claims of inclusion, exclusion, and belonging – smoothing away past tensions to sustain hope for a better future. However, memories are problematic when a sense of belonging entails 'a nostalgia that elides exclusion, power relations, and difference' (Espiritu 2003, 15). By 'forgetting' familial tensions and gendered relations of power, migrants may imagine a sense of unity – the crisis of reunification may be overcome, subsumed under the rubric of family solidarity that affirms a 'common cause' in sending remittances to the Philippines to improve familial and economic conditions.

The promise of material security coupled with upward class mobility provides a foundation for sibling solidarity across national terrains. In this manner, the family home in the Philippines represents a locus in which the confluence of familial relations and transnational capital takes form. The family home is thus remembered as a place of belonging and made meaningful through the collective economic and social achievement of the family. Moreover, the idea of home within the Filipino imagination is a site of familial bonds strong enough to withstand the impact of distantiation and 'non-Filipino' influences, such as Western ideals of individualism (Espiritu 2003).

However, the desire to transform familial class status vis-à-vis home-building is also a self-disciplining practice. Parreñas (2005) astutely observes that 'the project of building a house never seems to end … expanding because resources are available' (70). Yet, the ongoing process in developing the home is not simply due to a material availability, it is also relative to an imagination of the household, envisioned as a place in need of constant improvement. In the Philippines, it was explained to me that many Filipinos feel as if they cannot return and resettle in the Philippines, as a return 'home' would be seen as a 'failure' and damaging to one's self-esteem. Similarly, Constable (1999) observed that migrant Filipinos experienced ambivalence in returning to the Philippines as they had gained alternative experiences and identities that contrasted with social and familial relations 'at home,' which had also changed during their absence. However, the ambivalence of returning 'home' also intersects with an unconscious reconstitution of a 'colonial mentality,' whereby some Filipino migrants experience 'home,' especially rural homes, as 'simple,' 'traditional,' and 'primitive,' specifically when migration to North America is equated with and recognized as the promise of success.

Helping or Working?: A Labour of Care Work within the Family

As techniques in assimilation, the exploitative working conditions of live-in caregivers are well documented, demonstrating the vulnerability of domestic workers to unregulated employment standards (Stasiulis and Bakan 2005; Parreñas 2008, 2001; Pratt 2008; Constable

2007; Cohen 2000). Many of the Filipinas whom I interviewed were grateful to their relatives for the opportunity to migrate to the West, yet they noted that their experience and status as live-in caregivers working within the domain of their own family were not what they expected. They imagined that reunification with family members would give rise to activities expressing unity, friendship, and companionship, along with increased freedom in terms of equitable employment opportunities and an improved capacity for leisurely pursuits, all of which represented success and the fulfilment of their hope for a better life. Yet, working within the domain of the family did not entail the experiences of hope that they expected. Family sponsorship via the program was not simply an invitation to reunify with family and experience a sense of liberation from parental surveillance, but also to labour with little pay and limited leisure. This point is elucidated by Joy, who migrated under the LCP under the sponsorship of her sister in 1997:

LISA: *How would describe your LCP experience?*
JOY: *Hell! If I think back, I can't imagine how I got through it. Because first of all, my first employer was my sister so I was expecting better treatment, but it was the opposite. She was expecting a domestic helper not a sister, not even a friend! So it's an employer-employee relationship. I didn't get as much freedom as I was expecting to get ... She was demanding and demanding. She wasn't paying the right amount anyways!*

To make sense of her experience, Joy frames her labour in the family through the role of a domestic *helper* rather than a domestic *worker.* In the Philippines, a 'helper' is a young woman from a poor household, who 'in return for domestic service ... is typically provided with resources, social and economic, necessary to complete high school and sometimes university education' (Barber 2000, 403). Although it is facile to render domestic *help* commensurate to domestic *work,* commensuration may be acknowledged as an exercise in power through its capacity to efface particular ways of knowing, thereby limiting fields of possibility (Povinelli 2001). For Joy, distinguishing between *help* and *work* is a necessary tactic in explaining her sense of degradation and the moral breakdown she experienced among family members as she became a marker of elevated prestige, an object signifying her sister's middle-class status in Canada. Expanding on a Marxian analysis in considering how migrants subjectively experience limitations in their labour-time, Fikes (2008) suggests that 'attention to the relationship between labour-time and cultural practice illuminates how particular configurations of gender [and social relations] impact on the kinds of expressiveness in which people might engage' (65). In this way, family members of caregivers, in their role as Canadian employers, may conduct themselves in 'non-emancipatory' and capitalist-oriented ways by accessing and manoeuvring within fields of possibilities, situated within and defined by the contours of the LCP, for more labour-time flexibility and increased leisure for themselves – a strategy that fulfils their own immediate hope of becoming middle-class Canadians (cf. Fikes 2008). Thus, expanding on the observation made by Parreñas (2008) on the tactics of migrant Filipinas in relying on the unpaid work of female kin in the Philippines, naturalized Filipinas in Canada similarly rely on the transnational migration of female relatives to balance work and family in the West.

In experiencing employment as a helper, Joy explains that she was without rights and that her well-being was dependent on the goodwill of her sister for remunerating her domestic services. She narrates:

> *A lot of people have helpers in the Philippines and they are treated like slaves. No specific laws as like two days off here. Here, you are treated like equals . . . There are regulations to protect you, you don't get abuse by your employers . . . you have the right to complain . . . There is a lot of protection.*

Joy's narrative may be interpreted as a diasporic practice by which she orients her understanding on domestic labour in relation to Canadian governance and authority, subjectively experiencing the presence of the state by situating and recognizing herself within an imagined Canadian labour community. In Joy's view, domestic *help* in the Philippines is incommensurable to domestic *work* in Canada, since her experience provided the impetus for a more critical reflection on Philippine domestic help and, by extension, the Philippine state. Canada remains a desirable context, imagined as a place for hope and transformation where one can become more 'free,' equal, and protected, thus reifying liberal democratic principles that sketch Canada as a place for equitable work relations. The Philippines, however, is recalled as a place of stagnation in the light of its lax or absent labour policies, unethical patronage relations, and corrupt governmental practices. Some Filipina caregivers, such as Joy, thus experience their work and family life under the LCP as a contradiction, becoming extensions of the discontent associated with the Philippine homeland, which is made understandable by distinguishing between Philippine and Canadian domestic work worlds.

This, in turn, points to changes in power dynamics between differently classed family members through their roles of employer and employee. In framing her sister as a Philippine employer, Joy's narrative is a technique for critiquing her sister's conduct as a familial relative and as a Canadian employer.

Alternatively, incommensurability between work and leisure shaped everyday labour-time practices for some Filipino caregivers. The tension between labour-time and leisure-time also characterizes the plight of live-in caregivers in Filipino and non-Filipino families. From the context of Hong Kong, Constable (2007) demonstrates that the spatial and temporal separation of live-in work from leisure time is difficult to distinguish and does not fall into clear-cut boundaries of 'time on' and 'time off' work schedules (96). As Joy's sister owned a garment factory, Joy's timetable was regulated by her sister's work schedule, which lasted from 6:30 a.m. until 7 p.m. This timetable, however, was not stipulated in her written contract, though she was expected to abide by it as a member of the family. Joy says,

> You cannot just leave a note that says, 'OK, my time is up, I have to go back to my room. It's all yours, you do the rest!' No, you have to help ... and then, sometimes, the kid will follow you to your bedroom. You know, you don't have privacy. It's very hard ... You cannot just leave them, even if you're in the same house, you cannot just go in your room and lock them out.

The work-leisure divide is rendered incommensurate through caregiver relations with their nieces and nephews. Children are positioned in ambivalent roles as they take part in regulating the conduct and spaces of their live-in caregiving relatives – a practice in which caregivers participate and give constrained consent to implicitly identify as a 'good' Filipina within the Filipino family and community in Canada. Interview participants conveyed that they were expected to comply with unethical conduct that infringed on their privacy yet was deemed conducive to the moral upbringing of children. As a technique in shaping the 'good' character of children, care work included the inculcation of hospitality as Filipina caregivers were expected to welcome and receive their nieces and nephews as respected guests within the privacy of their bedrooms. As such, caregivers experience the home in a contradictory manner, where hope for a better life is expected, yet remains not fully attainable as private accommodations are turned into a 'public' domain, a place of surveillance, open to all in the household.

The Cultivation of Hope and Self

It is important to note that some Filipinas do experience positive work conditions, yet take issue with stipulations within the program that impede their professional development. One requirement raised by interview participants is the condition limiting live-in caregivers from upgrading their educational and vocational skills while working under the program. Under this stipulation, caregivers may only enrol in non-credit courses that are less than six months in duration. As most live-in caregivers are educated professionals, this contributes to their deprofessionalization by restricting their ability to upgrade in preparation for professional work after completing the LCP. On the Citizenship and Immigration Canada website, there is a caveat stating to potential caregivers that 'it is important to remember that you are in Canada to work as a live-in caregiver,'[5] a warning that is taken up by familial employers.

LISA: *So how would you describe your experience as a live-in caregiver?*
JULIA: (laughing) *It's depressing, depressing because . . . yeah, I enjoyed taking care of my nieces, because they are my nieces but you cannot do anything! You cannot go to school, you want to study but you cannot do that, and then you want to get a part-time job but you cannot do that because it's not allowed – that's the policy of Canada Immigration.*
LISA: *Did you know this before you came?*
JULIA: *No. My sister told me [when I arrived], 'No you cannot go to school, you cannot study. If you take First Aid, sure! You can do that, but you cannot go to university.'*

Even though Filipina caregivers have a desire for self-improvement in becoming productive members of the family and Canadian society, Filipino family members in the role of employers become representative of the Canadian state in regulating the actions of their caregivers, aiding in asserting labour policies. As a technique in governmentality, Julia's dialogic exchange with her sister demonstrates how caregivers experience vulnerability to 'governance and discipline [that] occurs within and not outside diasporic production,' and attends to the ways in which migrants 'experience self-management' through non-emancipatory ethics (Fikes 2008, 53, 58, 64).

Over time, some Filipina caregivers take action by leaving their employers before fulfilling their two-year contract. Despite initiatives taken by caregivers in breaking labour and familial relations with their employers, employers still have the capacity to govern caregivers from a distance. In order to find domestic employment, caregivers require a letter of reference from their employer evaluating their work ethic and care work. Here, Joy recounts how her sister used coercive tactics to impede her departure from care work within the family.

LISA: *She [Joy's sister] gave you a bad recommendation?*
JOY: *Yeah . . . [the employment agency] phoned me and said, 'Joy! We cannot find you a new employer. Your last employer said that you shouldn't be a nanny because you are not good with children' . . . And she [her sister] promised me that she would help me to find a new employer and she is giving me bad feedback? She really made it hard for me.*

Joy's sister was exercising her authority through her claims of knowing Joy best through a negative diagnosis regarding her work ethic – an attempt to constrain and narrow Joy's employment opportunities that reinforces economic and social dependency on the family. However, through her relations with other caregivers and participation in informal study groups, Joy was situated in a supportive community of Filipina caregivers who were able to provide her with connections to other employers, while offering insights and advice about the labour practices of potential employers.

For some live-in caregivers, the contours of the program create a depressing existence as ordinary life under the LCP entails everyday experiences of unfulfilled hope. This is not to say that a sense of hopelessness is maintained, as they actively recultivate hope through innovative strategies that transcend the restrictions of the program. Some Filipina caregivers forge alliances with other Filipino live-in caregivers and professional Filipino Canadians in establishing informal study collectives to develop their language skills in preparation for vocational entrance exams, while sharing information and advice on potential employers and their labour practices.

Conclusion

In this chapter, I have attempted to broaden an understanding of the creative ways in which Filipinos engage with the Live-In Caregiver Program. Following Hirokazu Miyazaki (2006), I look to the subject of hope 'in its capacity to reorient the directionality of critical knowledge' (166), while maintaining a lens on the LCP as a domain of governmentality in shaping diasporic Filipinas and guiding the conduct of the Filipino Canadian community. It is clear that some Filipinas transcend the restrictions placed on family sponsorship by looking to the LCP for reunification and for experiencing middle-classness in Canada through their ability to employ family members as caregivers, thus reconstituting a salient practice in the Philippines within a Canadian context. In this way, the Live-In Caregiver Program is a domain of possibility that enables different ways of thinking, where problems 'at home' in Canada and in the Philippines may be rethought and action towards satisfaction modified. As transnational subjects, Filipina live-in caregivers and their familial employers have differential capacities to develop, realize, and improve their strategies for a better life as they are differently positioned within Canadian and Philippine state governance. Both LCP workers and employers negotiate their experiences and make choices that may, at times, reconstitute the rationale of one nation-state over the other.

Hope for a better way of being is a process of change and reflection as the measure of success, contentment, and happiness is rethought and reformulated. Because of its enduring indeterminacy, hope entails freedom and unfreedom, resentment and fulfilment, and despair and pleasure as one hopes for more happiness, more satisfaction, and more success. As such, strategies and rationalities deployed to realize the hope held by one subject may curtail and regulate the hopes of others. Familial relations as employers take on the regulatory presence of the Canadian state in everyday domestic experiences. For some Filipina live-in caregivers, their discursive practices in distinguishing between *domestic worker* and *domestic helper* are part of a sense-making process to understand the conditions they experienced under the LCP, while maintaining Canada as a site in which hope of a better life remains attainable and realizable.

NOTES

1 This stipulation has been amended since the period of this research. As of April 1, 2010, live-in caregivers may apply for permanent residency: (1) after completing twenty-four months of full-time work, or (2) within twenty-two months after working 3,900 hours. Interview participants in this chapter, however, fell within the former stipulations in applying for permanent residency: two years of full-time employment within a three-year period.

2 The identities of all interview participants are represented under pseudonyms, as many expressed concerns over shame and stigma they may
encounter with family and members of the Filipino community.
3 See http://www.cic.gc.ca/english/information/faq/work/caregiver-faq22.asp.
4 Ibid.
5 http://www.cic.gc.ca/english/information/faq/work/caregiver-faq01.asp.

REFERENCES

Barber, Gardiner Pauline. 2000. Agency in Philippine women's labour migration
and provisional diaspora. *Women's Studies International Forum* 23 (4): 399–411.
Bloch, Ernst. 1998. Can hope be disappointed? In *Literary essays,* ed. Werner
Hamacher and David E. Wellberry, 339–45. Stanford, CA: Stanford
University Press.
Borneman, John. 2001. Caring and being cared for: Displacing marriage, kin-
ship, gender and sexuality. In *The ethics of kinship: Ethnographic enquiries,* ed.
James D. Faubion, 29–46. New York: Rowman and Littlefield.
Chamberlain, Mary, and Selma Leydesdorff. 2004. Transnational families:
Memories and narratives. *Global Networks* 4 (3): 227–41.
Choy, Catherine Ceniza. 2005. *Empire of care: Nursing and migration in Filipino
American history.* Durham, NC: Duke University Press.
Cohen, Rina. 2000. 'Mom is a stranger': The negative impact of immigration
policies on the family life of Filipina domestic workers. *Canadian Ethnic
Studies* 32 (3): 76–88.
Constable, Nicole. 1999. At home but not at home: Filipina narratives of
ambivalent returns. *Cultural Anthropology* 14 (2): 203–28.
– 2007. *Maid to order in Hong Kong: Stories of migrant workers.* Ithaca: Cornell
University Press.
Domingo, F.A. 1977. Child-rearing practices in Barrio Cruz-na-Ligas. *Journal of
Psychology* 10(2). July–December.
Espiritu, Yen Le. 2003. *Home bound: Filipino American lives across cultures, com-
munities, and countries.* Berkeley: University of California Press.
Faubion, James. 2001. Towards an anthropology of ethics: Foucault and the
pedagogies of autopoiesis. *Representation* 74 (1): 83–104.
Fikes, Kesha. 2008. Diasporic governmentality: On the gendered limits of
migrant wage-labour in Portugal. *Feminist Review* 90: 48–67.
Foucault, Michel. 1982. Afterword: The subject and power. In *Michel Foucault:
Beyond structuralism and hermeneutics,* ed. Hubert L. Dreyfus and Paul
Rabinow, 208–26. Brighton: Harvester.

– 1984. Selection from *History of sexuality, volume II*, 23–32. New York: Penguin.

– 1991. Governmentality. In *The Foucault effect: Studies in governmentality*, ed. Graham Burchell, Colin Gordon, and Peter Miller, 87–104. Chicago: University of Chicago Press.

– 1997. The ethics of the concern of the self as a practice of freedom. In *Essential works of Michel Foucault, Volume 1: Ethics, subjectivity, and truth*, ed. Paul Rabinow, 281–301. New York: New Press.

Fox, Robert. 1956. *The Filipino family and kinship in the Philippines (volume 1), Subcontractor's monograph*, 415–24. New Haven, NJ: Human Relations Area Files.

Guthrie, George. 1961. *The Filipino child and Philippine Society*. Manila: Philippine Normal College Press.

– 1966. Structure of maternal attitudes in two cultures. *Journal of Psychology* 62: 155–65.

Mahmood, Salma. 2001. Feminist, theory, embodiment, and the docile agent: Some reflections on the Egyptian Islamic revival. *Cultural Anthropology* 16 (2): 202–36.

Medina, Belen T.G. 1991. *The Filipino family*. Quezon City: University of the Philippines Press.

Miyazaki, Hirokazu. 2006. Economy of dreams: Hope in global capitalism and its critiques. *Cultural Anthropology* 21 (2): 147–72.

Papastergiadis, Nikos. 2002. Faith without certitudes. In *Hope: New philosophies for change*, 78–97. New York: Routledge.

Parreñas, Rhacel Salazar. 2001. *Servants of globalization: Women, migration and domestic work*. Stanford, CA: Stanford University Press.

– 2005. *Children of global migration: Transnational families and gendered woes*. Stanford, CA: Stanford University Press.

– 2008. *The force of domesticity: Filipina migrants and globalization*. New York: New York University Press.

Povinelli, Elizabeth. 2001. Radical worlds: The anthropology of incommensurability and inconceivability. *Annual Review of Anthropology* 30: 319–34.

Pratt, Geraldine. 1999. From registered nurse to registered nanny: Discursive geographies of Filipina domestic workers in Vancouver, B.C. *Economic Geography* 75 (3): 215–36.

– 2008. Waiting, and some limits to transnational mothering. Lecture at Munk Centre for International Studies, Southeast Asia Seminar Series. February 12.

Stasiulis, Daiva K., and Abigail B. Bakan. 2005. *Negotiating citizenship: Migrant women in Canada and the global system*. Toronto: University of Toronto Press.

Stoodley, B.H. 1957. Some aspects of Tagalog family structure. *American Anthropologist* 49: 236–49.
Zournazi, Mary. 2002. *Hope: New philosophies for change.* New York: Routledge.

INTERNET RESOURCES

Citizenship and Immigration Canada
http://www.cic.gc.ca/english/work/apply-who-caregiver.asp
http://www.cic.gc.ca/english/immigrate/sponsor/relatives-apply-who.asp
http://www.cic.gc.ca/english/information/faq/work/caregiver-faq01.asp
http://www.cic.gc.ca/english/information/faq/work/caregiver-faq26.asp
http://www.cic.gc.ca/english/information/faq/work/caregiver-faq22.asp

Chapter 7

Debunking Notions of Migrant 'Victimhood': A Critical Assessment of Temporary Labour Migration Programs and Filipina Migrant Activism in Canada

ETHEL TUNGOHAN

Introduction

Temporary labour migration is increasing globally. Statistics from the Organisation of Economic Cooperation and Development (OECD) indicate that 2.5 million legal temporary labour migrants resided in developed countries in 2006, three times the number of permanent migrants residing in these states (Abella 2006). The same numbers also show that temporary labour migrants' entry into developed countries has increased by 4 to 5 per cent annually since 2000.

Migration trends in Canada follow this pattern. There were 79,509 temporary labour migrants entering the country in 2008, a significant increase from 2007 and 2006, when 74,038 and 71,786 temporary labour migrants arrived in Canada respectively (Citizenship and Immigration Canada 2009). In total, there were 363,494 temporary labour migrants residing in Canada in 2008, an increase of 62,598 from 2007 (Citizenship and Immigration Canada 2009).

Based on these figures, it is clear that temporary labour migration has become a permanent part of today's labour landscape. Indeed, it is telling that a substantial number of temporary labour migrants are 'temporary' in name only; whereas some migrants work only for a few months, most stay longer by either renewing their work contracts indefinitely or by applying for landed immigrant status. Despite temporary labour migrants' 'permanent' presence, however, very little academic and policy work has been undertaken to understand the political situation of temporary labour migrants in receiving states; the bulk of academic and policy theorizing, in fact, has focused on the *economic* benefits temporary labour migrants bring to both sending and receiving countries (Stahl 1982; De Haas 2005). With the exception of legal and political theorists such as Joseph Carens (1996, 2008) and Linda Bosniak (2006), receiving states' *political* responsibility towards temporary labour migrants has not been discussed. A rhetoric of gratefulness prevails among policymakers in receiving states, whereby the assumption that migrants should be thankful for the opportunity to work abroad overshadows recognition of the tangible contributions migrants make and thus prevents any discussions on whether temporary labour migration programs are politically tenable.

This is especially true for migrant caregivers, specifically live-in caregivers in Canada. In spite of the benefits Canada derives from the labour of live-in caregivers, the belief that they should be indebted to Canada prevails. Although the image of the Filipina live-in caregiver is deeply ingrained in the popular imagination – as evidenced by frequent references to Filipina 'nannies,' 'maids,' and 'servants' in the news media and in movies, film, and television – scant attention has been paid to the structure of the Live-In Caregiver Program (LCP) itself. For instance, news articles that emerged following the Ruby Dhalla scandal, whereby a Liberal Party member of Parliament was accused of mistreating two Filipina live-in caregivers, focused on the racial attributes of all parties rather than on the restrictions imposed by the LCP. Reactionary headlines dominated the airwaves: the focus was primarily on how the two Filipinas were 'modern day slaves' acting without agency (Cleroux 2009), with little consideration for the structural elements of the LCP that make migrant workers vulnerable to abuse. All of these news reports implied that the abysmal labour conditions faced during this incident were isolated incidents. More significantly, analysis of the important labour contributions live-in caregivers make to Canada or of deficiencies in the welfare state and in the labour market that have increasingly made foreign workers responsible for care work was minimal.

Seeing that the live-in caregivers conveniently disappear from popular consciousness in the absence of sensationalistic scandals, the efforts undertaken by some live-in caregivers to change deleterious work conditions are ignored. Despite being non-citizens, live-in caregivers have the political agency to change the policies set by the LCP. This chapter uses the case study of Filipina migrant workers entering the country through the Live-In Caregiver Program as a springboard from which to explore notions of temporary labour migrants' political engagement in Canada. I argue that temporary labour migrants such as Filipina live-in caregivers, far from being the compliant 'slaves,' are full political agents who do not allow non-citizenship status to hinder their political participation in Canada.

This chapter is accordingly structured in three sections. The first section explores the history of migrant care work in Canada, highlighting the way racial bias motivated the establishment of temporary migrant care work programs in Canada. These biases negatively affected the experiences of live-in caregivers from the Caribbean, who dominated the industry in the earlier part of the twentieth century, and now affect Filipina caregivers, who make up 95 per cent of all live-in caregivers in the country (OCAP 2005). The second section discusses why and how live-in caregivers are political agents. I provide a theoretical assessment of *why* temporary labour migrants – specifically live-in caregivers – should be politically integrated in receiving states. Then, in the third section, I look at the ways Filipina live-in caregivers have fought against these restrictions and discuss the way they have carved a political space in Canada *despite* lacking formal citizenship status.

Migrant Care Giving in Canada

In Canada, foreign domestic workers have historically been relied upon to provide care work. A racial hierarchy ranking domestic workers from most to least desirable existed, with Europeans on top and Asian and Caribbean women at the bottom. Academic work on the experiences of the latter is minimal. While there have been numerous accounts of how European women – primarily from Ireland and Finland – came to Canada as 'nannies,' 'nursemaids,' and 'governesses' from the eighteenth to the early twentieth century (Macklin 1992; Sharpe 2001), much less is known about Chinese and Japanese men working as 'domestic servants' and as 'coolies' (Ty 2004, 21–2) or about the Caribbean women who worked as 'servants' but were later sent back to their countries (Calliste 1989) during the same time period. The only information that is really known about Chinese and Japanese 'coolies' can be derived from historical records showing that these men originally came to Canada to work as labourers for the Canadian Pacific railway and for the agricultural industry but later sought work in domestic service, probably as a result of endemic discrimination preventing them from working in other professions.

On the other hand, there have been comparatively more academic studies on Caribbean domestics during this time period, with most studies concluding that domestic service was one of the few industries open to Caribbean women (Calliste 1989; Henry 1998). Since Afro-Caribbean people were considered 'reserve labour,' Canadian immigration authorities loosened immigration criteria for them during the two world wars, when Canada was facing labour shortages, and preferred to allow these groups entry on a temporary 'trial' basis during regular time periods (Henry 1998, 71).

It is clear from such analysis that arguments pertaining to individuals' ability to assimilate into Canadian society affect the perceptions of care workers. While the argument has been made that 'race has been crucially important to the nature and the status of the work' only in the twentieth century (Miranda 2007), historical records seem to show that this was the case even before that. Migrants' racial attributes and countries of origin determine the type of work they are seen as doing, subsequently explaining why European women were more likely to be seen as 'nursemaids' and why people of colour were seen as 'servants.'

These perceptions affected migrants' access to permanent settlement. For instance, in the middle of the twentieth century, European women seeking employment as care workers were given permanent resident status automatically, whereas Caribbean domestic workers allowed into Canada under the Caribbean Domestics Scheme – which was established in 1955 as a bilateral trade agreement between Canada, Barbados, and Jamaica – were only allowed to apply for permanent residency after a year working in domestic service (Daenzer 1997). Under this scheme, Caribbean women were monitored regularly, were subjected to regular pregnancy tests, and were also paid less compared to their European counterparts. This scheme asked prospective applicants to fulfil criteria that European domestics were not asked to meet; to be more specific, women were required to be between the ages of eighteen and thirty-five and were asked not to have any dependents because immigration officials were concerned that these women were from the 'lower classes' and would therefore sponsor the entry of relatives of similarly 'dubious' qualities (Henry 1998, 74).

There were attempts in the 1960s and 1970s to eliminate such racial and cultural criteria. Prime Minister Lester B. Pearson abolished Canada's White Settlement Policy and invoked the vision of a 'multicultural' Canada where cultural diversity reigned. His White Paper on Immigration, published in 1966, indicted racial and cultural discrimination and endorsed an immigration system that allowed individuals from 'all corners of the globe to come to Canada' (Canada Manpower and Immigration 1966). At the same time, however, Pearson also saw immigration as a way to bolster the Canadian economy, whereby 'skilled' migrants were preferred to 'unskilled' migrants because the latter were seen as being more likely to be poor and thus a drain on the welfare system (Canada Manpower and Immigration 1966). Canadian immigration policy has since been structured according to the twin goals of attracting a diverse populace and improving Canada's economic standing, though it is clear, based on the way migrants are classified on the basis of 'skill,' that the latter is prioritized. In short, economics, reinforced by pervasive racial and cultural preferences, are more important than multiculturalism.

Because immigration criteria were couched using the language of economics, it is initially difficult to understand how racial bias continues. The points system, established in 1967 and formally enshrined into law in 1976, ranked migrants using 'objective' criteria that prioritized migrants who were deemed to have high potential in bolstering the Canadian economy. While permitting the entry of multitudes of skilled migrants, the points system was unable to meet Canada's caregiving needs. Rather than considering potential migrants' care work contributions as fulfilling a permanent and ongoing need, Canadian officials deemed such labour 'unskilled' not only because of the low status care work had socially but also because the majority of applicants were from developing countries such as the Philippines. The fact that British and European 'nannies and nursemaids' are consistently seen as fulfilling enough criteria under the points system and are therefore quickly eligible for citizenship, whereas Caribbean and Asian 'servants and domestics' are not given enough points to qualify for entry under the points system and have to enter through temporary migration schemes, shows that despite both groups being employed in the same profession, Canadian policy still prioritizes the inclusion of 'assimilable' groups (Arat-Koç 2003). Hence, the objective nature of immigration policy is in question. Immigration criteria have to be modified and new reasons have to be given to limit the entry of individuals from 'other' countries. A discursive shift thereby transpires when considering the potential migration of individuals whose cultural and racial backgrounds are deemed at odds with Canadian norms. Rather than viewing the entry of these individuals as an opportunity to enhance Canadian multicultural nation-building imperatives, Canadian immigration officials see their entry as evidence of Canadian benevolence; their migration into Canada is constructed as a 'favour' to 'poor' individuals, subsequently masking the benefits Canada derives from their arrival (Sharma 2006).

The Temporary Employment Authorization Scheme in 1973, which issued temporary labour visas for care work (Daenzer 1997), consequently established a way for the Canadian state to limit the entry of undesirable groups. While immigration criteria still technically allowed women coming under this scheme to apply for permanent residence, they were 'effectively barred' from gaining permanent residence because the low wages they were given as domestic workers made it difficult for them to meet immigration criteria of 'economic self-sufficiency' (Khan 2009). Far from meeting Canada's multicultural ideal, Canadian immigration law at this time merely consolidated pre-existing racial hierarchies, spuriously adding 'economic' criteria as a way to justify its decision to classify migrants as 'permanent' and as 'temporary.' As Nandita Sharma (2006, 147) argues,

> It was in the nexus of the simultaneous production of Canada as a tolerant [multicultural] society and the representation of non-Whites as a foreign threat that legitimacy for categorizing people as migrant workers was organized. By problematizing the permanence of 'too many' non-Whites while shifting Canadian immigration policy away from admitting the majority of people as immigrants towards one that admitted people as migrant workers, the Canadian state was able to assert that it was simply protecting the integrity of the nation and the state. The making of migrant workers and the discrimination against them that resulted was effectively depoliticized ... Indeed, discrimination was most often presented as part of the state's duty to its citizens.

Unsurprisingly, there is a lack of oversight on the Temporary Employment Authorization Scheme by the federal and provincial governments. Such disregard, which likely stems from the presumption that 'temporary' workers are disposable commodities who do not merit integration into Canada, has led to numerous documented cases of abuse. Since Filipinas dominated migrant care work in Canada during this period as a result of the Philippine government's vigorous endorsement of its labour export policy, Filipinas were especially vulnerable to racial and gender discrimination. Documented cases of abuse under this program, as articulated by Filipina caregivers, compelled a policy shift (Bakan and Stasiulius 1997). The 1981 report written by the Task Force on Immigration Practices highlighted the concerns of Filipina caregivers. The results of these reports, as well as the efforts undertaken by Filipina caregivers and other concerned civil society groups, led to the institutionalization of the Foreign Domestic Workers Movement (FDM) in 1981 (Daenzer 1997). This means that Canada's temporary foreign worker program continued unabated. In fact, blatant racial preferences formed the heart of Canada's temporary foreign worker policy. For instance, migrants of European descent are issued open temporary work permits giving them 'the right to choose in which province, in which occupation and for which employer they want to work' (Depatie-Pelletier 2008), in contrast to live-in caregivers, who are placed in a special migrant worker category subjected to more strenuous restrictions.

The FDM was conceived by the Task Force on Immigration Practices and was deemed a suitable compromise between the Canadian government's interests in maintaining control over the entry of 'suitable' groups and its recognition that migrant workers were made vulnerable by existing arrangements. Thus, the FDM stipulated that migrant workers could apply for permanent residency after twenty-four months of continuous live-in employment in the same household following a 'post-entry' evaluation that evaluated the migrants' 'suitability' to Canada. This evaluation gave immigration authorities the right to act as gatekeepers and to use arbitrary criteria judging migrants' suitability, alternately judging migrants on their assimilation into Canadian culture, on their economic performance, etc. (Daenzer 1997). More significantly, immigration authorities are able to judge migrants on these criteria on the basis of the evaluations given by migrants' employers, who are deemed to be reliable, trustworthy, and unbiased enough to indicate whether the migrants they have employed are 'good workers.' This stipulation then magnifies the power held by migrants' employers, making migrants depend on their employers for access to good labour and living conditions and, crucially, also for access to permanent settlement. It is clear that the Canadian government then instituted a policy that admitted migrants into Canada partially on the basis of the length of time they had stayed in Canada but mostly on the basis of their assimilability. The FDM showed that the Canadian government was not interested in the 'question of how policies should change to affect greater fairness and justice for immigrant non-citizen servants' but was rather invested in 'how Canada can continue to serve the interests of influential Canadians while purporting to redress domestic exploitation' (Daenzer 1997, 91).

The LCP, founded in 1992, attempted to redress some of the short-comings of the FDM, again primarily as a result of the activism of various civil society actors (Khan 2009). The biggest change pertains to more stringent training requirements, which mandated that potential applicants should show that they are qualified to undertake care work (Bakan and Stasiulus 1997, 39); this emphasis on 'better' training was seen by most as a way to limit the entry of 'undesirable' nationals. The terms used to describe migrant care workers also shifted in order to 'professionalize' the program. Rather than calling migrant care workers foreign domestic workers, which was the case under the FDM, the government made clear that the LCP recruited caregivers. Such a change in terminology theoretically ensures that live-in caregivers are employed specifically to provide unsupervised 'care work,' a category that encompasses a broad range of activities like childcare, elderly care, and care for people with disabilities. As such, more systematic checks were implemented to allow for the entry of 'qualified' migrants: migrants are now required to be high school graduates and to be fluent in either English or French and are also supposed to show that they have received sufficient training as caregivers, either through a six-month intensive education course or through prior work experience (Macklin 1992).

Nonetheless, efforts to professionalize the program failed. Though caregivers are 'professionals' and are not supposed to perform menial household tasks, they are oftentimes asked to do so by their employers (England and Stiell 1997), thereby calling into question the effectiveness of the shift from 'domestic worker' to 'caregiver.' Moreover, while the LCP promised more thorough governmental interventions in the event of migrant abuse and eliminated the requirement that caregivers needed to upgrade their educational credentials and do volunteer work in order to be eligible for permanent residency (England and Stiell 1997), the live-in requirement and twenty-four-month 'temporary' status remained mandatory.

While one could make the point that the FDM, and later the LCP, at least allow live-in caregivers to apply for permanent residency and eventually become Canadian citizens – a significant improvement from previous schemes – the program locks workers into potentially deleterious working conditions with little opportunity to mitigate harms. The desire to achieve permanent status irrevocably places live-in caregivers in a position of extreme duress, particularly in cases where their employers are abusive. In these circumstances, the decision to leave one's employer is tempered by the reality that doing so may jeopardize one's permanent residency application not only because finding new employment is onerous but also because the clock is reset when one changes households. These conditions therefore make it difficult for caregivers to consider political action. Indeed, if live-in caregivers seek citizenship status, the desire to be politically active may seem at first glance to be at the bottom of their priorities.

The LCP therefore continues to be a target of criticism and controversy, particularly among live-in caregivers themselves. The next section discusses the political advocacy of live-in caregivers, assessing both the ways in which their political activism expands notions of political participation and also the differences in strategy adopted by live-in caregiver advocates.

The Political Integration of Live-In Caregivers

To see live-in caregivers as political actors at first appears counterintuitive. After all, the structural restrictions posed by the LCP increase the isolation live-in caregivers face, making political activity difficult. From the perspective of the Canadian state, the question of why live-in caregivers merit political inclusion arises; since the right to participate in formal politics (i.e., voting) is reserved for citizens, making allowances for the needs of live-in caregivers with temporary status seems preposterous. In this section, I first discuss normative reasons why live-in caregivers deserve inclusion into the Canadian political sphere. Then, I discuss the ways in which Filipina live-in caregivers are already involved in political processes, a trend which belies the stereotype of Filipina caregivers as lacking agency. While it is not my intention to romanticize these activist pursuits, I hope to show that political action should not be – and is not – the purview of citizens alone.

Justifying the Political Inclusion of Live-In Caregivers

Conventional analysis of political participation is limited to the political activities of citizens. Live-in caregivers, like other temporary migrants, are seen as outsiders whose capacity to influence policies within the receiving state is limited because their national allegiances purportedly lie in another state. Nonetheless, Filipina live-in caregivers – again like other migrants – inhabit a grey area, where they are members of both Philippine and Canadian society. Ignoring their presence in Canada and maintaining that their allegiance remains solely with the Philippines is therefore misguided.

Equally misguided are attempts to ignore the relevance of the nation-state. Live-in caregivers find that international human rights legislation is supportive of their claims for recognition, which may eventually lead to a form of 'post-national citizenship,' where national governments have become obsolete (Sassen 2006, 311). The reality remains, however, that live-in caregivers are still reliant on receiving states like Canada; even if shifts are gradually dismantling the power held by the state in determining the treatment of individuals within their borders, receiving states still wield tremendous power in determining migrants' experiences. Even transnational social movements, whose campaigns span national borders, find that their campaigns are still reliant on the state: 'the structures of the international system oblige movements to pursue their social and political goals through the different organs of the sovereign state' (Colas 2002, 80). Ergo, while it is tempting to endorse the eradication of inequalities between migrants and non-migrants and between sending and receiving states through the establishment of open borders, such a cosmopolitan ideal will not be realized any time soon.

A more productive way of assessing why live-in caregivers deserve to be politically integrated is to use the terms set by the receiving state to one's advantage. In this particular case, justifying live-in caregivers' political inclusion requires a thorough reconsideration of Canada's political commitments to 'liberal democracy.' Canada's live-in caregiver policy was clearly an economic imperative, with little to no thought to whether the LCP lives up to the 'liberal democratic' values that the Canadian state claims to uphold. While Canada's immigration policy more generally and the LCP specifically are largely informed by the state's economic needs, Canada cannot ignore its political commitments within its borders. Pearson's White Paper, as mentioned, may have stressed how immigration should be economically motivated, but it also emphasized how racial and cultural discrimination should be abolished. Paying equal attention to the latter, instead of only prioritizing economic needs, becomes important.

Thus, live-in caregivers can tactically claim political space in Canada because Canada abides by liberal values. Such liberal values are an integral part of Canada's national identity, as numerous scholars have asserted (see, e.g., Lipset 1990; Wiseman 2007). After all, even if liberal doctrines have entrenched the values of national self-determination and hold that Canada has the national autonomy to place immigration restrictions, the same liberal doctrines also espouse 'legal and constitutional protections' for all members of society regardless of identity. Since temporary labour migration programs promote citizenship as a 'strategically produced form of capital' (Bauder 2008), with formal and informal processes being used to promote the exclusion of economically 'undesirable' migrant workers, they directly contravene Canadian liberal values. Citizenship therefore does not concern 'the right to have rights,' as is popularly believed in Canada. In this case, 'personhood' – one's status as an autonomous moral agent whose equality is not predicated on citizenship status – should be sufficient for the provision of rights (Bosniak 2006, 117), since Canada's commitments to liberal doctrines bind it to doctrines of equal treatment and non-discrimination. The discrepancy between Canada's support of liberal doctrines and its concurrent violation of such doctrines through its temporary migration programs highlights the contradictions that exist between its economic agendas and its political values. In short, live-in caregivers may not be citizens but are entitled to make claims for just treatment, as guaranteed by liberal provisions. Using the terms set by Canadian liberal discourse exposes the contradictions inherent in the LCP.

Live-in caregivers who are part of civil society groups that criticize the LCP draw attention to these liberal contradictions through their political activism. In doing so, live-in caregivers bypass conventional means of political participation such as voting, which are 'passive' ways to instigate change. Instead, they are active in civil society groups, thereby 'transcending politics "as usual"' (Bauböck 2003) by showing that political involvement is not limited to passive actions like voting and does not only involve citizens. A full range of political activities accompanies live-in caregiver activism. This includes – but is not limited to – lobbying political officials to change the terms set by the LCP, marching in demonstrations to express solidarity with live-in caregivers who have been abused by the system, creating support networks for live-in caregivers, providing counselling services and advice, and spreading awareness through information campaigns. All of these activities show that it is erroneous to assume that temporary labour migration policies produce static outcomes whereby the affected stakeholders blindly accept existing legislation. Live-in caregivers show that the absence of citizenship does not lead to an absence in activism.

Disaggregating rights from citizenship status opens the possibility of considering the divergent ways in which the LCP breeds inequality. If one agrees that citizenship is not a prerequisite to the right to participate politically or the right to live with one's family, for example, then it becomes easier to accept the changes demanded by live-in caregivers because one is not hindered by the belief that live-in caregivers belong to a 'special' category exempt from liberal democratic protections. To maintain that only citizens deserve fair treatment becomes fallacious, for doing so would counter the requirements of equality enshrined in Canadian law. In a way, the political activism of live-in caregivers reverses Marshall's (1950) account of the evolution of citizenship. While Marshall contends that citizenship developed through the gradual expansion of civil, political, and social rights, live-in caregivers exercise these rights despite lacking citizenship status. Unlike Marshall's belief that full citizenship coincides with full access to civil, political, and social rights, live-in caregivers show that personhood and not citizenship is relevant.

Filipina Live-In Caregivers' Political Actions[1]

The pervasiveness of Filipina live-in caregiver advocacy shows that live-in caregivers do not need to be citizens to be politically involved. Despite the fact that their lack of citizenship limits the types of political actions they can legally pursue, Filipina live-in caregivers' activism is exceedingly varied. Indeed, their advocacy work expands the definition of the 'political,' since such activism has to take place outside formal political arenas. Because they are restricted from accessing formal methods of political participation such as voting and running for public office, Filipina caregiving advocacy – like other forms of migrant activism (Bosniak 2006, 117) – takes the form of civic activity. It occurs in multiple scales and engages a variety of actors, from other social movements like the feminist and labour movements to different non-state and state actors such as international, federal, provincial, and municipal bodies. Such activism spans different movements because the experiences of Filipina live-in caregivers resonate with demands for gender justice and workers' rights, though it remains to be seen whether some alliances are more fruitful than others. Furthermore, Filipina live-in caregiver activism transpires in different sites because different government actors are involved; though the LCP is administered federally by Human Resources and Skills Development Canada (HRSDC) and Citizenship and Immigration Canada (CIC), the promotion of temporary foreign workers' well-being is a provincial mandate, with municipal governments becoming increasingly involved with ensuring that live-in caregivers are protected from abuse. The fact that such activism is so multi-varied corroborates the reality that civil society campaigns in support of related causes like the movement to combat violence against the children of caregivers (Catungal in this volume) need to occur in multiple sites and to use diverse tactics in order to be effective.

Needless to say, Filipina live-in caregiver activism cannot be easily characterized. The only similarities these groups have are in the high level of involvement of Filipina live-in caregivers in all cases. In most organizations, not only are they the ones to establish these organizations, they are also the ones to determine the types of campaigns these groups engage in and to represent the demands of these groups in national forums such as Canadian parliamentary gatherings and in international forums such as the United Nations in Geneva, Switzerland.

Nevertheless, there is no cohesion or 'unity' to such activism, nor is there consensus on goals, agendas, or strategies. Different types of activism take place simultaneously, with hardly any interactions between organizations that are not part of the same network. The organizations representing Filipina live-in caregivers in Canada differ in size and scope. Organizations have their own histories, priorities, and tactics. Some organizations such as the National Alliance of Philippine Women have co-ordinated national, regional, and provincial campaigns and have centres in British Columbia, Ontario, and Quebec. Other organizations like the Caregivers' Action Centre in Toronto, and the Migrant Workers Family Resource Centre in Hamilton have a smaller membership base, are more grassroots, and focus on the needs of live-in caregivers in their specific areas, although some of these smaller groups are currently attempting to work together to achieve common goals and to jointly administer programs, such as 'skills-sharing' initiatives that will allow Filipina live-in caregivers to get together to share their advocacy tactics. Yet other organizations, such as Migrante Canada, have a broad network of affiliated organizations in British Columbia, Manitoba, Ontario, and Quebec, yet this organization also partakes in transnational activist work because it is part of Migrante International. To be specific, Migrante Canada has provincial, regional, national, and international campaigns, all of which are closely co-ordinated to advance Migrante International's goals of improving the situations of migrant workers, including live-in caregivers, and eventually curbing sending countries' reliance on migrant labour. Thus, different organizations may choose to be politically engaged in different scales, or they may choose to concentrate their efforts only on one or two sites.

Organizations also differ in the ways they choose to be political. All Filipina live-in caregiver organizations inevitably have to engage with the state. Since state policies like the FDM and the LCP create identities and produce grievances (Pierson 1993), civil society groups that emerge to redress these grievances have to make tactical decisions on the best way to deal with the state. Civil society activity, in turn, affects state policy. State and society are therefore locked into a symbiotic relationship, whereby the actions of one invariably determine the actions of the other, although ruptures, contradictions, and inconsistencies are found within this relationship. As such, Filipina live-in caregiver organizations alternate between co-operating with the state and protesting state activity, with most organizations straddling the fine line between collaboration and dissent. Of course, some organizations are more likely to work with – rather than against – the state. Specifically, some groups may choose to work directly with state officials to induce policy changes. For example, Intercede's campaigns in 1980 led Canada to accede to live-in caregivers' demands that they be given the right to apply for permanent residency (Bakan and Stasiulus 1997, 38). A more recent example can be found through the Caregiver Action Centre, which worked closely with Ontario Labour Minister Peter Fonseca to implement provincial protections on behalf of live-in caregivers and other migrant workers (Brazao 2009). In contrast, other groups have opted to work against the state. They are more vigilant in exposing the detrimental effects of state activity by organizing ongoing protests against state policy; these protests take the form of media campaigns, marches, awareness-raising workshops, and alliance-building with local organizations that also have an interest in exposing state atrocity. Of these groups, the National Alliance of Philippine Women is the most prolific and the most vocal in protesting the LCP. Their campaign to 'scrap the LCP' seeks the abolition of migrant care work in Canada. Though their demands to curb migrant care worker abuse through the elimination of the live-in requirement and the availability of landed immigrant status for live-in caregivers upon arrival coincide with those of other organizations, their espousal of the establishment of a national childcare policy in Canada and their desire to end the LCP are distinct demands (National Alliance of Philippine Women in Canada 2009).

These variations in political tactics expose long-standing debates among Filipina live-in caregiver organizations on the necessity of reforming or abolishing the LCP. While addressing this debate is not the purpose of this chapter, suffice it to say that these divisions highlight long-standing ruptures on political strategies. The decision to advocate one political stance over another, however, should not make it appear as though these decisions occur in a vacuum. All organizations consider context, and assess the needs and interests of their members. The decision to endorse reform or abolition illustrates organizations' determination to promote the interests of Filipina live-in caregivers, albeit from opposing perspectives. If anything, these divisions highlight the diverse ways in which Filipina live-in caregivers act politically.

On that note, it becomes imperative to point out that Filipina live-in caregiver organizations may also choose to be political by choosing to engage in activities away from state purview. Some groups like Pinay in Montreal, the Caregiver Support Services, Intercede, and Migrante in Toronto, the Migrant Workers Family Resource Centre in Hamilton, and the West Coast Domestic Workers Association in Vancouver provide services for live-in caregivers. They give live-in caregivers psychological counselling, legal aid, and immigration advice. In some cases, they provide live-in caregivers with a 'safe space' in Canada by facilitating networking opportunities with other community members and helping live-in caregivers form social networks. While the provision of social services and the creation of safe social spaces may not necessarily lead to concrete policy changes and may not be construed as 'political' in the formal sense, the act of 'being there' for live-in caregivers is transgressive in that it promotes a form of activism outside the state (Brown 1997), thereby leading to the promotion of a modified form of 'citizenship' that binds individuals together on the basis of empathy, affect, and shared goals. It rejects the bifurcation of individuals into citizens/non-citizens, non-migrants/migrants, desirable/undesirable that is promoted by the Canadian state, instead showing that citizenship and membership can be re-imagined outside the state.

Filipina live-in caregiver organizations engage with the state and outside the state, thereby showing that they wage campaigns on different scales. Filipina live-in caregiver activism takes numerous forms and exists on multiple levels because of the need to promote different agendas, from policy change/policy abolition to awareness-raising to service provision. Creating a 'typology' of Filipina live-in caregiver activism therefore becomes an exercise in futility because of its diverse nature. Despite these differences, Filipina live-in caregiver activism exemplifies Filipina live-in caregivers' resilience; their involvement in civic activity – both through formal and informal politics – underscores their resilience in combating the deleterious circumstances caused by the LCP and their ability to transcend the limitations posed by their 'temporary' migrant status. They show that rights need not only come with citizenship; rather, fair and equal treatment should be granted to everyone regardless of migration status.

Conclusion

I had two goals in writing this chapter. First, I highlighted how the LCP is a 'natural' successor to racially discriminatory temporary labour migration programs that have been in existence in Canada for the last century. The same patterns of racialized and gendered exclusions can be found at the LCP, thereby showing how Canadian immigration policy – then and now – relies on classifying individuals according to their perceived desirability and compatibility with Canadian 'norms.' That live-in caregivers are subjected to numerous restrictions before acquiring citizenship shows that they have to 'prove' that they are worthy of Canadian permanent residency and later, Canadian citizenship. The LCP, as a result, leads to numerous harms. Live-in caregivers are more inclined to withstand abusive labour conditions in order to avail themselves of permanent residency and citizenship. As such, the LCP goes against liberal standards of just treatment by normalizing oppressive treatment.

Second, I showed how live-in caregivers' political activism criticizes prevailing notions of political participation. Their activism highlights how political activity is not restricted to citizens, thereby disrupting the association made between 'rights' and 'citizenship'; instead, Filipina live-in caregivers show that 'personhood' – i.e., the fact that they are human – matters. I also discussed how their activism expanded notions of the political; not only did they interact with the state to press for reform or for abolition, they also participated in informal politics through the creation of safe spaces for live-in caregivers.

Has Filipina live-in caregiver activism therefore led to improvements in the labour and living conditions of live-in caregivers? The preceding examples of activism clearly show that Filipina live-in caregiver organizations force the Canadian government to be accountable to their demands. Even if the activities of different organizations do not result in concrete political changes, their very presence denotes a constant 'opposition' presence to state policy and, more crucially, signals to live-in caregivers and other migrant workers that there are groups that are actively promoting their interests. Nevertheless, challenges persist. Romanticizing Filipina live-in caregiver activism would ultimately be harmful, for doing so masks the current struggles these caregivers face. In fact, the need for civil society actors to form coalitions and to wage effective campaigns has never been stronger. The Dhalla case cited earlier is not anomalous. There are still numerous cases of live-in caregivers facing maltreatment at the hands of their employers, recruitment officers, and immigration officials. Moreover, a decreasing number of live-in caregivers are being given permanent residency status (Valiani 2009), which inevitably prolongs their temporary – and thus, their precarious – status; while live-in caregiver activism may show that citizenship status does not determine political activism, citizenship status is still needed in order to avail oneself of rights such as the ability to choose one's profession or to live with one's family. Even more insidiously, the Canadian government has expanded temporary foreign worker programs to encompass other professions, with the Philippines remaining its preferred source of workers. Unlike the LCP, however, these new temporary foreign worker programs do not provide the option of applying for citizenship after a period of employment, instead mandating that migrant workers be repatriated to their home countries at the conclusion of their work contracts.

The continued existence of Filipina live-in caregiver activism becomes especially important in light of these harms. Perhaps at this stage, different organizations need to consider forming coalitions despite opposing agendas. Exploring alliances with other groups also becomes crucial. After all, the evolution of migrant care worker policy in Canada shows that civil society organizations need to be persistent as well as creative in their responses to state abuse. The formation of partnerships at this stage may create the impetus to create stronger measures against migrant worker abuse and to provide live-in caregivers and other migrant workers access to citizenship.

NOTES

1 It should be noted that live-in caregiver activism has existed for as long as migrant domestic worker programs have been in place in Canada, with Caribbean women active in political organizing in the late 1960s and early 1970s, when they dominated domestic worker programs. While little is known about Caribbean live-in caregivers' political activism, suffice it to say

that much like Filipina live-in caregivers' activism today, Caribbean women's organizing was crucial in providing an ongoing response to migrant domestic worker policies, forcing the Canadian government and Canadian employers to be accountable for their policies and their actions. Filipina women took over from Caribbean women and became active in organizing on behalf of live-in caregivers once the Philippines became the most popular source country for these workers.

REFERENCES

Abella, Manolo. 2006. *Policies and best practices for management of temporary migration.* Turin: UN Secretariat Department of Economics and Social Affairs.

Arat-Koç, Sedef. 2003. Good enough to work but not good enough to stay: Foreign domestic workers and the law. In *Locating law: Race, class, gender connections,* ed. Elizabeth Comack, 125–51. Halifax: Fernwood.

Bakan, Abigail, and Daiva Stasiulius. 1997. *Not one of the family: Foreign domestic workers in Canada.* Toronto: University of Toronto Press.

Bauböck, Rainer. 2003. Towards a political theory of migrant transnationalism. *International Migration Review* 37 (3): 700–23.

Bauder, Harald. 2008. Citizenship as capital: The distinction of migrant labour. *Alternatives: Global Local Political* 33 (3): 315–33.

Bosniak, Linda. 2006. *The citizen and the alien: Dilemmas of contemporary membership.* Princeton: Princeton University Press.

Brazao, Dale. 2009. Nannies anti-exploitation law passes. *Toronto Star,* December 11, 2009. http://www.thestar.com/news/canada/article/737520-nannies-anti-exploitation-law-passes.

Brown, Michael. 1997. *RePlacing citizenship: AIDS activism and radical democracy.* New York: Guilford.

Calliste, Agnes. 1989. Canada's immigration policy and domestics from the Carribbean: The second domestic scheme. In *Race, class, gender: Bonds and barriers,* ed. Jesse Vorst, 136–68. Toronto: Society for Socialist Studies and Between the Lines.

Canada Manpower and Immigration. 1966. *White paper on immigration.* Ottawa: Queen's Printer.

Carens, Joseph. 1996. Realistic and ethical approaches to the ethics of migration. *International Migration Review* 30 (1): 156–70.

– 2008. Live-in domestics, seasonal workers, and others hard to locate on the map of democracy. *Journal of Political Philosophy* 16 (4): 419–45.

Citizenship and Immigration Canada. 2009. *Facts and figures 2008 immigration overview: Permanent and temporary residents.* Accessed August 10, 2009. http://www.cic.gc.ca/english/resources/statistics/facts2008/temporary/01.asp.

Cleroux, Paul. 2009. Ruby Dhalla is in one heap of trouble. *Seaway News.* http://www.cornwallseawaynews.com/article-335575-Ruby-Dhalla-is-in-one-heap-of-trouble.html.

Colas, Alejandro. 2002. Agencies and structures in IR: Analyzing international social movements. In *International Civil Society,* 64–100. Cambridge: Polity.

Daenzer, Patricia M. 1997. An affair between nations: International relations and the movement of household service workers. In *Not one of the family: Foreign domestic workers in Canada,* ed. Abigail Bakan and Daiva Stasiulus, 89–118. Toronto: University of Toronto Press.

De Haas, Hein. 2005. International migration, remittances and development: Myths and facts. *Third World Quarterly* 26 (8): 1269–84.

Depatie-Pelletier, Eugenie. 2008. Under legal practices similar to slavery according to the U.N. convention: Canada's 'non white' 'temporary' foreign workers in 'low-skilled' occupations. Paper presented at the 10th Annual National Metropolis Conference, April 3–6, 2008, Halifax, NS.

England, Kim, and Bernadette Stiell. 1997. They think you are as stupid as your English is: Constructing domestic workers in Toronto. *Environment and Planning* 29 (2): 195–215.

Henry, Annette. 1998. *Taking back control: African Canadian women teachers' lives and practices.* Albany: State University of New York Press.

Khan, Sabaa. 2009. From labour of love to decent work: Protecting the human rights of caregivers in Canada. *Canadian Journal of Law and Society* 24 (1): 23–44.

Lipset, Seymour. 1990. *Continental divide: The values and institutions of the United States and Canada.* New York and London: Routledge.

Macklin, Audrey. 1992. Foreign domestic workers: Surrogate wives or mail order servant? *McGill Law Journal* 37: 681–760.

Marshall, Thomas H. 1950. *Citizenship and social class and other essays.* Cambridge: Cambridge University Press.

Miranda, Susana. 2007. Exploring themes in the scholarship on twentieth century domestic work in Canada and the US. *Left History* 12 (2): 113–29.

National Alliance of Philippine Women in Canada. 2009. *Scrap Canada's live-in caregiver program: End violence against Filipino women.* Accessed October 30, 2009. http://kalayaancentre.net/pwcofbc/?p=210.

Ontario Coalition against Poverty (OCAP). 2009. Canadian government rejects calls to stop deportation of Filipino caregivers. Accessed August 10, 2009. http://update.ocap.ca/node/534.

Pierson, Paul. 1993. When effects become cause: Policy feedback and political change. *World Politics* 45 (4): 595–628.

Sassen, Saskia. 2006. *Territory, authority, and rights: From medieval to global assemblages.* Princeton: Princeton University Press.

Sharma, Nandita. 2006. *Home economics: Nationalism and the making of migrant workers in Canada.* Toronto: University of Toronto Press.

Sharpe, Pamela. 2001. Gender and the experience of migration. In *Women, gender, and labour migration: Historical and global perspectives,* ed. Pamela Sharpe, 1–14. London: Routledge.

Stahl, Charles. 1982. Labour emigration and economic development. *International Migration Review* 16 (4): 869–99.

Ty, Eleanor. 2004. *The politics of the visible in Asian North American narratives.* Toronto: University of Toronto Press.

Valiani, Salimah. 2009. The shift in Canadian immigration policy and unheeded lessons of the live-in caregiver program. *MRZine.* Accessed July 10, 2010. http://mrzine.monthlyreview.org/2009/valiani030309.html.

Wiseman, Nelson. 2007. *In search of Canadian political culture.*

Chapter 8

Toronto Filipino Businesses, Ethnic Identity, and Place Making in the Diaspora

CESAR POLVOROSA, JR

At one Filipino remittance company, it is customary for the staff and the manager to start the workday by gathering around the altar and saying a short prayer for guidance and blessings. The staff then chat in Tagalog about their families and about Philippine politics and show-business personalities while having a hurried breakfast of coffee and *pan de sal* (Filipino bread) before their first clients come in. While such practices are replicated in many companies in the Philippines, this particular company is on St Clair West near downtown Toronto. This early morning office ritual is an example of the spread of Filipino workplace practices to distant shores, a phenomenon increasingly made common by the migration of Filipinos all over the world.

As of December 2009, overseas Filipinos are estimated to total 8.62 million (Commission on Filipino Overseas 2010) or roughly 9.3 per cent of the Philippine population. Located in different host countries, these overseas Filipinos have highly diverse experiences and impacts on the Philippines. Research on overseas Filipinos deals mostly with Filipino Americans, who are large in numbers (about 2.9 million) and have a long history in the United States (Aguilar 2002; Bonus 2000; Espiritu 2003; Tiongson 2006). Given this, there is still a need to consider other major destination societies, such as Canada. Where Filipino migration to Canada has been investigated, the focus has largely been on labour migration, especially of live-in caregivers (further explication of the centrality of live-in caregivers to Filipino Canadians can be found in Kelly et al., Pratt, Davidson, Tungohan, and Angeles in this volume). The major objective of this chapter is to examine another critical aspect of the economic and cultural life of Filipinos in Canada by investigating the role of Filipino entrepreneurial activities and spaces in Toronto.

Traditionally, ethnic enterprises are viewed from economic and cultural frameworks (Light 1972; Marger 2001; Kloosterman and Rath 2003). The economic framework emphasizes the ethnic enterprise as a source of livelihood and the immigrants' fulfilment of financial objectives in the host society. The cultural framework highlights the role of community resources, practices, and values in the formation of ethnic business enterprises. Ethnic enterprises are also significant, I argue, as an assertion of diasporic identity and place making. Thus, this chapter has two objectives: (a) to analyse the linkages among entrepreneurial activities, national identities, and place making in order to better understand their dynamics and the motivations of ethnic entrepreneurship; and, (b) to fill a vital gap in the scholarly literature on Filipino Canadians' entrepreneurship, which has broad policy implications, considering the community's rapid growth in Canada.[1]

The major sections of the chapter proceed as follows. Part 1 discusses the ethnic entrepreneurship literature and its main schools of thought. Part 2 presents the research methodology. Part 3 examines the geographies of Filipino business space in Toronto from the viewpoints of entrepreneurs, employees, and consumers. For the conclusion, part 4 summarizes the main points and stresses the contested notions of home in diaspora and trajectories of the immigrant.

The Diaspora and the Filipino

The concept of 'diaspora' has transcended its origin in Jewish history and the dispersal of Jewish people. Scholars have now begun deploying the term more generally as 'a metaphoric designation to describe different categories of people – expatriates, expellees, political refugees, alien residents, immigrants and ethnic and racial minorities' (Cohen 1997, 21). The wider meaning of diaspora captures the large-scale and long-term movements of people across boundaries rather than the earlier migration terminology grounded in Jewish history. San Juan (2000) points out that the central features of diasporic groups include a historical connection to a homeland, a desire for eventual return, and a collective identity centred on homeland myths and memories. (On the utility of these myths and memories for Filipino artists, see Balmes in this volume.) With the divide-and-conquer policy of the colonizers and facilitated by the archipelagic nature of the Philippines, national cohesion was never achieved. Filipino immigrants to other countries maintained their ties with their homeland, primarily to their regions and not to the nation-state. Thus, Bicolanos may immigrate to Canada and maintain ties mostly with other Bicolanos in the settlement society and with Bicolano friends and relatives back in the homeland. On the other hand, the criterion of Okamura (1998) for a diaspora is simply the maintenance of transnational linkages with the homeland. Whether these transnational linkages are with specific regions in the homeland as in the diaspora concept of San Juan or with the heritage nation in general does not appear to be significant for Okamura.

For Filipinos, the experience under U.S. rule engendered a colonial mentality that glorified the United States as a vastly superior culture and a prosperous country overflowing with milk and honey (Bonus 2000; Tiongson 2006; Espiritu 2003; although see McElhinny in this volume, on how U.S. superiority was produced through the denigration of Filipinos as 'inferior Others'). As immigration to the United States became more restrictive, Filipinos focused on the country north of the U.S. border – Canada – which was perceived to provide good economic opportunities (see chapter 1 and chapters by Damasco and Eric in this volume). From the perspective of Filipino immigrants, the main goal is to escape the underdevelopment of the 'East' and take part in the prosperity and high status of the 'West.'

Entrepreneurship, Cultures, and Identities

In the process of uprooting themselves from the homeland, entrepreneurship presents itself to Filipinos as an avenue to prosperity and a mode of adaptation in the capitalist countries of the 'West' that had become the settlement societies (such as Canada). Discovering the linkages of entrepreneurship with culture and identities will lead to a richer understanding of the process of adaptation for different ethnic groups, aside from helping to fill up an underresearched area in the literature. While earlier approaches to entrepreneurship follow a neoclassical conception of entrepreneurship as an individualistic economic action (e.g., Wennekers and Thurik 1999), my focus on entrepreneurship, cultures, and identities is reflective of the recent move of scholars to go back to Max Weber and his theory of the embeddedness of the economy in culture. For Weber (1930), the motive of entrepreneurial energy is generated by 'exogenously supplied religious beliefs' (Kilby 1971, 6). Entrepreneurship is also embedded in broader societal values, role expectations, and social sanctions (Kilby 1971). Similarly, Morrison (2000) invokes the cultural embeddedness of the economy in terms directly relevant to entrepreneurship by arguing that 'there is a significant relationship between entrepreneurship and cultural specificity' (59–60). This emphasis on the linkage of culture and economy contrasts with the mainstream neoclassical economic thinking that assumes that culture is a given in business and that profit maximization is the be-all and end-all of economic activity.

What is the relevance of ethnic identity in ethnic entrepreneurship? The ethnic entrepreneurship literature has centred on cultural and mainstream economics and the combination of the two to explain ethnic business activities (Ibrahim and Galt 2003). In the cultural approach, the explanatory variables are social capital, values, and modes of social organization to explain the propensity and motivations (e.g., higher status) of certain ethnic groups to become entrepreneurial, while in mainstream economics the focus has been on maximizing the benefits or profits from any economic undertaking. Culture as it pertains to 'every aspect of life' (Verhelst 1990, 17) is often not considered in this literature; neither is the way it is 'learned and shared' (Spradley and McCurdy 1987, 4) in social relationships. In entrepreneurship literature, the way that ethnic cultures are circulated and reproduced within workplaces and entrepreneurial networks remains understudied. Heberer's (2005) study on the Nuosu of China and Pecoud's (2004) research on German-Turkish businesspeople in Berlin are two cases in the literature linking entrepreneurship and ethnic identity within specific cultural and spatial contexts.

Furthermore, there is a dearth of research on the link between culture, economy, and identity formation in relation to ethnic entrepreneurship, despite increasing recognition of identity formation as a more-than-individual phenomenon. The idea that culture is tied to the social construction of identity rejects the conventional idea that 'an individual is unique, stable and whole entity, and asserts that an individual should be seen as a socio-historical and socio-cultural product' (Hytti 2000, 3). Often, identity needs a mechanism through which it can be expressed. Social roles serve this function and, in the context of this study, the firm created by the entrepreneur is another.

Theories of Immigrant Entrepreneurship

The significance of entrepreneurship in the successful integration of immigrants to the receiving society has been recognized in the literature (e.g., Light and Gold 2000). Immigration especially to Canada and the United States during the past decades has generated research on the modes of integration into the receiving societies, including immigrant entrepreneurship (e.g., Hiebert 2002; 2003). Theories have been proposed in the immigration literature to explain the motivations, advantages, constraints, and varying rates of entrepreneurship among different ethnic groups, and these are as follows: (a) blocked mobility theory, (b) theory of middleman minorities, (c) interactive theory, and (d) mixed embeddedness.

Under the blocked mobility theory or disadvantage theory, immigrants pursue the self- employment route because of many structural constraints in the receiving society such as racial discrimination (e.g., Anderson 1990) and cultural barriers that hobble their success in the regular labour market. The concept of ethnic enclave economy is derived from a dual labour market theory (Light and Gold 2000, 11), which suggests that immigrant ethnic groups face numerous obstacles in succeeding in the mainstream labour market and cope by starting ethnic enterprises or being employed by co-ethnic enterprises. However, as Hiebert (2002) observed, even if immigrants face many barriers in the labour market, those who succeed as entrepreneurs are those who are the best prepared in terms of human, social, and financial capital. Many of these enterprises are formed into enclaves, which can be defined as 'spatially clustered networks of businesses owned by members of the same minority' (Portes 1995, 27; Wilson and Portes 1980). Enclaves take advantage of the benefits of clustering, including agglomeration economies, knowledge sharing, community formation, and place branding, which can compensate for the disadvantages faced by immigrants in the dual market.

The middleman theory asserts that ethnic entrepreneurs engage in business to use existing networks and linkages and act as middlemen, e.g., specializing in commercial and financial services in generally poorer communities with other ethnic groups. In the literature, Jews in Europe and Indians in Africa have been described as middlemen entrepreneurs (Bonacich 1973). Ethnic groups which historically performed the middleman role, such as Chinese in Southeast Asia, have an advantage when they become entrepreneurs in the receiving society. Thus, the Chinese perform the role of middlemen in the GTA for the Filipino community; e.g., Filipino food, DVDs, and toiletries can be found in Chinese supermarkets.

Scholars utilize interactive approaches to examine the congruence between supply and demand of the economic environment (Waldinger 1986; Waldinger, Aldrich, and Ward 1990; Light and Gold 2000).

Waldinger (1986) emphasizes the 'opportunity structure' as an important determinant of immigrant and ethnic businesses. The theory argues that immigrants become entrepreneurs because they sense business opportunities. Management theorist Kirzner refers to this as the entrepreneur's quality of 'alertness' or sensitivity to profitable opportunities (Boettke and Coyne 2003). Related to this is the notion that ethnic groups have cultural characteristics that predispose them to avail themselves of opportunities in the open market (e.g., Light 1972; Waldinger 1986). By combining cultural factors and opportunity structures in the economy, the interactive model is considered a more comprehensive theoretical approach.

In their work on immigrants in Western Europe, Kloosterman and Rath (2003) propose the concept of mixed embeddedness, which combines agency and structure perspectives. In their view, their model goes beyond the social embeddedness of the actors themselves and incorporates the wider societal and operating environment: 'The mixed embeddedness approach takes into account the characteristics of the supply of immigrant entrepreneurs, the shape of the opportunity structure, and the institutions mediating between aspiring entrepreneurs and concrete openings to start a business in order to analyze immigrant entrepreneurs in different national contexts' (Rath and Kloosterman 2000, 4–5).

In short, there are numerous factors that one should take account of in order to have a more complete picture of why immigrants go into business and why they may vary according to ethnic group and the settlement society.

Immigrant Entrepreneurship Research in Perspective

Immigrant entrepreneurship theories continue to evolve and are in a state of flux. Considerable ground in the literature is still contestable territory, suggesting that the theories are incomplete rather than outright erroneous. Hiebert (2003), for example, comments that 'immigrants are more likely than the native born to be self employed though analysts are not agreed whether this is the result of blocked-mobility or other factors' (44). There may be evidence to support the original blocked mobility and middlemen theories (Bonacich 1973), but others have expanded on these and have made the current theory of mixed embeddedness the most prominent (Kloosterman and Rath 2003). The dynamics fuelling debate in the immigrant entrepreneurship literature may be traced to ethnic diversity, various immigration contexts and spatial variations, and the opportunities and constraints in different business niches. The time period in an ethnic group's settlement may be a factor as well: as the initial years are spent on survival so the immigrants are 'pushed' into entrepreneurship. Consequently, after adjusting and building up financial, social, and human capital in the 'host' society, the entrepreneurially minded in the ethnic group take advantage of profitable opportunities or are 'pulled' into entrepreneurship.

Research Methodology

My main research methodology consists of interviews with twenty-five Filipino business owners and key members of their families involved in the business as well as in-depth case studies of four businesses, which involved several interviews and discussions over the course of several months. These methods were combined with on-site observations and conversations with some customers and employees. On the average, each interview lasted about two hours.

The immigrant entrepreneurs I interviewed came to Canada through the Skilled Workers or family reunification streams. Some of the families are recent arrivals, while others have been in Canada for as long as thirty-eight years. The majority of the owners are middle-aged, with a few in their sixties and early thirties, and with one only twenty-seven, representing the extreme of the age range. Most of the respondents are business-owning couples. The recent arrivals tend to come from business and professional groups in the Philippines. The interviews with Filipino business owners in Toronto were across a wide range of industries – restaurants and groceries, cookware marketing and distribution, publishing, IT consultancy, remittance services, and healthcare. Supplemental information came in the form of conversations with clients and employees of the Filipino-owned enterprises.

The topics of identity formation and place making were explored through discussions about the workplace roles, performances of the owners and their key family members, and their perceptions of the enterprise. Major themes from the ethnic entrepreneurship literature were explored through the interviews. For example, the middleman role theory was analysed through questions about where the Filipino businesses secure their supplies and market their products. The issues of dual markets and personal motivations – common themes in the blocked mobility and mixed embeddedness literatures – were examined through discussions on the respondents' reasons for entrepreneurship.

I am critically aware of my own position in conducting research on my own co-ethnic group and I faced both advantages and disadvantages because of this position. More specifically, my ethnicity and some personal contacts based on my own professional affiliations in the Philippines secured me access to interviews and business sites. I also gained insights into my profession as a strategic planner, socio-economic consultant, and business plan writer. However, as an international student who had been in Canada for only a few years to pursue a doctorate, I also constantly negotiated my own identity as I realized that I am neither completely in nor out of my own ethnic group in Toronto (Chatterjee 2003, 51). My student status, short history in Toronto, and consequent lack of social capital were constraints in securing appointments with some Filipino business owners. As a senior bank officer in the Philippines, I was accustomed to being accorded priority when talking to business owners in the home country, which stood in sharp contrast to my fieldwork experience in Toronto.

Filipino Entrepreneurial Identities, Place Making, Social and Power Relations

Given that Toronto is a major site of various ethnic enterprises, it provides rich materials for research on Canadian ethnic entrepreneurship (Lo, Texeira, and Truelove 2002; Marger 2001). However, the relationship between entrepreneurship and ethnic identity formation among immigrants remains under-theorized. In fact, ethnic identity formation *through* entrepreneurship does not appear to be a common theme in the literature.

I contend that what may be less understood is that ethnic entrepreneurs frequently view their business as a platform to assert and reinforce their ethnic identities by showcasing the achievements of their ethnic group. For instance, in my discussions with a group of Filipino IT businessmen, they cited Filipino pride as a motivation for setting up the enterprise: '*When we set up this IT company we did so not only because we think it will be profitable but because we want to show Canadians that we Filipinos can excel in the IT field. We want to show that the Philippines is a country with a lot of professional and technical skills.*'

The goal of ethnic pride consistently resonated in my conversations with other Filipino business owners. For example, a Scarborough businessman who imports Filipino-authored children's books said: '*I want the Filipino children and youth here in Toronto to be able to read books by Filipino authors so as to take pride in what we can do and for the other people to see that we can write good books.'* Similarly, a restaurant owner also pointed to ethnic pride as a motivation for entering the food sector business: *'I want to show the people here in Canada that we Filipinos have a lot of wonderful and interesting dishes.'*

The Filipinos in Canada that I have interviewed acquire entrepreneurial identities when they assume entrepreneurial roles. As they have related, they sense opportunities in the market, but as immigrants they also perceive the barriers in the labour market. Entrepreneurship is their mode of adaptation in a less-than-open system of capitalism, echoing the view that ethnic entrepreneurship celebrates 'hybridity, deterritorialization and fluidity' (Ong 1999, 172).

As the opening example of the remittance centre on St Clair West Avenue shows, Filipino place making in a major cosmopolitan space of North America is socially constructed and invested with human meaning. 'People are active participants in the historically contingent process of the making of place ... and that place making is situated in specific time-space contexts' (Kong and Yeoh 1995, 2). This raises the question: How do Filipino businesses in the diasporic space of Toronto relate to the identities and social and power relations of Filipino entrepreneurs, employees, and clientele?

Filipino Businesses as Entrepreneurial Spaces

For many Filipinos, becoming entrepreneurs in a destination society like Canada can profoundly shape their identity and feeling of self-worth. Since those with sufficient social and economic capital have better chances of starting a business, entrepreneurship is an affirmation of one's likely privileged position in the homeland. It is also a response to the loss of status that results from de-skilling and deprofessionalization of immigrants and from the perception of blocked mobility in the job market. (See de Leon in this volume for a discussion of the role of class and socio-economic status in Filipino youth's understanding of their Filipino identities.) For example, one Toronto-based Filipino businessman explains that he owns a big company in the Philippines and it felt good to own even a small business in Toronto, as it is better than being a clerk. In the case of the United States, a National City (California) Filipino store owner notes, 'At least, I have managed to start up a business on my own. The other Filipinos cannot do the same. It takes a lot of money' (Bonus 2000, 60). A Filipina entrepreneur in Toronto related to me with embarrassment that another Filipina told her about a nanny opening, without knowing that she was a senior Manila executive. Opening her own business in Toronto after a few months enhanced her class status in the local community.

There are other practices that reproduce hierarchical status in Philippine society that can be found in the diasporic space of Toronto. In the Filipino workplace, it is a standard practice to address superiors as 'sir' and 'ma'am,' and to continue to be addressed as such in a North American setting is a re-creation of Philippine socio-economic power relations. To the extent that Philippine society is highly stratified and hierarchical, entrepreneurship can serve as the institution that reinforces existing social inequalities. In this way, the economic rewards that come with entrepreneurship can serve to widen the distance from those who do not have the means to become business owners. Through the business owners' ability to hire and fire especially co-ethnic employees, entrepreneurship is a form of social power and is manifested in the mode of communication. For example, when asked if he allows himself to be addressed as 'sir,' a Filipino food business owner replied in the affirmative: *'I really don't think of it as so important but it's already part of our traditional practice back home and it's a sign of respect from my employees.'*

Since the work setting is North America, the Filipino entrepreneur's use of his Filipino ethnicity is contingent and situational – becoming Filipino where required especially in the workplace. Echoing Chatterjee's (2003, 51) notion that identity is a matter of constant negotiation, immigrants may disregard Filipino-ness but revive it on certain occasions (Aguilar 2002). Immigrant entrepreneurs have wide latitude in following ethnic practices, as the workplace is their dominion.

However, entrepreneurship in the settler society of Canada can also promote socio-economic mobility, especially for immigrants who lack social and economic resources and who did not own businesses in their homeland, but who have saved money and are innovative and creative enough. A number of my respondents who are business owners in Canada did not have business backgrounds in the Philippines. However, it appears that the more successful entrepreneurs among the respondents are those who immigrated with ample financial and human capital. For example, one Filipino travel agent in Toronto explains that he felt encouraged to set up his own travel agency so he could put his experience as a former employee of a Philippine airline to good use: *'Having my own business would not be possible back home. The Philippine travel agency industry is overcrowded and all I need here in Toronto to operate are a few computers and a small office space.'*

Does ethnic identity endure in a diasporic space such as Toronto? What is the role of the ethnic enterprise in perpetuating such identities? A North York Filipino restaurant owner who had been in Toronto for twenty years addressed the issue emphatically: *'I am Filipino and no matter how long I stay in Canada nothing can change that fact! My skin is brown, I prepare Filipino dishes, we speak Tagalog here and most of our clients are Filipino so what else can I be? I am therefore Filipino.'*

Here, the endurance of ethnic identity is the result of the confluence of racial appearance, the nature of the business, workplace performance, professional role, and the clientele. While ethnic identity is by its nature self-identification, the lack of affirmation from one's co-ethnics can lead to self-doubt and personal ambiguity. Asked if she considers herself Filipina, an artist who owns a studio paused before replying:

You know I always consider myself as Filipino period. However, when I went to the Philippines, I began to feel that I am actually a foreigner. I cannot understand many of the language nuances of the locals, the context of the conversation and they, in turn, cannot appreciate many of my jokes and what I am trying to say. They regarded me as not totally a Filipino. So, what am I? I realized then that I am a Filipino Canadian.

This is similar to the experience of some Soviet Greeks who were able to use their ethnic resources when they returned to Greece permanently after the fall of the Soviet Union and yet were not considered as truly Greek (Popov 2010). I noted from my research that even if Filipinos have been residents of Canada for a long time (e.g., fifteen years or more), if they arrived in Canada as adults, they tend to continue to regard themselves as Filipinos. On the other hand, Filipinos who arrived as teens or as children in Canada tend to identify themselves as Filipino Canadian in their adulthood. This suggests that ethnic self-identity formed in the socialization process up to adulthood can become a lifetime marker and is manifested and reinforced by later roles in the ethnic economy.

Filipino Businesses as Workplaces

For many employees, working in the Filipino enterprise is being in their comfort zone – it feels like being back home. While for many the re-creation of power relationships in a Toronto workplace may make it a far from ideal situation, it is often preferable to the uncertainty of working with other ethnic groups and having a non-Filipino as a supervisor. It is as though they were working in a Filipino company in the Philippines and the sense of the familiar can compensate for any perceived disadvantages.

In the Filipino workplace, as all my fieldwork respondents have informed me, they speak Tagalog, Taglish (combining Tagalog and English), or one of the Philippine dialects common to the group. When employees share similar values, the ground rules for social interaction are clear, and as Hirschman (1987) puts it, 'among the many dimensions that may serve to define or reinforce ethnicity in a plural society are cultural characteristics such as language, dress and cuisine' (557). Management, especially in a Filipino ethnic economy that is dominated by family-owned and small firms, tends to be patriarchal and is often bound by kinship and regional ties. Several of my respondents explained, for example, that their employees come from their province in the Philippines and that some are relatives or friends of close relations. This facilitates bonding between co-ethnic employers and employees and the formation of specific work practices. Employees can request special favours such as salary advances and personal loans or leave early to attend important family functions. In return, the company owners expect loyalty, hard work, and an unquestioning attitude in the workplace.

Both Filipino entrepreneurs and employees within the confines of Filipino space engage in 'spatial introversion': they tend to 'reorder internal relations within the existing social milieu through experienced spatial practices that refer to production and social production and perceived spatial practices which allow these experienced spatial practices to be understood and articulated' (Liu 1997, 96). In other words, Filipinos behave how they feel a Filipino should behave in Filipino space. While potentially materially explicit in directly Filipino-oriented businesses (especially grocery stores and restaurants), Filipino-ness can also exist in coded and symbolic forms in other mainstream market-oriented Filipino businesses (e.g., travel agencies), especially through language and workplace practices. Thus, a travel agency which is not outwardly Filipino-owned in its appearance could 'sound' like one when employees converse in Tagalog and address co-ethnic customers and employees as *'kuya'* (elder brother) or *'ate'* (elder sister).

Filipino Businesses as Consumer Landscapes

For the mostly Filipino clientele of Filipino businesses in Toronto, the 'myths and memories of the homeland' (San Juan 2000, 236) are re-created in the Filipino business spaces, comprising part of the process of business place making. It enables Filipinos in Canada to become like Filipino consumers by buying the same or similar products and services as their compatriots back in the homeland.

Favourite Philippine brands and cuisine are familiar reminders of home. They also bring nostalgia because one is reminded of being 'abroad,' since these products are not generally conveniently accessible daily. The presence of Filipino businesses can signal the idea that one has not really left all of 'home.' For example, Filipino new arrivals to Toronto are often pleasantly surprised to find Filipino stores with appearance and décor replicating those found in the homeland and encountering many Filipinos in the immediate neighbourhood. One gets this sense of being 'home' at the intersection of St Clair and Bathurst or Wilson and Bathurst because of the proliferation of Filipino stores and the numbers of Filipinos that one bumps into. Such is also the case in the United States – as a Filipino in Stockton, California, shares regarding the town's 'Little Manila': 'I was so happy! The people walking around were all Filipinos! When I look at the street from the shop, my goodness, it looks like the Philippines!' (Mabalon 2006, 73). This is best typified by the *sari-sari* stores (small variety stores) and *turo-turo* (small eateries) that dot the Philippine landscape and are re-created in Toronto city-space.

The locations of many complementary Filipino businesses as clusters facilitate the pursuit of Filipino customs and practices. At St Clair West and Bathurst and to some extent in Scarborough, Filipino businesses are located near churches. After Sunday mass, many Filipino churchgoers partake of their meals in Filipino restaurants nearby, echoing a common Filipino practice of having a special meal after Sunday mass. In small Philippine towns, the church is at the village centre and the surrounding area becomes a focal point of social interactions after religious festivals and occasions. In this way, the juxtaposed spaces of religion and business are significant factors in maintaining and reinforcing ethnic identities, even in Toronto.

While eating a Filipino lunch after Sunday mass, the Filipino clientele make small talk with the Filipino restaurant staff and other clients, read Philippine newspapers, and watch Filipino movies or the Filipino Channel, a cable TV channel in North America devoted to Filipino programming. Philippine DVDs of Filipino singers and celebrities are also widely available in these spaces, and there is typically *karaoke* for parties and special occasions.[2] There are Philippine paintings with rural themes and a crucifix or altar that manifests religiosity. Just as in Philippine eateries, the usually female staff are addressed frequently as '*ate*' (older sister), a sign of both respect and familiarity, and in turn typically answer with '*kuya*' (older brother). Similar terms of *manong, manang,* and *inday* in the major Philippine dialects are used. After their meal, the customers proceed to a nearby remittance agency to send money back home.

The Filipino business becomes a venue for social interaction – even in remittance agencies – where clients and staff chat about their seemingly never-ending financial obligations to the family in the homeland. 'That's why we remain poor because we have to send money back home regularly' is a common lament. In this manner, in the span of a few hours on a Sunday, the Filipino client is able both to address his/her spiritual and bodily needs and to meet financial obligations to family in the homeland. The various Filipino goods and services in Toronto can be regarded as 'cultural representations of the diasporic identity and consciousness,' since they signify 'cultural, economic and social connections with the Philippine homeland ... [and] the various ways by which spatial boundaries are being transcended' (Okamura 1998, 102).

Are these spaces exclusionary? These transnational spaces actually function as 'contact zones' on the Filipino entrepreneur's own terms. Pratt (1992) defines a 'contact zone' as 'an attempt to invoke the spatial and temporal copresence of subjects previously separated by geographic and historical disjunctures, and whose trajectories now intersect' (7). In these spatial intersections of ethnic interactions, other ethnic groups get to discover Philippine culture through its products, lifestyles, customs, and social interaction, and the differences from other 'Oriental' stores become apparent. Thus, someone who has been to, say, Korean, Chinese, and Filipino stores in Toronto will be able to discern the highly significant differences among the three that repudiates the Orientalist notion of lumping all things Asian into a homogeneous whole. Especially in the food industry, where clients walk into the business premises, it is often the business owner who engages in conversation with the non-Filipino client.

Filipino enterprises and their spatiality partly address the marginalization of Filipinos in Toronto (and in Canada) that is shown in what I personally call 'the invisible visible minority.' I use the latter term to refer to Filipinos as a visible minority that is largely 'invisible' or an ethnic group that remains economically, culturally, socially, and politically marginalized as explicitly manifested in lower earnings, the absence or invisibility of high-profile achievers in the areas of the arts, government, business, and politics of the Canadian mainstream, and the subsequent stereotyping of Filipinos as low-paid workers. As Kelly (2009) notes, 'it is not uncommon to find that non-Filipinos believe that all Filipinos arrive in Canada as caregivers' (31). Thus, integral to place making in the diasporic space of Toronto is also the re-creation of historical and cultural constraints of Filipinos.

Sometimes, socio-economic realities play out in this North American city in terms of relationships with other ethnic groups and the manifestation of subaltern roles. The interviews reveal that many Filipino enterprises remain small-scale and depend on other ethnic groups for their trading and distribution networks. For instance, at *Lone Tai* supermarket, a major Chinese supermarket in Scarborough, there is a large and prominent section marked 'Canadian and Philippine Goods.' This scene is similarly replicated in numerous Chinese supermarkets in the Greater Toronto Area, e.g., Bestwin on Victoria Park Avenue and T & T in Thornhill. This highlights the historical middleman role of Chinese businesses in the Philippine economy (see Yeung 2004). The sizes of these middleman-owned businesses dwarf Filipino business enterprises in comparison, mirroring the status of the Chinese in the Philippines, where they comprise 1 per cent of the population yet contribute 40 per cent of the country's GDP (Yeung 2004, 13).

The Filipino entrepreneur in the diasporic space of Toronto might represent both pride and small-mindedness – displaying one's ability to establish a business that promotes Filipino culture and ethnic pride and yet hampered by a continuing perception of one's own limited business capabilities through small operations and the unwillingness to venture beyond the relative safety of the secure but narrow co-ethnic market. In interviews, it consistently emerged that Filipino business owners just wanted to focus on Filipino clientele and had no definite plans to target the mainstream market for long-term growth. Subsequently, it becomes difficult to name Filipino enterprises that have really become big in the mainstream Canadian economy.

Turning Full Circle: Notions of Home in the Diaspora and Immigrant Trajectories

Memory is persistent like a recurring dream
and the promise is certain
as winter's end.
I have to hurry.

This wind-swept, snow-smothered road
though it may meander, though it may disappear
in blinding whiteness is the course that leads
to the warm hearth of home. (Polvorosa 2005)[3]

For Espiritu (2003), the immigrant is forever 'homebound,' which can be understood as not necessarily a physical return to the homeland but as the lived experiences of imaginations of finding home. (Balmes in this volume discusses artists' return trips to the Philippines as reclamations of homeland and Filipino-ness.) Entrepreneurship is seen as a route to achieve this objective, despite perceptions of limits to capital accumulation in a segmented and inaccessible labour market. Evidence suggests that among Filipinos in Toronto, 'the return to home' has various meanings and desirability. The notion of a physical return to the homeland is an area of contestation. San Juan (2000) questions home as the Philippines itself, given the impact of imperialism on the home country and its fragmentation. On the other hand, 'home is anyplace; it is temporary and it is moveable; it can be built, rebuilt, and carried in memory and by acts of imagination' (Espiritu, 2003, 10–11), so that all immigrants can and do 'return home' in both literal and figurative senses.

The imagination of the homeland is articulated spatially in the Filipino enterprise. The Filipino owner, employees, and clientele 'return home' every time they are within the physical confines of the Filipino business. The 'foreigner' visits the Philippines every time he or she goes to a Filipino establishment. The Filipino firm therefore functions as more than the source of livelihood for newly arrived immigrants. The ethnic enterprise may represent a transitory stage in the career trajectories of many immigrant Filipino entrepreneurs and employees. As gleaned from many of the interviews, for entrepreneurs, the challenge to grow their firms is to enter the mainstream market. For employees, many find it necessary eventually to leave the Filipino enterprise for financial reasons, despite the cultural advantages of working in the same Filipino space. Many interviewees also noted that they thought that working daily with other ethnic groups in non-Filipino-owned enterprises would hasten their cultural integration into the mainstream multicultural society in Canada.

Tracing the trajectories of Filipino enterprises in Toronto and their ultimate implications for place making, negotiations, and constructions of identities offers insights into the settlement strategies of Filipino immigrant families in Toronto. Even as Filipino enterprises represent an adaptation to the settlement society, they not only function as sources of livelihood for the immigrating families, but also become a means to re-assert ethnic identities and place making in the diasporic space of Toronto. Finally, by conferring an advantage on those Filipinos who arrived in Canada with enough financial and human capital to become employers, entrepreneurship in the settlement society tends to re-create the socio-economic relations prevalent in the homeland. However, there are those individuals who by being innovative and creative can overcome the lack of capital and are able to establish their own business enterprises. As played out in the settlement society and in the diasporic space of Toronto, ethnic entrepreneurship as represented by Filipino businesses is a multidimensional endeavour that can be critically examined through various lenses of inquiry and that has significant implications for scholarship and research.

NOTES

1 From my review, the only academic work on Filipino entrepreneurs in Canada is that of the Laquians on Filipino businesses in British Columbia (2008).
2 Karaoke singing is a very popular mode of entertainment in the Philippines, as in many Asian countries. Contrary to popular perception of its Japanese origin, it was actually invented by a Filipino, Roberto del Rosario (see www.geocities.com/kodikos/karaoke.htm and www.inventors.about.com).
3 This is the last stanza of my poem 'Going Home to Scarborough in Mid-Winter,' which I read during the Cultural Night of the 'Making the Filipino Community Count in Ontario' Conference on November 10, 2006.

REFERENCES

Aguilar, Filomeno, Jr. 2002. *Filipinos in global migrations: At home in the world?* Quezon City, Philippines: Philippine Migration Research Network and Philippine Social Science Council.

Anderson, Kay. 1990. *Vancouver's Chinatown: Racial discourse in Canada.* Montreal and Kingston: McGill-Queen's University Press

Boettke, Peter, and Christopher Coyne. 2003. Entrepreneurship and development: Cause or consequence? *Advances in Austrian Economics* 6: 67–81.

Bonacich, Edna. 1973. A theory of middleman minorities. *American Sociological Review* 38: 583–94.

Bonus, Rick. 2000. *Locating the Filipino American.* Philadelphia: Temple University Press.

Chatterjee, Partha. 2003. My place in the global republic of letters. In *At home in diaspora,* ed. Jackie Assayag and Veronique Benei, 44–51. Bloomington: Indiana University Press.

Cohen, Robin. 1997. *Global diasporas.* Seattle: University of Washington Press.

Commission on Filipino Overseas. 2010. Stock estimates of overseas Filipinos. http://www.cfo.gov.ph/pdf/statistics/Stock%202009.pdf.

Espiritu, Yen Le. 2003. *Home bound: Filipino American lives across cultures, communities and countries.* Berkeley: University of California Press.

Heberer, Thomas. 2005. Ethnic entrepreneurship and ethnic identity: A case study among the Liangshan Yi (Nuosu) in China. *China Quarterly* 182: 407–27.

Hirschman, Charles. 1987. The meaning and measurement of ethnicity in Malaysia: An analysis of census classifications. *Journal of Asian Studies* 46 (3): 555–82.

Hiebert, Daniel. 2002. The spatial limits to entrepreneurship: Immigrant entrepreneurs in Canada. *Tijdschrift voor Economische en Sociale Geographie* 93: 173–90.

– 2003. A false consensus. In *Immigrant entrepreneur,* ed. Robert Kloosterman and Jan Rath, 39–60. Oxford: Berg.

Hytti, Ulla. 2000. The concept of identity and its relevance for entrepreneurship research. Paper presented at the RENT XIV Conference in Prague, Czech Republic, November 23–4.

Ibrahim, Gamal, and Vaughan Galt. 2003. Ethnic business development: Toward a theoretical synthesis in policy framework. *Journal of Economic Issues* 37 (4): 1107–20.

Kelly, Philip, et al. 2009. Explaining the deprofessionalized Filipino: Why Filipino immigrants get low-paying jobs in Toronto. Toronto: CERIS-The Ontario Metropolis Centre CERIS Working Paper No. 75.

Kilby, Peter, ed. 1971. *Entrepreneurship and economic development.* New York: Free Press.

Kloosterman, Robert, and Jan Rath. 2003. *Immigrant entrepreneurs: Venturing abroad in the age of globalization.* Oxford and New York: Berg.

Kong, Lily, and Brenda Yeoh. 1995. The meanings and making of place: Exploring history, community and identity. In *Portraits of places: History, community and identity in Singapore,* ed. Brenda S.A. Yeoh and Lily Kong, 12–23. Singapore: Times Edition.

Light, Ivan. 1972. *Ethnic enterprise in America: Business and welfare among Chinese, Japanese and Blacks.* Berkeley: University of California Press.

Light, Ivan, and Steven Gold. 2000. *Ethnic economies.* San Diego, CA: Academic.

Liu, Xin. 1997. Space, mobility and flexibility: Chinese villagers and scholars negotiate power at home and abroad. In *Ungrounded empires,* ed. Aihwa Ong and Donald Nonini, 91–114. New York: Routledge.

Lo, Lucia, Carlos Texeira, and Marie Truelove. 2002. Cultural resources, ethnic strategies and immigrant entrepreneurship: A comparative study of five ethnic groups in the Toronto CMA. Toronto: Centre of Excellence for Research on Immigration and Settlement CERIS Working Paper No. 21.

Mabalon, Dawn. 2006. Losing Little Manila. In *Positively no Filipinos allowed,* ed. Antonio Tiongson et al., 73–89. Philadelphia: Temple University Press.

Marger, Martin. 2001. The use of social and human capital among Canadian business immigrants. *Journal of Ethnic and Migration Studies* 27 (3): 439–53.

Morrison, Alison. 2000. Entrepreneurship: What triggers it? *International Journal of Entrepreneurial Behavior and Research* 6 (2): 59–71.

Okamura, Jonathan. 1998. *Imagining the Filipino American: Transnational relations, identities and communities.* New York: Garland.

Ong, Aihwa. 1999. *Flexible citizenship.* Durham, NC: Duke University Press.

Pecoud, Antoine. 2004. Entrepreneurship and identity: Cosmopolitanism and cultural competencies among German-Turkish businesspeople in Berlin. *Journal of Ethnic and Migration Studies* 30 (1): 3–20.

Polvorosa, Cesar. 2005. Going home to Scarborough in mid-winter (unpublished).

Popov, Anton. 2010. Making sense of home and homeland: Former Soviet Greeks' motivations and strategies for a transnational migrant circuit. *Journal of Ethnic and Migration Studies* 36 (1): 67–85.

Portes, Alejandro. 1995. *The economic sociology of immigration.* New York: Russell Sage.

Pratt, Mary Louise. 1992. *Imperial eyes: Travel writing and transculturation.* London: Routledge.

Rath, Jan, and Robert Kloosterman. 2000. Outsiders business. *International Migration Review* 34 (3): 657–81.

San Juan, Epifanio, Jr. 2000. Trajectories of the Filipino diaspora. *Ethnic Studies Report* 18 (2): 229–38.

Spradley, James, and David McCurdy. 1987. *Conformity and conflict: Readings in cultural anthropology.* Boston: Little, Brown and Company.

Tiongson, Antonio, et al. 2006. *Positively no Filipinos allowed.* Philadelphia: Temple University Press.

Verhelst, Thierry. 1990. *No life without roots.* London: Zed.

Waldinger, Roger. 1986. *Through the eye of the needle: Immigrants and enterprise in New York's garment trade.* New York: New York University Press.

Waldinger, Roger, Howard Aldrich, and Robin Ward. 1990. *Ethnic entrepreneurs: Immigrant business in industrial societies.* Newbury Park: Sage.

Weber, Max. 1930. *The Protestant ethic and the spirit of capitalism.* London: Routledge.

Wennekers, Sander, and Roy Thurik. 1999. Linking entrepreneurship and economic growth. *Small Business Economics* 13: 27–55.

Wilson, Kenneth, and Alejandro Portes. 1980. Immigrant enclaves: An analysis of the labour market experiences of Cubans in Miami. *American Journal of Sociology* 86 (2): 295–319.

Yeung, Henry. 2004. *Chinese capitalism in a global era.* London and New York: Routledge.

Chapter 9

Between Society and Individual, Structure and Agency, Optimism and Pessimism: New Directions for Philippine Diasporic and Transnational Studies

LEONORA C. ANGELES

Spectre: fr Latin: Spectrum appearance, fr Specere to look at, 1. a visible, disembodied spirit: GHOST, 2: something that haunts or perturbs the mind: PHANTASM <the spectre of hunger> – *Webster's New Collegiate Dictionary* (1981)

Introduction

The meanings of *spectre* in this dictionary definition frame well the chapters in part 2: they made visible to us the ghosts, nay, phantasms of contentious issues that continue to haunt and perturb our individual and collective existence as Filipinos or people of Philippine ancestry living in Canada. I offer a tentative framing of the haunting question implicitly raised in these five chapters: How and why has a nation with highly literate and industrious people, an Asian nation second only to Japan in terms of all social and economic indicators in the early postwar period, been reduced to a country crushed by poverty, which has earned a dubious reputation for being the biggest source of caregivers and domestic workers around the world?

For Filipinos in Canada, a version of this haunting question might be: How and why have Filipinos, already the fourth largest visible minority group in Canada, remained invisible as a social and political force, as an overlooked successful professional force, yet visible as workers in the domestic-like service sector? These five chapters taken collectively bring to our attention the spectre of this in/visibility, but also the invisibility of the spectre of this haunting question. The necessity of asking this haunting question is often obscured by the Canadian state's emphasis on multiculturalism and labour policies that remain dependent on temporary foreign workers – of which 45,000 who entered and remained in Canada by year's end in 2008 came from the Philippines.

While reading the chapters, I was reminded of a question posed in 2000 by eminent geographer Terry McGee, now Professor Emeritus at the University of British Columbia. He asked me, 'Nora, how has your relocation and resettlement in Canada transformed your perspectives when you are studying or writing about the Philippines?' I have known Terry long enough to expect such a provocative question from a great scholar. He was challenging me, nay us, hyphenated Asian and Filipino Canadians raised in the region, but working in global places, to think of how diasporic existence and identities shape scholarship, and by implication, how scholarship transforms diasporic loyalties and dispositions.

I must admit that I did not think much about my initial answer to Terry's question until I wrote 'The Filipino Male as *Macho-Machunurin:* Bringing Men and Masculinities in Gender and Development Studies in the Philippines' (Angeles 2001). Revisiting that article made me realize how my positionality as a Filipino academic in a North American setting has coloured and adjusted the analytic lenses I am using in looking at Philippine political economy, culture, history, and gender relations. From my new position as a transplanted émigré feminist academic in Canada, my experiences and identities were shaped by my relocation from Ontario (Kingston) to Saskatchewan (small-town Esterhazy, Regina, and Saskatoon) and British Columbia (Vancouver), as well as my new roles, responsibilities, and identities. These include my being in an interracial marriage to a third-generation Canadian of British ancestry, having two mestizo children who looked different from me and my husband, teaching in the top universities in the provinces where I resided, my tenured cross-appointment in two interdisciplinary fields – planning and women's and gender studies – and engagements with fascinating colleagues, students, and community organizations in the cities where I lived. My rethinking and sharpened consciousness of race, hybridity, gender, (dis)ability, sexual identities, transnationality, and postcoloniality, and my bringing these lenses more centrally into my own research and writing, were heightened by encounters with both multicultural and white Canada, some poignant, some funny – even hilarious – often shaped by mistaken identities and stereotypical assumptions about Filipinos in particular and Asian women in general.

But those new analytical lenses were not thickened and coloured by white Anglo-Saxon Canadian cultures alone, or by my encounters in multicultural Canada, but also by Canadian exploits and experiments in transnational linkages. I began the article by narrating how my Vietnamese colleagues interrogated gender identities and hierarchies in the Philippines while I took them on a study tour in Manila, as part of a capacity-building project funded by the Canadian government. Much of my own writing since has been shaped by new issues and questions confronting the Philippines and the Filipino diaspora, using lenses crafted and coloured by my trips to other countries, from Brazil to India, from Nepal to New Zealand, as well as my frequent trips to the Philippines – at times going for extended periods two or three times a year – to do research, accompany my graduate students, and visit my natal family and friends on the side. For three years now, I have taught for the University of British Columbia the Philippine Planning Field Studio course where I bring graduate students to learn about the challenges of local and regional development planning and get them to research and undertake planning-related projects. Seeing my country of origin, its cultures, people, and politics, in new kaleidoscopes through the eyes of my students in itself would merit a lengthy reflection paper.

So I ask myself then and now, am I still doing critical Philippine studies in the strict sense of how I, as a former student and later assistant professor at the University of the Philippines, came to know and defined the field when the Philippine Studies Program was developed in the 1970s? The field was after all, already embedded within the critical-analytical tradition in that it was clearly anti-colonial, progressive, steeped in political economy, but being rapidly cross-pollinated by other interdisciplinary perspectives. Or am I doing Philippine diasporic studies? Or am I doing Philippine transnationalism studies more broadly? Are these three initially distinct fields that started from different directions now converging and dissolving into one common sphere? What new species has their cross-pollination generated? And what roles have transplanted academics like me and the second- and third-generation academics of Filipino ancestry been playing in spawning, grafting, re-grafting, and reproducing these fields? Are we cultivating the traditional seedlings of academic inquiry framed by Philippine-driven questions and Philippine-generated urgencies, or are we promoting the high-yielding, genetically modified organisms germinated in Canadian multicultural, multiethnic laboratories, or are we interbreeding these varieties to create new knowledge organisms?

In the Philippine context in the 1970s–1980s, Philippine studies as a field developed as a multidisciplinary (note: not inter- or trans-) field of scholarship led by faculty researchers from Philippine studies, anthropology, political science, sociology, psychology, and Asian studies – many of whom shared similar political views towards the Marcos dictatorship and the neocolonial relations with the United States. At the University of the Philippines, the program was initially based at the old College of Arts and Science (CAS) before it was restructured in 1984 into three separate colleges: Science, Social Science and Philosophy, and Arts and Letters (where Philippine studies was later housed). The institutional site of knowledge production of what could be called nascent Philippine transnationalism studies came, not from the various College teaching units, but from the research arm of CAS – the Third World Studies Centre, founded in 1977, whose fellows were drawn from various disciplines. The Centre was the first to develop a long-term research agenda on transnationalization of export commodities, the transnational technocratic elite, overseas labour migration, and global commodity chain studies. Researchers doing studies on Filipino construction workers in the Middle East, domestic workers in Hong Kong or Singapore, entertainers in Japan, and mail-order brides in Australia or Germany, given their permanent residential location in the Philippines, initially tend not cast their research as falling within Philippine diasporic studies. This is understandable, given the original association of the term 'diaspora' with dispersed communities in exile (e.g., Jewish, Armenian) that long for an eventual return to a homeland yet to be constituted (see Polvorosa in this volume), in contrast to the temporary or contract nature of Filipino overseas employment. Since the 1990s, the use of the term 'diaspora' has become more common to refer more loosely to various categories of returning, circular, chain, and permanent (im)migrants. Still, there are migration studies programs within academic institutions (e.g., Miriam's College) and non-government research organization (e.g., SCALABRINI), but they have yet to evolve into diasporic studies.

Antecedent Scholarships and Debates

The five chapters could be well situated within Philippine transnational and diasporic studies, given their emphasis on Filipino permanent residents and temporary workers. The writers' own positionalities (e.g., Canadian-born second generation, Philippine-born first generation) and locations in multicultural Toronto, Hamilton, or Vancouver, as well as their erstwhile travels as émigrés (e.g., permanent resident, live-in caregiver, or international student), enable them to speak comfortably of 'diasporic' spaces, identities, and desires. Their writings also demonstrate shifts in theoretical approaches and analytical perspectives that have challenged the social sciences and interdisciplinary studies in recent decades.

The Philippines and the Southeast Asian region have been very productive sites of scholarship that generated many landmark works considered trail-blazers in their time. Southeast Asian peasant and industrial labour studies exploded in the 1950s–1960s largely because of the agrarian crises, labour unrest, and insurgency problems that peaked during the Cold War. The rather heavy focus on structural and class determinism, shaped by Marxist analysis in many of these studies, found a refreshing rebuttal in James Scott's analysis (1985) of the 'weapons of the weak' and their 'hidden transcripts.' Shaped by his fieldwork on the peasantry in Malaysia, his thesis influenced many postcolonial and feminist scholarly writings about the interplay of politics, structures, and agency in everyday life in Southeast Asia (e.g., Hart et al. 1989; Hart 1991; Kerkvliet 1990; Ong and Peletz 1995; Wolf 1992).

By the late 1970s and 1980s, as neoliberal market-oriented development reached ideological and organizational maturity, Southeast Asianists were producing voluminous works on the role of the state and the bourgeoisie in development, particularly the contributions of local entrepreneurs and domestic capitalists in the East Asian 'economic miracle.' Some of these materials (e.g., Deyo 1987; McIntyre 1994; McVey 1992; Yoshihara 1988) examined the dynamics of 'state penetration,' 'crony capitalism,' 'rent-seeking,' and 'neo-patrimonialism' of elite families, the internal structure of the domestic capitalist class, the interlocking directorates, kinship and family connections in huge corporations, and their connections with transnational elites and foreign capital. Most of these works were silent on the role of migration, migrants, and migrant communities and the contributions of their economic and social remittances. By the 1990s, there emerged a parallel body of literature (e.g., Robison and Goodman 1996; Sen and Stivens 1998) on the 'new rich' and emergent middle classes in Asia, placing more emphasis on how migration and social remittances in the region influenced local identities, consumption patterns, and ideologies, shaped by what geography of migration and diaspora researchers earlier call 'transnational social fields' or 'transnational social space' that transcend national territories and geographic boundaries (Basch et al. 1994; Massey 1984). These studies opened up new vistas on the relationships between structure and agency, individuals and society, and hope and fatalism within the spaces of engagement and scholarship in the Philippines and Southeast Asia.

I situate these five chapters within this long scholarly tradition of analysing how structures and agency connect in non-linear ways, how society and individuals shape each other, and what prospects lie ahead as academics ponder past trends and future directions. Note that three of the chapters (Davidson, Eric, Tungohan) deal with the Live-In Caregiver Program (LCP) and the people and agencies implicated in this program, whereas two (Damasco, Polvorosa) tackle professionals in the fields of nursing and business. Of the three chapters on Live-In Caregivers, one examines the possibilities for their political engagement in their host country (Tungohan), another examines Filipinas' socialization within the LCP, which sets the stage for their labour market segmentation (Eric), and the third considers consequences for family reunification and possibilities for fulfilling the desired 'better' middle-class life in Canada (Davidson). One of the two chapters on Filipino professionals in Canada focuses on the significance of ethnic enterprises in place making and identity construction of Filipino business professionals in Toronto (Polvorosa), while the other provides a historical analysis of the organized recruitment and communication transactions involving Filipino healthcare professionals in Ontario (Damasco).

I will discuss each of these binaries cum explanatory propositions, and position the five chapters along the continuum between holism and methodological individualism, structure and agency, optimism and pessimism, while highlighting an interesting conversation between them on the nature and structure of the Philippine and Canadian states and governments, and the construction of Filipino diasporic identities in Canadian society.

Between Structure and Agency, Society and Individual

The five chapters have grappled directly or indirectly with academic debate on structure-agency relationships, or the dualism of society and the individual, determinism and voluntarism – one of the most established dualisms in social theory. As Giddens (1979) argues, the structure-agency relationship cannot be explained by the simple opposition between (social) determinism and (individual or collective) voluntarism, nor can their opposition be overcome by bringing these two rival perspectives together. Instead we must develop an institutional analysis and analysis of power and social change that provide 'an adequate account of human agency [that] must, first, be connected to a theory of the acting subject; and second, must situate action in *time* and *space,* as a continuous flow of conduct rather than treating purposes, reasons, etc. as somehow aggregated together' (2, emphasis in original). Giddens underscores the interdependence of action/agency and structure/system, and the need to examine the *'time-space relations inherent in the constitution of all social interaction'* (ibid.). In place of the dualisms of society/structure/determinism and individual/agency/voluntarism, he proposes a *theory of structuration* based on the 'central notion of the *duality of structures.'* Structure is considered as 'both a medium and outcome of the reproduction of practices' that 'enters simultaneously into the constitution of the agent and social practices, and "exists" in the generating moments of this constitution' (5). All five chapters, without making explicit their theory of social action and practices, follow the above notion of duality of structures, although at times they also tend to violate some of its basic propositions. There are sections, for example, where some of the authors could have been more explicit in articulating historical nuances and spatial analytic comparisons (e.g., provincial and/or rural-urban variations), as well as the role of other Canadian social practices besides multiculturalism and racialized labour recruitment (e.g., educational policies, popular culture, media representation, public discourses) that enter into subjectivities and constitution of agents they examined.

Following classical political economy and critical feminist analysis, Eric, Damasco, Davidson, and Tungohan render the 'structural' and 'agentive,' the 'economic' and 'social,' the 'material' and 'representational' as integrated in their analysis of gendered migration. Polvorosa likewise scrutinizes the limitations of traditional analyses of ethnic business enterprises that tended to focus on their 'economics' or their 'culture,' shown in their interests in viability and competitiveness or the level of their social capital, networks, and values. And yet, the writers of these chapters differ in their explanation and understanding of structure-agency interaction and their examination of time-space relations in social interaction. To Eric, the LCP represents ideologically a double-edged rite of passage: an escape from poverty in the Philippines and an entry to precarious living and working conditions in Canada. Tungohan, in contrast, debunks the victimhood narrative embedded in many accounts of the LCP, while offering possibilities for their political engagement.

Eric, Tungohan, and Davidson provide a similar reading of the 'hegemonic-ideological-representational' in their chapters. They implicitly understand hegemonic ideologies as products of the capacity of dominant classes and institutions (e.g., states, private recruitment agencies, middle- and upper-class employers) to make their interests appear universal or beneficial to many. All three scholars are clear in their support of domestic workers as potential and real Canadian citizen-subjects, not as disposable foreign workers. This is most clear in Eric's call for policy changes to improve the status of LCP workers, particularly in enabling them to access the services of immigrant settlement agencies. Eric's chapter confirms Damasco's findings that earlier cohorts of Filipina nurses and domestic workers lead more successful and well-integrated lives than recent arrivals. Although cautioned by an 'old-timer' to keep her 'shameful' past as a nanny a secret, as she is 'already successful,' Eric uses her 'in-between position' to uncover the differences in the rites of passage – marked by education, professional preparation, prior overseas work experience, entry status, and first employment in Canada – between earlier and newer cohorts of Filipina immigrants, best exemplified in the contrasting lives of Delia and Madonna.

All five chapters recognize that migrants and live-in caregivers, as social actors, are still knowledgeable about the social structures and systems which they constitute and reproduce in their action. But this knowledge and consciousness need to be carefully elucidated. While simultaneously arguing that live-in caregivers themselves are free agents, Eric attributes their agency to the superpower-overseer-gatekeeper role of the state and the mediation of private recruitment agencies: 'in the Live-In Caregiver Program (LCP), there are no agreements between states, and the sending and receiving countries are not involved. Rather, private employment agencies mediate the flow of caregivers. Consequently, Canada saves costs as labour and migration gatekeeping move from the state to private agencies. Canada's shift in its gatekeeping role is in line with its alignment to neoliberal policies and its restructuring of the welfare state' (127).

Parallel to Eric's elucidation of caregivers' agency and conciousness amid neo-liberal restructuring, Davidson brings agency and consciousness even closer, under the microscopic within the home and household. She acknowledges the perceptions, discursive consciousness (i.e., the knowledge people express at the level of discourse, or their 'hidden transcripts'), and strategies (i.e., 'the inventive practices and rationales' such as 'commensuration' considered as 'an exercise in power through its capacity to efface particular ways of knowing') of live-in caregivers working within the homes of their Filipino Canadian family members who differentiate *domestic worker* and *domestic helper* to make sense of the regulatory and exploitative conditions they experience under the LCP. Cognizant of the social knowledge and agency of temporary migrant workers, Tungohan, like Davidson, argues that Filipina live-in caregivers are not compliant 'modern-day slaves,' but are full political agents who do not allow their non-citizenship status to hinder their political participation in Canada. By showing how live-in caregivers' political activism criticizes prevailing notions of political participation, now extended to non-citizens, she considers the ways in which civil society action was decisive in implementing changes to the LCP.

Of the five chapters, Damasco's, Tungohan's, and Davidson's provide perhaps the most careful and consistent analysis following the Giddensian plea to examine the 'time-space relations inherent in the constitution of all social interaction.' Davidson, Eric, Tungohan, and Damasco have the most explicit analysis of the temporal dimension of social relations and practices, while Polvorosa has the most pronounced analysis of their spatial dimension. Analysing the links between space and identities, Polvorosa contends that the study of ethnic businesses established in a diasporic and multicultural spaces like Toronto can help us examine the constructions of identity, particularly how Filipino business owners negotiate and construct their national identities and contribute to place making. Davidson examines the difficulty of spatial and temporal separation of leisure and work, which do not have clear-cut boundaries in the everyday lives of live-in caregivers. Eric, in her data analysis, examines how the timing of migration and the immigration category used to enter Canada create different outcomes for women. Tired of functional explanations that frame Filipino migration within the context of 'global economies' and the 'economic logic' of unequal exchange, Damasco provides an alternative historically sensitive analysis that examines the mechanisms of migration, specifically through a systematic and well-organized recruitment scheme that revealed how dependent Canada was on Philippine skilled professional labour in the 1960s. Tungohan's chapter provides a similar analysis in its historical examination. Her account of the political-philosophical foundations of political engagement of non-citizens could be enriched by more empirical data gained from actual interviews and ethnographic research.

Between Holism and Methodological Individualism

The debate on the merits and pitfalls of holism and methodological individualism has preoccupied thinkers since Thomas Hobbes and the Enlightenment, as well as more recent scholars in the social sciences and philosophy (Lukes 1968, 119). Holism, or methodological collectivism, accords greater priority to collective phenomena in any explanation, whereas methodological individualism accords importance to individual actions, motives, and purpose. This dualism is best explained in the following summary:

> When the individualist contends that only individuals are responsible actors on the social and historical stage, the holist retorts that society is more than a collection of individuals ... To the holists ... people's aims do not constitute a society but rather depend on society. The individualist [sees] ... the social setting ... as explicable in terms of human action. The holist argues in turn that human action does not determine, but is rather constrained by, or is directed by, the social setting (perhaps because social forces are much stronger than any single individual). (Agassi 1960, 244)

This debate has been resurrected in the works associated with Analytic Marxism (e.g., Cohen 1978; Elster 1985; Roemer 1982a, 1982b). Gidden's own theory of structuration offers a strong variety of methodological individualism when he argues in favour of non-functionalist theories: 'Social systems have no purpose, reasons or needs, whatsoever; only individuals do. *Any explanation which imputes teleology to social systems must be declared invalid*' (Giddens 1979, 7, emphasis in original). More recent writings on this debate, however, contend that there is no necessary conflict between the two approaches, as there are different versions of both, and some versions combine the elements from both, given similarities in the insights generated by thinkers from both camps (Udehn 2001). Hence,

> the main divide is between strong versions of methodological individualism, which suggest that all social phenomena should be explained only in terms of individuals and their interaction, and weak versions of methodological individualism, which also assign an important role to social institutions and/or social structure in social science explanations. (Udehn 2002, 479)

Of the five, Damasco, Polvorosa, and Davidson demonstrate a strong variety of methodological individualism, whereas Eric and Tungohan follow a weaker form. Eric's bifurcated analysis demonstrates an attempt to straddle between holism, when she explains the reasons for migration in the form of structural determinism, and methodological individualism, when she presents her interview data.

Contrary to studies that emphasized the liberalization of Canadian immigration policies and the Philippine state's labour export policy, Damasco contends that the migration of Philippine-trained health professionals to Ontario in the 1960s was the outcome of very specific institutions and mechanisms (e.g., recruitment schemes) run and used by individuals connected with the Philippine and Canadian healthcare, educational, and governmental institutions, and Canadian professional regulatory bodies and travel agencies. She argues for the need to examine *when* and *why* Filipino professionals immigrated to Canada during specific periods, and *which* policies, practices, and processes facilitated their migration and the post-1970s dramatic shift from professionalization to deprofessionalization.

Polvorosa argues that the motives and intentions of members of the Filipino diaspora cannot be separated from colonial and capitalist histories while using these as a backdrop to focus on individual choices, motives, and circumstances. Using interviews with Filipino business owners in Toronto, he uncovers how ethnic pride and identity become a motivating factor for the business, thus linking ethnic pride and entrepreneurship, which becomes 'an institutionalized response to the loss of status that results from de-skilling and deprofessionalization of the immigrants and the perception of a blocked mobility in the job market.' His analytical approach follows the tenets of methodological individualism by analysing the perspectives of the Filipino entrepreneurs, complemented by views of employees and clients. The research methods (i.e., life histories, interviews) used in the chapters by Davidson, Eric, and Polvorosa easily lend themselves to methodological individualism. Yet, this methodological approach could be weaker or stronger, depending on whether one gives prominence to individual actions and intentions, or to social systems. Ultimately, one cannot make a holistic, integrated, and comprehensive analysis without accounting for the dialectic or interplay between structures and agency, individuals and systems, histories and biographies.

Gender is a central organizing concept of migration. All chapters mention the relevance of gender in their analyses of social differences, and yet, there is much room to bring this more centrally into the discussion of diasporic and migrant identities, ideologies, place making, and lived experience, especially in Polvorosa's chapter. His conscious use of the term 'business owners' instead of the more common 'businessmen' could be further queried in terms of the relative position and market share of female and male entrepreneurs within the Filipino diaspora in Toronto. This question is especially relevant, given overall statistical data on Canadian immigration showing that men predominate in the category of 'primary applicants' or 'sponsors' while women and children dominate the 'family-class' and 'dependents' category (Statistics Canada 2009). Are these businesses to be seen as 'family businesses' – a term that might obscure the actual labour and financial investments of members – or are the owners to be seen as 'self-employed entrepreneurs' who rely on occasional family help and pooling of income from other sources?

As Clifford (1994) notes, diasporic experiences are always gendered, and discussions of diaspora and people's journeys in unmarked terrains serve to normalize male experiences. Similarly, Pratt and Yeoh (2003) point out that concepts such as 'hyper-mobility' and 'transnational flows' that are dominant in globalization and transnationalism studies are implicitly gendered and often read as masculinist.

> In traversing transnational space, men often feature as entrepreneurs, career-builders, adventurers and breadwinners who navigate transnational circuits with fluidity and ease, while women are alternatively taken to be truants from globalised economic webs, stereotyped as exotic, subservient or victimised, or relegated to playing supporting roles, usually in the domestic sphere. (Pratt and Yeoh 2003, 159)

Gender relations, along with class and race hierarchy, may be transformed in transnational social, political, and cultural spaces, as migrants form and reform their identity. There are a number of potent openings for such transformative changes to take place. First, transnational migration potentially subverts one of the fundamental premises of capitalist globalization, namely, that labour stays local, whereas capital's range is global (Portes et al. 1999). Second, transnational migration creates opportunities and necessities to challenge unfair social structures in both home and host countries (Basch et al. 1994). Lastly, transnational migration creates cross-border networks that may help migrants build economic success in a new country as well as cushion the effect of discrimination they experience as minorities (Portes 2001), outcomes already stressed in the chapters by Polvorosa and Tungohan. And yet, optimistic analyses of transformation in new transnational spaces are tempered by findings in many case studies – ranging from the study of Haitian immigrants in the United States (Fouron and Glick-Schiller 2001), pan-Chinese business connections (Ong 1999), Thai women in transnational marriages (Angeles and Sunanta 2009), migrant domestic workers from Sri Lanka (Gamburd 2000), and children of Filipino migrant workers (Parreñas 2005) – which suggest that while transnationalism both transforms and reinforces existing gender relations, it is premature to assume that gender hierarchy will be destabilized in transnational spaces.

Between Optimism and Pessimism

The divide between optimism and pessimism is not the main concern of the five chapters. Hence, positioning their take on this divide is based on my interpretation of their prognoses and predictions. Damasco's initial motivation to do her research was born out of a desire to question the 'collective amnesia' behind our ignorance of earlier histories of migration, and to challenge the long-held stereotypes and misconceptions about Filipino women, in particular, and the history of Filipino immigration, in general. Eric's bleak historical account of women's migration and the equally dim employment prospects of some of her research subjects was followed by clear and pointed recommendations on how to make the lives of immigrant women better. I read them both as a form of 'pessimism of the intellect' tempered by the 'optimism of the will' to contribute to social change. Polvorosa, on the other hand, began with an optimistic and celebratory account of Filipino entrepreneurship-as-resistance to de-skilling and deprofessionalization, but ended his chapter with 'The Filipino firm therefore functions as more than the source of livelihood for newly arrived immigrants. The ethnic enterprise may represent a transitory stage in the career trajectories of many immigrant Filipino entrepreneurs and employees. As gleaned from many of the interviews, for entrepreneurs, the challenge to grow their firms is to enter the mainstream market' (196). This reveals a measured optimism over the possibility of eventual entry of Filipino entrepreneurs into the mainstream commercial and financial capital markets in Canada.

Davidson's chapter celebrates optimism in the discursive consciousness and 'inventive practices and rationales' of Filipinos 'within a domain of hope,' a strategy to transcend LCP restrictions and experience middle-class life in Canada. Tungohan's chapter positions itself as an optimistic piece in stressing how live-in caregivers become active in forms of political engagement that draw attention to the liberal contradictions of the LCP through their political activism. One outcome of this activism is the recent reform of this program, including the Tejada Law (named after Juana Tejada, who campaigned tirelessly for the passage of the law before she succumbed to cancer), which enables live-in caregivers to apply for permanent residence without being required to undergo a second medical examination. Yet, the collective power and voice of domestic workers and other temporary foreign labourers remain to be seen. Indeed, immigrant women and other minority voices are beginning to be heard in Canada (Andrew 2008); but as Ong (1999) argues, they are still less influential in state policy than transnational corporations and capitalists.

Conclusion: Place, Privilege, and Identity Formation

The level of personal disclosure in these chapters by the five researchers range from Eric's sharing her own experience as a former caregiver, to Polvorosa's admission of his status as a recent immigrant, and Damasco's intimate familial and kin relations with the nurses she interviewed. These experiences all affected their respective research. Their chapters share a common passionate tone, tempered by academic analysis, and at times are punctuated by surprises, identification with their subjects, and frustration over de-skilling and retrogressive policies. Only Davidson and Tungohan are silent in positioning themselves vis-à-vis their research topics. One can only guess why this is so, especially in this day and age of postmodern pleas for self-reflexivity and the popular use of autoethnographic narratives to locate oneself in the research.

Like Eleanor Ty (in this volume), I have met many Filipinas who, like Daisy, have mistaken me for a fellow domestic worker or live-in nanny. This automatic association of Filipina identity with this job designation is so ingrained in the minds of many that my friendly and well-meaning question, 'So, what do you do here?' – an attempt to decouple identity from job assignation – was once seen as inappropriate. One *kababayan* responded with, *'Nagtanong ka pa. E di ano pa, nanny?'* (Why did you even have to ask? Nanny, what else?)

The question 'What do you do?' is often asked in Canadian circles not only as a way of slotting you into the social class hierarchy, but also as a way of social networking that places value on work-derived identities. In a society where one's work is not only the source of income and life satisfaction, but also the basis of status and estimation of your education and residential neighbourhood, *not* to ask that question and assume that the Filipina before us must be a nanny, or a former nanny, not only insults our own collective intelligences, but also perpetuates the intragroup racialized stereotyping discussed in these five chapters. If identity formation is indeed tied to power and privilege (or lack thereof) as well as to specific places and spaces, then all five chapters have done great service to Philippine diasporic and transnationalism studies in Canada by illuminating the mechanisms and dynamics of diasporic (trans)formations induced by increasing transnational linkages between Canada, the Philippines, and the rest of the world. These chapters collectively provide the next generation of scholars in Canada, and elsewhere, who are interested in Philippine-Canadian linkages, a good reason indeed to celebrate and be optimistic about the future where we will no longer be haunted by the spectre of in/visibility. Their potential contributions to alternative policy uptake and to activist social movements will hopefully make Filipinos in Canada a more visible and decisive social and political force.

REFERENCES

Agassi, Joseph. 1960. Methodological individualism. *British Journal of Sociology* 11 (3): 244–70.

Andrew, Caroline, et al., eds. 2008. *Electing a diverse Canada: The representation of immigrants, minorities and women.* Vancouver: University of British Columbia Press.

Angeles, Leonora. 2001. The Filipino male as macho-*machunurin:* Bringing men and masculinities in gender and development studies in the Philippines. *Kasarinlan Journal of Third World Studies* 16 (1): 9–30.

Angeles, Leonora, and Sirijit Sunanta. 2009. Demanding daughter duty: Gender, community, village transformation and transnational marriages in northeastern Thailand. *Critical Asian Studies* 41 (4): 549–74.

Basch, Linda, Nina Glick-Schiller, and Christina Szanton. 1994. *Nations unbound: Transnational projects, postcolonial predicaments, and deterritorialized nation states.* Langhorne, PA: Gordon and Breach.

Clifford, James. 1994. Diasporas. *Cultural Anthropology* 9 (3): 302–38.

Cohen, Gerald Allan. 1978. *Karl Marx's theory of history: A defence.* Princeton: Princeton University Press.

Deyo, Frederic. 1987. *The political economy of the new Asian industrialism.* Ithaca: Cornell University Press.

Elster, Jon. 1985. *Making sense of Marx.* Cambridge: Cambridge University Press.

Fouron, Georges, and Nina Glick-Schiller. 2001. All in the family: Gender, transnational migration and the nation state. *Identities: Global Studies in Culture and Power* 7 (4): 539–82.

Gamburd, Michele R. 2000. *The kitchen spoon's handle: Transnationalism and Sri Lanka's migrant housemaids.* Ithaca: Cornell University Press.

Giddens, Anthony. 1979. *Central problems in social theory: Action, structure and contradiction in social analysis.* Berkeley: University of California Press.

Hart, Gillian. 1991. Engendering everyday resistance: Gender, patronage and production politics in rural Malaysia. *Journal of Peasant Studies* 19 (1): 93–121.

Hart, Gillian, Andrew Turton, and Benjamin White, with Brian Fegan and Lim Teck Ghee, eds. 1989. *Agrarian transformation: Local processes and the state in Southeast Asia.* Berkeley: University of California Press.

Kerkvliet, Benedict. 1990. *Everyday politics in the Philippines: Class and status relations in a central Luzon village.* Berkeley: University of California Press.

Lukes, Steven. 1968. Methodological individualism reconsidered. *British Journal of Sociology* 19 (2): 119–29.

Massey, Doris. 1984. *Spatial divisions of labour: Social structures and the geography of production.* London: Macmillan.

McIntyre, Andrew, ed. 1994. *Business and government in industrializing Asia.* Ithaca: Cornell University Press.

McVey, Ruth, ed. 1992. *Southeast Asian capitalists.* Ithaca: Cornell University Southeast Asia Program.

Ong, Aihwa. 1999. *Flexible citizenship: The cultural logics of transnationality.* Durham, NC: Duke University Press.

Ong, Aihwa, and Michael Peletz. 1995. *Bewitching women, pious men: Gender and body politics in Southeast Asia.* Berkeley: University of California Press.

Parreñas, Rhacel Salazar. 2005. *Children of global migration: Transnational families and gender woes.* Stanford: Stanford University Press.

Portes, Alejandro. 2001. Introduction: The debates and significance of immigrant transnationalism. *Global Networks* 1 (3): 181–94.

Portes, Alejandro, Luis. E. Guarnizo, and Patricia Landolt. 1999. The study of transnationalism: Pitfalls and promise of an emergent research field. *Ethnic and Racial Studies* 22 (2): 217–37.

Pratt, Geraldine, and Brenda S.A. Yeoh. 2003. Transnational (counter) topographies. *Gender, Place and Culture* 10 (2): 159–66.

Robison, Richard, and David S.G. Goodman, eds. 1996. *The new rich in Asia.* London and New York: Routledge.

Roemer, John. 1982a. *A general theory of exploitation and class.* Cambridge, MA: Harvard University Press.
– 1982b. Methodological individualism and deductive Marxism. *Theory and Society* 11: 513–20.
Scott, James. 1985. *Weapons of the weak: Everyday forms of everyday resistance.* New Haven: Yale University Press.
Sen, Khrishna, and Maila Stivens. 1998. *Gender and power in affluent Asia.* London and New York: Routledge.
Statistics Canada. 2009. Facts and figures 2008 – Immigration overview: Permanent and temporary residents. http://www.cic.gc.ca/english/ resources/statistics/facts2008/permanent/05.asp.
Udehn, Lars. 2001. *Methodological individualism: Background, history and meaning.* New York: Routledge.
– 2002. The changing face of methodological individualism. *Annual Review of Sociology* 28: 479–507.
Wolf, Diane. 1992. *Factory daughters.* Berkeley: University of California Press.
Yoshihara, Kunio. 1988. *The rise of ersatz capitalism in Southeast Asia.* Singapore: Oxford University Press.

PART THREE

Representation and Its Discontents

Balikbayan Express (acrylic on canvas)
Celia Correa

Artist Statement

Celia Correa

Darna, the most popular Filipina comic superhero, is on a mission to deliver a balikbayan (back to country) box to a family in the Philippines. Sending these boxes (full of clothes, shoes, canned goods, etc.) to relatives and family in the homeland is a ritual performed by most Filipinos overseas. Each item in the box is picked with care, love, and anticipation of joy. The image explores the migrant realities of how distances and absences are lived and transformed in concrete and idealistic terms.

Chapter 10

Meet Me in Toronto: The Re-exhibition of Artifacts from the 1904 Louisiana Purchase Exposition at the Royal Ontario Museum

BONNIE MCELHINNY

I have traveled to every part of the United States and I have been saddened to learn how many misapprehensions exist here as to the real conditions in the Philippine Islands, due, probably as much as anything else, to the exhibition of the native Igorrote village at the St. Louis Exposition ten years ago. (Then Philippine Resident Commissioner Manuel Quezon, cited in Fermin 2004, 202)

Introduction

In 1904 the United States mounted a World's Fair in St Louis, Missouri, popularly memorialized in the movie *Meet Me in St. Louis* starring Judy Garland. One of the fair's most popular, and controversial, features was the Philippine exhibit, a twenty-hectare section with five 'tribal' villages in which 1,100 Filipinos lived for the duration of the fair in a human-zoo setting, demonstrating arts and crafts, selling products, and being observed in their daily lives. At the fair's end, the artifacts were sold to notable U.S. cultural institutions. A largely unknown part of the story is the afterlife of some of these artifacts in Canada. By 1910, a University of Toronto zoologist, Ramsay Wright (1933), had purchased several hundred of them for the university. When the Royal Ontario Museum (ROM) split from the University of Toronto, they were stored in its collections, until the fall of 2008, when curator Trudy Nicks mounted what is the first known re-exhibition of these artifacts in over a hundred years.

In this chapter, I trace the history of the debates about the fair, and then discuss the politics of representation encoded in the new exhibition. I argue that the exhibit, while challenging some of the racist and evolutionary narratives of its predecessor, is nonetheless still caught within, rather than transcending, the arguments and structures of the earlier exhibit. Moreover, I argue that the new exhibit largely foregrounds issues of culture over discussions of race and imperialism, which simultaneously allows for a depiction of the Philippines as primitive and contributes in contradictory ways to a hegemonic and celebratory narrative of official Canadian multiculturalism.

The St Louis Fair and the Philippine Reservation

The 1904 Lousiana Purchase Exposition

The six-month-long World's Fair in St Louis commemorated the hundredth anniversary of the Louisiana Purchase (Rydell 1984, 157). It attempted to portray the recent overseas imperial actions of the United States in the Philippines, Cuba, Puerto Rico, Hawai'i, and Guam as part of its manifest destiny. The Louisiana Purchase territory was meant to serve as a historical model for how society had evolved from a wilderness populated by primitive savages to its current civilized state. Indeed, the two physical endpoints of the fair were the Indian School Building and the Philippines display. The exposition was, at 1,270 acres, the largest international exposition the world had ever seen, attracting nineteen million visitors.[1] During the fair, four hundred meetings occurred in St Louis, including the Olympics, the national Democratic and Republican conventions, and the annual meeting of the National Education Association, exposing an array of political, educational, and cultural leaders to the fair exhibits (Breitbart 1997, 36).

The Lousiana Purchase Exposition was distinguished by having the most extensive anthropology department of any World's Fair. It included the participation and exhibition of roughly two thousand indigenous people. People of colour were displayed as craftsmen, curiosities, trophies, and objects for scientific study, while White people, when in exhibits, were generally displayed as technicians and workers. Approximately twelve hundred of the people displayed were Filipinos. The second largest group was First Nations. Other groups displayed included the Ainu from Japan and African pygmies. The fair was meant as a summary of existing knowledge in all fields, structured within a narrative of Social Darwinism. It asked questions about whether newly occupied territories should be colonies, states, or independent territories, and whether the people in captured territories could be civilized.

To White Americans disoriented by imperialism, industrialization, and consumerism, and at a moment when labour action was at its peak (there were two hundred strikes against the exposition company alone during the construction of the fair), the White working class – the intended audience for the exhibition – was also being tutored in racial unity and White supremacy.

W.J. McGee, a former anthropologist at the Bureau of American Ethnology and the director of the fair's anthropology exhibit, had developed the social evolutionary theories that underlay the fair in his 1899 article 'The Trend of Human Progress.' He divided people into four racial groups: savage, barbaric, civilized, and enlightened. The first two were meant to distinguish between peoples of colour that he felt could not be civilized and those who could. The last two were meant to distinguish White ethnic populations from southern and eastern Europe from Anglo-Saxons. Deploying languages of scientific objectivity (compare Anderson 1995), he argued that the driving forces behind social evolution were *cephalization* (the gradual increase in the cranial capacity of different races) and *cheirization* (the gradual increase of manual dexterity along racial lines). He suggested that mental and manual abilities increased as one moved up the ladder of civilization. Displaying Native Americans, Ainus, or Filipinos making baskets or carving did not simply show how products were made, but the particular evolutionary niche such groups were purported to inhabit. The emphasis on manual dexterity dovetailed with a pedagogical focus on vocational education for Filipinos (May 1980), which in turn suggested that they would have a place similar to that mapped out for African and Native Americans as manual labourers within burgeoning industrial capitalist systems.

The Philippine Reservation

The Philippine Reservation (and the name marked a further continuity with Native issues) covered more space (forty-seven acres) than that used for several previous international expositions. Its cost of $1 million was funded by the U.S. government and the colonial administration, both of which believed it had a crucial role in influencing Americans' attitudes towards the new colonial possession. It was organized into three cultural spheres, depicting the civilizing influence of the Spanish past, the current ethnological state of the islands, and benefits expected from the U.S. takeover (Rydell 1984, 170).

Groups within the Philippine Reservation were organized according to the same evolutionary narrative that structured the exposition, one consistent with the 'benevolent assimilation' ideology of the U.S. colonial government. Filipinos were displayed on a continuum from least civilized (Negritos and Igorots) to semi-civilized (Bagobos and Moros) to civilized (Visayans, the Constabulary, and Scout Organizations). Although signs around the exhibit noted that 'true savages' (U.S. anthropologists placed Igorots, Moros, Bagobos, and Negritos in this group) made up only one-seventh of the population in the Philippines, and although the largest group of Filipinos at the fair were the seven hundred members of the Constabulary and Scouts, the exhibits overwhelmingly concentrated on the groups deemed 'savage.' Negritos were portrayed as the missing link between apes and humans, even more primitive than the African pygmies who occupied this slot in European fairs.

The most popular attraction at the fair was the Igorot village, in part because of the controversies associated with it. The minimal clothing of Igorots was a subject of fascination for the press, and became a preoccupation of pro-imperialist forces. The Roosevelt administration became concerned that furor over the absence of clothing could undermine the government's efforts to show the possibility for progress, and might throw an upcoming presidential election to anti-imperialist forces. The president issued an edict requiring clothing, which was ridiculed in the press and critiqued by anthropologists concerned about compromising the scientific value of the exhibit. Another controversy was about dog-eating, a stereotype which arose at this fair and is persistently attached to Filipinos (Choy 2003; Hagedorn 1990). Although dog-eating was associated with ritual practice among certain mountain-dwelling groups, it was presented at the fair as a daily habit, and Filipinos were unjustly blamed for the disappearance of St Louis dogs during the fair.

By portraying the Philippine islands as a jumble of tribes, U.S. administrators meant to suggest that Filipinos were not capable of governing themselves. Dean Worcester, a former zoology professor and secretary of the interior in the colonial government from 1900 to 1913, divided the country's eight million inhabitants into eighty-four tribes (twenty-one Negrito, sixteen Indonesian, and forty-seven Malayan) (cited in Breitbart 1997, 54). Challenges from Filipino elites noted that the Philippines was less ethnically heterogeneous than the United States, and that groups that ethnologists portrayed as distinct tribes were often merely separated by living in different places and/or by speaking related but dissimilar languages. Many elite Filipinos, and some Americans, protested that the racist representations of Filipinos as savage barbarians was a dishonest attempt to justify U.S. imperial rule.

Filipino elites were never convinced that it was in their interests to participate in the Exposition, in part because of bitter memories of ilustrado encounters with earlier such expositions under the Spanish regime. In 1887, Filipino Propagandists had been scandalized by the display of Igorots at the Madrid exposition (Kramer 1999, 90; Scott 1975). Indeed, early protests by Filipino elites led to the inclusion of an honorary commission as part of the final exhibit plan to ensure that Filipinos were not represented only by what Taft called the 'wild and uncivilized tribes' (Kramer 1999, 102). A board of forty-two lawyers, physicians, landowners, and politicians had a nationwide tour, purportedly to study the conditions of the U.S. cities with the aim of replicating the same, before arriving in St Louis. The Exposition was immediately denounced by the group's leading figures, who argued it was shrewd political work to emphasize one million 'backward and non-progressive races,' at the cost of seven million civilized Christians (cited in Kramer 1999, 103).

The Afterlife of the Fair

At the fair's end, artifacts were sold to prominent U.S. cultural institutions, including the Smithsonian Institution and the Philadelphia Commercial Museum. The American Museum of Natural History in New York City purchased the entire Philippine Ethnological Collection, and staged a Philippine Hall until 1961. Some of the materials remain on display in the museum's Hall of Pacific Peoples (Fermin 2004, 194).

Elite Filipinos were so outraged that the Philippine legislature passed a law in 1908 prohibiting the exposition of tribal people, except those who were customarily fully clothed. In 1914 further legislation was passed penalizing those who exhibited or exploited tribal people (Fermin 2004, 200). Nonetheless, because of the popularity of the Filipino exhibit in St Louis, tribal peoples were displayed throughout the United States and Europe, including the Lewis and Clark Centennial and American Pacific Exposition and Oriental Fair in Portland in 1905, the Alaska-Yukon-Pacific exposition in Seattle in 1909, the Ghent Exhibition in Belgium in 1913, and the Panama-Pacific International Exposition in San Francisco in 1915. Some participants in the St Louis Exposition were said to have joined a troupe that toured the United

States, performing at world expositions, state fairs, and amusement parks.

The fair's influence extended well beyond the actual six months that it was open. Most crucially for this chapter, in the fall of 2008, a new exhibit, 'The Philippines at the 1904 World's Fair in St. Louis/Les Philippines à l'exposition universelle de St. Louis, 1904,' was installed on the third floor of the new Michael Lee Chin Crystal at the Royal Ontario Museum. The crystal was funded by a donation from the Chin family, and is widely touted as a symbol of immigrant contributions to Canada.

The ROM Exhibit

This relatively modest exhibit in the Royal Ontario Museum is in the section entitled 'Africa, Americas, Asia Pacific, Middle East, South Africa,' which is to the right as one comes up the stairs from the very popular dinosaur exhibit. To the left is 'Europe and Twentieth-Century Design.' The areal groupings convey, as Rafael (1994, 1999) notes in critical discussions of area studies, a construction between a presumed European self and racialized others, a distinction between tradition and modernity evident at the St Louis Fair. The official message of the gallery of 'Africa, the Americas, and the Asia-Pacific: A Celebration of Cultures' is 'a space which celebrates the diversity of mankind,' a message linked to certain kinds of cultural relativism and multiculturalism. However, the intended meaning may be taken up differently – a point highlighted for me as I was taking notes and a young White boy shouted, 'Nobody look at the shrunken heads!'

Multiculturalism has been official state policy in Canada since Pierre Trudeau announced support for 'multiculturalism within a bilingual framework' in 1971. Multiculturalism has been enshrined in the 1982 Charter of Rights and Freedoms and in Bill C-93 (the Canadian Multiculturalism Act) in 1988. It has received various forms of material assistance, including the creation of a Department of Multiculturalism and Citizenry in 1991. The Act notes that multiculturalism is a fundamental characteristic of Canadian heritage and identity, and promotes the full participation of all individuals and communities in shaping Canadian society, while pledging assistance to the elimination of barriers to such participation. The policy responded to a range of conflicts, including Quebec separatism, demands for recognition by immigrants, First Nations' activism, differentiation from the United States and

Great Britain, and the need for immigrants to fuel economic prosperity. Critics, however, point out that the Act is 'primarily concerned with mobilizing diversity for the project of nation-building, as well as limiting that diversity to symbolic rather than political forms' (Mackey 2002, 67), with the power to delimit tolerable difference remaining with the dominant group. Multiculturalism has enabled certain kinds of claims on the state, while co-opting, pre-empting, or suppressing anti-racism activism (das Gupta 1999). Thobani (2007) also considers how the focus on cultural parity in official multiculturalism disrupts the potential for multiracial solidarity among communities of colour intent upon socio-economic parity. The emphasis on 'culture' has a communalizing effect, seeing communities as neatly bounded and untouched by migration and dislocation, with resources allocated on the basis of cultural distinctions undermining multiracial organizations.

The Filipino exhibit at the ROM is opposite 'Africa – Themes and Collections' and sandwiched between a case on the Ainu (also featured in St Louis) and exhibits on the Maori, Aboriginal peoples of Australia, and the Sepik. Much of the new exhibit was installed in the fall of 2008; some of the images for the walls behind the exhibit were still not installed when I saw it (though notes indicating what was slated to appear were in the exhibit). The display was curated by Trudy Nicks, curator of world cultures at the ROM, whose most extensive experience is with First Nations groups.[2] It is ironic, but perhaps not accidental, that First Nations and Filipinos continue to be grouped in the curatorial mind. The analogy between Filipinos and Aboriginal people is one that has recurred in Filipino history, from the way that U.S. military men whose experiences were forged in battles with First Nations groups approached warfare, to the way that U.S. educators drew on the models of industrial and vocational schools designed for African Americans and Indians at Hampton and Tuskegee Institute, to developing models of industrial education in the Philippines, to the way the St Louis Fair was structured, with Native groups holding a position in the history of the Louisiana Purchase that was seen as analogous to the Filipino experience in the 1898 imperial acquisitions. It is not only analogies which are at stake, however; some American teachers who taught in Philippine schools were seen as not fit to teach White students upon their return to the United States and were hired in residential schools instead. While it is helpful to draw attention to shared histories of imperial occupation, there are limits to such a discussion. Immigrants can be complicit in the politics of a settler colonial state.

One of the ideological effects of official multiculturalist discourse can be to treat First Nations as analogous to other ethnic groups in Canada, in ways which undermine their distinct political identity and claims, and may even cast them as ethnocentric and premodern for failure to embrace multicultural difference (Thobani 2007, 172–5).

There are some distinctions in curatorial practice linked to the relative roles of the two groups in Canadian or American imperial histories, linked to the questions of (hyper)visibility and invisibility that are the subject of this volume. Nicks (2003a) has written about the importance of consulting First Nations groups; however, Filipino community groups were not consulted for this exhibit, which is admittedly much smaller than some of the others. The exhibit is structured in ways that suggest how curators currently meet some of the challenges of displaying First Nations material. For instance, curators are keen to challenge the stereotype of the vanishing or vanished Native by introducing materials on contemporary life.

Following Kramer's (1999) thoughtful analysis of the contradictions structuring the meaning of the St Louis Fair, it might be helpful to outline at least four tensions that structure the re-exhibition: (1) the tension between historical contextualization and ethnographic exemplification; (2) the tension between challenging and transcending colonial classifications and collections; (3) the tension between strategies specific for the Philippines and established strategies for exhibiting other colonized groups; and (4) the tensions between staging exhibits exemplary of diversity in Canada and avoiding uncritical accounts of Canadian multiculturalism. Each of these tensions is evident in the three key points that I take up in this chapter: (A) the ways the history of the artifacts in and from St Louis is, or is not, referenced; (B) the relationship between the past and the present constructed in the exhibit; and (C) the lingering influence of the World's Fair in the continued prominent focus on the Igorot.

How the History of the Artifacts in and from St Louis Is Referenced

One of the crucial questions these artifacts raise is what kind of story we can tell with histories – whether based on artifacts, texts, or images – originally produced within colonial narratives, and whether, when, and how those stories disrupt or perpetuate colonial stereotypes. One could imagine exhibiting these artifacts as a sort of education about the history of the fair, and the controversies it excited, to consider the politics of any and every exhibition in the context of imperialism, colonialism, nationalism, and racism. Such an exhibit might even showcase debates that one sees between historians Robert Rydell (1984) and Paul Kramer (1999) about whether the meaning of the exhibit is determined by elite narratives, or that compare the reactions of different historical actors, as the recent films *A World on Display* and *Bontoc Eulogy* do (with the former focusing on the impressions of White viewers and the latter on Filipino participants and their descendants). However, the history of the circulation of the objects is only lightly referenced in the ROM exhibit. The longest is the following text:

(1) From the Philippines to St. Louis to Toronto many of the objects still bear tags and labels which trace the history of the collection. Tags attached in the Philippines indicate the name of the object, the district of origin, and sometimes the cultural affiliation. American customs stickers and a label bearing the insignia of the 'Philippines Reservation' relate to the Philippines exhibits at the St. Louis World's Fair. Sale tags reflect the dispersal of Philippines material at the end of the fair, and the beginnings of the ROM collection.

The text is descriptive, rather than analytic, and refers largely to the material characteristics of the objects that are evident to viewers. It does not allude to the selectivity of the original collection, or the contrast that viewers were explicitly and implicitly asked to make between the cultural products of the Philippines and other parts of that exhibit. Other panels in the exhibit address sales stickers, customs labels, and the procedure used for identifying various objects in the exhibit.

The only explicit mention of the original evolutionary narrative within which the display is embedded is the following paragraph, which is oddly found under the heading 'Official Logo of the Philippine Reservation':

(2) The Philippine Reservation housed nearly 1200 Filipinos living in 6 villages arranged around a central plaza on a 47-acre site. It was a very popular destination for visitors to the 1904 World's Fair in St. Louis. The organizers of the fair intended to celebrate the recent American acquisition of the Philippines, and to illustrate the nineteenth century theory of cultural evolution. A century later, objects from Philippines exhibition are more valued for the insight they can provide about the rich cultural heritage of Filipino peoples.

Note that the text does not indicate why the villages were popular, and it uses the term 'acquisition' rather than 'occupation' to describe the U.S. relationship to the Philippines. The description of cultural evolution as a nineteenth-century theory might be accurate in dating the temporal origins of such theories, but obscures their vitality in the early twentieth century, at the time of the St Louis Fair, and in the twenty-first century, at the time of the re-mounting of the exhibit. Indeed, the continuing assignment of individuals and groups into a taxonomy of types and the arrangement of these types into a hierarchy is precisely the definition of *racialization* (Hill 2008; Omi and Winant 1994). Finally, the text provides a very explicit statement of the curator's hope as to the meaning viewers will take away from the exhibit: a culturally relativist tribute to the contributions made by Filipinos that echoes the gallery's tribute to the diversity of the world's people. It is, perhaps, worth asking if viewers take away a message of 'richness,' or whether these are the cultural products from the Philippines most likely to create such an impression.

The focus on the culturally relativist challenge to cultural evolutionary theories in the present also does not highlight the challenges in 1904 to a racial evolutionary narrative. The selectivity in the St Louis display means that the artifacts and objects were skewed to portray lifestyles that are as far as possible from that which is construed as 'civilized,' 'modern,' or 'advanced.' The ROM re-exhibit repeats this selectivity, without commenting on its impact. Anti-racist critics have argued, as Thobani (2007) notes, that multiculturalism 'diverts attention from the power relations that reproduce racial hierarchies, reframing these instead as conflicts arising from ignorance and cultural intolerance' (162), requiring education in cross-cultural communication. The funding practices of the multiculturalist bureaucracy authenticate certain aspects of culture (a process Thobani calls 'culturalism'), with 'source countries of immigrant communities [being] constructed in the western imagination as pre-modern, tradition bound, and culturally backward' (163).

*The Relationship between the Past and the Present
Constructed in the Exhibit*

BLURRED DISTINCTIONS BETWEEN THEN AND NOW
The introductory text of the exhibit suggests that the artifacts displayed represent the lifestyles of Filipinos around a century ago. However, the exhibit blurs the distinction between past and present, in a variety of texts and images. This is, in some ways, linked to an interpellation of

Filipino history into a curatorial framework for discussing First Nations issues. The strategy for organizing displays in the exhibit and for understanding the relationship between the present and the past is shaped by narratives for exhibits focused on the First Nations, where some of the work are invested in challenging the stereotype of the disappearing Native, or colonialist narratives which treat Aboriginal people and sites as antecedent to, but not part of, contemporary Canada (Mackey 2002). This framework, where it has a cultural rather than political emphasis, is also a problematic format for representing First Nations issues, and can serve to deepen the integration of First Nations into a multiculturalist discourse as just another cultural group.

How are the past and present blurred? For instance, the exhibit includes a wooden model of a traditional mill used for crushing sugar cane to extract liquid. It is accompanied by a 1998 colour image showing a man processing cane using a similar device in a northern province. This juxtaposition suggests the exhibit is not just about the past, but an ethnographic report on the present. But is this present indicative of actual use, or something more like the historical re-enactments one finds at, say, Black Creek Pioneer Village in Ontario? And, in a broader question about representation, what does it mean to represent contemporary processing of sugar cane in this way, as the somewhat bucolic work of an individual farmer, rather than with, say, an image of Victoria's Mill in the Philippines, reportedly the world's largest integrated sugar mill and refinery? Or to represent the controversial hacienda conditions of large numbers of sugar workers, rather than export processing zones in the Philippines (Chant and McIlwaine 1995)? Similar images document coconut processing or fishing to similar representational ends. This is not to question that many Filipinos engage in small-scale fishing or coconut processing, but rather to draw attention to the ways that a systematic erasure of more industrial, large-scale forms of production continues to establish the traditional/modern, agricultural/industrial hierarchy that structured the St Louis Fair.

DISPLAYING CONTEMPORARY PRODUCTS

The final section of the exhibit focuses on contemporary products from the Philippines. This portion of the exhibit, the curator reports, will regularly change with a rotating set of objects. Again, both challenging and staying within the narrative provided by the St Louis Fair, this section highlights the creative expansion of the materials used, especially for weaving, and the forms constructed (e.g., a cell phone holder made of buri palm and bamboo). Ironically, these contemporary objects were largely purchased from another exposition – the Canadian National Exhibition. The focus on materials and form stays within a narrowly defined material culture focus of the exhibit; its focus on wood carving, the production of piña (pineapple fibre) cloth, and weaving is shaped by the original St Louis Fair hierarchies of manual labour and dexterity. Even more striking is the continuing focus on consumption, aligned with Breitbart's (1997) observation that perhaps the most compelling aspect of the St Louis Fair was in teaching viewers that anything could be bought. This section of the exhibit notes that the materials used have been 'greatly expanded as a result of production for tourist and international markets,' that luxury piña clothing is woven for 'both local and international consumption,' and that 'today, a great array of products made in the Philippines are available around the world, including in the marketplaces of modern fairs such as the CNE in Toronto.' This could be seen to contrast with the display in twentieth-century design, where the focus is on aesthetic appreciation, rather than ingenuity or consumption. Nonetheless, the products available for consumption stop short of any objects associated with industrial production – cell phone holders but no cell phones, slippers but not computer components from factories in export processing zones, buri palm but not the largest sugar cane processing plant in the world. Indeed, the focus on products, rather than the challenges to strategies for representation, represents a continuity with St Louis. The ROM exhibit thus participates in the 'folklorization' of Filipino culture, an overdetermined motif in Canadian multiculturalism where products for consumption – food, dance, music, arts, and crafts – stand in for diversity, and other discussions of historical and current structural antecedents for inequitable relations linked to gender and racialization are obscured. Hence we can flag the ways that multiculturalism as a discourse coincides with consumerism. Hage (2000) notes that a 'discourse of enrichment' enables normative national subjects to consume multicultures within their vicinity by eating ethnic foods and buying ethnic arts at multicultural fairs and restaurants. The price of an adult ticket for a day visit to the ROM when I visited was $22, a price only affordable by certain consumers.

The Continued Prominent Focus on the 'Igorot'

One lingering way in which the selectivity and narrative of the St Louis World's Fair shape the ROM exhibit is in the continuing over-emphasis on the Igorot. The designers of the exhibit used the term 'Igorot' throughout, and noted that it was once a controversial term, but is now understood as a positive form of group identification. This, perhaps, prematurely forecloses discussion, since not all individuals or groups (especially some Kalinga and Ifugao) accept the term as a positive, or appropriate, group designation, preferring instead 'Cordilleran' as an ethnic or political group designation. The term 'Igorot' is in the spirit, however, of the widely cited quotation from columnist Jose G. Dulnuan: 'I am an Igorot. Let me be treated as I deserve – with respect if I am good, with contempt if I am no good, irrespective of the name I carry. Let the term, Igorot, remain, and the whole world will use it with the correct meaning attached to it.'[3]

The emphasis on the 'Igorot' is evident in several ways, including:

- The two large panels behind the exhibited artifacts are slated to be a view of the Philippine Reservation at the St Louis Fair, and an image of Igorots preparing a meal at the fair.
- The panel and portion of the exhibit entitled 'Ifugao carved spoons' discuss Ifugao wood-carving abilities generally and carved wooden spoons specifically that depict human figures, 'sometimes referred to as ancestor figures or deities.' (A textual note asks viewers to look at a large image of the stone-walled rice terraces to be installed on one of the back walls of the exhibit.)
- The panel and portion of the exhibit entitled 'backpack with rain-shield' describe Igorot men's traditional use of backpacks covered with palm leaf stalks, which repelled rain on hunting expeditions. It is accompanied by a slightly over-exposed early twentieth-century image of Igorot men and boys with backpacks.
- The focus, in the 'clothing, adornment and personal items' section of the exhibit, is on objects associated with the Igorot, the Bagabo, and the Moro.[4]

The 'Igorot' receive markedly more attention in text and in artifacts than any other group in the Philippines. Some of the text does challenge the primitivizing stereotypes of the St Louis World's Fair, for instance, by noting Igorot achievements in the construction of rice terraces and mentioning Igorots as miners and farmers, and not just hunters or headhunters. However, the connection is not made explicitly. Like many studies of colonial discourse, the exhibit is able to critique the arguments of the earlier exhibit – but in doing so, it stays within the limits for discussion set by precisely that discourse, one in which those groups who live in the highlands become central to, almost constitutive of, Filipino identity. Furthermore, because what is at stake in this critique is always implicit, viewers may find the argument too subtle.

Conclusion: What It Means to Re-exhibit Colonial Artifacts

Paul Kramer notes that colonialism is always accompanied by a crisis in colonial representation, for politicians and historians alike (1999, 76). Scholars have extensively debated the meaning of the Louisiana Purchase Exposition, looking at its significance for the various people who organized it, for the people on exhibit, for the photographers who documented it, and for the large crowds that flocked to the fair. Breitbart (1997), in debating how to reprint photographs taken at the fair, wonders if they can simply speak for themselves, or if his task is instead to find a way to 'bridge the gap between the reader, the photographs, and the vanished world they represent by describing the cultural context in which the images were produced and distributed' (4). He asks what historical audiences made, and what contemporary audiences will make, of photographs taken at the fair. What does the re-exhibition of material artifacts – like baskets, models of agricultural and fishing technology, and textiles – from the fair do? Has meaning been 'liberated' from contingencies of use? In the absence of any other cultural artifacts, texts, or context, does the meaning of the re-exhibited artifacts remain similar to the former meaning (suggesting that these artifacts are the primary cultural achievement of Filipinos), or does the meaning change?

One interpretation of this exhibit is that it is nervous and timid about describing racism, for fear of being labelled as racist. It even manages to be dull. This exhibit moves quickly to critique earlier modes of display (though not, notably, as racist), in ways that claim the (White) virtue of this exhibit. Indeed, it never names race, preferring to talk about a framework for cultural evolution. When does informing people about racism constitute the recirculation of racist language, practices, or stereotypes? In *The Everyday Life of White Racism*, anthropologist Jane Hill (2008) argues that the obsessive amount of attention paid to racial slurs and gaffes in contemporary media serves to reproduce racism, since the media endlessly repeat and re-circulate racial slurs and stereotypes. They also reproduce Whiteness, since they allow Whites to reproduce their folk theory understandings of racists and racism (understood as always elsewhere) and accounts of White virtue (since a White person shows herself to be a good person by recognizing racism, elsewhere).

These are motivations from which I cannot claim to excuse myself, of course, in the writing of this chapter.

Hill wonders whether to use racist epithets when analysing racist language. She notes her own compromise: she does not use racist epithets in speaking, since she feels that uttering them, even when carefully framed as examples, does incalculable harm and causes pain; however, she spells out racist words in writing, while noting that it may not simply be a rational choice made on theoretical grounds but perhaps, at some deep level, a form of shamefully pleasurable catharsis, which still causes pain for readers, for which she must take responsibility. The principle to extract from her example is that the need to name, analyse, and criticize racism needs to be balanced with the necessity of attending to the evidence one offers, understanding that some images, words, and artifacts, in different contexts, can have a stronger effect on audiences, and that others should not, in some circumstances, be re-analysed. Certainly, there are images, practices, or discourses so deeply embedded within imperial and racial optics that they cannot be reproduced without inciting troubling forms of racial voyeurism.

To be sure, we need to go beyond critical accounts of colonialist, imperialist, or racist ideologies, since to give these accounts is to stay within the terms of that discourse, without considering other ways to talk about cultural, political, and aesthetic contributions to material culture.[5] However, the exhibited baskets, agricultural and fishing equipment, jewellery, and textiles are, arguably, not in this category. The exhibit errs in the other direction; it is too cautious about unpacking the racist logics of colonial exhibition. The existence of this collection is embedded within certain colonial logics which, if they are not carefully elucidated and critiqued, can be (re-) produced.

Crucial, also, is not just the form of the exhibits but the institutional contexts for them – who the curators are, what their backgrounds are, who is consulted in the preparation of different exhibits, and in what ways. This is highlighted by the controversy associated with the 1990 ROM exhibit Into the Heart of Africa, which likely shaped the form of caution that this new Filipino exhibit displays. Into the Heart of Africa was a museum exhibit curated by a White Canadian anthropologist, Jeanne Cannizzo, who attempted to present colonialism and museum collections in a reflexive and critical way, by looking at the world-view of colonialist collectors of objects. It elicited outrage and accusations of racism from, especially, Black individuals and organizations throughout Toronto. The curator's stated aims were to critique the ethnocentrism and cultural arrogance of the Canadian colonialists in Africa. Among the concerns raised by critics were that the exhibit did not address the contributions Africa had made to the history of civilization, that its design had not incorporated sufficient or appropriate community feedback, that in distinguishing Canadians from Africans it excluded historical African voices and present-day African Canadian ones, that its presumed ideal viewer was a White Canadian, and that the net effect was that viewers were being asked to venerate and respect not just African art but also the ideology of its colonialist collectors (Mackey 1995; Schildkrout 1991). Certain images, particularly a wall-size image of a White British lord on horseback plunging his sword through the shield and heart of a Zulu man, attracted particularly strong forms of critique, as overly vivid and traumatic images of past and continuing White violence. The exhibit was defended by the ROM: Cannizzo (1990, 1991) published defences in prominent newspapers and academic journals; protestors received a legal injunction to keep away; the police arrested eleven protestors; and the museum sued one protest group for $16,000 in damages.

There are a variety of lessons from such an incident. The ROM is in some ways now more attentive to drawing more fully on community input for certain exhibits, including the new African section of the gallery.[6] Community consultation was not part of the strategy for this exhibit; yet even that is not a panacea. What is required is significant interrogation of what is meant by 'community' and 'consultation' and what the outcomes of such consultations are. Consultations are not, in the end, collaborations.

The ROM exhibit of the artifacts from the St Louis World's Fair flinches from fuller discussion of the colonial context and ideologies of the artifacts perhaps because of a wariness about being perceived as re-inscribing racist attitudes as it attempts to critique them with colonial artifacts. Instead, it promotes a culturally relativist account consistent with a form of multiculturalism that promotes fragments of cultures, constructed from folkloric and culinary remnants, the process that Handler (1988) calls cultural objectification and that Moodley (1983) pithily summarizes as the 3 Ss model of culture (saris, samosas, and steel bands) rather than the 3 Rs (resistance, rebellion, rejection).

It is important, also, to place the importance of this exhibit within a larger context, to focus on the reception of the exhibit and not just a textual analysis of it. In my longest stretch of time at the ROM while preparing for this chapter (three hours), the exhibit only attracted three groups. One pair of Asian or Asian Canadian women paused briefly by the exhibit of contemporary products to look at the shirts made from piña cloth, and reacted in a way framed by consumption and use. 'This is famous,' said one, 'but it's very starchy, not at all soft to wear.' Another, older White couple stopped to look at the section of the exhibit entitled 'clothing, adornment, and personal items.' The woman's attention was caught by some jewellery – she spent time tracking down what they were on the explanatory panels: '#17 – anklets.' Her attention then moved to a sword identified as Kampilan, a sword used as a personal weapon by the Moro. She noted: 'That's a weapon all right.' These first two reactions are overdetermined by a focus on objects, commodities, and perhaps consumption. The last is overdetermined perhaps by recent militarized images of Muslims. This exhibit does tell part of the history of Filipinos that Coloma's chapter (this volume) notes that we need, but not in a critical way. One challenge here is how to use material objects to get audiences to focus on history; another is to figure out how to take this history of colonial racism and its continuing ramifications to a wider audience.

The fair continues to attract the attention of artists. In 1995, Marlon Fuentes wrote, directed, and narrated *Bontoc Eulogy*, a film which interweaves fiction and non-fiction to tell the story of Filipinos at the fair from their perspective. The film presented the story of a first-generation Filipino American who tries to trace what happened to his grandfather, a Bontoc Igorot warrior, who was taken from the Philippines to be displayed at the fair and never returned to his village.[7] Screening this film, or fragments of it, alongside the exhibit could move the story from a focus on objects to a focus on the people whose objects these are. Another alternative is evident in community-based art exhibits, which engage with continuing colonial legacies of racism, including the contemporary manifestations of racism in Canada (see chapters by Balmes, Largo, and Pratt in this volume; see also Johnston and Pratt 2010). With such input, the St Louis Fair exhibit could be informed by the representational strategies of socially informed artists also working through the implications of colonialism and global migration for Filipinos, creating a different kind of dialogue between imperial and immigrant pasts and presents. To forge such exhibits will be, indeed, to forge a weapon to challenge the emotional, economic, and cultural impacts of racism and colonialism.

NOTES

1 This is nearly six times the size of the Canadian National Exhibition in Toronto, an annual thirteen-day fair and the largest in Canada. The CNE

takes place on 192 acres, and attracts 1.3 million visitors annually, making it the fourth largest such fair in the United States and Canada. See http://www.theex.com/site.php?menu=06:01, accessed August 24, 2009.

2 Nicks kindly gave me a personal tour of the exhibit. She has also offered to do the same for other individuals or groups who are interested in the exhibit. The exhibit includes about 120 of the over 500 objects in the collection. Nicks also showed me the artifacts that are off exhibit; those displayed are representative of the larger collection.

3 The name issue is not new. See Gerard Finin's *The Making of the Igorot* (2005). Dulnuan is quoted by William Henry Scott in his essay, 'The Origin of the Word Igorot,' in *Of Igorots and Independence* (Baguio City: A-Seven Publishing, 1993), 67.

4 Particularly troubling is the text introducing the adornment section, which draws upon generalizing ethnographic discourse and a colonial discourse which associated certain groups with a fascination with trinkets in the phrase 'The Bagabo love of ornament is illustrated in the man's . . . wooden comb and beaded necklaces.'

5 See Rafael's 2008 commentary on recent contributions to 'Philippine' studies in the United States, in which he notes that some of the most effective historical critiques nonetheless remain firmly within the realm of American studies.

6 Note, though, that community requests to exhibit Egyptian artifacts alongside other African ones are still not honoured.

7 See Fermin (2004, 208–9) for more on the afterlife of the fair.

REFERENCES

Anderson, Warwick. 1995. 'Where every prospect pleases and only man is vile': Laboratory medicine as colonial discourse. In *Discrepant histories: Translocal essays on Filipino cultures*, ed. Vince Rafael, 83–112. Manila: Anvil.

Breitbart, Eric. 1997. *A world on display 1904: Photographs from the St. Louis world's fair*. Albuquerque: University of New Mexico Press.

Cannizzo, Jeanne. 1990. Into the heart of a controversy. *Toronto Star*, June 5.

– 1991. Exhibiting cultures: 'Into the heart of Africa.' *Visual Anthropology Review* 7 (1): 150–60.

Chant, Sylvia, and Cathy McIlwaine. 1995. *Women of a lesser cost: Female labour, foreign exchange and Philippine development*. London: Pluto.

Choy, Catherine Ceniza. 2003. Salvaging the savage: On representing Filipinos and remembering American empire. In *Screaming monkeys: Critiques of Asian American images*, ed. M. Evelina Galang, 35–50. Minneapolis: Coffee House.

Fermin, Jose. 2004. *1904 world's fair: The Filipino experience.* West Conshohocken, PA: Infinity.

Finin, Gerard. 2005. *The Making of the Igorot: Contours of Cordillera Consciousness.* Quezon City: Ateneo de Manila University Press.

das Gupta, Tania. 1999. The politics of multiculturalism: 'Immigrant women' and the Canadian state. In *Scratching the surface: Canadian anti-racist feminist thought,* ed. Enakshi Dua and Angela Robertson, 187–206. Toronto: Women's Press.

Hage, Ghassan. 2000. *White nation: Fantasies of white supremacy in a multicultural society.* London: Routledge.

Hagedorn, Jessica. 1990. *Dogeaters.* New York: Penguin.

Handler, Richard. 1988. *Nationalism and the politics of culture in Quebec.* Madison: University of Wisconsin Press.

Hill, Jane. 2008. *The everyday life of white racism.* West Sussex: Wiley-Blackwell.

Johnston, Caleb, and Geraldine Pratt with the Philippine Women's Centre of BC. 2010. *Nanay* (mother): A testimonial play. *Cultural Geographies* 17: 123–33.

Kramer, Paul. 1999. Making concessions: Race and empire revisited at the Philippine exposition, St. Louis, 1901–1905. *Radical History Review* 73: 74–114.

Mackey, Eva. 1995. Postmodernism and cultural politics in a multicultural nation: Contests over truth. *Public Culture* 7: 403–31.

– 2002. *The house of difference: Cultural politics and national identity in Canada.* Toronto: University of Toronto Press.

May, Glenn. 1980. *Social engineering in the Philippines: The aims, execution and impact of colonial policy.* Santa Barbara, CA: Greenwood.

McGee, W.J. 1899. The trend of human progress. *American Anthropologist* 1: 401–47.

Moodley, Kogila. 1983. Canadian multiculturalism as ideology. *Ethnic and Racial Studies* 6 (3): 320–31.

Nicks, Trudy. 2003a. Museums and contact work: Introduction. In *Museums and source communities,* ed. Laura Peers and Alison Brown, 19–27. New York: Routledge.

– 2003b. Dr. Oronhyatekha's history lessons: Reading museum collections as texts. In *Reading beyond words: Contexts for Native history,* ed. Jennifer S.H. Brown and Elizabeth Viert, 459–89. Peterborough, ON: Broadview.

Omi, Michael, and Howard Winant. 1994. *Racial formation in the United States: From the 1960s to the 1990s.* 2nd edition. New York: Routledge.

Rafael, Vicente. 1994. The cultures of area studies in the United States. *Social Text* 41: 91–111.

– 1999. Regionalism, area studies, and the accidents of agency. *American Historical Review* 104 (4): 1208–20.

– 2008. Notes on the study of the Philippines in the United States. *Philippine Studies* 56 (4): 345–58.

Rydell, Robert. 1984. *All the world's a fair: Visions of empire at American international expositions 1876–1916*. Chicago: University of Chicago Press.

Scott, William Henry. 1975. The Igorots who went to Madrid. In *History on the Cordillera: Collected writings on mountain province history*. Baguio City: Baguio Printing and Publishing Company.

Schildkrout, Enid. 1991. Ambiguous messages and ironic twists: Into the Heart of Africa and the other museum. *Museum Anthropology* 15 (2): 16–23.

Thobani, Sunera. 2007. *Exalted subjects: Studies in the making of race and nation in Canada*. Toronto: University of Toronto Press.

Wright, Ramsay. 1933. Obituary. *Nature* 132: 631.

FILMS

A World on Display. 1994. Written and directed by Eric Breitbart. Produced by Eric Breitbart and Mary Lance. Narrated by Leona Luba. New Deal Films, Inc. 53 min. VHS video.

Bontoc Eulogy. 1995 Produced, written, directed and narrated by Marlon Fuentes. 57 min. VHS video.

Meet Me in St. Louis. 1944. Directed by Vincente Minnelli. Produced by Arthur Freed. Metro-Goldwyn-Mayer.

Chapter 11

From the Pearl of the Orient to Uptown: A Collaborative Arts-Based Inquiry with Filipino Youth Activists in Montreal

MARISSA LARGO

Introduction

In my work as an artist, researcher, educator, and activist with community organizations in Montreal, I have come to know the pressing concerns of immigrants and their families, particularly those faced by Filipino Canadian youth. Kabataang Montreal is one community organization that addresses those concerns. The following chapter examines my collaboration with them to promote positive change within the community. My primary inquiry question is: *How can collaborative art production assist a youth activist organization in furthering its goals for individual and collective empowerment?* This question was answered through the production of two art projects; first, a mural was created focusing on participants' lived experiences and their hopes for the future; and, second, a video piece was created using footage collectively composed and performed by the community participants. Based on the data collected from questionnaires, focus groups, my personal journal, and the artwork itself, I identified what the youth gained through the collaborative art projects. These findings, in conversation with social reconstruction, a discourse which at its centre aims to challenge inequality and promote social and cultural diversity, elucidated the connection between collaborative art production and activism with implications for the fields of community art education and community organizing (Johnston and Pratt 2010; Stuhr 1994).

Community Organizing and in Kabataang Montreal

In late 2005, I began community organizing with Kabataang Montreal (KM), a youth organization that deals with issues affecting the Filipino community in Montreal. I became interested in how issues pertinent to the community could be addressed through art and how this could be a form of activism, or, in other words, community organizing. *Community organizing* is a process that creates social change by 'developing leadership among individuals or by building power for collectives' (Ratcliff 2003, 432). In such processes, social problems are identified and acted upon by affected community members. KM exemplifies community organizing because it is dedicated to addressing problems which affect Filipino Canadian youth and their community. According to founder Roderick Carreon,[1] community organizing for KM is recognizing the needs of the community and working towards making positive change a reality:

> *Because the way KM understands the situation of the migrant here, is that yes, we are here, but it doesn't mean that we have to suffer here. We have to improve our situation as well. There's various ways of improving it. We could do lobbying, we could push for this, we could push for that, we know as KM members as activists for Filipino [change in the Philippines]. We know that the change would have to come from the Philippines 'cause migration will still continue until the system is changed. Until the system allows its people to starve, until the system doesn't answer the need of its own people, migration will continue.* (Personal interview, June 3, 2006)

Formed in October 2000, KM is a Filipino youth outreach organization based in Côte-des-Neiges, a neighbourhood with a high population of new immigrants in Montreal (Meintel 1997). This part of Montreal saw, and continues to see, an influx of migrant workers from the Philippines, many of whom are women. Under the Canadian government's Live-In Caregiver Program (LCP), women can migrate to Canada as domestic workers, oftentimes leaving their own families behind (Pratt 2004; see Davidson and Tungohan chapters in this volume). After their twenty-four-month contract has been fulfilled, these women can then begin the process of sponsoring their families to come over.[2] Family reunification, however, does not always happen swiftly and happily. Owing to financial problems, many years may pass before a mother may see her children again. In some cases, children have grown into adults by the time reunification occurs. The children of these migrant workers, once reunited with their mothers in a new society, are often forced to deal with dramatic cultural adjustment. In this context, many newly arrived Filipino youth form gangs as *'a defence mechanism'* (Carreon, personal interview, June 3, 2006) against the difficulties experienced in schools and the streets, and as a way to form a sense of belonging often missing from the reconstructed family. The formation of gangs among Filipino youth, as explained by Carreon, was but a symptom of a larger problem relating to forced migration[3] because of the poor economic conditions of the Philippines.[4] It was in this context that KM emerged.

Current members include Filipino immigrants and Filipinos born in Canada. They comprise middle and high school students and young adults who are either in post-secondary studies or in the workforce. Several members, including founder Carreon, are past gang members. Their lived experiences give them an empathetic perspective that informs their outreach efforts among other Filipinos who are experiencing difficulties. In this community-based organization, 'empowerment' is not a gift given from socially well-adjusted individuals to the 'oppressed,' but is a dialogical process in which empowerment is mutually achieved by youth organizers and young community members working closely together.

Participatory Action Research and Community Art

As an arts-based inquiry, this project presupposes that art production is a form of research. As the production of knowledge and culture is a practice of power, in order to share the power inherent in these processes, I carried out *participatory research,* which according to Deborah Barndt (2004) 'democratize[s] research by involving communities in defining the issues to be researched as well as in the data gathering, analysis, and action to be taken' (222). Participatory research lends itself to community art initiatives; just as community art involves people in a collective process of meaning-making, so too does participatory research. With this in mind, I aimed to conduct this research through collaborative processes, which directly implicated the participation of KM members.

Through *action research,* I constructed knowledge from my practice as a community artist and art educator. Facilitating the art workshops and partaking in collaborative art production allowed me to reflect on my practice and link it to theory. Action research in combination with the collective data gathering and analysis processes of participatory research is known as *participatory action research* or PAR (Pratt 2010; Barndt 2004; Marino 1997). In PAR, the results of the research have benefits for all those involved. According to Morris and Muzychka (2002), PAR blurs the boundaries between the researcher and researched by enabling the 'two way exchange of information' (10). However, because the researcher is inextricably linked to that which is researched, the researcher loses the ability to examine from a distance, presenting a methodological dilemma, as it complicates data collection from observation. In spite of this, the purpose of PAR remains the mutual attainment of knowledge and skills by participants and researchers alike in order to help the community reach longer-term goals.

Creative Process: The Mural and Video Projects

In autumn 2005, I conducted a pilot project with KM members that involved the collaborative creation of a video reflecting on their lived experiences of family separation. The pilot project included analysis and production components; after a discussion on how personal experiences are linked to the political (as with their experiences of forced migration), we went through basic interviewing techniques and simple videography. Working collaboratively, the participants shared their stories, and took turns interviewing and filming each other (figure 11.1). The result was a short video produced for and with KM members for the purposes of educating others about the problems facing newly arrived Filipino youth. Based on the positive feedback from the focus group, I concluded that the collaborative mode of learning and creating was a successful way in which the youth activists could express their concerns on both an individual and collective level. Members of KM and I wanted to extend this work. As a result, we developed two collaborative arts-based projects. For these projects, I used two major approaches for community-artist collaborations that I identified from my reading of Kester (1995) and Lacy (1995). They are Community Artist as Facilitator of the collaborative creative process, and Community Artist as 'Gatherer.' The two approaches are elucidated in the following projects and act as a framework in negotiating 'collaboration' with the community group. While collaboration in the first project refers to the direct participation of the community group members in the creation of the artwork, in the second project, collaboration occurs in the creative process while I produce the final work.

Figure 11.1. Collaborative video production

Collaborative Mural Project – Approach #1: Community Artist as Facilitator of the Collaborative Creative Process

In Febuary 2006, I proposed a collaborative mural project that would examine the context of Filipino youth in Montreal as a way of naming problems within the community and to visually represent these problems and, also, hopes for the future. The creation of the mural would not only serve as a critical and reflective practice for the youth activists, but would also act as a tool for outreach, awareness raising, and a catalyst for dialogue. Most importantly, the creation of the mural would provide an opportunity to envision alternatives for the community. From conception to completion, the creation of the mural took five workshops, which were each approximately five hours long. Eleven people, not including myself, participated in the workshops, and among them, seven participants were active members of KM. Four were not, but were familiar with the work of KM. Two participants of the group of 'non-active' members were thirteen-year-olds. Everyone else ranged from twenty to twenty-seven years of age. Of the eleven participants, five were Canadian-born Filipinos, five had emigrated from the Philippines, and one person was born in Singapore.

Acting as a facilitator, I assumed more of a pedagogical role in the collaborative creation of a mural. Thinking about our specific context in Montreal as immigrants or children of immigrants, we brainstormed how to visually represent our lived experiences as such. Based on the survey completed at the beginning of the workshop, participants cited the exploitation of Filipino domestic workers, family separation due to migration, racial profiling by the police, lack of support for new immigrants, high school drop-out rates, gang violence, and the gap between Canadian-born Filipino youth and newly arrived Filipinos as problems affecting the Filipino community in Montreal. I proposed that the theme of the mural be 'Our Past, Present, and Future,' to which the participants agreed.

Once a general plan was established, participants enacted the different scenarios that were needed for the mural (e.g., a group of youth gathering around the Métro) while other participants digitally photographed these poses. This activity turned into something that I had not anticipated. While enacting poses of youth 'hanging out' in the local schoolyard, two participants began a dramatic re-enactment of 'outreach,' the act of approaching youth and engaging them in a dialogue about their present conditions. One participant, in particular, who was an ex-gang member, began recounting his past as such. While the rest of us listened, he explained that instead of continuing with self-destructive patterns caused by poverty and family separation, he decided to discontinue his gang involvement and begin community organizing. He went on to describe how, through learning about the root causes of his social conditions and how they arise from Third World exploitation, he began to understand why his parents were forced to migrate. The resulting photographs from this activity were exceptionally powerful. This process may be likened to Augusto Boal's *Theatre of the Oppressed,* in which dramatic re-enactment becomes a performance in which participants' subjectivities are actively engaged and become part of the creation of meaning. As a demonstration of 'life as art,' this photography activity created 'a space to practice and prepare for activism' (Cohen-Cruz 2002, 7). For participants who were new to the work of KM, it became an education in how the past experiences of KM members inform their present-day work.

In the second workshop, participants began sketching out the design onto the canvas and painting the background. The photographs that were taken during the first workshop were digitally projected onto the canvas while participants traced them. This strategy proved to be a quick and an accessible way of transferring images to the support surface for individuals with little art background. Regardless of technical skills, all participants were able to immediately engage in the collaborative creative process. Participants who were more confident with their drawing skills outlined the background and added hand-drawn elements in the mural.

Collaborative work proved to be challenging at times because of fluctuating attendance and variable group dynamics. For instance, in the third workshop, only five participants attended. To complicate the matter, participants arrived late and then left early. However, the fourth workshop was a full and rich experience. The mural at this point was materializing nicely and at a steady pace, validating participants' commitment to the project. Seven members and I were in attendance. The workshop began with individuals working on designated areas. Gradually, participants became more at ease with these detailed tasks. At some points, participants were working five to a panel. One participant volunteered to paint all of the clothing in the mural. After a little coaching on painting shadows and highlights required for the wrinkles in the fabric, he continued on his own and became increasingly skilled as he went on. The mural was becoming a shared space in

Figure 11.2. From the Pearl of the Orient to Uptown: *Pag-Asa Ng Kabataan* (6 x 12 feet)

which participants could build on each other's work. For example, one participant painted the foundation colour of the red wall in the second panel, while another participant painted the bricks. Yet another participant added the 'tagging' or graffiti on top of the brick wall. It became apparent to me that participants were realizing the total vision of the mural and working as a team towards the final product.

The final workshop was for finishing touches. Once it was completed, I asked KM members to come up with a title for the work. Participants brainstormed a series of possible titles in English, French, and Tagalog. There were two suggestions that appealed to most of us, so I suggested amalgamating them. The title, *From the Pearl of the Orient to Uptown: Pag-Asa Ng Kabataan* (Hope of the Youth), encapsulates several themes addressed in the mural in a playful way. 'Pearl of the Orient' is a popular and romanticized nickname for the Philippines, while 'uptown' refers to Côte-des-Neiges (the neighbourhood in which the majority of the organizing work takes place) and calls to mind the idea of migration. The Tagalog phrase refers to how the youth envision change.

The mural is in triptych form (representing the past, present, and future), with each panel approximately six feet wide by four feet tall. In the first panel, the image of a Filipino woman longing for home highlights the emotional struggle of migrant workers in Canada. A live-in caregiver is standing in the Philippine countryside wearing a winter coat and holding a baby that is not her own. This dramatic juxtaposition represents the harsh contradictions that she must face in a new society. In the second panel, a group of youth is gathered in front of a red brick wall covered with graffiti or tagging. These tags are the names of Filipino gangs, now dissolved, that once plagued Côtes-des-Neiges before KM's formation. The third panel illustrates a community centre in the heart of the neighbourhood, which would provide a place for young Filipinos to gather instead of the Métro. A golden road leads to a brighter future and one of the youth organizers points back as if to recall their history of struggle (figure 11.2).

**Collaborative Video Project – Approach #2:
Community Artist as 'Gatherer'**

Unlike the mural project, in which collaboration took place from start to finish, in the video project, collaboration occurred only in the process, while the final product was edited and composed by me. Here, I took on the approach of the community artist who acted as a participant-observer and who gathered material in the form of interviews and performance to create a new work of art. Throughout the mural workshops, a video recorder was set up to capture the creation of the mural. It was positioned in the same place each time to consistently tape the evolution of the mural as best as possible. Although the participants were aware of the video recording, they paid little attention to it. In total, eight hours of footage were collected.

Capturing the video onto the computer offered me an opportunity to review the mural-making process and provided me with a critical distance from which I could observe interactions among participants and myself. This was a helpful strategy that captured all the subtleties that I had missed while I was immersed in facilitating. It was interesting to see the participants' confidence in their art-making abilities grow as the mural developed. One scene shows a participant beginning to paint the brick wall in the second panel. He tentatively begins painting, applies one dab of colour, and quickly steps back to admire his handiwork. He laughs and continues to paint the entire wall. Moments like those would have been easily overlooked, without the aid of the video. Thus, video documentation solved one methodological challenge of PAR and participant-observation.

In addition to being used as a form of data collection, this video was also used in the creation of a work of art. I produced a video using the footage collected from the mural workshops, combined with the documentary interviews produced from the pilot project. My intention in creating this video was to reveal the collaborative processes and personal narratives that were behind the finished mural. Judging from the mural alone, it is not evident that it is the product of many hands. The video acts as documentation of group participation.

The video begins with an entire screen shot of the completed mural. After about a minute, the static camera zooms in to the painted image of one of the female participants. At that point, it transitions into documentary footage of the same youth speaking about her experience of family separation. The video continues to pan across the mural, zoom in to other figures, and transition to their interviews of other hardships experienced in Canada. This editing provided the personal context that was behind the mural's imagery. These transitions create a dynamic between action and reflection, past and present, as the video switches from documentary footage to the image of the painting. The last three minutes of the video include time-lapsed clips selected from the eight hours of footage collected. This was a multilayered montage of key scenes of varying speeds in which the youth and I are seen before the blank canvas, and after sketching and painting, the mural gradually emerges. The fast speed of the video encapsulates the high energy and excitement of the participants during the project. It demonstrates the youth activists engaged in collective action. While the documentary interviews poignantly describe the problems of the youth, the creative process illustrates the collective will to work together to create solutions. The result is a narrative in which individual problems of family separation and forced migration are not seen as isolated events, but are seen as patterns of oppression. In that collective recognition, the community group members can consolidate a vision for the future. The last scene is a static shot of the completed mural, which then loops to the beginning, where the narrative begins again.

The video shares the same name as the mural, but it can be shown independently from it. For exhibition purposes, it may be looped and projected onto a wall. The projection would ideally have dimensions similar to that of the physical mural (approximately six by twelve feet). Although I edited the video piece, it represents the collective efforts of the youth. Working as a community artist as gatherer allowed me to incorporate the voices of the community members, yet create a work in a single aesthetic.

The work was shown in May 2007, at the MAI Gallery (3680, rue Jeanne-Mance, Montreal), as a part of the Accès Asie Festival. The exhibition was an opportunity for the greater community to learn about the concerns and experiences of these Filipino youth. The month-long run included an opening and an artist talk, in which members of KM participated. The artist talk was attended by a group of Haitian refugees organized by a local social agency. This resulted in a dynamic sharing of experiences of displacement and concerns about the formation of youth gangs in the Haitian and Filipino communities. The exhibition created a relational space in which such an intercultural dialogue could occur.

Although public reception of this work is not the focus of this research, I asked the participants how they felt about the work being seen by the greater community. They expressed pride in sharing their stories with others, the opportunity of raising awareness of the issues among visitors, and the possibility of mobilizing others to become involved in their cause. One participant, Bonifacio, spoke of the importance of creating a visual history of Montreal's young Filipinos – a history that might not otherwise be told, if it was not shared by the youth themselves.

What We Learned

Based on these research findings and supported by the relevant literature, I will provide an interpretation of the findings organized into seven themes: (1) learning through visual representation and collaboration; (2) learning to connect the personal to the political through collaboration; (3) gaining knowledge of others within the collective; (4) gaining a sense of agency; (5) collaborative art production as a mode for consolidating individual experiences into collective expression; (6) collaborative art production as awareness of social problems and circumstances; and (7) collaborative art production as catalyst for critical dialogue through the creation of critical visuals. This analysis suggests that collaborative art production can be a mode for community organizing. Pseudonyms are used in the following analysis.

Learning through Visual Representation and Collaboration

LAYA: *For me, it [the mural] signifies two different things; first, it's KM's work, but ... it also signifies that if you put youths together, they're not just hanging around and doing nothing. They're actually doing something very important, you know. And the second significant thing about this mural is ... it actually represents a lot of things in everybody's lives. It's basically based [on] what's going on in our society.*

For Laya, the mural demonstrated the active participation of the youth in representing the conditions of their lives. Through visual representation, problems are given a face and hopes become tangible, and they begin to circulate in the public sphere. None of the members of KM had any formal art training. Production skills were demystified by collaboration, along with facilitation, solving the mystery of artistic production. The interactions that occurred within the collaborative process exposed youth to new art-making skills, such as colour mixing, shading, and drafting. These skills were learned in a constructivist manner, allowing non-specialists to immediately participate in production. In the following quote, Enna describes the demystification of art-making techniques that allowed a 'non-artist' like herself to participate in the mural's creation. She also alludes to the sense of achievement brought on by a collective effort:

ENNA: *I thought people doing the mural actually had to be really good and talented in painting, but with the projector, the one we used to draw the people, it was really neat. I was so happy to see that. Because I never thought we could do it that way, the way we traced the live-in caregivers. And, um, what I learned about others is that, we can actually work in groups. I was very surprised and we're very progressive in our organizing, but also, like, we can do anything in groups.*

Emphasizing the creative process over the product and making the conceptual stages participatory democratized the art-making experience. Recognition of the fact that all individuals have something to offer is important for community organizing. Art as a means of problem-posing and problem-solving allows community members to contribute to bottom-up, democratic exchange needed for collective action (Marino 1997).

Learning to Connect the Personal to the
Political through Collaboration

The elusive and dangerous character of oppression is the way it becomes naturalized and invisible. By understanding that certain problems are the social effects of oppression, communities can start working towards solutions. In the video, participants connected their experiences to the real effects of globalization, especially with regard to family separation. As elucidated by Laya and Mark in the film, their mothers, along with countless others, migrated to Canada because of economic oppression in the Philippines. In immigrating, the youth had to deal with a host of problems including language barriers, discrimination, and difficulty at school. The youth activists articulated how their present conditions were linked to larger, global problems.

By interviewing each other, hearing each other's stories, and then seeing them on video, the activists created a critical distance from each other's lives which allowed them to see how their activism is informed by their lived experiences. Through the video and mural, the participants realized that they are not only linked by their cultural background and their organizing work, but also by the struggles that they, in one way or another, have experienced in their lives. This is supported by Laya's comments from the focus group:

LAYA: *We're no longer just like members of KM, we're more like, we're together now in this. We see that we have a lot of problems and we can really co-operate altogether, not just because we're in KM – that's what we do in KM – but also as friends and by doing this we got really closer because I don't think you can just say something like that, so I think it was one step forward towards each other.*

As evidenced in the workshops and focus group, participants increased empathy through the exchange of experience and knowledge. According to Lacy (1995), it is empathy that motivates the desire for change: 'Empathy begins with the self reaching out to another self, an underlying dynamic of feeling that becomes the source of activism' (36). Linking personal affect and empathy to larger social realities promotes a sense of agency, or the sense that one can effect change in one's life or community. This sense of empowerment fosters social action (Stevens 2001). In this way, collaborative art-making facilitates the motivation needed for activism.

Gaining Knowledge of Others within the Collective

ENNA: *We saw in the movie that we all have similarities; our stories have similarities ... and we're all hiding in our own shell, you know. And it's not something that we should hide; it should be something that we're proud to say that: You know what, this and this happened to me and we're doing this now because of that.*

Enna's comments reveal how the exchange of lived experiences in the video resulted in the increased knowledge of others and a sense of solidarity. At first, the participants were nervous about sharing their lived experiences, many of which dealt with personal, sometimes painful issues. Since they knew this video was meant for a large viewing public, some participants were uncertain if they could go through with the process. However, for these activists, the project was tied to issues they strongly cared about. Temporary nervousness faded in light of knowing that their work could be used as an organizing and educating tool for others.

Although members of this community group are tied together by shared social and political consciousness, it is still, to use Hicks's phrase, a 'community of difference' (1994, 153), in which our experiences as Filipinos in Canada are different. Mameng, a child of a migrant worker, elucidates this in the mural focus group. He describes how the second panel of the mural depicts a difficult time when he was growing up. The scene shows the youth beginning to listen to a youth organizer. For Mameng, this is representative of his past gang involvement and his transformation into a youth organizer. Mameng left his tag on the wall as a way of acknowledging that past and marking his transformation (see figure 11.2). For those of us who did not share his experience, the images in the mural and the explanation that followed provided an education in the specific struggles faced by individual members of our group. The mural, as the externalization of lived experience, helps others within the group empathize with their fellow members, contributing to a nuanced understanding of community, which can help in outreach efforts with other youth, as one participant explains:

LASALLE: *I think it is beneficial to get more youth involved in this and it would be good because everyone gets to know each other, too. Also to get to know each other, see their experiences through the pictures, get to know their stories too. You get to learn more about each other.*

Gaining a Sense of Agency

JOVI: *Without collective work we would not get this done. Ah, also, you know, when I was painting, I'd go once and a while and look at the camera, you know. You can go far away from the painting and you can see the progress, you know. Augmenting by the minute. You look at it and it's a relief: 'Oh, I'm so good, man! I'm so good!' you know.*

Jovi's feelings of personal satisfaction in light of collective efforts are indicative of how participants gained an individual and collective sense of agency. Agency, or the sense that they can affect change, was fostered through the affective experiences of the collaborative process. Bayani describes how knowledge of video production gives rise to the ability to empower others: *'There are those skills of using the camera and . . . we are able to express ourselves and be more articulate . . . We can encourage others to articulate their stories as well.'* The very act of creating is a form of activism as individuals become engaged in sharing and expressing truths about their lives.

The collaborative production of the mural underlined the effectiveness of collective work, demonstrating the adage *the whole is greater than the sum of its parts:*

BAYANI: *Also I liked the fact that we did the work together [as a] collective. It's like the work with KM. We realize that with individual efforts you feel the work that everybody else [is doing] so your work is sometimes bigger . . . and you can relate it to this kind of work too and it feels that much bigger.*

The resulting product of the collaboration acts as a collective vision of where the youth have been, where they are, and where they hope to be. When art making is motivated by the deep concerns of a community, personal affect is connected to a bigger group reality (Stevens 2001). The realization that one is not alone in tackling these issues – but is a part of a larger effort – inspires action and change. Here, collective art production becomes collective action.

Collaborative Art Production as a Mode for Consolidating
Individual Experiences into Collective Expression

Because the participants were both Filipino immigrants and Filipinos born in Canada, there was a vast array of experiences among them. Although it was experienced differently, the participants, including myself, have all been affected by forced migration. In the first panel of the mural, an idealized homeland is represented with two Filipino women: one in a winter coat and another longing for home, showing displacement of the migrant worker. Whether it happened to the participants themselves or to their parents, forced migration was collectively expressed through symbols in the mural. For community organizing, collaborative art becomes a way to consolidate many individual experiences into key symbols that represent common concerns. According to Cary (1998), this sharing and creation of symbols connects individual experiences to larger collective realities. People within a collective can use these shared symbols to better identify inequalities in their community.

However, KM is also a 'community of difference' (Hicks 1994, 153), in that members, both immigrant and Canadian-born, have a wide range of experiences of life in Canada. As a participant observer, facilitator, and as the primary researcher, I was very much in an 'insider-outsider' position. Although I am a second-generation Filipino Canadian who can empathize with the realities of Filipino immigrants because of my work in the community and my family, I will never fully understand their lived struggles. My parents, immigrant themselves, came to Canada during the 1960s and felt that assimilation was key to their children's success. As a result, I did not grow up with the ability to speak Tagalog or even my family's dialect of Ilongo. Conducting the focus groups and the art workshops in my mother tongue, English, presented barriers to fuller participation for some youth. The youth who had a better grasp of English were more inclined to participate in discussions. As well, it seemed that the female participants were more articulate in speaking of their lived experiences of family separation. Several of the male participants immigrated in their late teens and struggled with family life and school. Mameng was one such male and he was the most reticent. Second-generation youth, who were fluent in Tagalog, English, and French, were able to freely communicate with everyone. Many times, they acted as co-facilitators and translators who helped others express themselves in English. This allowed for a freer exchange of ideas and experiences.

The process of collaborative art production becomes a means of examining social difference in community and learning about each other's experiences, however similar or different they may be. Collaborative art production, then, can contribute to the development and sustenance of this shared consciousness that we call community.

Collaborative Art Production as Awareness of
Social Problems and Circumstances

In both projects, the youth activists demonstrated an ability to visually represent problems and hopes. Specifically, in the video project, the harsh realities of forced migration were described by several youth. As addressed in the video, the social problems that stem from forced migration include family separation, gang involvement, and difficulty adjusting to a new society and language. Our understanding of these problems did not come from statistics, but from the lived reality of the youth. The video revealed the specificities of social problems affecting the community, which can be used to raise awareness among other Filipino youth. This video collectivizes the narratives of the youth's struggles, so when it is viewed by other youth going through similar struggles, they may come to understand that their situations are not isolated events. In building this awareness that the hardships of Filipino youth are symptoms of bigger issues relating to Third World exploitation, youth may begin to realize that they are not alone. This collective realization of oppressive patterns within a community can influence one's actions in public life (Stuhr 1994), which ultimately is the driving force for community activism (Stevens 2001). Here, community art education becomes a critical practice where collaborative art production develops a 'critical consciousness' (Freire 1993) in those who create and receive the work.

Collaborative Art Production as Catalyst for Critical
Dialogue through the Creation of Critical Visuals

The youth were asked to create their vision of the future for the community in the mural. In the second panel, participants illustrated a community centre in the heart of the neighbourhood. Jovi explains: *'Not only [does] it shows our future plans ... but the mural itself, you know, it's very intriguing 'cause there are a whole lot of different contradictions happening.'* The creation of the mural provided a space in which the youth activists could envision positive change for their community. The mural, full of possibilities and contradictions, provides alternative visions of the development of the community. According to Marino (1997), *critical visuals,* or imagery produced to identify issues and generate ideas within groups, act as tools for integrating the ideas of many individuals and identifying common concerns and goals. Such rich imagery stirs curiosity and generates dialogue; thus the creation of the mural becomes a mode of inquiry. While KM members envision the creation of a community centre, Laya suggests that the imagery in the mural will spur discussion and inquiry:

> *I think it will bring out a lot of discussion. It's going to bring out a lot of people talking about:* No, I think this future, this and that. No, I think ... *So, slowly, slowly, among themselves, among the society, I think, the light will finally shine ... They would make their own reflections and slowly they would understand by themselves, so that by doing this kind of mural it's probably going to boost up their interest in organizing as well. So, it's probably a good attraction, especially for youths.*

It is also the hope of the group that the artworks will create a critical awareness outside the Filipino community. Demonstrating a critical multiculturalism, the mural and video show the marginalization of Filipinos in Montreal and actions taken to counteract it. It is our hope that members of dominant society and other minority groups, in viewing these works, can learn about the harsh realities of difference. Jovi imagines how the greater community may view this work and how it may instigate critical dialogue:

> *If I was, you know, non-Filipino, I wouldn't understand none of these things, you know ... But, I would also be intrigued, you know.* Why are these kids like this? How come my kids aren't like this? How come my kids aren't, you know, like hanging out in this kind of neighbourhood? Why is their neighbourhood like that? *Maybe it helps to wonder.*

This research illustrates the fundamental purpose of community art education, that is, the creation and reinvention of public life: 'The point is not just to produce another thing for people to admire, but to create an opportunity – a situation – that enables viewers to look back at the world with renewed perspectives and clear angles of vision' (Phillips 1995, 70). The opportunities to wonder, dialogue, and envision alternatives for a community are several ways in which collaborative art production in the community setting can become a mode for community organizing for social change.

Conclusion

When community art education is combined with community organizing, art learning, teaching, and making become activated for a social cause and become a living process full of the possibility of change. The creation of knowledge and culture is extended from its traditional institutional confines and is brought back to the grassroots level. The cultural production becomes democratized when the perspectives of individuals and communities who have been historically ignored are brought to the centre.

The youth identified problems in their world and connected those problems to the political dimension. They gained art production skills as demystified by collaboration, and gained a sense of community based on their shared experiences and hopes. Most importantly, this learning fostered a sense that their creative work could empower others to speak of their lived experiences, difficult as it may be. By sharing our experiences, we created culture and knowledge that calls for action and change. Through collaborative art production, the Filipino youth activists realized that they, and their art, could be agents of change.

The youth is this study challenged existing oppressive conditions through discussion and art production. In identifying and externalizing these conditions through visual means, they examined unequal structures in their community. As an art educator in this context, I facilitated this process and aligned myself with their goals for social transformation. Here, art teaching and production were politicized and activated for positive social change and I, too, became agent in this process.

Social change can only happen when there is a change of consciousness among individuals. Collective art production can assist in change-making by consolidating individual efforts and experiences and by creating a context for shared visions. When problems affecting community members are identified, either through words or images, problems no longer remain isolated, but emerge as patterns of societal oppression. It is then, when problems experienced at the personal level are understood at the systemic level, that the need for action is recognized.

Collaborative art production has the ability to raise critical consciousness of community problems and is a way of developing individual and collective agency. In doing so, it becomes a form of activism. This research opens up a discursive space where those on the margins can create meaning from their lived experiences. These spaces are required to expand cultural democracy, in which art and education can reflect the lived experiences of minority youth who are often ignored by society at large.

When stepping into a community group, artists and educators alike must adopt democratic practices in order to truly address the needs of a community. Artists/educators are never just artists/educators in collaborative relationships with marginalized communities, but are agents in either challenging or reproducing existing power relations. In order to align goals, artists/educators must first understand the values of the community before a mutual, creative learning experience is established. This research also has implications for activists who are interested in incorporating art education into community organizing. Collaborative art production as community organizing can facilitate capacity-building by calling on concerned community members to identify and visually represent critical issues affecting them, connect personal experiences to larger group reality, and envision change in their community.

Community art education becomes a strategy of engaging people whose social, political, and cultural participation in society has been limited by race, social class, economic factors, etc. By activating aesthetics in a creative process, which challenges the dominant structures that have constrained the participation of ethnic minority youth in society, community art education crosses borders within social and cultural work. For community organizers, collaborative art processes can involve people in group decision-making and problem-solving while providing opportunities to recognize the diverse strengths of individuals within the collective. Such a process activates the imagination in envisioning future possibilities, providing a context for collective and individual change. In this context, community art education becomes a mode for community organizing and, thus, positive change.

NOTES

1 No pseudonym used here. Roderick Carreon is a labour organizer and one
  of the main founders of Kabataang Montreal in 1999. He continues to be a
  prominent activist with the Filipino community in Montreal.
2 As of 2009, the time requirement for the LCP was changed to 3,900 hours
  within a minimum of twenty-two months.
3 'Forced migration,' in this context, refers to Filipinos, particularly women,
  who are compelled to emigrate in order find economic opportunities that are
  not available in their homeland. The poor economy of the Philippines, the
  national endorsement of labour export policies, and the pull from the global
  North for cheap labour factor into this understanding of forced migration.
4 For more information about Roderick Carreon and the formation and
  dissolution of Filipino youth gangs, see the documentary *When Strangers
  Re-unite*.

REFERENCES

Barndt, Deborah. 2004. By whom and for whom?: Intersections of participa-
  tory research and community art. In *Provoked by art: Theorizing arts-informed
  research*, ed. Ardra L. Cole et al., 221–34. Halifax: Backalong.
Cary, Richard. 1998. *Critical art pedagogy: Foundations for postmodern art educa-
  tion*. New York: Garland.
Cohen-Cruz, Jan. 2002. An introduction to community art and activism.
  Accessed October 1, 2007. http://www.communityarts.net/CAN/API.
Freire, Paolo. 1993. *Pedagogy of the oppressed*. New York: Continuum.
Hicks, Laurie E. 1994. Social reconstruction and community. *Studies in Art
  Education* 35 (3): 149–56.
Johnston, Caleb, and Geraldine Pratt, with the Philippine Women's Centre
  of BC. 2010. *Nanay* (mother): A testimonial play. *Cultural Geographies*
  17: 123–33.
Kester, Grant. 1995. Aesthetic evangelists: Conversations and empowerment
  in contemporary art. *Afterimage* 22 (6): 5–11.
Lacy, Suzanne. 1995. Cultural pilgrimages and metaphoric journeys.
  In *Mapping the terrain: New genre public art*, ed. Suzanne Lacy, 19–47.
  Seattle: Bay.
Marino, Dian. 1997. *Wild garden: Art, education, and the culture of resistance*.
  Toronto: Between the Lines.

Meintel, Deirdre, Victor Piché, Danielle Juteau, and Sylvie Fortin, eds. 1997. *Le quartier Côte-des-Neiges à Montréal: Les interfaces de la pluriethnicité.* Paris: L'Harmattan.

Morris, Marika, and Martha Muzychka. 2002. *Participatory research and action: A guide to becoming a researcher for social change.* Ottawa: CRIAW/ICREF.

Phillips, Patricia C. 1995. Public constructions. In *Mapping the terrain: New genre public art,* ed. Suzanne Lacy, 60–71. Seattle: Bay.

Pratt, Geraldine. 2004. *Working feminism.* Philadelphia: Temple University Press.

Ratcliff, James L. 2003. Community-based organizations, agencies, and groups. In *Encyclopedia of education,* 2nd edition, 432–6. New York: Macmillan.

Stevens, Caroline Alexandra. 2001. Making art matter: Narrating the collaborative creative process. Doctoral dissertation, Concordia University, Montreal, Quebec.

Stuhr, Patricia L. 1994. Multicultural art education and social reconstruction. *Studies in art education* 35 (3): 171–8.

Chapter 12

Borrowing Privileges: Tagalog, Filipinos, and the Toronto Public Library[1]

VERNON R. TOTANES

Many new Filipino immigrants to Canada might be excited, one imagines, upon learning that they have borrowing privileges at the nearest public library, an institution practically unknown in the Philippines. Perhaps they are even delighted to learn that obtaining a library card allows them to check out not just English or French materials, but also Tagalog books, CDs, and DVDs for a few days or weeks, with the possibility of renewal. Eventually, however, they might just come to realize that the available materials in Tagalog are rather meagre in number compared to those in other collections that are intended for the use of minority groups even smaller than the Filipino population in Canada. But all this remains in the realm of speculation because no studies have been published about how Filipinos choose to exercise their borrowing privileges at public libraries in Canada.

This chapter examines the extent to which Tagalog materials – and by extension, Filipinos – are underrepresented on the shelves of the Toronto Public Library (TPL) as of 2009, and offers possible reasons for what seems to be an inequitable situation. The first section provides background on Filipinos in Canada and the languages they use, and highlights the need to distinguish between 'Tagalog,' 'Pilipino,' and 'Filipino.' The second section reviews the history of multilingual collections in Toronto as an introduction to the third section, which analyses the available evidence related to TPL's Tagalog collection, specifically in terms of location, collection, circulation, and staffing. Finally, the fourth section appraises the efforts exerted to acquire appropriate materials for Filipino library users, as well as the constraints that prevent TPL from offering the kind of service it provides other minority groups.

Filipinos and Tagalog

Filipinos began migrating to Canada in the 1940s, but as Damasco (in this volume) points out, it was not until the mid-1960s that they arrived in significant numbers. In 2006, there were more than 400,000 Filipinos in Canada, with one-fourth residing in the City of Toronto (2008a). Of these Filipinos in Toronto, almost 37 per cent most often speak a Philippine language at home, with Tagalog as the dominant language at 33 per cent, and Ilocano, Bisayan, and Pampango accounting for less than 4 per cent (Statistics Canada 2007). The rest, presumably, speak English in their homes, which is a phenomenon among second-generation Filipinos that Bustamente (1989) observed as early as twenty years ago. In her article, Bustamente made a case for passing on the Filipino heritage language to the next generation, but – like many Filipinos – did not feel it was necessary to distinguish between 'Filipino,' 'Pilipino,' and 'Tagalog.'

A look at a few official Canadian websites shows that there is some confusion surrounding the language spoken by Filipinos. For example, Statistics Canada indicates in the 2006 Census that Filipinos speak 'Tagalog (Pilipino, Filipino).' Settlement.org (2009) provides information for newcomers to Ontario in thirty-four languages, including 'Pilipino/Tagalog.' On TPL's primary page for 'Multicultural Resources' (2009b), videos may be found introducing the library's services in seventeen languages, one of which is 'Filipino.' Finally, TPL's list of 'Multilingual Collections' (2009c) shows that 'Tagalog' is one of the forty-one languages represented on its shelves.[2]

Despite the seemingly interchangeable use of 'Filipino,' 'Pilipino,' and 'Tagalog' to refer to the language spoken by many Filipinos in their Toronto homes, these terms are in fact different. The word 'Filipino,' for instance, officially refers to the people of the Philippines *and* the Philippine national language (Philippines 1987). 'Pilipino,' meanwhile, is the Tagalog word for 'Filipino.' Hence, the Tagalog translation of 'I am Filipino' is 'Pilipino ako.' And finally, 'Tagalog' can refer to a person from the Tagalog region *or* the language s/he speaks. Tagalog *people* are, of course, Filipinos, but not all Filipinos are Tagalogs. Other Filipinos refer to themselves as Cebuanos, Ilocanos, Bikolanos, etc. The same is true of the Tagalog *language*. The very fact that Tagalog had to be selected in 1937 as the basis for the Philippine national language, which was later called Pilipino, indicates that Tagalog is not the only language spoken by Filipinos, many of whom also speak Ilonggo, Kapampangan,

Chavacano, etc. Filipino itself only officially became the national language courtesy of the 1987 Constitution (Aceron 1994).

The reality, however, is that Filipino is the national language of the Philippines only on paper (Rafael 2000). Filipino, the language, is supposed to be a fusion of all the languages used in the Philippines, but very few Filipinos when asked will say that they speak 'Filipino.' Instead, more Filipinos are probably familiar with English than most Philippine languages because, aside from being the language that appears on government and business documents, it is also the medium of instruction in schools. In fact, based on anecdotal evidence, Filipinos who travel to regions or provinces other than their own and address the locals in English tend to receive warmer welcomes than those who speak Tagalog or another Philippine language. Tagalog, in short, is not the national language.[3]

To avoid confusion, this chapter uses 'Tagalog' to refer to the language, and 'Filipino' to indicate a person born in the Philippines or descended from someone who was born there. In addition, this chapter singles out Tagalog – and no other Philippine language – because it is the only one that has been privileged with its own collection on TPL's shelves, which thankfully enough are consistently labelled 'Tagalog.' While some may question the primacy given to the Tagalog language on TPL's shelves, the most basic reason for such a decision may be traced to the 2006 Census and even previous censuses, which show that more Filipinos in Toronto speak Tagalog than any other Philippine language.

Toronto Public Library's Multilingual Collections

The Toronto Public Library (2009a), with ninety-nine branches, is the largest public library system in Canada, and is the second busiest in the world (next only to Hong Kong) in terms of circulation or the number of items borrowed by its users. These items include books, magazines, CDs, and DVDs. Its multilingual collection held almost 750,000 such items in 2006, with more than a hundred languages represented. TPL began acquiring materials written in languages other than English in 1885, but it was not until 1957 that a Foreign Literature Collection was officially established and the acquisition of such materials was systematized (Zielinska 1980).

Although there was already a significant Filipino presence in Ontario by the time multiculturalism became a formal government policy in 1971, it seems the Filipino population was still not large enough by 1978 for Tagalog or any other Philippine language to be considered a major language in Ontario's libraries (ibid.). Even then, acquisition policies for the multilingual collection were not entirely dependent on population counts or the number of individuals who spoke a particular language. Other factors included the ease of procuring foreign-language materials, the degree to which existing ones were utilized, and a few other considerations that varied depending on the language concerned. These policies, of course, were not static, but were adjusted periodically as years and decades passed.

While a significant number of scholarly articles have been written about TPL's multilingual collection, especially because of its long history with foreign-language materials, no such studies have been published focusing on its Tagalog collection.[4] The few articles that have been published in relation to specific languages – such as Turkish (Skrzeszewski 1997), Russian (Dali 2004), and Slavic and East European languages (Dali and Dilevko 2005) – were primarily descriptive and/ or survey-based, and did not devote much attention to comparisons between existing populations and the available collections, and the reasons for any disparities between the former and the latter.

Curiously, though Filipinos are the fourth largest visible minority group in the City of Toronto (2008a) – after the South Asians, the Chinese, and the Blacks – TPL's Tagalog items, according to unpublished data, numbered fewer than 7,000 or less than 1 per cent of TPL's entire multilingual collection in 2006. 'Visible minority' is a term used in Canada to refer to 'persons, other than Aboriginal peoples, who are non-Caucasian in race or non-white in colour' (Statistics Canada 2009).[5] Population counts of visible minorities in Canada were derived initially from 1981 Census responses to the ethnic origin question, but beginning with the 1996 Census, respondents have been asked to self-identify as White, Chinese, South Asian, Black, etc.[6]

It is important to remember, however, that TPL does not rely on statistics on visible minority group populations to determine its acquisition policies. Instead, it uses the relatively smaller figures on language most often spoken at home for this purpose, perhaps because individuals who speak a language at home are the ones more likely to read books or watch movies in that language as well. But as table 12.1 shows, even if home language – and not population – is used to verify whether TPL's different users are adequately represented in its multilingual collection, it is clear that individual language collections are not always proportional to the number of home language speakers.

Table 12.1. Tagalog collection as percentage of Toronto Public Library's multilingual collection in relation to population and home language*

2006	Population (%)[a]	Home Language (%)[b]	TPL Collection (%)[c]
South Asians[1]	12.0	7.4	18.8
Chinese	11.4	8.1	31.9
Filipino[2]	**4.1**	**1.5**	**0.9**
Korean	1.4	1.0	2.0
Japanese	0.5	0.1	1.7

Sources: Statistics Canada 2007, unpublished 2006 TPL data

* All data are for the year 2006, Census Division of Toronto. Data for 'Blacks' and 'Latin Americans' are not used for comparison purposes because these do not have clear language equivalents in TPL's multilingual collection. ('Latin Americans,' for instance, are not the only ones who speak Spanish and Portuguese.)

[a] Percentage of entire population. n = 2,476,565

[b] Percentage of language spoken most often at home. n = 2,476,565

[c] Percentage of TPL's multilingual collection. n = 746,578

[1] Total of Indo-Aryan and Dravidian languages in 2006 Census. Major languages included are Hindi, Tamil, Gujarati, Urdu, Panjabi, and Bengali – the languages for which there are separate collections at TPL.

[2] Includes Tagalog, Bisayan languages, Ilocano, and Pampango; but TPL figures are only for the Tagalog collection.

While the South Asian population may be the largest in Toronto, the Chinese speakers outnumber those who speak South Asian languages, and thus, it may be deemed appropriate that the aggregate of TPL's different South Asian collections is smaller than its Chinese collection. The same is not true for other groups. Statistics show that the Korean and Japanese populations in Toronto – combined – were not even close to approximating the size of the Filipino population. The total number of Korean- and Japanese-language speakers is also smaller than the number of Philippine-language speakers, but each of the Korean and Japanese collections was about twice as large as the Tagalog collection. This imbalance may be traced in part to TPL's longer history of acquiring materials in the Korean and Japanese languages, but there are other factors – addressed in the next section – that must be considered as well.

Figure 12.1. Toronto Public Library branches with Tagalog collections on map showing density of Tagalog speakers. Sources: City of Toronto 2008b, Toronto Public Library 2009

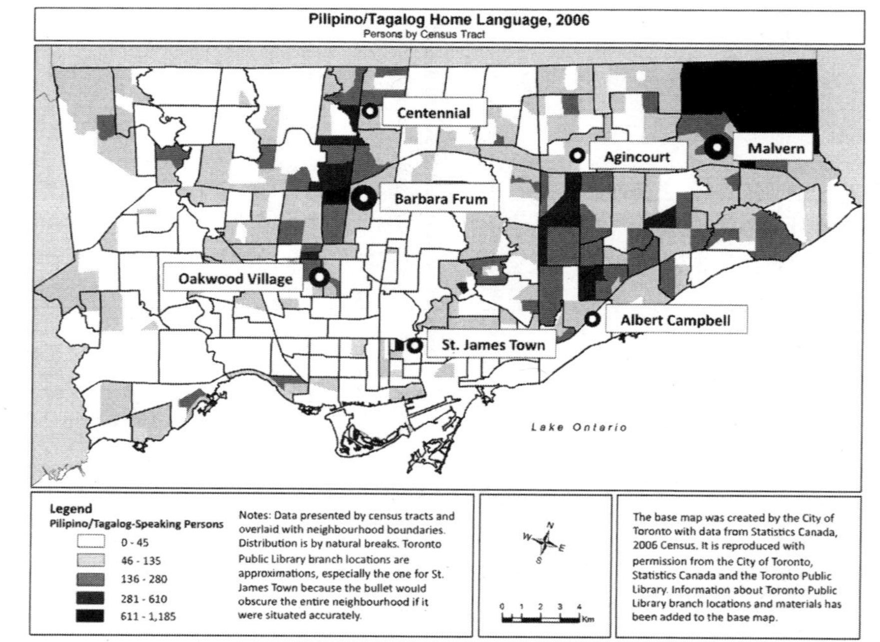

The Tagalog Collection

The following comments on location, collection, circulation, and staffing highlight the ways in which the Toronto Public Library could perhaps better serve the Filipinos living in Toronto.

Location: Are the Collections in the Right Place?

The map of Toronto (figure 12.1) shows where, according to the 2006 Census, those who speak Tagalog at home are concentrated (City of Toronto 2008b). The darker areas are those where more Tagalog speakers live.

In 2009, TPL had eight branches with Tagalog collections across the City of Toronto. The biggest one – but the least relevant for this study – is the Toronto Reference Library, which has small, representative collections for most of the major languages spoken in Toronto. The remaining seven branches are indicated on the map. As the TPL website indicates, two of them are classified as having large collections (1,500 items or more), one has a medium collection (750–1,500), and the rest are considered small (less than 750). Ideally, the larger Tagalog collections would be found in neighbourhoods where there are more Tagalog speakers. But as figure 12.1 shows, the branches with Tagalog collections are not always strategically located or appropriately stocked. The large collections at Barbara Frum and Malvern make sense, of course, considering that these branches are positioned at or near the intersection of several areas where Filipinos live. But the small collection at St James Town looks rather inadequate, because the relatively tiny neighbourhood is home to a huge number of Tagalog speakers, whereas the other libraries with small or medium collections are located in areas with fewer Filipinos.

It is possible that collection locations were selected based on a previous census, but even if this were true, there is no evidence that Tagalog speakers moved to different locations between 2001 and 2006, when censuses were conducted. Besides, there were other areas, according to the 2001 Census, that had a higher density of Tagalog speakers compared to the areas in which the Oakwood Village, Agincourt, and Albert Campbell branches were located. Thus, it seems more likely that no effort was made after the release of the 2001 Census to align the collection locations with the data it provided.

Collection: What Is Available?

In 2007, according to unpublished data, the items in the Tagalog collections at different branches included almost 4,000 books, 1,500 DVDs, 700 CDs, and 700 VHS tapes.[7] Note, however, that these are 'items,' not 'titles.' 'Title' is a technical term used by librarians, and each title can have more than one copy. Hence, it is very likely that the Tagalog *items* available in 2007 were not all unique *titles.* An ocular inspection conducted in 2009 revealed that some titles had multiple copies: at least one for each branch, and in some cases, more than one copy of a few titles at a specific branch. Thus, a search for all the Tagalog children's books, for instance, through TPL's online catalogue would have returned fewer *titles* than the 815 *items* available. It must be noted, though, that there are also titles with only one copy. In such cases, users need not travel to the library where an item is located, but can request that it be delivered to the nearest branch. This may be done through TPL's website, which also makes it possible for users to join a virtual queue to borrow a title for which demand is high. But a book that TPL does not own – like many bestsellers written by Filipinos – obviously cannot be checked out.

Of the dozens of books written by four bestselling authors published by Anvil (Bolasco 2008) – the most successful Philippine publisher for almost two decades – only two titles, with one copy for each, may be found on TPL's shelves. One is a Tagalog translation of an anthology by Margarita Holmes, and the other is a children's book by Ambeth Ocampo. It is perhaps understandable that none of the other bestsellers by these authors are currently available in TPL's Tagalog collection because – like those by Jessica Zafra – most of their works are in English. But it is curious that not one of the books by Pol Medina, the artist known for his Tagalog comic strips, has been acquired by TPL. What is even more perplexing is that unlike many Philippine publications, Medina's books – as well as those by Holmes, Ocampo, and Zafra – are still in print and can easily be purchased.

Based on a physical examination of shelves and anecdotal evidence provided by staff at the branches with Tagalog collections, it is clear that paperback romances and melodramatic movies are borrowed more often than award-winning novels and films. In fact, it is very likely that some of the latter have never been borrowed at all, as suggested by their pristine condition. While it may be interesting and perhaps useful for librarians, as well as those concerned about the

Figure 12.2. Stock and circulation percentages for different kinds of media in Tagalog collections. Source: Unpublished 2007 TPL data

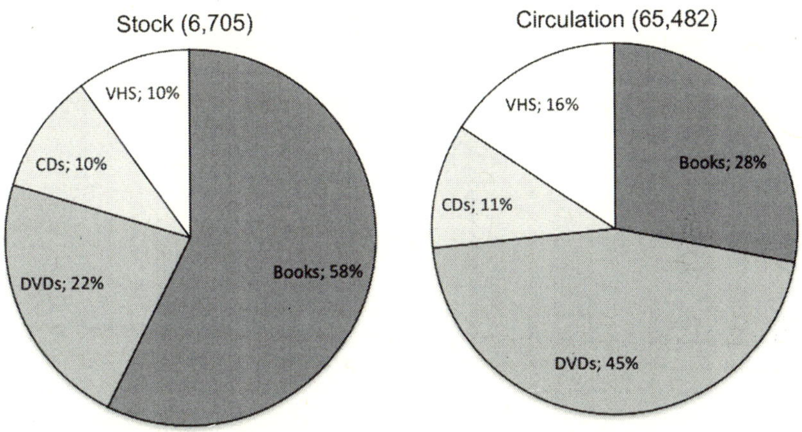

plight of Filipino women, to ascertain whether the fact that there are more women (58 per cent) than men among the Filipinos in Toronto (Statistics Canada 2007) – and that many of the women are caregivers and nannies – has anything to do with the popularity of romances and melodramas, it is not possible, unfortunately, to obtain circulation data for specific titles or demographic information on their borrowers.

Circulation: Are the Materials Being Used?

It has been suggested that while most Filipinos residing in the Philippines are literate, many of them do not really like to read books (Bolasco 2006). The latest data from the National Statistics Office (2005) indicates that Filipinos seeking knowledge or information are more likely to turn to TV (62 per cent), radio (57 per cent), and newspapers (47 per cent) than magazines/books (36 per cent). In addition, according to the nationwide survey conducted by the National Book Development Board (2007), 92 per cent of Filipinos could read, but only 39 per cent had read a non-school book in the last two months. These figures are not necessarily true for Filipinos outside the Philippines, but the circulation percentages for TPL's Tagalog collection (see figure 12.2) certainly imply that Filipinos in Toronto are more likely to pick up DVDs (45 per cent) than books (28 per cent). But these pie charts can be deceiving.

Table 12.2. Circulation-to-stock ratios for Tagalog collection and total multilingual collection

2007	Stock	Circulation	C-S ratio Tagalog[1]	C-S ratio Total MLC[2]
Print (books)	3,849	18,337	4.76	3.25
Audio (CDs)	697	7,125	10.22	6.64
DVD	1,498	29,755	19.86	32.37
Video (VHS)	661	10,265	15.53	12.49
Total	6,705	65,482	9.77	6.20

Source: Unpublished 2007 TPL data

[1] C-S ratio = Circulation/stock

[2] MLC refers to multilingual collection

While it is obvious that there are more books in stock (58 per cent) than any other format, and CDs (11 per cent) and VHS tapes (16 per cent) circulate at a lower rate than books, computing for the ratio of circulated items to stock available (C-S ratio; see table 12.2) – which provides an indication of how frequently an item is borrowed in one year – can be a better gauge of consumer demand. The C-S ratio for the Tagalog collection shows, in fact, that CDs (10.22) and even VHS tapes (15.53), not just DVDs (19.86), were also more popular than books (4.76). Another way of looking at it is that the average VHS tape was borrowed 15.53 times, while the average book was checked out only 4.76 times.[8] In short, even though there were fewer CDs, VHS tapes, and DVDs compared to books, such items were more than twice as likely to be borrowed.

But if the Tagalog ratios are compared with those of the entire multilingual collection, it is obvious that this observation is true not only for Filipinos. Clearly, users of other language collections also prefer DVDs, VHS tapes, and CDs over books.[9] If population and home language are examined in relation to the total C-S ratios for different languages (see table 12.3), it becomes apparent why the Chinese collection is so much larger. Not only are there more Chinese in Toronto (11.4 per cent), there are also more of them who speak a Chinese language at home (8.1 per cent). Plus, the C-S ratio (11.3) for the Chinese collection, when compared with those of other collections, proves that the materials available are actually being used.

Table 12.3 highlights another reason the use of the C-S ratio is better than relying on actual stock and circulation figures. For instance,

Table 12.3. Circulation-to-stock ratio for specific visible minorities in relation to population and home-language percentages

2006	Population (%)	Home language (%)	Stock	Circulation	C-S Ratio
South Asians	12.0	7.4	140,456	1,197,624	8.5
Chinese	11.4	8.1	238,332	2,689,514	11.3
Filipino	**4.1**	**1.5**	**6,967**	**58,884**	**8.5**
Korean	1.4	1.0	14,884	52,839	3.6
Japanese	0.5	0.1	12,386	24,410	2.0

Sources: Statistics Canada 2007, unpublished 2007 TPL data

although the circulation figures for the South Asian collections (1,197,624) are much higher than those for the Tagalog collection (58,884), both have the same C-S ratios of 8.5, which indicates that even though the latter has fewer materials, the demand for them is just as strong as for those in the former. In short, there may be fewer Filipinos than South Asians, but the smaller Tagalog collection is used just as often as the larger South Asian collections. But it is not so clear why the Korean and Japanese collections are individually larger than the Tagalog collection. Not only are there fewer Koreans and Japanese in Toronto compared to Filipinos, the C-S ratios for their collections (3.6 and 2.0, respectively) show that these are also not circulating as much as the smaller Tagalog collection (8.5). In other words, although the Tagalog materials are checked out more often, it has fewer items than other collections that are not used as much.

The disparity between the sizes of the Korean and Japanese collections and their current populations may be attributed to several factors, including the longevity of the collections, the relative ease of acquiring materials, or even statistical declines in their populations towards the end of the twentieth century. It is possible, for instance, that the number of Koreans and Japanese in Toronto has remained constant over several decades, but as the populations of other minority groups increased, the percentage of Koreans and Japanese decreased in relation to the total population with no commensurate decrease in the acquisition of materials for their respective collections. There is no evidence available, however, to either prove or disprove this theory.

Staffing and Representation

Another plausible reason that the Tagalog collection is smaller than the Korean and Japanese collections is that there are fewer Filipino librarians at TPL than Korean- and Japanese-speaking librarians. Filipino librarians, after all, would be more likely to appreciate the significance of requests made for Tagalog books, CDs, and DVDs and could then advocate the need for such materials. But there is also no evidence to support this hypothesis because information about the ethnicities of TPL's staff is not readily available. Even questions regarding the number of Filipinos or Tagalog-speakers at TPL were answered with a statement that this information was 'an HR question,' which presumably means it is confidential.

What is known is that there was one senior Filipino librarian at TPL in 2006, who was later joined by two more newly minted librarians in 2009. The senior librarian, currently a library service manager responsible for four branches, migrated to Canada with her husband and children in 1974 and has been working as a librarian in Toronto libraries since 1976. The new librarians moved to Canada from the Philippines with their respective parents and siblings as children, and began working as library assistants when they were still high school students. It must be noted, though, that it is only the senior librarian who can speak and read Tagalog fluently. The other two, though able to understand spoken Tagalog, are more likely to converse freely in English. All three may be said to represent and can relate to the different generations of Filipinos in Canada. Not one, however, was working at any of the eight branches with Tagalog collections in 2009.

The Filipinos whom users looking for Tagalog materials are more likely to encounter are library assistants. At least two of them work at branches with Tagalog collections, but since their responsibilities are limited to answering directional questions and attending to clients at the circulation desk, it would not be reasonable to expect that they would be able to influence acquisitions policies beyond making occasional suggestions. Perhaps the Filipino at TPL who is best able to shape the composition of the Tagalog collection is someone whom library-card holders very rarely meet. The selector who chooses the Tagalog materials that TPL acquires does not have to be a librarian, but s/he does have to speak and read the language. Unfortunately, it was not possible to interview the Tagalog selector because she was on extended leave when this chapter was finalized.

Practical Considerations

In fairness to TPL, the efforts it has made for the benefit of its Filipino clients must be acknowledged. First, the budget for acquiring Tagalog materials, according to unpublished data, has increased from less than $4,000 in 1999 to almost $38,000 in 2009.[10] Second, the number of branches with Tagalog collections was to be expanded from eight to seventeen by the end of 2009. So it would not be correct to say that TPL has ignored the needs of its Filipino clients. In fact, it must also be recognized that there are certain constraints that limit TPL's options in serving the Filipino community.

One, the Tagalog collection is fairly new compared to the other language collections. TPL only began actively building up its Tagalog collection after the 1998 amalgamation that resulted in the current City of Toronto.[11] Two, the lack of Filipino librarians at TPL is merely part of a larger problem, which is that very few members of visible minorities even consider becoming librarians (8Rs Research Team 2005). Three, Filipinos in Toronto, especially new immigrants, are not necessarily keen on obtaining a library card because public libraries in the Philippines are virtually non-existent. As the 2007 Readership Survey commissioned by the National Book Development Board of the Philippines (2007) indicates, the majority of Filipinos do not even know where the nearest public library is located. This lack of awareness is probably partly due to the reality that there is approximately only one public library for every 100,000 Filipinos (Cruz 2009; National Statistical Coordination Board 2009).[12] In contrast, there are four times as many public libraries for every 100,000 people in the City of Toronto (TPL 2009a; Statistics Canada 2007). And of course, very few public libraries in the Philippines are even comparable to the ones in Toronto. It is possible that Filipinos in Toronto have already discovered the advantages of having borrowing privileges and are just not interested in availing themselves of them, but it is also very likely that many of those who grew up without access to any kind of library in the Philippines need assistance and encouragement in exploring and taking advantage of TPL's resources.

Four, Tagalog is not the language spoken or read by most Filipinos, especially those in Toronto, where 63 per cent speak English at home. According to its official government website, the Philippines (2010) has eight major languages and almost five hundred dialects, but the languages of its mass media are limited to English and Tagalog, and it is not always easy to discern why one is more popular than the other. For instance, Tagalog shows dominate Philippine television today, but Hollywood movies are much more popular than locally produced ones, especially if the sales of pirated DVDs are taken into account (Baumgärtel 2006). When it comes to music, Filipino singers are just as likely to perform Tagalog songs as English ones, and the titles of the songs they sing in concerts, on TV, and on their CDs reflect this reality.

While it is possible that the nature of the medium influences patronage – i.e., TV is free, but movies cost money, which English-speaking Filipinos are more likely to have – this explanation does not fully account for previous decades when English programs dominated primetime TV schedules, and Tagalog movies regularly trounced foreign films at the box office (Fernandez 1981). The same is true for pop music, which may be seen and heard on free TV and radio, but songs played – when not exclusively American – are likely to be either Filipino singers' cover versions of U.S. hits, original compositions by Filipinos in English, or foreign-sounding Tagalog tunes.

The scenario for books is even more puzzling. Although evidence shows that Filipinos prefer to read Tagalog materials (Jurilla 2008; National Book Development Board 2007; Hidalgo 2007), more titles in English are published in the Philippines than Tagalog ones. Filipino

Table 12.4. Percentage of visible minority population that most often speaks a non-official language at home[1]

2006	Population	Home language	HL/Pop[2](%)
South Asians	298,375	183,985	61.7
Chinese	283,075	200,230	70.7
Filipino	**102,555**	**37,610**	**36.7**
Korean	34,215	23,785	69.5
Japanese[3]	11,965	2,910	24.3

Source: Statistics Canada 2007

[1] The official languages in Canada are English and French.

[2] HL/Pop = home language/population

[3] The number of Japanese who speak Japanese at home is even lower than the number for Filipinos, which suggests that most of the Japanese in Toronto speak English at home.

publishers, however, continue producing more titles in English. Thus, local bookstores, whose stock is largely devoted to imported books in English, also carry more Philippine-related titles in English than in Tagalog (Bolasco 2008). Video and music stores also stock more imported DVDs and CDs, but even the Filipino items on their shelves are not always exclusively in Tagalog. While the prevalence of books, CDs, and DVDs in English in the Philippines may be viewed as evidence of the miseducation of the Filipino by their American colonizers (Constantino 1966), and is perhaps further evidence of the Filipino's lingering colonial mentality (David and Okazaki 2006), there is really not much that TPL can do about the situation. What this means in practical terms is that even if TPL wanted to drastically increase the size of its Tagalog collection, there probably would not be enough materials available for purchase (Arlante and Tarlit 2001).

But more importantly, if Canadian census statistics on home language are really a major component when it comes to acquisitions policies, it is probably time to acknowledge the biggest difference between Filipinos and other minority groups in Toronto (see table 12.4). In contrast to the Chinese, South Asians, and Koreans – most of whom speak their mother tongues at home – the majority of Filipinos in Toronto do *not* speak a Philippine language at home. Thus, the acquisition of more Philippine-related materials in English – and not Tagalog – may actually be more appropriate for the Filipino community. This, incidentally, would be much easier than acquiring Tagalog materials – especially books.

Conclusion

Although Filipinos and their culture are practically invisible at the Toronto Public Library and its shelves, it is clear that efforts are being made to improve the situation in spite of certain realities that prevent TPL from offering better service to Filipinos living in Toronto. But there is still more that can be done. For instance, although new Tagalog collections have recently been established at nine locations, the appropriateness of the current sites and/or the sizes of their Tagalog collections should also be reviewed. It would be even better if the branches with large Tagalog collections had at least one Filipino librarian. TPL's acquisitions policy also needs to be revisited, so that popular Tagalog works in the Philippines are not unintentionally overlooked. In addition, instead of focusing solely on Tagalog readers and publications, TPL needs to acknowledge that the majority of Filipinos in Toronto speak English as their home language, and that most titles published in the Philippines are written in English.[13]

But this does not imply that the Tagalog collection need not be developed any further. The majority of Filipinos in Toronto may speak English as their home language, but as the analysis of C-S ratios demonstrates, Tagalog books, CDs, VHS tapes, and DVDs are borrowed just as often as South Asian ones. This suggests that there is, in fact, a significant demand for Tagalog materials, even though Filipinos who most often speak Tagalog at home are not as numerous as the English-speaking ones. Thus, more research needs to be done on Filipinos and their awareness of TPL's services and resources. Are most of them new immigrants or second-generation Filipino Canadians? Why do some exercise their borrowing privileges and others do not? Do the Filipinos who are regular library users already know Tagalog or are they trying to learn it? Would those who are not regular users be interested in Tagalog materials or would they rather read Philippine literature in English? These are just some of the questions that can be asked. The answers will contribute not only to a better understanding of just how Filipinos in Canada view the resources available at public libraries, but even of the ways in which the needs of Filipinos are different from those of other visible minority groups.

NOTES

1 The information provided in this chapter was obtained from the official websites of Statistics Canada, the City of Toronto, and the Toronto Public Library, supplemented by personal visits, informal interviews with TPL employees, unpublished data, and formal correspondence with Diane Dragasevich, a senior collections specialist at TPL. All data provided, unless indicated otherwise, is as of 2009.

2 There is also anecdotal evidence that many non-Filipinos do not even know what people from the Philippines are called. Just recently, a librarian kept referring to me as 'Philippine,' even though I had already mentioned that I was 'Filipino,' which seems to be as unfamiliar to some as 'Pilipino' or 'Tagalog.'

3 In certain cases, what seems to be Tagalog may be the scholarly version that the literati invented, but which many find difficult to understand. What is more commonly used, especially on TV shows, is colloquial Tagalog or even

Taglish, which incorporates English words and phrases into Tagalog sentences as if one language was equivalent to the other.

4 Other Philippine languages are represented at TPL, but none has enough items to be listed separately on TPL's website as a major language.

5 The term has been in use for several decades, but is not without its critics, notably the United Nations' Committee on the Elimination of Racial Discrimination (2007).

6 One of the curious aspects of the census questionnaire is that even though the Philippines is considered part of Southeast Asia, respondents can choose 'Filipino' as a separate category from 'Southeast Asian.'

7 Only aggregate data is available for 2006, so the 2007 figures, which provide a breakdown of the number of different items available on shelves throughout TPL's branches, will be used.

8 While the C-S ratio does not account for the fact that some items are borrowed more than others and some are never borrowed at all, this ratio is helpful, nonetheless, because it gives librarians an idea of how often the materials in a collection are checked out.

9 It is worth noting, though, that Tagalog books are checked out more often compared to the average for the entire multilingual collection.

10 An additional, one-time allocation of $25,100 was also appropriated in 2009 for the purchase of DVDs, for a total expenditure of $63,000.

11 Specific information related to the sources of materials in the Tagalog, Korean, and Japanese collections is, unfortunately, not readily available.

12 There are more school libraries than public libraries in the Philippines, but since most school libraries are *public* school libraries – for which there is practically no funding at all – the state of school libraries in general cannot be said to be better than that of public libraries. In fact, the great majority of public school libraries are usually poorly stocked and/or rarely ever open to students. See Totanes (2004).

13 Philippine-related materials in English would not, of course, be part of the multilingual collection, but there are actually very few titles in TPL's main collection at this time that Filipinos interested in Philippine materials in English would be able to check out.

REFERENCES

8Rs Research Team. 2005. The future of human resources in Canadian libraries. Accessed January 1, 2010. http://www.ls.ualberta.ca/8rs/8RsFutureofHRLibraries.pdf.

Aceron, Eldrige Marvin B. 1994. Filipino with the 'F': A construction of the national language policy. *Ateneo Law Journal* 38: 76–94.

Arlante, Salvacion M., and Rodolfo Y. Tarlit. 2001. The state-of-the-art of Filipiniana collections in the Philippines. In *Sanghaya 2001: Philippine arts + culture yearbook,* 121–5. Manila: National Commission for Culture and the Arts.

Baumgärtel, Tilman. 2006. The culture of piracy in the Philippines. Paper presented at Asia Culture Forum, Gwangju, Korea.

Bolasco, Karina A. 2006. Issues of reading and languages. Paper presented at RAP Demofest, Legaspi, Albay.

– 2008. When the book became personal: 30 years of Philippine tradebook publishing. Paper presented at quadrennial meeting of the International Conference on Philippine Studies, Quezon City.

Bustamente, R.E. 1989. Filipino Canadians: Where is our heritage language going? *Polyphony: The Bulletin of the Multicultural History Society of Ontario* 11: 112–15.

City of Toronto. 2008a. Backgrounder: Release of the 2006 Census on ethnic origin and visible minorities. Accessed August 23, 2009. http://www.toronto.ca/demographics/pdf/2006_ethnic_origin_visible_minorities_backgrounder.pdf.

– 2008b. Pilipino/Tagalog Home Language, 2006. Accessed August 23, 2009. http://www.toronto.ca/demographics/atlas/cma/2006/language/ct06_lang_home_pilipino.pdf.

Constantino, Renato. 1966. The mis-education of the Filipino. *Weekly Graphic* (June 8), 35–40.

Cruz, Prudenciana. 2009. CDNLAO country report: National Library of the Philippines. Accessed April 21, 2010. http://www.ndl.go.jp/en/cdnlao/meetings/pdf/CR2009_Philippines.pdf.

Dali, Keren. 2004. Reading by Russian-speaking immigrants in Toronto: Use of public libraries, bookstores, and home book collections. *International Information and Library Review* 36: 341–66.

Dali, Keren, and Juris Dilevko. 2005. Beyond approval plans: Methods of selection and acquisition of books in Slavic and East European languages in North American libraries. *Library Collections, Acquisitions, and Technical Services* 29: 238–69.

David, E.J.R., and Sumie Okazaki. 2006. The colonial mentality scale (CMS) for Filipino Americans: Scale construction and psychological implications. *Journal of Counseling Psychology* 53: 241–52.

Fernandez, Doreen G. 1981. Philippine popular culture: Dimensions and directions – The state of research in Philippine popular culture. *Philippine Studies* 29: 26–44.

Hidalgo, Antonio A. 2007. Creative publishing. *University of the Philippines Forum* (July–August), 8–11.

Jurilla, Patricia May B. 2008. *Tagalog bestsellers of the twentieth century: A history of the book in the Philippines.* Quezon City: Ateneo de Manila University Press.

National Book Development Board. 2007. *NBDB readership survey.* Accessed August 23, 2009. http://nbdb.gov.ph/images/readership_highlights.pdf.

National Statistical Coordination Board. 2009. Population of the Philippines: Census Years 1799 to 2007. Accessed August 23, 2009. http://www.nscb.gov.ph/secstat/d_popn.asp.

National Statistics Office. 2005. *2003 Functional Literacy, Education and Mass Media Survey,* 33.

Philippines. 1987. Constitution. Accessed March 31, 2010. http://www.gov.ph/index.php?option=com_contentandtask=viewandid=200034andItemid=26.

– 2010. Language. Accessed March 31, 2010. http://www.gov.ph/index.php?option=com_contentandtask=viewandid=200020andItemid=26.

Rafael, Vicente L. 2000. Taglish, or the phantom power of the lingua franca. In *White love and other events in Filipino history,* 162–89. Quezon City: Ateneo de Manila University Press.

Settlement.org. 2009. In my language. Accessed September 24, 2009. http://www.settlement.org/inmylanguage/.

Skrzeszewski, Stan. 1997. Library services to Turkish communities in Canada. *Resource Sharing and Information Networks* 12: 8993.

Statistics Canada. 2007. *2006 Census.* Accessed September 24, 2009. http://www12.statcan.gc.ca/census-recensement/index-eng.cfm.

– 2009. Visible minority population and population group reference guide. *2006 Census.* Accessed September 24, 2009. http://www.recensement2006.ca/census-recensement/2006/ref/rp-guides/visible_minority-minorites_visibles-eng.cfm.

Toronto Public Library. 2009a. About the library. Accessed September 24, 2009. http://www.torontopubliclibrary.ca/abo_index.jsp.

– 2009b. Multicultural resources. Accessed September 24, 2009. http://www.torontopubliclibrary.ca/mul_index.jsp.

– 2009c. Multilingual collections. Accessed September 24, 2009. http://www.torontopubliclibrary.ca/mul_bks_guide.jsp.

Totanes, Vernon R. 2004. Factors influencing the development of the public secondary school libraries in the Third District of Quezon City. MLIS thesis, University of the Philippines.

United Nations. 2007. Report of the Committee on the Elimination of Racial Discrimination. Accessed March 31, 2010. http://daccess-ods.un.org/access.nsf/Get?OpenandDS=A/62/18andLang=E.

Zielinska, Marie. 1980. Public library services to Canadian ethnocultural communities: An overview. *Library Trends* 29: 275–92.

Chapter 13

Abject Beings: Filipina/os in Canadian Historical Narrations

ROLAND SINTOS COLOMA

In a history textbook for Canadian secondary schools, a photograph shows a multi-generational white family – a father, a mother, their son, and a grandmother. Located in a section called 'Generation X, Tweens/ Teens, and the Greying of Canada,' its caption reads: 'A family that must care for both a teen and an aging family member might face certain problems. Name them' (Bolotta et al. 2000, 360).[1] While the caption solicits a delineation of concerns confronted by today's families, it fails to consider the people brought in to address and resolve them. In another Canadian history book, a section on 'The Baby Boom' from 1945 to 1963 states that 'the burden of child-rearing largely fell on women' (Bothwell 2006, 367). Although this statement captures the gendered division of labour in Canadian homes fifty years ago, it continues to resonate. However, what is different in the current context is the shift in childcare and domestic burden to Filipina/os who work as live-in caregivers. Missing in Canadian historical and educational discourse are the Filipina/os whose labour as caregivers has become the solution to problems of family health, safety, and well-being, and has become a major support for work and life balance. Through their labour in Canadian homes, they enable the development of professional careers and the accumulation of material capital in upper- and middle-class families. Yet the significant role that Filipina/os play in Canada's welfare and prosperity remains absent in mainstream narrations.

To look for Filipina/os in Canadian history books is to experience a profound sense of abjection not only in the narration of Canadian history but also in the Canadian imaginary of nation, citizenship, and belonging. In *Bodies That Matter,* Judith Butler (1993) describes 'abject beings' as 'those who are not yet "subjects," but who form the constitutive outside to the domain of the subject.' They mark the '"unlivable" and "uninhabitable" zones of social life which are nevertheless densely populated by those who do not enjoy the status of the subject, but whose living under the sign of the "unlivable" is required to circumscribe the domain of the subject' (3). What I find productive in Butler's formulation is that, although abjection 'designates a degraded or cast out status within the terms of sociality' (243), those who are positioned as such also serve as limit-threats to the constitution of the subject. In other words, analysis into the status and position of Filipina/os as abject beings, as degraded and cast out entities in historical accounts of the nation, can throw into sharp relief the representational power of racial inclusion, exclusion, and denial in Canada. An investigation into Filipina/os as abject beings in Canadian historical narrations, therefore, can illustrate the processes and effects of abjection and the ambivalence in occupying unliveable spaces and positions.

The absence of Filipina/os in scholarly and pedagogical discourse captures the epitome of abjection – the erasure of one's presence and accomplishment, the denial of one's labour and contribution, and the emplacement of elites as the only legitimate and central subjects of history. Abject beings become a present absence who haunt those who are emplaced; they are the counterparts of Sunera Thobani's (2007) 'exalted subjects' whose experiences and needs are foregrounded, who benefit from the other's labour, and whose status and privilege derive from the other's abjection. To elaborate on the condition of Filipina/os as abject beings, this chapter will analyse twelve Canadian history books for details on race, gender, labour, and migration in general and on Filipina/os in particular. It will situate such an examination within the scholarly fields of critical race studies and history education, and will put forward three recommendations that address the structural, discursive, and affective realms when redressing invisibility in historical narrations.

Situating the Project:
Critical Race Studies and History Education

This chapter is grounded in a scholarly field that can be construed as critical race studies (Bannerji 2000; Razack et al. 2010). Critical race studies offers theoretical, methodological, and pedagogical insights in investigations of national formation and expression that account for the triangulated racialized relations among white Europeans, Aboriginal peoples, and racial/ethnic minorities. This racialized triangulation underscores the exaltation and emplacement of whites as rightful citizen-subjects, the genocide and displacement of Aboriginal peoples, and the ambivalent position of racial/ethnic minorities in a settler nation-state (Thobani 2007). My contribution to this field, through this chapter, is to address the invisibility and ambivalent position of a particular minority group – Filipina/os in Canada. With the themes of abjection and ambivalence in mind, I ask: What does it mean for Filipina/os to be the fourth largest racialized minority group in the country, yet remain absent in Canadian historical narration? How does representational invisibility produce abjection, and how might abjection consequently engender desires and actions to redress marginality? What are the material, discursive, and affective effects of desires and actions to move out of invisibility and become part of Canadian narratives?

In his analysis of racial difference and postcolonial conditions, Homi Bhabha (1994) suggests that racialized peoples experience ambivalence, a feeling generated from a desire 'almost [to be] the same, but not quite [white]' (89). I argue that ambivalence captures the situation of many Filipina/o migrants in Canada, which derived from their conflicting sense of entitlement and exclusion. They feel ambivalent, in part, because of a distorted sense of relative entitlement based on their linguistic and educational capital, compared to others whose home language or primary idiom of formal instruction is not English, and who have not attained a certain level of higher education (i.e., college or university).[2] Their sense of relative entitlement, deriving from their English proficiency and educational attainment in the Philippines, Canada, or elsewhere, enables them to stake claims for legitimate inclusion and integration in this country. In fact, according to Statistics Canada's 2006 census, 46 per cent of Filipina/os in Canada have a university degree or college diploma, and 99 per cent have linguistic proficiency or knowledge of English. Nationally, 33 per cent of all Canadians have a university degree or college diploma, and 85 per cent have linguistic proficiency or knowledge of English. In spite of their putative linguistic and educational advantage, however, Filipina/os confront socio-cultural, economic, and political barriers from racialized, gendered, and labour programs and practices which adversely impact their lives and livelihoods (Kelly et al. in this volume; Pratt 2004; Stasiulis and Bakan 2005). These barriers mitigate and disrupt Filipina/os' sense of relative entitlement and their desire for belonging and citizenship in Canada.[3]

Filipina/os' ambivalent position is further conditioned by the tensions and contradictions in Canada's policy and rhetoric of multiculturalism.

Sunera Thobani (2007) contends that multiculturalism as a national social policy 'furthered popular perceptions of the nation having made a successful transition from a white settler colony to a multiracial, multi-ethnic, liberal-democratic society. Imagined now as welcoming "diverse" immigrants and valuing their cultures, the nation-state came to be seen as particularly amenable to resolving ethnic and cultural divisions. This perception ... was also shared by many immigrants' (144). Canada's multiculturalism – in contradistinction to the United States' version of multiculturalism as melting pot assimilation – foregrounds, instead, the metaphor of mosaic, which claims to recognize and celebrate the nation's rich cultural diversity.[4] However, in *Inside the Mosaic*, Eric Fong and his colleagues (2006) demonstrate the persistent challenges faced by peoples of colour in employment, education, housing, and public services. Although Canada's multiculturalism policy aims to simultaneously value cultural differences and bridge cultural divisions, it remains as an unfulfilled promise, especially for abject beings who occupy the nation's unliveable spaces.

Moreover, this chapter engages with the scholarly field of history education, which is concerned with the ways in which history is depicted and disseminated. Ruth Sandwell (2006, 3) asks, 'Whose history *counts*? What people, events, and issues get to be included in social studies and history classrooms? Who and what are left out? And who decides these things?' She frames these questions in relation to intellectual and societal anxieties about the increasingly contested nature of history. She adds that concerns about the 'who' and 'what' in history are connected to how the past is construed and why certain details are included or not. The issue of race and racism, for instance, has generated a tremendous amount of questions and unease about historical narrations. Timothy Stanley (2006) argues that one of Canada's enduring myths is the absence of racism. He elaborates that 'by selectively representing the histories of the many people who live in Canada, by identifying certain people as Canadian and largely ignoring the others, and by sanitizing the histories through which some people have become dominant, public memory sets the stage for racist denial. Meanwhile, the relative silence of public memory on the racism that has helped to create Canadian life, spaces, and institutions can make it seem that there is indeed no racism in Canada' (32–3). I employ Sandwell's and Stanley's questions about history and arguments about racism, respectively, as points of departure in my analysis of how history textbooks represent Filipina/os in Canada.

Methodology: Texts and Analyses

This study examines twelve Canadian history texts – six secondary school textbooks, four university textbooks, and two general reference books – that were published from the years 2000 to 2007 (see table 13.1). It does not intend to be a comprehensive analysis of Canadian history textbooks; rather, by examining a range of texts for high school, university, and general readership, I aimed to investigate how Filipina/os are depicted in mainstream Canadian historical narrations. I also selected books with time periods that focus on the twentieth century, since the first large wave of Filipina/o migration to Canada started in the 1960s. In addition, I chose school texts that were recently published, because they are more closely aligned with current official curriculum guidelines.

The twelve books were written by history teachers and teacher educators who work in school boards and faculties of education, and by historians who are employed as professors in institutions of higher education. They were published by major academic, trade, and specialized presses, such as Oxford University Press, McGraw-Hill, Pearson, Nelson, Gage, and Fitzhenry and Whiteside. The secondary textbooks indicate that they are aligned with the province of Ontario's school curriculum and are for students in grades 10 and 12 enrolled in Canadian history courses. The websites of the publishers for the university textbooks describe their target readership as students who take introductory courses in Canadian history. The reference books are geared for a general audience: according to company websites, Key Porter offers 'mainstream books of national interest,' and Penguin taps into the 'broadest reading public and addresses leading issues of social importance.'

Similar to my other study on the representation of Filipina/os in secondary school textbooks for United States and World history courses (Coloma 2012a), methodologically I relied on book indexes as guides for my textual analyses. Initially, I used the terms 'Filipino' and 'Philippines' in my search through all twelve Canadian history books. Then my search included the keywords 'race,' 'ethnicity,' and 'visible minority.' I also added the keywords 'Asian,' 'immigration,' 'migration,' and 'diaspora' as well as 'gender,' 'women,' 'domestic work,' and 'labour.' I utilized the keywords 'race' and 'migration' since they provide general descriptors for the experiences of Filipina/os in Canada. I also searched for 'women' and 'labour' because of the gendered pattern in Filipina/o migration and employment. I used these keywords to search the indexes, and examined the indicated pages and sections

Table 13.1. Canadian history books

Main authors/editors	Title	Year of publication	Publisher
Secondary textbooks			
Don Bogle et al.	Continuity and Change: A History of Canada since 1914	2006	Fitzhenry and Whiteside
Angelo Bolotta et al.	Canada: Face of a Nation	2000	Gage
Nick Brune et al.	Defining Canada: History, Identity, and Culture	2003	McGraw-Hill Ryerson
Dennis DesRivieres and Colin Bain	Experience History: Canada since World War I	2006	Oxford University Press
Garfield Gini-Newman et al.	Canada: A Nation Unfolding	2000	McGraw-Hill Ryerson
Garfield Gini-Newman et al.	Canadian History: A Sense of Time	2006	McGraw-Hill Ryerson
University textbooks			
John Bumsted	A History of the Canadian Peoples (3rd ed.)	2007	Oxford University Press
Margaret Conrad and Alvin Finkel	Canada: A National History	2003	Pearson Longman
Alvin Finkel and Margaret Conrad	History of the Canadian Peoples, 1867 to the Present, volume 2 (3rd ed.)	2002	Pearson Longman
Douglas Francis et al.	Journeys: A History of Canada	2006	Nelson
General reference books			
Robert Bothwell	The Penguin History of Canada	2006	Penguin
Craig Brown	The Illustrated History of Canada	2007	Key Porter

in the books to glean informational and representational insights not only on Filipina/os, but also on how issues of race, gender, labour, and migration are framed.

Results: Filipina/os as Statistical Figures and Late Arrivals

My analysis of the twelve history books reveals that (1) the terms 'Filipino' and the 'Philippines' do not appear in any index; (2) out of the twelve, only three mention 'Filipino' or the 'Philippines' in the main text; the other nine do not have any information on Filipina/os at all; and (3) when these terms appear in the main text (and one has to read closely to find them), Filipina/os show up as statistical figures of immigrants and as late arrivals to Canada.

The terms 'Filipino' and the 'Philippines' appear as part of statistical tables in one secondary textbook and two university textbooks. In the secondary textbook *Canada: Face of a Nation,* the term 'Filipinos' appears in a table on 'Top Ethnic Origins in Canada, 1996 Census.' The table lists 'Filipinos' as the twentieth among all ethnic or nationality groups in Canada (Bolotta et al. 2000, 370). In the university textbook *A History of the Canadian Peoples,* the 'Philippines' appears in a table on 'Immigrants Arriving by Place of Birth, 1981–1990.' It is part of a larger 'Asia' category, which includes India, Hong Kong, China, Middle East, and Other (Bumsted 2007, 485). In *Journeys: A History of Canada,* another university textbook, the 'Philippines' is in a table on 'Top Ten Countries of Birth for Recent Immigrants and All Immigrants, 2001.' The Philippines is the third-ranked country of birth for immigrants who arrived in Canada between 1991 and 2001, behind China and India (Francis et al. 2006, 567). These three tables provide cursory statistical information about Filipina/os, but are devoid of substantive narrations about their lived experiences. Given their appearance in the latter pages of the textbooks and in the latter part of the twentieth century, Filipina/os are also literally and figuratively construed as late arrivals into the Canadian nation.

The other nine textbooks do not mention Filipina/os at all, but provide general details about immigrants, racial/ethnic minorities, demographic shifts, and multiculturalism from which readers may glean details about Filipina/os. For instance, in a unit on 'Changing Faces, Changing Values' in *Canadian History: A Sense of Time,* two pie charts compare the regional 'Origins of Immigrants to Canada' from 1961 to 1970 and from 1971 to 1980 (Gini-Newman et al. 2006, 240). Although the Philippines is not explicitly marked, it is presumably included in the 'Southeast Asia' category. According to the 1961–70 chart, there were 14,040 immigrants from Southeast Asia, compared to the 111,700 immigrants from the same region in the 1971–80 chart. The increase of close to 100,000 people arriving from Southeast Asia can be assumed to be due to the influx of migrants from the Philippines, since other Statistics Canada reports indicate that the Philippines is a major source of immigrants. The increase is also due to the large number of refugees from Vietnam who came to Canada in the late 1970s. A passing glance at the pie charts, however, does not reveal such details. Background knowledge on immigration and refugee patterns as well as disaggregated data on Southeast Asia would be needed to unpack these charts.[5]

My analysis of the representation of racial/ethnic minorities in general and Asian Canadians in particular provides insights into the depiction of race, racism, and race relations in Canadian historical narrations. *Experience History: Canada since World War I* provides a one-page description on racial/ethnic minorities in the 1920s. Whereas white Canadians enjoyed the 'roaring twenties,' Asian Canadians 'faced political, social, and economic discrimination.' The book elaborates on the Chinese, Japanese, and Sikh communities in British Columbia during this period: 'All three groups faced discrimination. For example, many employers refused to hire Asian workers, or paid them lower wages. In response, many Asian Canadians set up their own small businesses, such as restaurants or laundries. Others fished or farmed. All three Asian cultures lived in close-knit communities, largely shut out from the rest of society but determined to build their lives here' (DesRivieres and Bain 2006, 86). Later in the same book, a caption next to a picture of the 'Boat People' reads: 'More than 60,000 Vietnamese people were admitted to Canada between 1979 and 1981. The new immigration laws had made this possible. Canadians donated money, clothing, and furniture to help resettle the "boat people"' (240). By attending to the text's language, we can glean how Asian and white Canadians are depicted in history. On the one hand, Asian Canadians 'faced discrimination' yet relied on their abilities to fish, farm, and establish small businesses 'to build their lives.' The textbook positioned them as agentic individuals and groups who persevered, in spite of hostile conditions and labour market segmentation. On the other hand, the book does not identify white Canadians as the ones who perpetrated racial discrimination. Unidentified 'employers' refused to hire Asian workers or paid them lower wages. The phrase, Asians being 'largely shut out from the rest of society,' does not indicate who excluded them and why they were excluded. The preceding phrase, Asians living in 'close-knit communities,' seems to place the blame of exclusion upon Asians themselves, as opposed to government policies and popular sentiments geared to keep 'White Canada forever' (Ward 2002). Yet the book stresses the generosity of 'Canadians' towards those in need, both through their revision of immigration laws and their material donations to refugees. By naming white Canadians as compassionate providers of benevolent altruism but not as perpetrators and beneficiaries of racial injustice, the book not only elides the racism confronted by Asians in Canada, but also reinforces racist denial and consequently abdicates Canada's responsibility to address and redress this past and its legacy.

The textbooks' emphasis on the demographic shifts since the 1960s and the ensuing federal policy on multiculturalism since the 1970s further frame how Filipina/os fit within Canada's mosaic, even though Filipina/os are not explicitly mentioned in most books. In a section entitled 'The Government Chooses Multiculturalism,' *Defining Canada: History, Identity, and Culture* underscores the fact that Canada is 'the first country in the world to adopt an official multiculturalism policy.' This policy urges the government to 'support ethnic groups in their efforts to preserve their cultures' and 'help members of all ethnic groups to overcome cultural barriers to full participation in Canadian society' (Brune et al. 2003, 595). In a later section on 'Immigration and Demographic Changes: Shifting Identities,' the book states that 'given the importance of immigrants to Canada's growth and prosperity, it will be increasingly important for Canada to help new arrivals manage the transition into Canada's labour market and to place more emphasis on recognizing their education, skills, and language ability or helping them acquire those skills' (629). These statements on federal policies of multiculturalism and immigration indicate that late arrivals, like Filipina/os, are welcome in Canada so long as they contribute and are not a drain to the nation's economic welfare. This confirms the findings of critical race studies scholars – that the economic and labour dimension of immigration carries a heavier weight and priority, in comparison to the socio-cultural and humanitarian dimensions, even in the putatively more objective point system of the revised immigration policy (Li 2003; Thobani 2007).

Moreover, the virtual absence of Filipina/os in Canadian historical narrations indicates a failure to fulfil the official education mandate.[6] In the province of Ontario, Canadian history is a mandatory course for all grade 10 students, whether they are in the academic or applied pathway. Students can subsequently take an additional course in Canadian history either in grade 11 (for college or workplace preparation) or in grade 12 (for university preparation). All Canadian history courses, regardless of grade level or course type, address five organizational strands: (1) communities; (2) change and continuity; (3) citizenship and heritage; (4) social, economic, and political structures; and (5) methods of historical inquiry and communication (Ontario Ministry of Education 2005a, 2005b). For descriptive purposes, table 13.2 provides a small

Table 13.2. Ontario curriculum for Canadian and world studies

Grade	Course type	Strand	Curriculum expectation
10	Academic	Communities	Explain how local, national, and global influences have helped shape Canadian identity (OME 2005a, 46)
10	Applied	Change and Continuity	Explain some major ways in which Canada's population has changed since 1914 (OME 2005a, 57)
11	College preparation	Citizenship and Heritage	Explain the importance of active citizenship and respect for heritage in the lives of Canadians (OME 2005b, 156)
11	Workplace preparation	Social, Economic, and Political Structures	Describe the spectrum of political beliefs and social attitudes in Canada (OME 2005b, 168)
12	University preparation	Methods of Historical Inquiry and Communication	Locate, gather, evaluate, and organize research materials from a variety of sources (OME 2005b, 191)

list of curriculum expectations for each grade level, course type, and organizational strand to demonstate how the inclusion of content on Filipina/os can fulfil official school curriculum expectations in Ontario.

Perhaps the virtual absence of Filipina/os in historical narrations should come as no surprise, given the 'late' arrival of large waves of Filipina/os in Canada starting in the 1960s, and the politics and economics of textbook publishing which still privilege the grand narratives of the nation-state (Apple and Christian-Smith 1991). Nevertheless, the sense of abjection is acutely felt by those interested to learn about the ethnic-cultural diversity in Canada. Since textbooks work in the 'cultural construction of nationness as a form of social and textual affiliation,' they serve as a crucial intellectual, political, and pedagogical site in the nation's narration (Bhabha 1994, 140). So how does one narrate the rich and complex history of a nation? How do we account for and redress the absence of certain peoples, events, and issues? For abject beings like Filipina/os in Canada, what are the structural, discursive, and affective stakes in exclusion and inclusion? What are the benefits and limits of transforming from abject beings to legitimate subjects of history and the nation-state?

Redressing Abjection: On Structure, Discourse, and Affect

What I offer below are three recommendations to address the virtual absence of Filipina/os in Canadian historical narrations. They work within the structural, discursive, and affective domains of redressing the position of Filipina/os as abject beings in Canada.

The virtual absence of Filipina/os in history texts can be traced to two structural issues – the limited empirical studies on Filipina/o Canadian history and the small number of scholars who pursue historical research on Filipina/o Canadians. To date, there are three book-length studies that trace the history of Filipina/os in Canada: *From Sunbelt to Snowbelt: Filipinos in Canada* (Chen 1998), *Negotiating Citizenship: Migrant Women in Canada and the Global System* (Stasiulis and Bakan 2005), and *Seeking a Better Life Abroad: A Study of Filipinos in Canada, 1957–2007* (E. Laquian and A. Laquian 2008).[7] To my knowledge, there is no university faculty undertaking primary research on the history of Filipina/os in Canada. Among graduate students, one of the rare exceptions is Valerie Damasco (in this volume) at University of Toronto, who is completing a doctoral thesis on the life history of Filipina nurses who came to Canada in the 1960s. The limited number of empirical studies and researchers that focus on Filipina/o Canadian history consequently impacts the actual content in history books. Put differently, how can we expect to see the inclusion of Filipina/o information in Canadian history texts when there is limited scholarly knowledge from which to draw?

My first recommendation is the development of a mentoring and pipeline program that will support Filipina/o students in their pursuit of higher education and academic faculty positions. Out of 436,190 Filipina/os in Canada (according to 2006 Statistics Canada), there are only eight tenured and tenure-stream professors of Filipina/o descent in the humanities and social sciences in the country.[8] Given this number, the recruitment and mentoring of Filipina/o students to pursue higher education and academic positions needs to be a part of the agenda to redress their invisibility. This agenda has to be construed within a larger pipeline project from the K-12 to the university level. Research indicates that many Filipina/o youth are getting pushed out of schools and only a small number of Filipina/os complete post-secondary education (see Mendoza in this volume), a pattern which adversely impacts the number of Filipina/os pursuing graduate studies and academic faculty positions. This pipeline project also has to account for the structural issues of institutionalized racism, sexism, classism, and linguistic chauvinism, which create formidable barriers. In addition, the recruitment and mentoring of students who can pursue research on Filipina/o Canadian studies has to be an active and intentional commitment by university faculty, especially in the field of history. While non-Filipina/os can and should pursue research on Filipina/o Canadians, I especially encourage the training of Filipina/o students for the ontological, epistemological, and methodological insights and practices that they can bring to the scholarly and pedagogical enterprise.

While the quantifiable increase in the empirical studies and researchers on Filipina/o Canadian history can help broaden and deepen our understanding of race, nation, and diaspora, we also need to scrutinize the discursive frameworks within which these topics are construed. In other words, how we frame and present topics qualitatively shapes how they are conveyed, understood, and written. For instance, history textbooks hardly use the terms 'race,' 'racial,' or 'racism' to describe the experiences of Asian Canadians and the unjust government policies and societal treatment towards them. Let me use two university textbooks as examples: *History of the Canadian Peoples, 1867 to the Present* (2002) and *Canada: A National History* (2003), both co-authored by Margaret Conrad and Alvin Finkel and published by Pearson Education Canada. The 'Race and Racism' section in the chapter on 'Developing Colonies, 1815–1860' in the first textbook has specific sub-sections on 'Aboriginal Peoples,' 'The Métis,' and 'Blacks.' Although the introductory framing of the section reads: 'Treated with a mixture of disdain and paternalism, Aboriginal peoples and immigrants from Africa and Asia faced major obstacles in their efforts to get ahead,' the experiences of Asian immigrants do not receive any elaboration (Conrad and Finkel 2002, 184).[9] In a chapter on 'Community and Nation, 1945–1975,' 'Asian-Canadian Communities' receive almost identical half-page descriptions. Both books highlight Asians being 'discriminat[ed against] in their job searches,' being 'ghettoized in low-wage, supposedly unskilled factory jobs,' and 'living in converted barns without running water or electricity' (Conrad and Finkel 2002, 487–8; Finkel and Conrad 2003, 400–1). However, deleted in the 2003 version are sentences from the previous version that include phrases like 'racist' and 'prejudice from white [people].'[10] Another disturbing revision is the shift in the narration of the Japanese Canadian internment during the Second World War. The Canadian government's 'suspen[sion of] the civil liberties of the entire Japanese-Canadian population' receives three paragraphs in the 2002 book, including a photograph of 'internees packing to leave for camps in the interior of British Columbia' and ending with the government's official acknowledgment of its 'mistreatment of Japanese Canadians' and provision of 'compensation ... in recognition of their suffering' (Finkel and Conrad 2002, 295–6). However, the 2003 book downplays the government's violation of Japanese Canadians' civil rights by lumping their racially motivated internment with other groups that 'experienced the heavy hand of government control,' such as Jehovah's Witnesses, Jewish refugees, and anti-war dissidents. It also uses phrases like 'evacuation of the Japanese' and 'Japanese evacuees' (Conrad and Finkel 2003, 430), failing to mention that nearly three-quarters of the 22,000 Japanese Canadians who were interned were Canadian citizens by birth or naturalization, a fact provided in the previous version (Finkel and Conrad 2002, 295).

Why are there discrepancies between these two books that are co-authored by the same historians and published by the same company a year apart from each other? While my responses to this question are varied and speculative, the effect points to a narration of Canada's history of racism as a phenomenon which took place in the past (prior to Confederation), with aberrant moments of prejudice and discrimination during its first hundred years (1860s to 1960s), and has been diminished by the country's more welcoming policies of immigration and multiculturalism at the onset of its centennial celebration in 1967. The prevailing historical narration of Canada indicates that the nation has 'successful[ly] transition[ed] from a white settler colony to a multiracial, multi-ethnic, liberal-democratic society' (Thobani 2007, 144). Such celebratory discourse has so permeated mainstream understanding of race and race relations in Canada that charges of racism are met with outright denials or quizzical looks.

My second recommendation challenges us to rethink the discursive parameters of historical inquiries and narrations. Elsewhere, I introduce four interconnected heuristic frameworks to address the racialized conditions of Asian Canadians, which have relevance for our understanding of Filipina/o Canadians (Coloma 2012b). The four frameworks are: pan-ethnic and ethnic-specific, intersectional, transnational, and comparative. The pan-ethnic racial categories of 'Asians' and 'Asian Canadians' need to be understood as socio-political constructs that are formed through interpellation and identification that name and bring together a racialized mixture of diverse ethno-national cultural groups. How to recognize and value the unique divergences and parallel similarities within and across Asian Canadians is an intellectual, political, and pedagogical point for ongoing discussions. What is crucial to high-light, however, is the racialization of Asians in Canada. Racialization, according to Michael Omi and Howard Winant (1986), 'signif[ies] the extension of racial meaning to a previously racially unclassified rela-tionship, social practice or group.' Omi and Winant emphasize that race must be interpreted as 'an unstable and "decentred" complex of social meanings constantly being transformed by political struggle' (64). The concept of racialization with the signifier of race as epistemologically decentred and politically negotiated is a productive entry point when pursuing research on and teaching the history of Filipina/o Canadians.

The second framework for conceptualizing racialization is through intersectionality, which examines how race is constituted by other mark-ers of difference, such as gender, sexuality, class, ability, and migration. Developed and advanced primarily by feminists of colour, it under-scores the 'heterogeneity, hybridity, multiplicity' of subjects, and ques-tions the universal claims about and by a community (Lowe 1996). The third framework addresses transnationalism, which accounts for the border-crossing flows of people, culture, technology, finance, and ideas (Appadurai 1996). The intersectional and transnational approaches are useful in investigating Filipina/o Canadians and, in particular, the Live-In Caregiver Program. Combined, they offer insights to intellec-tual issues that concern feminist, labour, immigration, and interna-tional relations historians, including the blurring of public and private spheres in domestic and service work; the increasing liberalization and privatization of healthcare; the development of economic capital and work-life balance on the backs of women of colour; and Canada's par-ticipation in the global labour marketplace.

The fourth framework, using a comparative approach, provides new perspectives into the relational racialization of peoples of colour, or the ways in which racial/ethnic minorities share similar conditions or shape the conditions of others. The Live-In Caregiver Program, again, can function as a significant index to scrutinize the comparative experi-ences of other peoples of colour, such as Black Caribbean women who also served as domestics and caregivers, as well as Latina/os who are recruited into temporary work by agricultural and service industries. Analysis into the Foreign Domestic Movement, the Live-In Caregiver Program, and the Temporary Foreign Worker Program within the past thirty years can yield significant insights into the historical continuity of governmental policies and economic practices in relation to race, gender, labour, and migration.

What are the affective consequences of discussing Filipina/o caregivers and domestics as part of Canada's relatively recent history? (See Ty in this volume.) My third recommendation aims to address this question by focusing on the affective realm of inquiring into, writing about, and discussing what Deborah Britzman (1998) calls 'difficult knowledge.' My faculty colleagues and students at the university inform me of the emotional challenges faced by students, who were raised by Filipina nannies, when reading and discussing studies on the class, racial, and gendered exploitation of women of colour through the Live-In Caregiver Program. Many students contest and deny research findings which indicate that caregivers suffer from verbal, physical, and even sexual abuse, and find few recourses because of the mandatory length of employment contracts, the live-in requirement, and their limited status under Canadian law. Some are not aware that the program is part of Canada's healthcare policy, as caregiving for children, the elderly, and the differently abled is increasingly privatized, and that the program is primarily designed as part of a larger temporary foreign labour policy, as opposed to the prevailing notion that it is an official immigration initiative. Others have difficulty acknowledging that they participate and are complicit in broader dynamics of global diaspora that is conditioned by economic push-and-pull factors in global South countries like the Philippines and resource-rich nation-states like Canada. Human labour has become the largest export of the Philippines, making Filipina/os 'servants of globalization,' a phenomenon underpinned by foreign structural adjustment programs and national policies of economy and labour (Parreñas 2001). The Filipina nanny has become central in the lives of Canadian children and families for two generations, and has become ubiquitous in Canadian homes, parks, schools, and popular imaginary. The image of a brown woman pushing the stroller of a white child has become a cultural icon and metaphor for the racialized and gendered dynamic of domestic and transnational labour in Canada.

Confronting the difficult knowledge of one's participation and complicity in processes of exploitation requires a commitment to research and pedagogy that pursues self-reflection on and unlearning of what one has taken for granted or previously learned as normal or typical. Kevin Kumashiro (2000) argues that 'learning about oppression and unlearning one's worldview can be upsetting and paralyzing ... By teaching students that *the very ways in which we think and do things* can be oppressive [in spite of our best intentions], teachers should expect their students to get upset' (44). Since pursuing research, teaching, and learning of history from critical race and anti-oppressive perspectives can engender strong affective responses, it is crucial that we create spaces for ourselves and our students to work through these affective crises. The creation of such intellectual, emotional, and political spaces to work through affective crises, however, is without guarantees. In other words, becoming aware of or feeling empathetic towards other people's marginality does not automatically make one think or act differently. In fact, it could even generate resistance, denial, or paralysis. Britzman and Kumashiro thereby suggest that working through the affective realms of difficult knowledge involves unknowability, a seemingly paradoxical move in a project that aims to bring a marginalized minority group into visibility. The unpredictability of affect requires a vigilant commitment to working through its uncertain consequences, even in our hopes to redress marginality.

Conclusion: Persistent Critique of What One Cannot *Not* Want

In history, only certain stories are told, and certain beings are made absent. This much is openly acknowledged by some scholars. *The Illustrated History of Canada* showcases what is 'possibly the best-known Canadian photograph,' depicting the completion of Canada's transnational railway system in the late 1800s (Waite in Brown 2007, 363). It shows well-dressed white men, including prominent railway financiers and officials, surrounded by a crowd of other white men. Its caption states: 'Conspicuously absent [in the photograph] are the immigrant Chinese labourers whose toil made possible the completion of the railway through the Rockies' (ibid.). Although the absence of racialized labour is noted, what is not explicitly articulated is the importance of the Chinese in Canadian nation-building through their construction of the railway system, which facilitated travel, trade, and communication across the country. Like the Chinese workers whose labour was made absent in the historical photograph, the Filipina/o workers are also made absent in contemporary narrations of Canada's national development and well-being.

The sense of abjection, experienced by Filipina/os in reading for self-representation in history textbooks, produces an ardent desire to redress their virtual absence. I provide three recommendations, demarcating in broad strokes the structural, discursive, and affective domains through which such desire for redress can be channelled. From my discussions with other Filipina/os, it seems that Filipina/os as abject beings cannot *not* want to be integrated in historical narrations, for the move from invisibility to visibility heralds their arrival as legitimate subjects of history who belong in the nation-state. However, their move to representational visibility is fraught with tensions, contradictions, and compromises; hence, I put forward these recommendations provisionally, ambivalently, and without guarantees. Heeding Gayatri Spivak's (1988) call to persistently critique 'what one cannot *not* want' in order to call into question the non-innocence even of acts of redress and transformation, I close this chapter with three sets of questions for future investigation. First, in what ways does the desire of racial/ethnic minorities for visibility in Canadian history collude with the exaltation of whiteness and the displacement of indigeneity? What are the possibilities for cross-racial solidarity against white supremacy and settler colonialism? Second, under whose and what terms will the integration of abject beings depend? What are the seductions of compliance with parameters that regulate the narration and inclusion of racialized bodies in general and Filipina/os in particular? These questions are concerned with the reinscription of mainstream narrative frameworks, even as abject beings attempt to speak and intervene. Third, which Filipina/o Canadian histories are to be included, and why? And, how will they be integrated? These questions signal the potential hierarchy and priority-setting within Filipina/o Canadian histories, which can produce other forms of dominating and exclusionary scripts. As scholars, researchers, educators, and activists, we need to remain alert to the unforeseeable possibilities and effects of our desires and interventions, even in spite of our good intentions and transformative agendas. The redress of abjection may produce other forms of abjection, even in the name of giving voice, reclaiming the past, or opening up history. Ultimately, we need to take serious responsibility for the textual formation of national narrations, and persistently critique what one cannot *not* want in struggles for inclusion, legitimacy, and visibility.

NOTES

1 The titles for history books and textbooks being examined will be found in table 13.1.
2 Filipina/os' linguistic capital in English is valued quite differently in francophone Quebec.

3 Statistical data are derived from the Special Interest Profiles in the 2006
  Census: Data Products (http://www12.statcan.ca/english/census06/).
4 The distinction between Canadian and U.S. multiculturalism can be gleaned
  from one of the textbooks reviewed in this study. In *Continuity and Change*,
  a section on 'Assimilation or Integration?' reads: 'Some people believe that
  immigrants should be assimilated . . . This is comparable to the American
  idea of the melting pot where all immigrants become part of one identical
  society. Others suggest that immigrants . . . should be encouraged to retain
  important aspects of their original culture, such as customs, traditions
  or beliefs. Today, it is generally believed that Canada is a richer society
  because Canadians have been free to maintain their original culture while
  being integrated into a Canadian identity or cultural mosaic' (Bogle et al.
  2006, 340–1).
5 Disaggregated information is also needed in another textbook by Gini-
  Newman and his colleagues (2000). In *Canada: A Nation Unfolding*, a chart on
  'Immigration population by place of birth and period of immigration, 1991'
  shows five bars indicating particular time periods: Before 1961; 1961–70;
  1971–80; 1981–90; and Total. Each bar has six colour-coded sections which
  mark migration from certain regions of the world: Asia and the Middle
  East, Oceania and other; Africa; Caribbean; South and Central America;
  USA; and Europe. The caption reads: 'This chart shows that since World
  War II, immigration to Canada from European countries has decreased,
  while immigration from Third World and Asian countries has increased.
  Why has this change occurred?' (394). Aside from the book's aggregation
  of various 'Asian' and 'Middle Eastern' nations, the distinction between the
  Third World and Asia must also be questioned, given that the Philippines is
  a Third World nation located in Asia.
6 According to the Ontario curriculum for Canadian and World Studies, 'The
  compulsory Grade Ten course, Canadian History Since World War I focuses
  on the events and personalities that have shaped our nation since 1914.
  Optional Canadian history courses in Grades Eleven and Twelve provide
  opportunities to investigate Canada's past and examine issues that the country will face in the future' (Ontario Ministry of Education 2005a, 43). Since
  the grade 10 course is mandatory for all Ontario public school students, five
  of the six secondary history textbooks in this study are geared for grade 10
  students in Applied and Academic courses. *Defining Canada* (Brune et al.
  2003) is the only grade 12 textbook reviewed in this study, and is geared
  for the University Preparation course on 'Canada: History, Identity, and
  Culture.' Not included in this study are grade 11 textbooks for College and
  Workplace Preparation courses on 'Canadian History and Politics since 1945.'

7 Anita Beltran Chen also wrote the 'Filipinos' entry for the *Encyclopedia of Canada's People* by the Multicultural History Society of Ontario. Her 'Further Reading' section provides a list of scholarly and community accounts on Filipina/os in Canada from the early 1970s to the mid-1990s. See: http://www.multiculturalcanada.ca/Encyclopedia/A-Z/f1.

8 To my knowledge, the eight Filipina/o professors in the humanities and social sciences in Canada are Teresa Abad (Sociology, Western Ontario); Jeffrey Aguinaldo (Sociology, Wilfrid Laurier); Patrick Alcedo (Dance, York); Leonora Angeles (Community and Regional Planning, and Women's and Gender Studies, British Columbia); Glenda Bonifacio (Women's Studies, Lethbridge); Roland Sintos Coloma (Humanities, Social Sciences, and Social Justice Education, Toronto); Robert Diaz (Women and Gender Studies, Wilfrid Laurier); and Eleanor Ty (English and Film Studies, Wilfrid Laurier). This list does not include professors emeriti, such as Anita Beltran Chen (Lakehead), Aprodicio Laquian (British Columbia), and Romulo Magsino (Manitoba). Nor does it include professors in the faculties of sciences (such as M. Cynthia Goh of Chemistry in Toronto) and applied professional programs, such as medicine, law, business, or engineering. Not all of these professors pursue research on the Philippines or Filipina/os in the diaspora, and Filipina/o students should be encouraged to pursue a wide range of disciplinary and interdisciplinary research topics, including and beyond Filipina/o Canadian studies.

9 The grouping of Aboriginal peoples and immigrants from Africa and Asia can elide important political distinctions. Although these communities struggle against the workings and legacies of white supremacy, the experiences of Aboriginal peoples could be framed as another strand in Canada's multicultural mosaic. Such framing could consequently minimize not only Aboriginal claims for sovereignty, but also racial/ethnic minorities' participation and complicity in settler-nation governance.

10 The two deleted sentences are: 'Educational institutions and major employers gradually became less racist, opening new opportunities for more Chinese Canadians'; and in a paragraph referring to immigrants from India and Pakistan, 'they settled in communities throughout Canada and managed to survive the prejudice from their white neighbours and coworkers' (Finkel and Conrad 2002, 401).

REFERENCES

Appadurai, Arjun. 1996. *Modernity at large: Cultural dimensions of globalization.* Minneapolis: University of Minnesota Press.

Apple, Michael W., and Linda K. Christian-Smith, eds. 1991. *The politics of the textbook*. New York: Routledge.

Bannerji, Himani. 2000. *The dark side of the nation: Essays on multiculturalism, nationalism and gender*. Toronto: Canadian Scholars Press.

Bhabha, Homi K. 1994. *The location of culture*. London: Routledge.

Britzman, Deborah P. 1998. *Lost subjects, contested objects: Toward a psychoanalytic inquiry of learning*. Albany: State University of New York Press.

Butler, Judith. 1993. *Bodies that matter: On the discursive limits of sex*. New York: Routledge.

Chen, Anita Beltran. 1998. *From sunbelt to snowbelt: Filipinos in Canada*. Calgary: Canadian Ethnic Studies Association.

Coloma, Roland Sintos. 2012a. Invisible subjects: Filipino/as in secondary history textbooks. In *The 'other' students: Filipino Americans, education, and power*, ed. Enrique Bonus and Dina Maramba. Charlotte, NC: Information Age.

– 2012b. Theorizing Asian Canada, reframing difference. In *Reconsidering Canadian curriculum studies*, ed. Nicholas Ng-A-Fook and Jennifer Rottmann. New York: Palgrave Macmillan.

Fong, Eric, ed. 2006. *Inside the mosaic*. Toronto: University of Toronto Press.

Kumashiro, Kevin K. 2000. Toward a theory of anti-oppressive education. *Review of Educational Research* 70 (1): 25–53.

Laquian, Eleanor R., and Aprodicio A. Laquian. 2008. *Seeking a better life abroad: A study of Filipinos in Canada, 1957–2007*. Manila: Anvil.

Li, Peter S. 2003. *Destination Canada: Immigration debates and issues*. Toronto: Oxford University Press.

Lowe, L. 1996. *Immigrant acts: On Asian American cultural politics*. Durham, NC: Duke University Press.

Omi, Michael, and Howard Winant. 1986. *Racial formation in the United States: From the 1960s to the 1980s*. New York: Routledge.

Ontario Ministry of Education. 2005a. *The Ontario curriculum, grades 9 and 10: Canadian and world studies*. Toronto: Queen's Printer for Ontario.

– 2005b. *The Ontario curriculum, grades 11 and 12: Canadian and world studies*. Toronto: Queen's Printer for Ontario.

Parreñas, Rhacel Salazar. 2001. *Servants of globalization: Women, migration, and domestic work*. Stanford: Stanford University Press.

Pratt, Geraldine. 2004. *Working feminism*. Philadelphia: Temple University Press.

Razack, Sherene, Malinda Smith, and Sunera Thobani, eds. 2010. *States of race: Critical race feminism for the 21st century*. Toronto: Between the Lines.

Sandwell, Ruth W. 2006. Introduction. In *To the past: History education, public memory, and citizenship in Canada*, ed. Ruth W. Sandwell, 3–10. Toronto: University of Toronto Press.

Spivak, Gayatri C. 1988. Can the subaltern speak? In *Marxism and the interpretation of culture*, ed. Cary Nelson and Lawrence Grossberg, 271–313. Urbana and Chicago: University of Illinois Press.

Stanley, Timothy J. 2006. Whose public? Whose memory?: Racisms, grand narratives, and Canadian history. In *To the past: History education, public memory, and citizenship in Canada*, ed. Ruth W. Sandwell, 32–49. Toronto: University of Toronto Press.

Stasiulis, Daiva K., and Abigail A. Bakan. 2005. *Negotiating citizenship: Migrant women in Canada and the global system*. Toronto: University of Toronto Press.

Thobani, Sunera. 2007. *Exalted subjects: Studies in the making of race and nation in Canada*. Toronto: University of Toronto Press.

Ward, W. Peter. 2002. *White Canada forever: Popular attitudes and public policy toward orientals in British Columbia*. 3rd ed. Montreal and Kingston: McGill-Queen's University Press.

Chapter 14

Between the Sheets

GERALDINE PRATT

On the first day of the two-week development process that led to the creation of Nanay, a testimonial play on Filipina domestic workers and their families, a non-Filipino scenographer who was new to the issues suggested the following scene to communicate the experience of family separation. Audience members would be led into a large room filled with small cot-like beds. Each would be invited to lie down between the sheets of one of them, imagined to be a child's bed in the Philippines. Putting on headphones, lying in the child's bed, they would hear the voices of mothers testifying to their experiences of separation from their children and their time working as domestic workers in Vancouver. As one of the creators of the play, I recoiled at the thought of this scene, which seemed to embody the violence of intimate trespass and appropriation. But in the spirit of representational adventure, who is to say where the limits of experimentation should lie?

Filipinos in Canada: Disturbing Invisibility is an important moment of documenting the astonishing void in representations of Filipinos in Canada, and invites the reader to think critically, cautiously, and boldly about the challenges and pitfalls of bringing Filipinos in Canada into visibility. Roland Sintos Coloma shows us that Filipino migrants are virtually absent from Canadian history books, and Vernon Totanes reveals the relatively sparse collection of Tagalog books in Toronto's public library collection. There is subtlety and nuance to their analyses, as they trace the far-reaching effects of U.S. colonialism in the Philippines, and the Philippine state's investment in post-secondary education as part of its labour export policy. English competency and high rates of post-secondary education are common among Filipino immigrants to Canada, and this can both veil Filipino culture and create ambivalent tensions, between staking claims to inclusion and integration and carving out visibility as Filipino Canadians. Further, both Coloma and Bonnie McElhinny make abundantly clear that visibility is not enough and that well-meaning representations of Filipinos easily fall into old colonial scripts of primitivism or newer narratives of celebratory multiculturalism. As an alternative, Marissa Largo introduces, through her work with Filipino youth at Kabataang Montreal, a collaborative process of self-representation through mural drawing and video production. I would like to add to this already rich discussion of the challenges of representation by reflecting further on points of conflict or surprise that emerged throughout the creation and staging of *Nanay,* surely the most immediate, vigorous, and contentious series of discussions that I have ever had about the politics of representation.[1]

Nanay came into being as a collaboration between theatre artists Alex Ferguson and Caleb Johnston, a university researcher (me), and the Philippine Women Centre of BC (PWC of BC). The theatre artists came to the project because they wanted to experiment with theatrical form to create a testimonial play based on actual verbatim transcripts. The Philippine Women Centre and I had been engaged in collaborative research for over a decade and were keen to bring our research to new publics in innovative ways to deepen and stretch public discussion and debate about the ethics, justice, and consequences of the Live-In Caregiver Program (LCP). As a geography PhD student and theatre artist, Caleb Johnston brought the two sets of interests together. We had our first development workshop in February 2007 when we (theatre artists, researchers, and representatives from the PWC of BC and the Filipino-Canadian Youth Alliance) worked for a week with three professional actors at the Vancouver Playwright Centre, editing the most promising research interview transcripts into theatrical monologues and dialogues, and experimenting with staging. Very little of this material was used in the end, but documentation of four or five scenes worked up during the workshop convinced the PuSh International Performance Festival in Vancouver to include our play in their 2009 program. The work began in earnest in spring 2008 when Caleb and I and a member of the PWC (now designated as writers) began to work with a dramaturge, Martin Kinch. In July 2008 Alex Ferguson (now the director) took us (along with five professional actors, a stage manager, a scenographer, an additional set designer, lighting and costume designers, three Filipino youth paid as apprentices, and interested members of the PWC of BC and Filipino-Canadian Youth Alliance) through a further two-week development workshop. The play was first performed in Vancouver as part of the PuSh Festival in February 2009 and then in Berlin in June 2009 as part of the Your Nanny Hates You! Festival. In Vancouver, there were twelve performances and about six hundred people saw the play. Because of the expense of the tickets, we purchased sufficient numbers to ensure that at least five domestic workers and/or their family members could attend each performance (there was a maximum of forty-eight audience members at each performance); the PWC of BC facilitated this community audience involvement.

Filipina as Victim

Both Coloma and McElhinny rightly criticize the propensity to obscure contemporary forms of systemic racism in Canada through narratives of multiculturalism; racism is represented as existing only in the past. But, as they know, an explicit focus on racism offers no safe ground for representation, and Western feminists – even those explicitly concerned about racism – have long been criticized for casting so-called Third World women in a perpetual state of victimhood, and as the beneficiaries of 'First World' women's protection and advocacy (e.g., Chow 1991; Mohanty 1986; Spivak 1988). Outrage over racism and a cosmopolitan embrace of cultural difference historically have been markers of the liberal bourgeois subject, and sympathy and sentimentality for those victimized by racist structures and practices can buttress rather than dismantle white privilege (Berlant 1999; Baucom 2005; Thobani 2007). Though these points are made routinely, the tendencies that are criticized have a nasty habit of reoccurring. Let me give one example from *Nanay*.

The play is a series of monologues that were developed from research interview transcripts. Working with actors, we edited and rearranged text to produce compelling dramatic testimonies. One such monologue was created from an interview with a young woman who was separated from her mother for many years, while her mother worked in Vancouver as a live-in caregiver and she remained in the Philippines in the care of her father. We crafted her narrative to tell a story of the problems experienced by Filipino youths in Canada, highlighting her urge to drop out of high school, her conflict with her mother, and her compromised ambitions. Though she was enrolled in university in the Philippines, her ambitions shrank in Canada, and at the time of the interview she was pleased to have completed a six-month medical assistant course, selected in part because of its modest length and cost.

When the two youths from the Filipino Canadian Youth Alliance who had interviewed this young woman as part of our research project first saw her story being animated in the theatre during the second development phase, they were taken aback by how we had transformed it. They noted that in the actual interview the young woman had been optimistic, expressing her personal triumph over what she saw as the destiny of most youths migrating to Vancouver to join mothers who had come through the LCP: that is, to work in low-waged fast food restaurants. Through selective editing of her verbatim transcript, we had transformed her narrative into one of compromised success, indeed partial failure: she was rendered as a victim of the Philippines' labour export policy and Canada's LCP.

The urge to represent victims of structural violence as pure victims – to sharpen critique and provoke outrage and response – is very strong. But moments such as the above can startle us into thinking harder about casting those who suffer structural violence in different and more nuanced ways that are not reducible to victimization.

The dramaturge Martin Kinch, who worked with us as we drafted the script of *Nanay*, was persistent in his advice to move beyond victimization by including a monologue of a domestic worker who had had a positive experience immigrating to Canada through the LCP. He argued that it would make the entire play more believable by creating the impression that we had taken a measured approach to the issue. In response, we introduced a monologue of a woman we called Jovy, who extolled the unlimited opportunities in Canada: *'You can have everything you want when you have a job. [My nine-year-old daughter], she wants to design clothes. That's good. "If you excel in that, you can have your own business." I told her: "There's nothing impossible here."'* Jovy presented herself as a go-getter, who created her own successes, despite the odds: *'Despite the circumstances . . . I never lose hope. [It's just] a matter of mind conditioning. If I say I can do it. I can do it. You know. It's a combination of personality plus your experience, plus your confidence . . . That's what I learned.'* She admonished other Filipinas to do the same:

> *You know how many people from the Philippines get disappointed when they get here. They can't do what their true job is. It's hard to adjust. Me, I'm really sure that I will face difficulties. I prepare my heart for that. I actually put my pride aside. Because if one just has blind hopes, things won't happen that way. You'll get disappointed. When you get disappointed, you go very, very low. You're lonely . . . you cry. What will happen to you? That's why so many of us caregivers who are first timers going abroad [end up] going back [to the Philippines]. We learned about*

those cases. There are a lot. Either they commit suicide here from being so depressed or go crazy [or] return after eight months. It's almost at the end of their 24-month term and [they] couldn't make it and so went back. It's like, 'Why? Almost 24 months and you quit?' Types like that. If you're not strong here [points to head] *and you're not strong here* [points to heart], *you'll have a hard time.*

Through her story of her exceptional entrepreneurial spirit and personal strength, Jovy nonetheless tells a larger story of community despair. And within her narrative of her own success, she tells of the difficulties of years away from her children:

Everyday din yon, *we webcam! There are even times that the webcam is turned on and they're [her young children] just about. It is me who ... listens to what they are doing ... When I get homesick I just listen to the little noises they make, what conversations they are having, when the kids are playing even if the camera is not focused on them — I could still hear what they are doing around the house ... That's all. I just listen.*

What we learned through this process is that it is equally through the positive, agentful stories, as much as the stories of victimization and pure despair, that the full weight of the structural violence of the LCP, which legislates the separation of families for years at a time, is felt.

There are two further points to note here. First, there is no need to flatten the affective tonalities of those who suffer structural violence. Those who suffer need not be reduced to human vectors of sadness or victimization to solicit widespread identification and critical reaction to the conditions that structure their lives. And second, we need to resist the temptation to reduce those who suffer structural violence to a stereotype or ideal type. In her analysis of the myth of the disposable Third World woman 'who evolves into a living state of worthlessness,' Wright (2006, 2) makes the point that, although individual women are made to 'embody the tangible elements of disposability within their being' (5), their concrete lives exceed this myth and individual women do not live the myth in identical ways. In short, the experiences of Filipinas coming through the LCP are not identical and in all cases their lives exceed their experiences as migrant workers.

Our dramaturge also urged us to introduce more stories of domestic workers' lives in the Philippines to better understand their motivations for migrating to Canada and to more fully contextualize their experiences as migrants. Commenting on our first draft script, he said, '*It's as if they come alive somewhere over the Pacific Ocean.*' Gayatri Spivak (2000) has also criticized the tendency for U.S. feminists to begin their analysis of migrant stories at the moment of landing in the destination country, and to conceive migrants' lives within the critical nexus of race-gender-class (that is, critical multiculturalism). The effect, she argues, is to reduce analyses to the binaries of black/white, poor/rich, periphery/core, to minimize critical aspects of migrants' agency and responsibility, and to miss the nuances of complex and contradictory affective tonalities and emotional registers. Such analyses are, she argues, 'narcissistic, question-begging' (335). They allow privileged readers to remain within their own predicament of a multicultural society, even if in a critical way. If we want to represent Filipinas as something other than victims, we need to do the hard work of representing their lives with a specificity that transcends typification; this involves situating them in an expansive geography that reaches beyond Canada.

Indeterminacy of Reception

There was another facet of the staging of *Nanay* in Vancouver in February 2009 that made me uneasy. The director, Alex Ferguson, hired an accomplished artist, Tamara Unroe, to create a shadow puppet scene, reflecting his desire to allow the audience a short break from the otherwise monologue-heavy scenes. The shadow play told the story of a domestic worker leaving her village in the Philippines, represented as a rural tropical environment (a lizard figured prominently), crossing the ocean (apparently by ship: the ocean crossing was represented by fish leaping across the waves), to reach a suburban Canadian home (figures 14.1 and 14.2). All of my critical resources were activated by this scenario. I questioned the mode of presentation: is there a tradition of shadow puppetry in the Philippines and, if not, does the use of this dramatic tradition comprise an orientalizing, homogenizing gesture? Why would we not represent the Philippines as an urban place, for example, by starting from a Manila neighbourhood, rather than reinscribing stereotypical notions of difference between the Philippines and Canada in the form of the binaries of rural/urban, and primitive/technologically advanced?

And yet when the Philippine Women Centre held a community assessment following the play in March 2009, a long-term organizer at the Centre had the following to say:

> In terms of content I also would like to express appreciation for the visual part of it. Especially the puppet show. Because I appreciated having the chance to have different forms of expression within the one play. For me having heard a lot of the

Figure 14.1. Developing the Shadow Play

Figure 14.2. Representing Canada

stories from the women it was also nice for me having it coming to me in a diffe-
rent form. That's also the part I got very emotional . . . the whole pictorial visual
depiction of migration.

The point is a simple one: scholarly critical skills are essential for assessing representations but they cannot stand in for nuanced evaluation of the actual reception of these representations. Readings and reactions can be quite unexpected.

No Guarantees

During one performance of *Nanay*, Caleb and I, quietly chatting in the lobby, were surprised by a woman rushing past us in tears. Audience members travelled through the play in small groups of twelve to witness scenes staged in different rooms. She had left her group and was headed to a bathroom for privacy. The room from which she had fled was a model bedroom assembled from domestic workers' memories of their rooms in Canadian homes. An exact replica of a domestic worker's daily journal lay on the bedside table, inspirational and devotional religious passages interspersed with an unrelenting schedule of domestic duties. Christian iconography – images of Pope John Paul and a rosary draped on a small figurine of Christ – were carefully arranged in the small space. A small, ancient black and white television was turned on, positioned on a dresser at the end of her bed. Around the edges of the room were framed handwritten and drawn descriptions of different domestic workers' Canadian homes, as well as actual letters, cards, and photographs sent between family members in the Philippines and Canada.

In the talkback following the play, this woman identified herself as Colombian, and explained what lay behind her reaction:

I just wanted to know, do you ever have on this show actual Filipina workers?
Because I felt, I felt really weird. I have been in the same kind of situation and I felt
that looking at people [audience members] sitting on the bed [in the model bedroom],
it was like an invasion of my privacy. And for me it was awful to see Canadians
like, you know, for me it was a little bit offensive. During the whole play, I was
wondering, like I felt like a coloured person watching the white people watching
the play . . . Because when I have been in that situation and you're talking about
me, that's really different. I felt that they were looking at my room . . . I just felt
that this play is for Canadians. It's not for Filipinos and it's not for immigrants.

Ironically, it was in the model bedroom in particular that domestic workers from the PWC of BC had the most direct involvement in the creation of the play[2] (and, as noted above, this representation of the audience is not entirely accurate). Domestic workers told stories about their Canadian bedrooms, donated their own things to put into it, and were intimately involved in setting up the room. As Charlene Sayo, member of the Philippine Women Centre of BC and co-facilitator of the talkback, explained in reaction to this woman's comments: *'In a very hands-on kind of way [domestic workers] would say "Don't put that here. This has to go there. This has to go on the calendar" ... For the women who participated it was for them very liberating and empowering in the sense that people wanted to hear their stories and this was an opportunity to tell them.'*

Both Largo and McElhinny rightly argue in this book for the need to rethink the process of knowledge production. In the case of the Filipino exhibit at the Royal Ontario Museum, it is not just the content of the exhibit that is at issue, but the process of curation, and in particular a lack of consultation (and better yet active collaboration) with members of the Filipino community. Largo provides an excellent example of a collaboration that was as much about process, and in particular using this process to organize Filipino youths in Montreal, as the final research output: a mural.

But the results of even these collaborative processes can and most likely will be misunderstood, underlining Coloma's insistence on the necessity for persistent critique and dialogue, within and across various Filipino communities in Canada, and across Filipino and non-Filipino communities. Such conversations may be difficult, but the words of one white male audience member, in reaction to the anger of the Colombian woman who spoke out against the model domestic worker's bedroom and the play more generally, are instructive:

> *I'm interested in opening a dialogue about that because how do you [know]? I mean, I don't know. I mean, I'm only me as a person from Canada. And how do you? So I just want to open a dialogue because I don't know if it was a piece for white people. It feels to me like it was piece ... I don't know. So that's a question for you guys ... I would like to engage with that anger more. Because it's quite rare ... I think here in Canada, certainly here in Vancouver, we exist within a really politically correct environment, which is for a very good reason but it is also an environment that stifles conversation and dialogue and the ability for people to engage in that way. I don't know if what I'm saying is massively offending people. But I'd be really interested to hear more of that angle and more of that perspective.*

Collaborative process offers no guarantees that the resulting representations of Filipinos in Canada will transcend some of the problems identified by the authors of *Filipinos in Canada: Disturbing Invisibility*. Collaborative or not, representations of Filipinos in Canada will likely continue to put us – creators and those who experience them – 'between the sheets' in uncomfortable ways. We can only hope to sustain the kinds of difficult conversations about representation and its discontents that have been begun in this book.

NOTES

1 For a fuller description of the play, see Pratt and Johnston 2009.
2 The PWC was involved throughout and from the very first development workshop, but professional theatre can be surprisingly hierarchical and roles became more defined and exclusive as the process developed. For instance, the three Filipino youth paid as apprentices were apprenticed to the stage manager and the director; that is, one became an apprentice stage manager and two became apprentice directors. There were two spaces that were in some ways off-side from the rest of the production: the model bedroom and a 'soundroom' in which testimony of actual domestic workers and children who had been separated from their mothers was heard. Although domestic workers came and went during the development workshop (located only two blocks from the PWC), the less mediated and professionalized nature of these two scenes allowed PWC members the most direct involvement creating the play. The choice of 'going professional' was an important and considered one. The PWC embraced the opportunity to work with theatre professionals to develop their skills and contacts.

REFERENCES

Baucom, Ian. 2005. *Specters of the Atlantic: Finance capital, slavery, and the philosophy of history*. Durham, NC: Duke University Press.

Berlant, Lauren. 1999. The subject of true feeling: Pain, privacy, and politics. In *Cultural pluralism, identity politics, and the law*, ed. Austin Sarat and Thomas R. Kearns, 49–84. Ann Arbor: University of Michigan Press.

Chow, Rey. 1991. Violence in the other country: China as crisis, spectacle, and woman. In *Third world women and the politics of feminism*, ed. Chandra

Talpade Mohanty, Ann Russo, and Lourdes Torres, 81–100. Bloomington and Indianapolis: Indiana University Press.

Mohanty, Chandra Talpade. 1986. Under western eyes: Feminist scholarship and colonial discourses. *boundary 2* 12 (3): 333–58.

Pratt, Geraldine, and Caleb Johnston. 2009. Translating research into theatre: *Nanay*, a testimonial play. *B.C. Studies* 163: 123–32.

Spivak, Gayatri. 1988. French feminism in an international frame. In *In other worlds: Essays in cultural politics*, 134–53. New York: Routledge.

– 2000. Thinking cultural questions in 'pure' literary terms. In *Without guarantees: In honour of Stuart Hall*, ed. Paul Gilroy, Lawrence Grossberg, and Angela McRobbie, 335–57. London and New York: Verso.

Thobani, Sunera. 2007. *Exalted subjects: Studies in the making of race and nation in Canada.* Toronto: University of Toronto Press.

Wright, Melissa. 2006. *Disposable women and other myths of global capitalism.* New York and London: Routledge.

PART FOUR

Youth Spaces and Subjectivities

Colour Correction (acrylic on canvas)
Eric B. Tigley

Artist Statement

Eric B. Tigley

Whether I intend to focus on a personal feeling or idea, my work has always been an opportunity for me to explore different styles and mediums. This art piece builds upon a live painting I created in response to *Beyond Colour Lines,* a spoken word piece performed by Conely de Leon at the Spectres of Invisibility: Filipina/o Lives in Canada national symposium in 2009. This visual rendering of de Leon's performance begins on a painted black canvas as opposed to a white canvas to reflect the reality of living with one's skin colour. The decision to paint in grayscale using acrylics and markers adds to the starkness of the piece. *Colour Correction* is a visual manifestation of how de Leon's spoken word piece affected me in that moment. It also reflects the intense build-up of emotion in the room at the time of its creation.

Chapter 15

Scales of Violence from the Body to the Globe: Slain Filipino Youth in Canadian Cities

JOHN PAUL C. CATUNGAL

Introduction: Filipino Youth Bodies, Violence, and Politics

In the five-year span between 2003 and 2008, Filipino communities in Canada witnessed four high-profile cases of deadly violence against four Filipino youth. Far from a homogeneous set of events, the deaths of Mao Jomar Lanot (in 2003), Jeffrey Reodica (2004), Charle Dalde (2008), and Deward Ponte (2008) were born out of different circumstances, each with its own cast of characters, histories, and legal complexities (see table 15.1). Taken together, these incidents speak to a broad set of themes around the links between immigration, nation-building, violence, and politics. They include racial violence in public spaces, narrations of grief through immigrant stories, activist responses from community organizations, and a public amplification of often private anxieties about racialized bodies, local tensions, multicultural urbanisms, national policies, and transnational processes.

This chapter provides some reflections on the linkages between these themes, approaching them through an analysis of public discourses around the cases of the four slain Filipino youth as detailed in table 15.1. The public discourses I reflect on in this chapter are drawn from various sources, including mainstream and community news media and legal coverage and published academic analyses.[1] Taken together, these public discourses provide a glimpse into the messy politics of difference in the Canadian context, showing the decidedly contested nature of belonging to various scales and forms of political community.

In this chapter, I am principally concerned with the way these public discourses talk about slain Filipino youth *in relation* to broader issues of violence and immigration in Canadian cities. I argue that in order for

Table 15.1. Background information on slain Filipino youth

Name	Year of death	Location	Case details
Mao Jomar Lanot	2003	Vancouver, BC	Lanot, 17, was chased and beaten to death by a group of youth outside of Sir Charles Tupper Secondary School, where he was playing basketball with friends. One man, who cannot be identified as he was charged as a young offender, was sentenced to seven years in prison for manslaughter.
Jeffrey Reodica	2004	Toronto, ON	Reodica, 17, was shot to death three times by Detective Constable Dan Belanger, who, with partner Detective Constable Allen Love, responded to calls of a fight between two groups of youth as a plainclothes officer. The two officers were cleared of any wrongdoing by the Special Investigations Unit. A coroner's inquest was subsequently called; its findings included non-binding recommendations for Toronto Police Services.
Charle Dalde	2008	Richmond, BC	Dalde, 24, was killed in an altercation while on his way home. Police investigators charged Umut Ari with second-degree murder, but the presiding judge ruled, after psychological evaluations, that he was unfit to stand trial, and he was committed to a psychiatric facility.
Deward Ponte	2008	Vancouver, BC	Ponte, 15, was stabbed to death in an alley after an altercation between two groups of teenagers. Dillan Anthony Butler was originally charged with second-degree murder, but was subsequently charged with the attempted murder of another teenager who was with Ponte at the time. Roseller Salvacion, 19, was ultimately charged with second-degree murder in Ponte's death.

Source: various news sources

us to make sense of the violence that gives rise to the killing of Filipino youth in Canadian cities, we must view bodies – in this case, violated immigrant bodies – as sites in and through which we come to see the relationships between personal experiences, local processes, national policies, and transnationalities. In other words, my argument is rooted in a politics of scale or, to be more specific, in the notion that 'social relations are . . . played out *across* scales rather than confined in them' (Kelly 1999, 381, emphasis in original).

This chapter begins with perhaps a simple premise: that the slayings of Filipino youth in Canadian urban spaces are political moments that reveal much about the taken for granted re/production and politics of difference. This is not to say that they are just that ('moments'). Such a view might come close to saying that bodies do not have their own value, that they are immaterial on their own. This is not what I mean by my argument, and I want to be clear that the killing of Filipino bodies that I analyse in this chapter clearly shows us precisely that the materiality and life of bodies do matter. Foucault's (1979) theorization of bodies as sites in and through which power operates is instructive here, since it reveals how corporeal spaces are, de facto, social spaces, as it is through bodily experiences that we intimately experience inequality and violence. Moreover, bodies matter for political institutions like the state, since, in the Foucaultian sense of the 'biopolitical,' lives and deaths of populations are an important political concern for the state and its legal and juridical institutions (see Lemke 2001). Extending this Foucaultian notion, grounded as it is on a particular political geography of the state, it is crucial to note that the infliction of deadly violence against particular bodies produces what Mbembe (2003) calls necropolitical relations, or a mode of politics whereby certain people are rendered without value and whose bodies can therefore be abandoned and disposed of. From this standpoint, the deaths of Filipino youth could be treated as starting points for investigating how Filipino lives and deaths are organized by the state through legal and policy discourses and practices.[2]

But beyond the state, this chapter is also concerned with other political geographies. The deaths I discuss here matter not only to the state, but also to other forms of political membership – the family, the community, for example. Like the state, these political spaces are also produced through discourses and practices; they do not have pre-figured or universal characteristics. In a sense then, much like the state, the calling up of these political categories within public discourses about slain Filipino youth reveals much about the social construction of *particular kinds* of family and community. Hence, when I argue that the slayings of Filipino youth bodies are political moments, I aim to shed light on how these episodes of violence reveal that individual lives and deaths are not 'individual' in a strict sense, since they exist in relation to broader conducts of power and politics. Indeed, for one, the stories of the deaths reveal the violated body's affective and co-constitutive relationships to multiple socio-spatial units (family, community, and nation, among others). Such an approach hopefully lets us get past the liberal/libertarian argument that the body is a unit unto itself and instead proffer an alternative that pinpoints the body's entanglements with other bodies, spaces, and scales.

Before I proceed, I'd like to offer a word on the ethical difficulties of writing about violence. It is with much unease that I write this chapter, for I do not wish to turn the unjust and untimely deaths of Filipino youths into a purely intellectual exercise. The loss and the pain that family and community members experience and continue to experience cannot – and perhaps should not – be reduced to words on pages. Any attempt to render stories visible and knowable carries with it significant ethical and political responsibility. Indeed, in their own respective reflections on the ethics of telling sad and painful stories of social injustice, Pratt (2009) and Razack (2007) warn us not to reproduce privilege by simply consuming – and therefore profiting from – stories of anguish, a process which Razack notes is tantamount to 'stealing the pain of others' (376). A genuine and responsible act of witnessing that goes beyond consuming pain is one that demands ethical accountability and critical analysis (Pratt 2009). In engaging with these stories, I aim to reflect on what these episodes of violence can tell us about the multiple and contested locations of Filipino bodies in urban, national, and transnational spaces. The ways that diverse groups reacted, in visible ways, to the killings of these youths mean that these episodes of violence struck a chord for multiple publics and therefore produced public discourses that, I think, are worth examining, if only because they speak to the contingent and contested nature of claims to belonging. In mapping the discursive reactions to these episodes of violence, I follow Pratt (2009) in hoping to channel my own encounters with these stories towards a critical politics of social change.

The chapter is organized using scalar keywords as guide-posts. I begin with *the body* and pay close attention to the discursive constructions of corporeal violations. Following spatial theorists of 'the body' as a space marked with difference (Razack 2002), I build in this section on the notion that the Filipino body, killed by violence, is produced by multiple socio-spatial relations. I move from the body to *community* to explore how and why these Filipino bodies are often talked about in relation to schools, playgrounds, neighbourhoods, and other local political geographies. In this section, I ground the violated Filipino body in broader public anxieties about the perils of multiculturalism in the public spaces of Canada's dangerous 'mongrel cities' (Sandercock 2003). I follow this section with a discussion of *nations and borders.* In this section, I consider public discussions around state policies, especially focusing on the Live-In Caregiver program and the federal multicultural policy. I also look beyond Canada towards *the globe,* and focus on the construction and politics of transnational relations. I discuss how specific discourses about migrant mobilities and border politics enable and are enabled by geographical imaginations of global relations. I end by going back to the Filipino body in order to reflect on its locations and dislocations, sometimes but not always violent, in the Canadian context.

Damaged Bodies: Slain Youth and the Mediated Production of Spectacle

Media coverage of murder cases is, perhaps not surprisingly, awash with very visual descriptions of the killing of bodies and, notwithstanding journalistic claims to supposed objectivity, is filled with discourses of pathos and drama. Accounts of circumstances before, during, and after the acts of killing often rely on the vivid, sometimes sensationalistic, discussions about the body and its limits. In the case of articles about murdered Filipino youth, journalists generously pepper their writings with descriptions of the comportments and positions of the killed body and the breakages and damages done to it. In these media accounts, the violated Filipino body is produced in representation both as a spectacle to be consumed and as an event where we come to see violence as – ultimately – a corporeal experience.

In one account, for instance, Fong (2005a) writes about the limits of Jomar Lanot's body: 'Being the slowest boy in a group of terrified fleeing teenagers cost Jomar Lanot his life.' She then goes on to describe how Jomar and his group were pursued by a group of young attackers, armed with weapons, who were 'set on revenge for a broken van window.' Despite the fact that Jomar and his friends were not the group's original objects of pursuit, they nevertheless became available victims of violence as the angry group came upon them on a playground and instigated a confrontation through the hurling of insulting slurs (Fong

2005a). In the end, the attackers caught up with Jomar, and on 'the last glimpse one of Mr. Lanot's friends had of him, [Jomar] was on the ground and being kicked.' Fong continues:

> By the time the police and ambulance arrived, Mr. Lanot was beside a chain-link fence, his arm extended at such an odd angle that the first people on the scene knew automatically it was broken. His face was on the ground. Even in the dark, the large pool of blood around his head was unmistakable.

The vividness of this description calls on the reader to bear witness, by consuming textual reconstruction, the severity of the violence visited upon Jomar's body.[3] In such an account, the excesses of corporeal trauma – broken limbs, pools of blood – clearly describe a body beaten with force and malice. Jomar's final location too is telling – beside a chain-link fence – suggesting that his entrapment, along with his slowness, contributed to his body becoming the violated body in this attack. In another article, Fong (2005b) extends this journalistic representation of Jomar's body using witness accounts of the killing in court proceedings. Here, we learn further that a bat was used as a weapon, resulting in multiple blows to the head, and that, soon after arriving at the hospital, Jomar would succumb to the severe trauma visited upon his body.

In this and other cases of violence against Filipino youth, media representations of the violated body are *not* absolute truths relaying irrevocable facts about often developing criminal cases. In many instances, they contain accounts of profound uncertainty and often controversial views about violence and its causes. In some instances, it is not difficult to suspect sensationalism. In the case of Jomar, for example, the media was quick to present the story as an instance of conflict between Filipinos and South Asians in Greater Vancouver, a sensational framing that plays up long-standing conservative anxieties about immigrant groups in the Canadian context (Pratt 2009, 17).

Similarly, media coverage of the case of seventeen-year-old Jeffrey Reodica, who was shot to death in a police confrontation, was peppered with profound uncertainty. In most of the media coverage, the slain body is once again vividly portrayed through the strategic use of accounts from anguished family members. For example, Gray (2004) recounts the reaction of family members upon learning that Jeffrey's body was left to die without help. He quotes Flora Reodica, Jeffrey's mother, as saying: 'When my son was lying there already, they flipped him over ... like a piece of meat. But before that ... they left my son there bleeding with no medical help.'

In their discussion of 'the news media's devotion to drama' in the context of the homophobic slaying of Matthew Shepard, communications scholars Brian Ott and Eric Aoki (2002) note that media accounts of murders are typically told using particular scripts or story forms. They note the propensity, in the Matthew Shepard case, of news media accounts to rely on 'individual actors and human-interest angles' in a way that individuates crime and that '[downplays] institutional and political considerations that establish the social context for those events' (488). I would argue that the same is true for reportage of slain Filipino youth. Through their focus on the gruesome details of bodily position and trauma, the media has a general tendency to render violated Filipino youth bodies as individual spectacles to be consumed. In this sense, representations of the slain body constitute an important component in the production of the news.

Shaken (Imagined) Communities: Slain Youth in Socio-Spatial Context

The human-interest angle is further achieved through the strategic use of a balancing discourse of the slain youth's moral and social life. Indeed, in many cases, media accounts included pleas by family members, peers, and others for the public to consider these Filipino youth as more than 'bodies.' For, while media accounts are heavy in their portrayal of the killed body, they also contain within them accounts that seek to humanize representations of slain Filipino youth. For instance, Heath-Rawlings (2004) writes how Jeffrey Reodica's family and friends sought to honour him by invoking his vibrant personality – 'the happiest guy in the world' – and sense of friendship and loyalty – 'he loves his friends. [Jeff] was my boy.' In these accounts, we also learn that Jeffrey was an altar boy at St Rose of Lima Catholic Church and was still in high school at the time of his death (Keung 2004a). These strategies act as counter-representations of Filipino youth and are political insofar as they produce public discourses about lost lives and broken social relations. Therefore, they extend the scope of representation from the spectacular individualization of the material body violated and broken to one that pays much more attention to bodies as lived *in relation* to often idealistically constructed notions of family and imagined (ethnic) community.

Such pleas to refuse the individualization of slain Filipino youth and to render them part of community and family are a powerful way for family and friends to map the lives *and deaths* of Filipino youth in a wider social context. In this spirit, the affective invocation of lives lived-in-relation during public moments of grieving and commemoration is simultaneously an attempt to reconsider violence as occurring to more than just the individual body and as having impacts that cascade to other scales. Indeed, attempts to locate Jeffrey in the community spaces of his church and school can be viewed as ways to map the effects of violence against Filipino bodies onto Filipino and other communities more broadly. In media accounts of the killing of youth, for example, the re-scaling of violence from the individual to the collective is obvious in the active and *deliberate* invocation of a particularly idealized and singularized – and arguably, strategically essentialized – discourse of 'community' by community groups, kin relations, and also legal agents. This is particularly clear in the case of Jomar Lanot, wherein legal agents recognize how the impact of violence goes beyond individual bodies and extends into immigrant communities more broadly. In his sentencing of Muzil Abdullah, BC Supreme Court Justice Lance Bernard notes that the fatal beating of Jomar 'was the sort of crime that shakes a community to its core' (quoted in Bellett and Travis 2006).

Indeed, the notion that violence goes beyond the slain individual body does not necessarily deny the corporeal materiality of such killings. On the contrary, the very absence of the material body is unavoidably felt and grieved; called up by friends and family through rituals of memorialization; and sometimes even literally made concrete through the creation of commemorative landscapes that mark loss in space. These strategies of marking the materiality of the Filipino youth body lost through violence rely on, and indeed affirm, the fact that these bodies are situated in socio-spatial relations. In the case of Jomar Lanot's slaying, these relations are invoked as 'community,' as exemplified in Supreme Court Justice Lance Bernard's pronouncement above – community not just in the sense of an imagined ethnic community ('Filipino community'), although this is common, but also more broadly. For example, in the case of Jomar, classmates, teachers, and community members of Sir Charles Tupper High School, where Jomar was a student, formed the 'Hope into Action' committee, which sought to respond to the violent incident in ways that both grieve the loss and violence and also provide something of material benefit to the school community (Hansen 2006). This committee was instrumental in ensuring that the loss of Jomar is remembered in and through a 'healing garden' created in his memory. Located in the vicinity of the Sir Charles Tupper school grounds, the healing garden is meant as both a memorial landscape and a community space for contemplation. In this context, 'community' is not just an ethno-racialized one, though that is a component; it also includes members of the school and the neighbourhood for whom the garden will be available.

In a similar way, community reactions to Jeffrey's killing were vociferous, resulting in the formation of the 'Justice for Jeffrey Reodica Coalition' (JJRC), an unprecedented grassroots group of Filipino community members from all over the Greater Toronto Area.[4] This group sought to confront the Filipino community's fraught relationship with the police after Jeffrey's killing, with the ultimate goal of pushing for a public inquiry into Jeffrey's death (Keung 2004b). In other words, this coalition sought to link the loss of Jeffrey Reodica with the overt political goal of seeking accountability for the incident. Speaking about the formation of this coalition, Hermie Garcia, publisher of the community paper the *Philippine Reporter*, notes this outrage and loss: 'The community is just highly charged and mad. As journalists, we don't usually take sides, but we feel our voices have been muffled. Jeffrey did not deserve to be shot and killed like this. We need to speak up for him' (quoted in ibid.). In her analysis of the formation of JJRC, Mila Astorga-Garcia (2007) notes that, as one of several possible reactions to Jeffrey's killing, the formation and work of this coalition moves the Filipino community 'from crisis to . . . capacity building.'

In these cases, the invocation of 'community' both by media and legal actors and by public interest groups is often strategic. Perhaps most simply, it relays the idea of slain Filipino youth as belonging to social spheres. But beyond this, it also underpins the re/production of ethno-racial groupings like the 'Filipino community' that may have a stake in mourning and politicizing the killing of one of their own, as in the case of Jeffrey analysed by Astorga-Garcia. In this particular case, the use of 'Filipino community' is clearly idealized in its (temporary) erasure of massive differences among Filipinos, but it is also clearly politically strategic in noting that Jeffrey's killing is an affront to the racialized group by a member of the police force, a dominant institution of the state.

Mongrel Cities: Filipino Youth in Canadian Urban Space

The strategic invocation of 'community' discussed above needs to be understood in the context of the racial politics of the Canadian multicultural cities. Despite their official framing in the mass media and in government publications as predominantly sites of belonging and racial acceptance, Canadian cities are increasingly sites of intense ethno-racial and class inequality, as well as spaces of racial violence (Goonewardena and Kipfer 2005). This socio-spatial context conditions the field of possibilities for public responses to the cases described above. For example, the formation of 'positive' community alliances such as the JJRC was tempered by the fact that racial tropes continue to condition media and legal reactions to the slaying of Filipino youth. Most prominently, for example, in three of the four cases above, the idea of 'Filipino youth as gang members' framed early reactions to the violent incidents. Indeed, in Jeffrey's case, one of the major points of politicization by the JJRC is the police force's overt representation of Jeffrey and other Filipino youth as dangerous. Astorga-Garcia (2007, 6) quotes one participant in a meeting of the Coalition: 'Our kids are being painted as knife-wielding gangsters, just so people would buy the police version of the story. This is so unfair.'

In some cases, the racialized representation of Filipino youth so obvious in Jeffrey's case extends to a *more general* racialized representation of racialized youth as dangerous elements in the multicultural city. In early coverage of Jomar's case, for example, the violence was framed by the media and the police as a gang conflict between Filipinos and South Asians, resulting in some public tension between youth from these respective ethno-racial communities (Mickelburgh 2003). Reacting to this 'incident tinged with elements of racism,' the police very early on called on people to stay calm amid 'heightening tension' (Constable Anne Drennan, quoted in Mickelburgh 2003). The media's suggestion of inter-ethnic violence in Canadian cities is not one that gained a lot of traction, especially as the investigation carried on. Mickelburgh (2003), for example, notes that 'most [in the Filipino community] appear to have accepted police statements that Jomar's death was not racially motivated, despite the racial slurs tossed out by the Indo-Canadian group' that was implicated in the incident. What is more, youth organizations from both Filipino and South Asian communities actively formed alliances to combat the racial trope of inter-ethnic violence as a threat to the multicultural Canadian city, appearing together in media outlets to denounce further violence (see Pratt 2009, 17). Furthermore, South Asian leaders were quick to denounce violence between groups, noting that 'all of us feel responsible for this absolute tragedy' (former BC premier and three-time member of Parliament Ujjal Dosanjh, quoted in Mickelburgh 2003).

The immediate turn by many in the mainstream corporate media to the trope of inter-ethnic violence in Canadian cities as an explanation for Jomar's slaying was far from accidental. It can be traced to a broader discourse of youth of colour as perilous elements of the multicultural city (see Schissel 1997). Such a discourse not only *naturalizes* youth of colour as violent threats to order, but also *masks* the insidious processes of racialization that render Filipino and other immigrant youth 'other' in relation to the white settler nation. What this discourse achieves is the constant reiteration of racialized youth, including Filipinos, as not only outsiders but also threats to the Canadian nation. Given the incredible violence of this framing, other counter-discourses were put forward to combat the media reportage on Jomar's slaying. For example, representatives from the Filipino Canadian Youth Alliance, a civil society activist group that aims to politicize the lived realities of Filipino immigrant youth in Canada, provided a more critical analysis by linking violence against Filipino youth to broader problems with Canadian policy. They point out that Jomar is only one example of many children of live-in caregivers who are rendered vulnerable by inadequate support structures in multicultural Canadian cities.

Such active naming of the *racialized* political economy of Canadian cities is one strategic way of disrupting the common portrayal of violence against Filipino youth as exceptional individual cases. For example, in at least two cases, family and community members readily named the racism of white national institutions such as the police in their calls for justice for slain Filipino youth. In the case of Charle Dalde, a twenty-four-year-old Filipino youth slain in Richmond, BC in 2008, the Dalde family noted that they were subjected to unfair and violent treatment during the police investigation, in huge part because the police went into the investigation with the belief that Charle – and therefore also his family – were involved in criminal activity (Colebourn 2009). Charle's father Cezar went on record to accuse the RCMP of 'falsely believing the fatally wounded Charle was a gang member' when the family was 'held at gunpoint, handcuffed and bullied during the Mounties' probe' (quoted in Colebourn 2009). Reacting sharply to this accusation, Richmond RCMP Cpl. Nycki Basra noted: 'we do not police based on the colour of one's skin' (quoted in ibid.). Similarly, Det. Const. Dan Belanger, who fatally shot Jeffrey Reodica, sharply rebuffed suggestions of racism by noting that 'he is a full-status Indian' and that 'race played no role in his conduct' (quoted in Teotonio 2006). Of course, such an argument does not sit well with research on the role of men of colour in violent nationalist institutions such as the police and the military, which shows that the performance of violent hegemonic masculinity in the service of nation implicates men of colour in state racism despite their own marginalization (see Razack 2004).

The murders of Filipino youth in Canadian cities cast profound doubt on publicly circulated discourses of tolerance and liveability and therefore take as problematic the oft-mentioned notion that diversity and multiculturalism are Canada's greatest strengths (see discussion below). As noted in the examples above, criminal cases like those involving the killing of Filipino youth – especially when they re-circulate and shore up tired old notions of immigrant gang violence – bring to the surface often unspoken tensions about difference-as-threat in Canada's 'mongrel cities' (Sandercock 2003). In these city-spaces, multicultural demographic realities combine with uneven hierarchies of privilege to produce anxious public confrontations with sometimes violent results (Goonewardena and Kipfer 2005). In the cases described above, we see how discourses of gang violence and mob mentality reveal the marginalization of youth of colour in Canadian cities and produce uneven topographies of policing that order the Canadian city along colour lines (Wortley and Tanner 2004).

(B)ordering Identities: Filipino Youth and Trans/national Mythologies

Community-level mobilizations in reaction to the murders of Filipino youth are not limited to critiques at the local scale, however. Indeed, criticisms of national institutions discussed above (e.g., the police) already reveal the complicity of the nation-state in the debate. However, critiques of the nation are not limited to these. Media coverage of these violent incidents also brings into focus the intertwined production of the Canadian nation as, simultaneously, a space of liberal multicultural tolerance and a host nation for labour immigrants and their families. Critiques of these innocent portrayals of the Canadian nation serve to hide the incredible racialized and colonial violence that sustains the Canadian nation (Thobani 2007). They also point out as a particularly glaring example the injustices enabled by Canadian temporary labour policies against women of colour and their families (see Pratt 2004). In drawing attention to these unjust policies, these critiques show how violence against Filipino youth and other racialized populations is not incidental to the production of nation, but is actively and intimately tied to it.

In at least two cases – those of Jomar Lanot and Deward Ponte – the stories of immigration that recounted how these youth came to Canadian cities were very prominent features of public discourse around their killings. These stories were disseminated in the form of media coverage, legal testimonies, and activist statements. In a *Globe and Mail* article, for instance, Matas (2008) writes that Deward came to Canada through the sponsorship of his mother, who 'arrived in Canada seven years ago under a federal program for caregivers. She worked in Canada for five years before she was in a position to sponsor the immigration of Deward and her daughter Dea.' Similarly, in a later part of the same article, Matas draws attention to parallels between Deward's story and Jomar Lanot's, who was killed five years before. He notes: 'Similar to Deward, Mr. Lanot had arrived in Canada from the Philippines shortly before the incident. His mother had come earlier and worked hard to sponsor Mr. Lanot and her two other sons.'

The juxtaposition of these two immigrant stories in this single *Globe and Mail* article reveals the threads that bind Jomar's and Deward's cases. They both lived through the dislocations of immigration, but first had to experience separation from their mothers, who, similar to many other Filipino women, moved to Canada to seek employment under the Live-In Caregiver Program (LCP). Research on the LCP as well as Philippine emigration more broadly shows that harsh economic necessities and federal immigration policy in the Philippines combine with household-level visions of better futures to facilitate the creation of transnational circuits of mobile Filipino bodies, often as contract workers, but also as independent immigrants to Canada and elsewhere. Pratt (2004) shows, however, that these transnational Filipino mobilities are not necessarily always positive in outcome, nor do they always result in better futures for emigrant families. Oftentimes, immigrants face harsh socio-economic realities in their host nations, owing to a combination of racially segmented labour markets, problematic accreditation policies, and inadequate supportive institutions for immigrants. Furthermore, Pratt (2009) suggests that, at the level of the household, family separations resulting from labour and other immigration processes can create tense relationships between mothers and their children after unification and can have negative long-term impacts on children, particularly in terms of educational attainment and career futures (see also Parreñas 2009).

While some might view such an analysis as coming close to a pathologizing gesture that turns immigrant children into subjects at risk, the wisdom of Pratt's (2009) analysis has to do with its refusal to map the problems of the LCP solely onto the scales of the Filipino body and household. Indeed, her analysis reveals how implicated Canada, the nation-state, is in constructing national policies that facilitate traumatic family separations and in enabling transnational mobilities between Canada and the Philippines. In other words, violence against Filipino bodies in Canadian cities is tied up in a host of other processes: from the political economic linkages between the Philippines' labour exportation policies and Canada's Live-In Caregiver Program, to the concomitant formation of cross-border affective communities that are sustained by transnational modes of caregiving and to the fashioning of Canadian ideals of multiculturalism and tolerance as national identity 'brands.' And, of course, this is not 'new' in a strict sense *per se,* since transnational histories of imperialism and contemporary patterns of immigration are genealogically linked. As San Juan (2000) and Espiritu (2003) point out, in the case of the Philippines and its diaspora populations, the country's historical and contemporary 'colonial' relation to the West – particularly the United States – is, in huge part, premised on the spatial construction of modernity and opportunity as further afield, as somewhere else (i.e., in and of the West). It is this very geographical imagination (West as modernity) that shores up – and is also shored up by – the transnational flows of Filipinos throughout the world.

The jump in scale between the violated bodies of Filipino youth in Canadian cities and the global patterns of immigration might seem an extreme rhetorical move, but a view of violence that attends to what Žižek (2008, 1) calls 'the contours of the backgrounds that generate such [violent] outbursts' encourages us to look at individual incidents not as mere flashes in the pan but as 'normal' incidences. By 'normal,' Žižek does not mean that they are justified. On the contrary, he emphasizes that they are made 'normal' – i.e., normalized – because they arise out of taken-for-granted institutional arrangements whose everyday violence is not all that visible to us except in instances of obvious but exceptional violence, such as murders. From this light, we might view killed Filipino youths as examples of what Žižek calls 'directly visible "subjective" violence, violence performed by a clearly identifiable agent' (ibid.) – agents who, in this case, are the people who directly violated their bodies.

In contrast, the circumstances that bring Filipino families into Canadian diaspora locations may not be seen as 'obvious' forms of violence. In fact, state policies are even constructed as benevolent forms of Canadian nation-building, with multiculturalism, immigration policy, and transnationalism in Canada being hailed as evidence of the nation-state's moral standing (Razack 2002). Indeed, the policy, ideology, and demographic reality of multiculturalism and its neoliberal logic ('immigrants as economic necessity') sustain the narration of Canada as humanitarian in nature (ibid.). However, scholars have also argued that the use of multiculturalism as immigration and labour policy – and the neoliberal logics that underpin such policy – mask the structural violence that renders possible the abandonment of immigrant bodies by the nation (Roberts and Mahtani 2010). Indeed, Pratt (2005) argues, drawing on Agamben, that Filipino bodies, particularly live-in caregivers, are rendered 'bare life' by this logic, no matter their importance for Canada's social reproduction. What is more, the children of these 'abandoned women' (ibid.) are also rendered vulnerable to violence: not only are their ties to kin relations severed by separation-via-labour-migration, but their own precarious positions as immigrants to the Canadian nation render them 'outside' its protection. It is therefore not surprising that it is a common reaction to the killing of Filipino youth for some members of the Filipino community to name – and therefore politicize – their outsider status as a factor in the slowness or ineffectiveness of legal investigations.

Resisting Violence: Corporeality, Materiality, Scale

In this chapter, I have discussed how political discourses about slain Filipino youth allow us to think through the place of violence in the making of Canadian cities and nations. My argument affirms the corporeality of violence – that it is something done to bodies, especially in the case of killings – but goes beyond it to note, following Žižek (2008), how violence to immigrant bodies is tied up in broader, structural forms of violence that do so much for the production of ideas about Canadian tolerance and multiculturalism. The cases of Jomar, Deward, Jeffrey, and Charle brought into public discourse how individual episodes of slayings are intimately related to – and therefore call into focus – broader societal issues about, among other things, inter-group violence in multicultural cities, police-community relations, immigration policies, and transnational mobilities. Their cases also show that the materiality of violence does not end in the killing of just the Filipino youth themselves and that the impacts of this violence cascade across scales, affecting immigrant communities in particular but also implicating state institutions such as the police and policymakers.

It is difficult though necessary to link the structural forms of violence that sustain the 'normal' workings of society (e.g., nation-making technologies like immigration policies) to more 'subjective' (Žižek 2008) eruptions of violence such as the individual cases of violence against Filipino youth in Canadian cities. For, according to the liberal logic that underpins much Canadian law and policy, violent incidences are exceptional moments committed by individual people. Such a view treats violence as pathologies of the individual rather than lived realities enabled by the very structures that sustain the everyday workings of society. Speaking truth to power would necessitate not only the undoing of this liberal logic, but also calling into question the normalizing institutions that sustain social order itself.

This is not to say that activists in the Filipino community have not tried to link structural and 'exceptional' violence in their political work. The opposite is actually the case. For example, Mildred German, a spokesperson for the Filipino Canadian Youth Alliance, expressly avoids individualizing the cases of Jomar and Deward. She notes forcefully that the LCP '[takes] advantage of the desperation of the people [in the Philippines]' (quoted in Matas 2008). She further argues that such programs 'should include funds for integration and settlements of new immigrants . . . [and that they] should be allowed to bring their children with them' (ibid.). Such a radical call for treating temporary workers in Canada as people with familial relations is simultaneously a call to recognize these same people as more-than-individual cogs in the wheel of Canadian social reproduction. It therefore messes with the singularizing neoliberal logic of such programs as the LCP and reconfigures the discourse on temporary worker programs by pointing out the structural violence of alienating workers from their kin relations and from the nation more broadly.

I end this chapter by looking back at the body and inquiring again about its spatiality as a locus of violence. The question of 'the body' in discussions of the politics of difference has produced a veritable literature that deconstructs its construction as a category and object of analysis. In this chapter, I have attempted to think through the slain Filipino body's materiality, as a space in and through which violence is experienced. Simultaneously, I have also hinted at the construction of the Filipino body in relation to other political processes such as immigration and transnationalism. In a sense, then, my argument concerns the place of the Filipino body in local, national, and transnational spaces. What does it mean for Filipinos in Canada to be reduced to 'bodies' through fatal killings, but also 'normally' through labour practices, migration policies, and media discourses? To begin to engage this question, we must go back to the body and its disciplining.

I reiterate the utility of Foucault's (1979) work on power, particularly given its analysis of the production of subjects through the disciplining of particular people's bodies. His *Discipline and Punish* has inspired much work on how bodies are put to use in the service of power. As I did in this chapter, I think we can usefully mobilize this treatment of the body as a starting point for making sense of Filipino bodies in the Canadian context. Scholars of Filipino migration to Canada have noted how Filipino bodies are consistently 'groomed' as labouring bodies in the face of nationalist demands for docile economic subjects (Pratt 2004) and that many engage in acts of resistance by working beyond national boundaries to maintain transnational linkages (Kelly and Lusis 2006).

But beyond this, I think it is also important to consider how Filipinos in Canada engage in resistance by claiming and airing grievances against the nation (see Astorga-Garcia 2007). This is to say that despite the constant grooming of Filipinos as docile labouring bodies, they actually actively engage in political work that confounds state actors like the police and government officials. In the cases discussed above, for instance, we see that mourning families and communities courageously *name* flawed immigration policies to grieve the violence of these institutions at the same time that they grieve the loss of Filipino youth. In a sense, then, at the same time that the slain Filipino body allows us to think through the materiality and corporeality of violence against immigrant bodies in the Canadian context, it also sheds public light on the very acts through which activist communities – Filipino and others – attempt to make meaningful material changes to law, policy, and everyday lives more broadly.

The killing of Filipino youth in the Canadian context is a gruesome reminder of the materiality of violence even in urban contexts deemed safe and tolerant, but this should be treated with a grain of salt. For, if we are to take seriously the everyday lives of Filipinos in the Canadian context, I think it is imperative for us to think through these episodes of corporeal violence in relation to institutions that enable the racializations and political economies of Filipino lives in Canada. That is, if we are to politicize questions of Filipino Canadian belonging, we need to look for ways to name not just the violence in cases of killings, but also the violence that sustains Canadian economies, policies, and institutions more broadly.

NOTES

1   The public discourses I analyse in this chapter are drawn from publicly available published sources. Many of these are archived online through individual publications' websites. Since most are drawn from corporate news media sources whose audience is the generalized public, the bulk of the articles are written in English. Even those community-based sources I consulted were mostly written in the English language. This arguably enables the political participation of only particular segments of the Filipino community in Canada. While an analysis of the socio-linguistic politics of participation in media and legal discourse is beyond the scope of this chapter, I recognize the importance of this topic and encourage further work on it.
2   See Pratt (2005) for an analysis of the gendered nature of necropolitical relations. This is particularly relevant for Filipino/a lives in Canada: as Pratt notes, the lives of Filipina live-in caregivers are subjected to state-sanctioned forms of necropolitical violence through policies and practices related to the Live-In Caregiver Program.
3   While the consumption of media by immigrant Filipino communities is not an explicit focus of this chapter, Benito Vergara's work provides clues as to the importance of ethnic print media for immigrant communities. See chapter 4 of his book *Pinoy Capital* (2009).
4   Astorga-Garcia (2007) provides one history of the formation of the JJRC. In this paper, she generally weaves a seemingly smooth story of the organic formation of the coalition, though she does hint at the fact that the process of bringing organizations together was actually power-laden. She notes, for example, that 'an attempt to organise the Coalition more formally, however, was fraught with problems due to differing ideas on how this should be done' (8). She goes on further to note that the Coalition's Youth Committee remained organized and active and 'began to have a vibrant life of its own' (ibid.). See Astorga-Garcia (2007) for further details.

REFERENCES

Astorga-Garcia, Mila. 2007. The road to empowerment in Toronto's Filipino community: Moving from crisis to community capacity building. CERIS Working Paper No. 54. Available online: http://ceris.metropolis.net/Virtual%20Library/WKPP%20List/WKPP2007/CWP54.pdf.

Bellett, Gerry, and Heather Travis. 2006. Teen's killer given seven years in jail: A 'chilling act of random violence that shakes a community to its core.' *Vancouver Sun,* July 13, A1.

Colebourn, John. 2009. Father seeks public apology. *Province,* February 26, A4.

Espiritu, Yen Le. 2003. *Home bound: Filipino American lives across cultures, communities and countries.* Berkeley: University of California Press.

Fong, Petti. 2005a. Slowest runner was killed, trial told. *Globe and Mail,* November 1, A7.

– 2005b. Attacker beat up teen, then went to eat, trial told. *Globe and Mail,* November 3, S2.

Foucault, Michel. 1979. *Discipline and punish: Birth of the prison.* New York: Vintage.

Goonewardena, Kanishka, and Stefan Kipfer. 2005. Spaces of difference: Reflections from Toronto on multiculturalism, bourgeois urbanism and the possibility of radical urban politics. *International Journal of Urban and Regional Research* 29 (3): 670–8.

Gray, Jeff. 2004. Police slow to tend to dying teen, family says. *Globe and Mail,* May 28, A10.

Hansen, Darah. 2006. Garden proposed near site of boy's fatal beating. *Vancouver Sun,* February 14, B6.

Heath-Rawlings, Jordan. 2004. Hundreds mourn slain youth. *Toronto Star,* May 30, A01.

Kelly, Philip F. 1999. The geographies and politics of globalisation. *Progress in Human Geography* 23 (3): 379–400.

Kelly, Philip F., and Tom Lusis. 2006. Migration and the transnational habitus: Evidence from Canada and the Philippines. *Environment and Planning A* 38 (5): 831–48.

Keung, Nicholas. 2004a. Mourners still seek answers in shooting of 17-year-old. *Toronto Star,* June 10, B05.

– 2004b. Anger over teenager's shooting. *Toronto Star,* July 15, B02.

Lemke, Thomas. 2001. 'The birth of biopolitics': Michel Foucault's lecture at the Collège de France on neoliberal governmentality. *Economy and Society* 30 (2): 190–207.

Matas, Robert. 2008. Late-night teenage brawl led to slaying, police say. *Globe and Mail,* January 29, S1.

Mbembe, Achille. 2003. Necropolitics. *Public Culture* 15 (1): 11–40.

Mickelburgh, Rod. 2003. Two teens arrested in fatal BC beating. *Globe and Mail*, December 6, A1.

Ott, Brian, and Eric Aoki. 2002. The politics of negotiating public tragedy: Media framing of the Matthew Shepard murder. *Rhetoric and Public Affairs* 5 (3): 483–505.

Parreñas, Rhacel Salazar. 2009. *Children of global migration: Transnational families and gendered woes.* Stanford: Stanford University Press.

Pratt, Geraldine. 2004. *Working feminism.* Philadelphia: Temple University Press.

– 2005. Abandoned women and spaces of the exception. *Antipode* 37 (5): 1052–78.

– 2009. Circulating sadness: Witness Filipina mothers' stories of family separation. *Gender, Place and Culture* 16 (1): 3–22.

Razack, Sherene, ed. 2002. *Race, space and the law: Unmapping a white settler society.* Toronto: Between the Lines.

– 2004. *Dark threats and white knights: The Somalia affair, peacekeeping and the new imperialism.* Toronto: University of Toronto Press.

– 2007. Stealing the pain of others. *Review of Education, Pedagogy and Cultural Studies* 29 (4): 375–94.

Roberts, David, and Minelle Mahtani. 2010. Neoliberalizing race, racing neoliberalism: Placing 'race' in neoliberal discourses. *Antipode* 42 (2): 248–57

San Juan, Epifanio, Jr. 2000. Trajectories of the Filipino diaspora. *Ethnic Studies Report* 18 (2): 229–38.

Sandercock, Leonie. 2003. *Cosmopolis II: Mongrel cities.* New York: Continuum.

Schissel, Bernard. 1997. Youth crime, moral panics and the news: The conspiracy against the marginalized in Canada. *Social Justice* 24 (2): 165–84.

Teotonio, Isabel. 2006. Offended by racism charge, officer says. *Toronto Star,* June 30.

Thobani, Sunera. 2007. *Exalted subjects: Studies in the making of race and nation in Canada.* Toronto: University of Toronto Press.

Vergara, Benito, Jr. 2009. *Pinoy capital: The Filipino nation in Daly City.* Philadelphia: Temple University Press.

Wortley, Scot, and Julian Tanner. 2004. Racial profiling in Canada: Survey evidence from Toronto. *Canadian Review of Policing Research* 1 (1): 24–36.

Žižek, Slavoj. 2008. *Violence.* New York: Picador.

Chapter 16

Kapisanan: Resignifying Diasporic Post/colonial Art and Artists

CHRISTINE BALMES

I graduated from the University of Michigan in 2007 with a degree in Asian studies, focusing on Southeast Asia and the Philippines in particular. My aunt Adelwisa Weller, who was then the Filipino-language instructor there, encouraged me to take courses on Philippine history and literature, as well as classes taught by Filipino American professors. In her Intermediate Filipino language class, I read Zeus Salazar and his idea of 'Pantayong Pananaw' or 'Filipino history written by us Filipinos for Filipinos.' It was an eye-opening experience. No other university course that I had taken at the University of Michigan had given me the proper theoretical models and vocabulary for a Filipino-centred consciousness. Reading Salazar was my first exposure to the indigenization movement that he spearheaded with Virgilio Enriquez and Renato Constantino (see Mendoza 2002).

After completing my undergraduate degree, I moved back to Canada, where my family had emigrated from the Philippines nine years earlier. I sought a community with whom I could share my ideas and interests that matched Salazar's idea – Filipinos interested in the question of what constitutes a Philippine-inspired viewpoint. But in multicultural Toronto, my desire to become more connected to my heritage could not find an outlet. My immigrant family, living in the suburb of Thornhill, was not part of a strong Filipino community. I experienced a crisis that had to do with questioning not only the validity of pursuing an Asian studies degree but also the relevance of foregrounding my Filipino identity. I felt disconnected and more out of place in Toronto than I ever did in Ann Arbor.

During a summer night in 2008, however, I found the community I had been looking for in the Kapisanan Philippine Centre for Arts and

Culture. By chance I dropped by during a one-day performance of *The Corner*, a play written and directed by Jason Maghanoy about Jeffrey Reodica, a seventeen-year-old Filipino Canadian who was shot and killed by the police in 2004 (see Catungal in this volume). After the performance, the director and actors held a question and answer period. The entire cast and crew were Filipino Canadians who were, like me, in their twenties, college-educated, and interested in their Filipino heritage. Reodica's mother and siblings were in the audience, and I remember his mother weeping, thankful to everyone for their support. I later learned that the showing was a fundraiser for Kapisanan; the cast members were allowed to use the space for rehearsals as long as they agreed to give a show there. A strong sense of community, awareness, and empowerment permeated the room. The play's subject matter, the visibly Filipino cast, and the mostly Filipino audience helped me realize for the first time that there was a 'Filipino Canadian' community in Toronto.

From this experience, I strove to take an active role in Kapisanan. I became an administrative intern under its executive director, Caroline Mangosing, for almost a year. In helping to write grants, I read past proposals and learned about Kapisanan's history and mandate. I also became friends with different artists who were part of the Kapisanan community. Eventually, because of my skills in playing the kulintang gongs in the Maguindanaoan tradition,[1] a skill I gained at Michigan, I became part of an artist collective called Santa Guerrilla. Within a year, I was assigned to develop and teach the conversational Filipino-language curriculum, and I taught over twenty of my peers, most of them Filipino Canadian artists. As I spent more time at Kapisanan, I began to think about the socio-cultural relevance of our activities, and sought to find a framework that would help define what we do. This chapter is the result of that work. It is my way of introducing Kapisanan to the larger Filipino Canadian academic community and to put the activities of Filipino Canadian artists – specifically those connected with Kapisanan – into conversation with the indigenization movements in the Philippines and the United States, so that the larger Filipino diasporic community may learn about and perhaps support what we are trying to do. Cognizant of what Stuart Hall calls the 'positionality of identity' as something that is 'a production which is never complete, always in process, and always constituted within, not outside representation' (Hall 2003, 234), my aim is to demonstrate the emergence of a 'Filipino Canadian' cultural movement. Using Kapisanan as a case study, I will show how it operates and what it comprises. I will be examining artworks, music, and performances as well as the ideas of the artists who create them, in order to highlight how they might contribute to the decolonization of the Filipino mind and to what Renato Constantino calls the development of 'counter-consciousness,' that is, 'a consciousness that articulates [the Filipino's] own economic, political and cultural aspiration and contraposes itself in an all pervading consciousness that seeks to keep the Filipino people permanently integrated in a worldwide system that produces poverty, wars, and degradation for the underdeveloped nations of the world' (Constantino 1978, 82).

Since my involvement with Kapisanan is both as a community member and as a researcher, my research method drew from iterative-inductive ethnography (O'Reilly 2005, 3). I conducted formal and informal interviews with individual artists, read grant and marketing materials for the organization, helped organize events, attended art and history classes, and watched musical and theatrical performances. Through my involvement in Santa Guerrilla, I also took part in creating and performing music. As the Filipino-language instructor, I wrote 'lessons' that were used in instructional videos, in which I also starred. Recognizing that 'Asian subjects who reside in the United States and in Canada face many of same issues regarding identity, multiple and cultural allegiances, marginalization vis-à-vis mainstream society, historical exclusion, and postcolonial and/or diasporic and/or transnational subjectivity' (Ty and Goellnicht 2004, 2), I position Kapisanan's activities within post/colonial[2] and neocolonial theories espoused by Filipino intellectuals, such as Sarita See, S. Lily Mendoza, E. San Juan, and Renato Constantino. Kapisanan artists and culture makers are involved in the project of (re)creating and (re)covering Philippine culture and, in the process of narrating their stories in Canada, are (re)defining the Filipino Canadian imagined community. S. Lily Mendoza states that 'one totally immersed in a singular constructed reality cannot have the means with which to challenge his/her ideological inscription' (Mendoza 2002, 179). Filipino Canadians, precisely because of the liminal position they occupy between the Philippines and Canada, have the capacity to speak to and challenge the inequities they perceive in both cultures. The artists I write about here are among those who have heeded the challenge of imagining what that Filipino Canadian community is by 'resignifying their Filipino subjectivity with more culturally self-affirming images, [so that] members undergo psychic transformation that releases the mind from the burden of colonial domination and shame' (Mendoza 2002, 151).

To elaborate further, the chapter is divided into three parts. The first part consists of an overview of Kapisanan: its origins, mandate, and operations. The second part takes a look at more established members of the Kapisanan arts community, including their artworks, music, or performances, as well as their personal stories and viewpoints. The third section focuses on the performance collective Santa Guerrilla, whose origins attest to the possibilities that arise when a group of post/colonial people with a clear decolonization agenda come together in a space like Kapisanan.

About Kapisanan

The Kapisanan Philippine Centre for Arts and Culture is a non-profit organization founded in 2005 by two Filipina Canadian artists, Nadine Villasin and Caroline Mangosing, in their early thirties. Villasin later became the artistic director of the Carlos Bulosan Theatre, a professional theatre company comprising Filipino Canadians and a community partner that shares the same space as Kapisanan. Villasin, a theatre performer and actress, and Mangosing, a film actress and artist, envisioned Kapisanan as a hub where young Filipino artists could gather and explore their Filipino roots through arts and culture.[3] They also aimed to respond to problems of the Filipino Canadian community such as racism, invisibility, cultural shame, lack of role models and leadership, and divisions between different generations and between newcomers and those integrated into mainstream society. These problems occur both internally (e.g., tensions between newcomers and those already integrated) and externally (e.g., invisibility in mainstream culture, weak political clout, and racist labour policies) (see Ty and Philip et al. in this volume).

Understanding that these problems have a common foundation in the 'colonial mentality' and cultural shame that Filipinos suffer as post/colonial people, Kapisanan intends to change how Filipino Canadian youth view Philippine culture by promoting and providing examples of Filipino culture as young, 'cool,' and 'hip.' In 2008–10 when I conducted my study, it had regular programs, such as the Critical Filipino History workshops and Conversational Filipino classes, as well as short-term workshops on arts and culture, such as Poetry Is Our Second Language, where students are taught the history of poetry in the Philippines and its different forms. There are annual events co-organized with the Carlos Bulosan Theatre, like the Kultura arts festival held every summer, an event where Filipino Canadian artists show their video installations and art exhibits, and perform music and theatre readings. Kapisanan also supports a large network of artists, both established and emergent, who frequently collaborate on multimedia projects. More established artists are invited to hold or take part in workshops, events, or performances at the space, mentor younger/beginning artists, and rent the space for rehearsals or part-time gallery showings. Budding artists or young people interested in the arts are invited to take part in the programs or events facilitated by these established artists, or serve as interns for Kapisanan. Currently, the members who regularly attend activities or are actively volunteering range from seventeen-year-olds to people in their mid-thirties. Since marketing is crucial to attracting new members and fostering the organization's image, Kapisanan's advertising materials, both online and in real life, are professionally designed and art-directed by its members. Kapisanan is located in Kensington Market in the downtown Toronto area, which is recognized as a hub for the city's arts and culture scene.

Most of the artworks at Kapisanan are 'indigenous' in Mendoza's sense – that is, they are 'originating from within and directed mainly to community members' (Mendoza 2006, 117), but always with an ear to the mainstream Western pop culture. The videos and websites created by the Kapisanan production team, staff, and members are good examples. 'Channel K,' a YouTube channel hyperlinked to the Kapisanan website, has two shows: 'Kain Na!,' a cooking show, and 'Glossari,' a Filipino-language show designed to teach non-speakers basic, useful sentences. 'Kain Na!' features two young Filipino men cooking in a studio kitchen. They use recipes that are reminiscent of, but not identical to, Filipino dishes, such as 'roast beef adobo' and 'menudo with quail eggs.'[4] Adobo is a casserole of bite-sized pieces of pork and/or chicken, and is never a whole slab of meat like roast beef. Menudo recipes do not normally include quail eggs. The decision to change the dishes this way is an aesthetic one. The recipes are essentially the same, and changing them does not fundamentally change the taste of the food – but doing so presents them in a different light.

To understand the relevance of these changes, it is helpful to view them in terms of Sarita See's 'strategies of indirection' (See 2009, 128). See, who wrote about Filipino American artists, notes that 'strategies of indirection, trickery, and mimicry [are] at the heart of Filipino/

American decolonizing cultures' (ibid). According to her, 'strategies of indirection like camp, mimesis, joking, and punning [are] articulations of the conditions of possibility that constitute this contemporary post/colonial archive' (xxix). Because of the Spanish and American colonization of the Philippines, as well as the continuing invisibility of Filipinos in American culture and history, Filipino American artists and culture makers are forced to use these strategies so that their culture may survive. Filipino Canadians – who struggle with similar problems of post/colonization and invisibility within the dominant Western culture – adopt the same strategies. But an added layer to these 'conditions of possibility' exists for these artists, as the show's tagline indicates: 'Learn to cook contemporary interpretations of Filipino cuisine, and impress your Lola!' Inherent in this statement is the idea that ethnic dishes, such as 'adobo' or 'menudo,' are relics from the past, hailing from lola's (grandmother's) time, which need to be improved upon and modernized. That is, certain aspects of Filipino culture are old-fashioned or even bland. The show thus creates a binary between past and present, 'Filipino' versus 'Canadian,' and attempts to present what a pairing of the two might look, or rather taste, like. Therefore, Filipino food is adobo and menudo. But Filipino Canadian food is 'roast beef' adobo, and menudo 'with quail eggs.'

In the Channel K show 'Glossari,' which I wrote, two members in silhouette face each other. One person pronounces the first syllable in a phrase ('Mag'), and the text appears from the mouth of the silhouette and flies up. The other person pronounces the next syllable ('ka'), and the same thing happens. They take turns until the whole sentence is fully spelled and pronounced (in this case, 'Magkano po?'), and an English translation appears on the bottom of the screen ('How much?'). Because of its reference to the 'soft-shoe silhouettes' from the 1970s 'Electric Company' TV show,[5] the 'Glossari' show presents the recognizably U.S. show in a new way through Filipino faces, or rather silhouettes. It teaches Filipino phrases, which I arranged according to themes, like 'Riding a Jeepney,' 'Shopping,' or 'Giving Directions,' through a familiar Western frame.

We can read this artistic effort in two ways. One way is to critique it as the Westernization of Philippine culture, another case of Filipinos being 'imitative rather than creative' (Constantino 1978, 78). Or we can view it the other way around, as an empowered approach to 'Filipinizing' the colonizer's culture, wherein U.S. childhood entertainment and educational tools are mobilized to teach the Filipino language to all learners.

'Glossari' is an example of what Virgilio Enriquez calls 'indigenization from without,' where indigenization originates from 'the exogenous (colonial) culture; the West is the source of theoretic constructs and the indigenous (Filipino) culture is the target recipient of culture flow. Its main strategy is "content indigenization, test modification, and translation of imported materials"' (Enriquez in Mendoza 2006, 47). Rather than directly opposing the hegemony of Western culture, another strategy for these artists is to indigenize it and use it as a tool to teach the Filipino language.

Kapisanan Artists

The question of who Kapisan identifies as its main audience is central to understanding what role these artists and cultural workers play in the Filipino diaspora. I am in agreement with See that there is 'scholarly thickness that can emerge from specificity' (See 2009, xxviii), especially for these artists who have bonded together because of their common cultural identity. When speaking directly about the Filipino diasporic community undergoing a process of decolonization, '"community" is better conceptualized as an "audience"' (ibid.). As artists who self-identify as Filipinos and engage Filipino issues in their work, they are speaking for, and to, the Filipino community-audience. But whom they imagine as part of their community is a complicated question. These artists have varied, sometimes divergent and opposing viewpoints on the question of belonging and responsibility to the Filipino community, both in the Philippines and the diaspora.

For this section, I focus on Kapisanan's more established artists, who have been working on their craft for a longer time period and have larger bodies of work. All except for one travel to the Philippines regularly, and all were either born in Canada or moved to Canada from the Philippines at a very young age. These artists are in their late twenties to mid-thirties, and are associated with Kapisanan for different reasons. For them, their actions at the local level effect change in the diasporic Filipino community. For example, theatre practitioner Catherine Hernandez uses her play *Future Folk* to communicate the problems encountered by Filipinas in the Live-In Caregiver Program to the community-audience of mainstream Canada, but also to speak for migrant Filipinos in Canada and her fellow Filipino Canadians who are lacking in 'self-love.' The wife and husband team Caroline Mangosing and Romeo Candido use their film *Ang Pamana* to introduce Philippine supernatural folklore to Filipino Canadians and to share their Filipino Canadian point of view with the audience in the Philippines. Musician Alexander Punzalan uses his kulintang-inspired music to bridge the gap between what he describes as the 'two different worlds' of the Philippines and Canada. Photographer Alex Felipe uses his pictures of Canadian mining operations in the Philippines to show the inequity in the relationship between the two countries. Because these artists are leading the Filipino Canadian arts and culture scene, they are defining what it means to be Filipino Canadian through their creations. As artists who choose to work directly on community issues, these artists have a 'mandate to represent their communities' (Megan Wilson, as quoted by See 2009, 128) and should be understood as such.

Catherine Hernandez is a theatre practitioner born in Canada in the mid-1970s to a mother who taught Philippine folk dance. Catherine has given dance workshops at Kapisanan, read plays at events, and is a member of Santa Guerrilla. She also co-wrote and acted in *Future Folk,* which was rehearsed at the Kapisanan Centre. The play weaves together traditional Philippine dances like the kappa malong malong[6] with stories of three Filipina caregivers in Canada. It explores themes inherent in their line of work, such as missing their children, being victims of sexual abuse, remaining on call even after the end of the work day, and living with the uncertainty of deportation. In my email interview with Catherine, she stated that her work aids the community because it has the capacity to affect

> one person, [who] will leave the theatre and rethink their mentality towards caregivers. That's all. Small, attainable goals. So if my play helps one caregiver's employer to stop treating her like the house pet and more like a human being, then great. If this means one less Canadian who thinks migrant workers should be so . . . grateful for a chance to work here, then fantastic.

Evident in Catherine's comments is that *Future Folk* is a way to speak directly to Canadians who employ Filipina caregivers or whose lives are affected by migrant workers (see Davidson and Tungohan in this volume). But in embodying the collective experiences of Filipina caregivers onstage, she is also enabling them to speak through her. In an email interview, she describes this as an act of making the invisible 'visible as ever.'[7] One of the most memorable scenes in the play is when Catherine portrays the sexual abuse committed against Luz, one of the central characters. Onstage, Catherine is splayed and screaming, fighting off an invisible man. Although she is alone, the scene is violent, visceral, harrowing, even traumatic. Catherine's portrayal of the rape scene recalls See's 'subversive disarticulation' – specifically, depictions of bodily injury and degradation in artworks by Filipino artists in the diaspora that respond to 'a matrix of historical, psychic, and cultural dispossession by producing a visual and rhetorical grammar of violence that in turn "disarticulates" the empire' (See 2009, xviii). According to See, these depictions of violence are ultimately subversive acts because it is when this 'grammar of violence' is incorporated or ingested by Filipino Canadian artists in their language and art, and is appropriated by them for their own purposes, that 'the empire falls apart [and] is in fact cannibalized by its radical interior' (ibid). Part of the power of *Future Folk* lies in its ability to present the violence committed against Filipina nannies onstage. Doing so re-appropriates the violence of Canadians against Filipino migrant workers, and makes it less of an attack on individual survivors and more of a community issue. As a result, Catherine acts as the conscience for the Canadian nation that asks, How do we treat people who come to our shores to work? What are our responsibilities to migrant workers?

On the other hand, the portrayal of migrant Filipina caregivers as mothers and daughters, whose decision to leave their country affects families and communities, humanizes labour migration. Besides acting as a mirror to Canadian society and advocating for the rights of migrant Filipinas, Catherine also aims to speak to the larger Filipino community in Canada, as described in her email message:

> *Is it cheesy to say my work fosters a self-love in Filipinos? . . . But I think pride is a very important piece of the puzzle that's missing in our community and so easily welcomed. I find that when I see reactions to my work. When people saw [my play]* Singkil *one person said, 'This is the heartbeat of us.' . . . When some caregivers saw* Future Folk, *they were in tears at seeing themselves onstage, visible as ever.*

The need to tell the 'Filipino-Canadian story' is what drove this thirty-something filmmaker couple, Canadian-born and -raised Romeo Candido and Philippine-born and U.S.- and Canada-raised Caroline Mangosing. They produced, co-wrote, and directed the thriller *Ang Pamana* (2006). The film centres on a Canadian-born Filipino brother and sister who live in Vancouver with their parents, speak 'Canadian English,' and like to snowboard. In other words, they are Filipinos physically and ancestrally, but not culturally. When they inherit their family's ancestral home in Bulacan from their recently deceased grand-mother, they visit the Philippines for the first time, and find out that their house is already inhabited by denizens of the supernatural world, such as the *kapre, aswang, duwende,* and other ghouls and ghosts from Philippine folklore.

In my interview with Romeo, he explained that the film was meant to tell the story from the point of view of the filmmakers, who self-identify as Filipino Canadians. Unfortunately, although the film received criti-cal praise, it did not have mass appeal in the Philippines. The audience in the Philippines felt alienated from the actors, who spoke English with a Canadian accent and did not attempt to speak in Tagalog or even Taglish. Yet the filmmakers made the deliberate decision to hire Filipino Canadian actors and to shoot on location in Canada and the Philippines. Their intent was to show typical diasporic teens who had very little, if any, connection with their Filipino-ness. But the film's unpopularity in the Philippines revealed that catering to a Filipino Canadian audience can and does alienate a Filipino one. Put differ-ently, messages aimed specifically at one group are not as effective when directed towards another group. The language issue is one indi-cation that Filipino Canadians function in relation to a different system of signs and symbols from their Filipino counterparts.

The film nevertheless succeeds in revealing the creatures of night-mares to frighten and entertain Filipino Canadians, evident in the reg-ular screenings of *Ang Pamana* at Kapisanan. In many ways, the film keeps Philippine mythologies and folklore alive by enabling the super-natural world to access the minds and psyches of Filipinos outside of the Philippines. Presented this way, *Ang Pamana* can be read as an effort to contribute to the 'massive cultural reclamation project [that is] the indigenization movement [which] intends to recover (read: uncover) "indigenous" ways of knowing and being' (Mendoza 2006, 202).

Another Kapisanan artist elucidates the connection between Filipinos in Canada and in the Philippines. After graduating from university, the Canadian-born musician Alexander Punzalan Jr, or JR, travelled to the Philippines on his own, where he volunteered for non-profit organiza-tions and created a documentary on families who squatted in cemeter-ies. In an email interview with me, he said,

Coming back to Canada [after travelling to the Philippines] I started focusing more on my music and video and started to work on unifying ideals between Balikbayans and Filipinos from the Philippines. What that means is creating an understanding

between both DIFFERENT worlds. This means learning from Filipinos in the Philippines and educating the Filipino-Canadians with my videos and music.

For JR, Filipinos and Filipino Canadians inhabit 'different worlds' with different ideals and worldviews. But he is able to navigate this difference by positioning himself in between, not only as a student of Philippine culture, but also as a teacher of Philippine culture to Filipino Canadians. An example of how JR bridged two worlds was when he went to South Cotabato in late 2008 to purchase a kulintang instrument from the Maguindanaoan tribes. He did so in order to *uncover something that's been hidden from us by Westernized cultures.'* JR literally brought kulintang music to the Kapisanan community when a collective of musicians and performers formed around the kulintang and became Santa Guerrilla.

One of JR's songs, 'Oh Woman,'[8] exemplifies his project to create this Philippine-inspired music. It is carried forth by the resonance of the agong and woven with a kulintang rhythm and the expelled breaths of a vocalist. It also integrates handclaps, guitar strings, scampering drumbeats, and phrases in Filipino. The song is melancholy and nostalgic: the chorus is 'Oh woman / you're five years from home / love breaks down / so free your mind some.' JR wrote the song in response to and as a dedication to the thousands of women who leave the Philippines to become caregivers in Canada. Neither he nor his parents went through the Live-In Caregiver Program. Yet he chose to write a song inspired by the plight of his compatriots, using instruments that are indigenous to the Philippines. He released this track on his website and posted its music video online to allow the public free access. That JR is involved in a project of 'affirming communal identities and autochthonous traditions' (San Juan 1998, 7) is obvious in his statement:

In order for me to accept my background and be proud of my bloodline I need to reach far back into time when these Islands first beat the drum to the sounds of the tropics. Not American and not Spanish . . . It's like we've been given a bunch of American propaganda on our Philippine walls and now we're slowly taking it down and uncovering the truth. It hurts. But that's what I provoke in my music, especially for the Philippines. Whatever I personally make, it's always for the Philippines. That includes my family, friends and people I meet. They all know that and you can hear it in my music.

What stands out from JR's comment is the clear intent he has of 'uncovering' that which has been 'plastered over' by U.S. and Spanish colonization. Like Romeo and Caroline's *Ang Pamana*, JR's Philippine culture–inspired music is another instance of Mendoza's 'massive reclamation project' of Philippine culture. The fact that there might be 'invention' and 'addition' as much as recovering or uncovering is part and parcel of this project. Artistic works like JR's are important because they offer hope and provide more productive alternatives to Western Enlightenment thought and postcolonial nominalism, which, according to San Juan, obscure the historical reasons for the 'asymmetry between North and South' (San Juan 1998, 22).

Alex Felipe, a photographer at Kapisanan, is another artist involved in this 'unearthing and reconstructing' project. During the course of my research in 2009–10, Alex was the facilitator of the Critical Filipino History workshops, where he taught history from the viewpoint of Filipinos. Alex was born in the Philippines but moved to Canada with his family in the late 1970s. He graduated from the University of Toronto intending to become a lawyer. But after graduation he travelled around Asia and discovered that he had a talent and interest in photography. He now works as a photographer whose focus is on poverty and human rights issues. He regularly travels between the Philippines and Canada, and works with non-governmental organizations in both countries, *'advocating for both changes here in Canada to improve our situation as invisible minorities, and for changes in the Philippines that were the root causes of our coming to Canada in the first place.'* He published a photo essay on Canadian mining operations in the Philippines, focusing on their horrific effects on communities and the environment, in *This* magazine (Felipe 2009). His interests in the economic and political relationship between the Philippines and Canada led him to conclude that the distinction between the two nations is insurmountable. As he learned more about the inequitable relations between the two nations, his alliance shifted from his Canadian to his Filipino identity. In an email interview with me, he said,

> *I also hope that the biggest help [I contribute] might be in the fact that to have a Filipino-Canadian interested in the Philippines may help other Filipino-Canadians (who suffer from a notorious problem with their identity) feel like it's OK to actually self-identify as Filipino, to care about their people, and to stop feeling like they have to drop their ethnicity to be respected by others.*

His interest in the Philippines is what he hopes will inspire others to feel proud of their heritage. He added, *'I began photographing at the same time that I became fully aware and accepting of my identity as a person from the Philippines. I feel that acceptance of one's identity and our shared past necessarily results in needing to focus on the improvement in the lives of our people.'* His audience is clearly other Filipino Canadians *'who suffer from a notorious problem with their identity'* – what Catherine described as the missing 'self-love' in the community.

For these artists, making art that is relevant to issues in the Filipino Canadian community and that uses Philippine instruments or ideas is also a very personal project. But this is not a project limited to artists. Other scholars and culture makers in the diaspora, especially in the United States, are involved in the same movement.[9] They are part of what San Juan calls 'subjects-in-process,' which he describes as 'a community of persons who inquires into the way things are, how they have been, and how they can be and should be' (San Juan 1998, 17). Filipino Canadian artists are tackling but one front in this massive project. Scholars and community members who are interested in decolonization are allies to these artists. As Mendoza says, 'the task of seizing initiative in the production of "ethno-centered" knowledge entails a deliberate and massive excavation project of the submerged discourses of the (cultural) nation which historiography must now take the lead in unearthing and reconstructing' (Mendoza 2002, 179). As evidenced by the artists' statements, the final goal is to aid other Filipino Canadians so that they may acquire 'self-love' or pride, and become empowered. Constantino calls this 'the liberation of consciousness,' and connects it to economic liberation. According to him, there is an important relationship between the two: 'Economic liberation will surely produce the liberation of consciousness in its advanced stage but it is possible, and indeed necessary, to work for some liberation of consciousness so that people may act to secure their economic liberation' (Constantino 1978, 22). While it may be too much to ask these Filipino Canadian artists to be culture bearers as well as entrepreneurs and intellectuals, I believe that they need to be at least aware of the theories and modes of thinking that are arising from these different fronts. Similarly, those who are working towards the same goals of decolonization and 'liberation of consciousness' from the different disciplines can benefit from taking part in the conversation that these artists have initiated.

Santa Guerrilla

The final section of this chapter is about an independent Filipino Canadian arts and music entity that traces its origins to Kapisanan:

Santa Guerrilla. Santa Guerrilla is a solid example of creative collaboration when a group of artists with different backgrounds and familiarity with Philippine and Canadian culture are given a safe and supportive space to work together on a common agenda. I met musician Alexander Punzalan Jr (JR) when I first joined Kapisanan in 2008. JR and I shared a similar desire to bring kulintang music to Toronto, and with the contacts I had from the United States, I was able to connect him with the kulintang master player Danongan Kalanduyan from San Francisco State University. Mr Kalanduyan's family, who still resides in South Cotabato in Mindanao, continues to create kulintang ensemble instruments and incorporate the music in their lifestyles. In late 2008, JR was able to travel to South Cotabato, meet Mr Kalanduyan's family, and buy a kulintang set from them. He also took video footage of his trip, which he shared in Kapisanan. The scenes that he captured during his three-day stay portrayed a Philippines that was unfamiliar to me and my peers: tribal, Islamic, and rooted in indigenous cultures. But the video footage energized us, and the richness of the culture we were seeing inspired the creative spirit within us.

Out of the kulintang JR brought from the Maguindanaoan peoples, a handful of us came to form Santa Guerrilla. Myk Miranda and JR had collaborated in the past, performing together at the Filipino Making Waves Festival in 2008 with Jennifer Maramba, who is a visual artist and a dancer. Romeo Candido, who directed the film *Ang Pamana,* is the other vocalist for Santa Guerrilla, and plays the kulintang in a non-traditional way. Kevin Polangco, another community member, has the talent for playing toms. Eventually, other individuals, including former Kapisanan administrator Kevin Centeno, Catherine Hernandez from *Future Folk,* and dancer and vocalist Robin Lacambra, became part of Santa Guerrilla.[10] All members of Santa Guerrilla, except for me, were born and raised in Canada to Filipino parents, yet I was the only one who had experience playing the traditional kulintang. However, it was not traditional kulintang music that my peers were initially interested in playing. Kulintang music has been thriving in San Francisco, largely because of the presence of Danongan Kalanduyan, who has taught dozens of students in traditional playing. But we in Toronto have no such teachers, so our ensemble was driven by our own creative aesthetics. It seemed more productive to use the instruments in novel ways, creating new beats that sounded good to our ears, incorporating musical styles that were more reminiscent of hip-hop than of traditional kulintang music.

Our first performance was in 2009 during the annual SuperSkillz talent show hosted by the Filipino student associations from York University and Ryerson University in Toronto. Although most of the other performers were Filipinos, we were among the few whose performance was visibly Filipino: we incorporated *kulintang* instruments, a spoken word poet who rapped in Filipino and English, and dancers who performed a variation of a traditional *malong* dance. We had only one song, and it was entitled 'Supernatural.' A *kulintang* melody began the song and was repeated for two bars. Romeo hauntingly crooned, 'You say you know your name, but do you / Wasting, wasting your time.' Tom drums entered, followed by a second *kulintang* melody. In this performance, I played the time-keeping instrument *bandir*, which came in at the same time as the second *kulintang*. JR sang the verse, 'We throw it on the floor / How you feel about that / The struggle's on the front / But we push it to the back / You don't know now / You don't know / Why we push them away.' Myk interjected with a spoken word solo, intermixing Filipino phrases with his message of cultural pride: 'With our fists gripping life everlasting / We will shine our light / Your past is mine / And our future intertwined / I'm proud to be Filipino / Taas noo, Filipino / Ngayon ang ating panahon / Our time is now.'

After this performance, we experienced a singular rush as we received accolades from fellow performers, calls for collaboration, and questions about our instruments. But in the beginning, my relationship with Santa Guerrilla was challenging. Although I recognized the relevance of incorporating tribal music in our project for decolonization, I felt some ambivalence about our use of Maguindanaoan instruments in non-traditional ways. I believe that the 'massive cultural reclamation project' must include tribal voices and viewpoints that have been marginalized and oppressed. Onstage performing for our peers, I felt deeply how much our Filipino Canadian community needed something 'ours' like this. As diasporic people living in Canada and away from the Philippines, the *kulintang* which is indigenous to the Philippines symbolized a key to formulating a sense of community.

But as non-indigenous, diasporic people, we are far from understanding what it really means to be oppositional to the Western hegemony. The Maguindanao, Maranaw, and T'boli people whose lives are intimately woven with *kulintang* music are still marginalized even within the Philippines (Asian Development Bank 2002). Our use of *kulintang* instruments, disconnected from their original purposes, provoked me to think about the question of appropriation, and made me realize that we are responsible for ensuring that we are not using them without an awareness of their origins. These concerns weighed heavily in my mind when, serendipitously, JR, Jennifer Maramba, and I attended the first ever Babaylan Conference at Sonoma State University in March 2010. We ended up travelling and living together in northern California, and in our time there, JR arranged for us to meet with and learn kulintang music from Danongan Kalanduyan in San Francisco. For three days, we took lessons with the master and learned the music by demonstration. Personally, taking the time and effort to learn traditional music with some of my band members from Mr Kalanduyan, who is deeply rooted in the culture and yet has lived for most of his adult life in the United States, has been a way of giving myself permission to then use the kulintang instruments and music to create new songs with and for my diasporic peers. Along with email discussions with other band members, particularly Romeo, the trip has helped me realize that our efforts in Santa Guerrilla were in line with the larger project of diasporic people to (re)cover and (re)create Filipino culture. This is the strategy that we have to adopt to allow our stories and our culture to thrive. Furthermore, it is our imperative to create music that is as authentic and relevant to our experiences as diasporic, post/colonial young people. Later, I encountered Stuart Hall's warning, writing about the African diaspora, that 'the original . . . is no longer there. It too has been transformed. History is, in that sense, irreversible. We must not collude with the West which, precisely, normalizes and appropriates Africa by freezing it into some timeless zone of the primitive, unchanging past' (Hall 2003, 241). Although our reclamation project as Filipino artists has significant differences from the one described by Hall, his statement provides a light into how we as Filipino Canadians can both problematize our identity and still move forward. I recognize that research and recovery do not end from learning from a master. But hand in hand with the efforts to find out about the aspects of Philippine culture that have been occluded by a history of colonization, we have the agency – and I would say, even the responsibility – to create something new that reflects our positions and lived realities as Filipino Canadians who have our own experiences and understanding of living in the diaspora.

Conclusion

Since its founding in 2005, the Kapisanan Philippine Centre for Arts and Culture has striven to be an integral part of the Filipino Canadian community. As a space that supports not only artists but also young people interested in the decolonization project, it plays an important role in contributing to a sense of common identity so necessary in the 'massive reclamation project' of Filipinos as post/colonial people. The artists and young people who have found their way to Kapisanan combine Filipino- or Filipino Canadian–inspired issues and art with aspects of Western culture because of the conditions of possibility specific to us as post/colonial diasporic people. But in the process we aim to promote self-love and pride among other Filipino youth, who, like us, may be more attuned to Western than to Filipino modes of thinking. That is, we are setting up the parameters for a Filipino Canadian identity – we are making our place and stories here, in Canada, but the Philippines remains a constant, if not easily defined, presence in our artistic and cultural projects.

NOTES

1 The kulintang gongs are a set of eight gongs that are pentatonic in scale, usually made of brass, from the southern part of the Philippines. The ones we use in Santa Guerrilla are from the Maguindanaoan peoples of South Cotabato. The word 'kulintang' can also denote the kulintang ensemble, which in Maguindanaoan tradition comprises the agung (large hanging gongs), the bandir (time-keeping gong), the dabak (rhythm drum), and the gandingan (talking gongs).

2 I borrow Sarita See's use of the solidus in 'post/colonial' to 'indicate the unfinished business of American colonialism' which she says largely accounts for the invisibility of Filipinos in Western culture and imagination (see 2009, xvi–xvii).

3 In 2009, during the writing of this chapter, the centre also had two part-time staff members: administrator Kevin Centeno and program co-ordinator Jodinand Aguillon, both in their late twenties. Centeno is also a musician member of Santa Guerrilla, and Aguillon has directed several Kapisanan videos.

4 These recipes are the brainchild of Kapisanan program co-ordinator Jodinand Aguillon.

5 The structure of the show was thought of by Caroline Mangosing. The Kapisanan staff and production team shot, edited, and directed the short film.

6 A dance from the Marano peoples in Southern Philippines that incorporates a colourful, tubular cloth called the 'malong.'

7 To become authentic spokespersons for caregivers, Catherine and her fellow actors in the Sulong Collective, Aura Carcueva and Karen Ancheta, spent almost a year meeting and interviewing caregivers, watching YouTube videos of hopeful applicants from the Philippines, and reading news articles about the Live-In Caregiver Program. During the run of *Future Folk*, the Sulong Collective provided one show free to caregivers, so that those whose stories they were telling could attend the play and watch their stories told and performed.

8 The song samples a track made by Folklorico Filipino Canada, a Toronto-based folk dance group. JR added voice, guitar, and synths to the kulintang rhythm. Santa Guerrilla member Myk Miranda also contributed lyrics in Filipino to the song.

9 Examples from the United States include scholars S. Lily Mendoza, and Leny Strobel. Virgil Apostol writes about traditional healing methods, and Lane Wilcken writes about ancient and modern tattooing traditions.

10 In 2010, two other musicians joined Santa Guerrilla: poet Haniely Pableo and producer Rudy Boquilla.

REFERENCES

Asian Development Bank. 2002. *Indigenous peoples / ethnic minorities and poverty reduction – Philippines*. Manila: Asian Development Bank.

Clifford, James. 1994. Diasporas. *Cultural Anthropology* 9: 302–38.

Constantino, Renato. 1978. *Neocolonial identity and counter-consciousness*. London: Merlin.

Felipe, Alex. 2009. 'All that glitters: Canada's toxic legacy in the Philippines.' May 29. Accessed August 1, 2010. http://this.org/magazine/2009/05/29/canada-philippines-gold-toxic/.

Hall, Stuart. 2003. Cultural identity and diaspora. In *Theorizing diaspora: A reader*, ed. Jana Evans Braziel and Anita Mannur, 233–46. Malden, MA: Blackwell.

Mendoza, S. Lily. 2002. *Between the homeland and the diaspora: The politics of theorizing Filipino and Filipino American identities: A second look at the post-structuralism-indigenization debates*. New York: Routledge.

– 2006. A different breed of Filipino balikbayans: The ambiguities of returning. In *Positively no Filipinos allowed: Building communities and discourse*, ed. Antonio T. Tiongson, Jr, Edgardo V. Gutierrez, and Ricardo V. Gutierrez, 199–214. Philadelphia: Temple University Press.

O'Reilly, Karen. 2005. *Ethnographic methods*. New York: Routledge.

San Juan, E. 1998. *Beyond postcolonial theory.* New York: St Martin's Press.

See, Sarita. 2009. *The decolonized eye: Filipino American art and performance.* Minneapolis: University of Minnesota Press.

Ty, Eleanor, and Donald C. Goellnicht. 2004. Beyond hyphenated identities. In *Asian North American identities: Beyond the hyphen.* Bloomington: Indiana University Press.

Chapter 17

Educated Minorities: The Experiences of Filipino Canadian University Students

MAUREEN GRACE MENDOZA

The classroom is where I initially questioned my experience as an immigrant, Filipina student. My undergraduate years at the University of British Columbia (UBC) inspired exploration into unarticulated parts of the Filipino Canadian experience: that of an educated minority who, despite their successes, still remain marginalized, wary of their identities and place in the future of Canadian society. This chapter attempts to capture those understated sentiments with a case study of eleven UBC Filipino Canadian students, exploring how the setting of higher education exposes deeply fragmented minority narratives. My study underscores influences of the Filipino diaspora upon the education of students. With respect to class reproduction, my research focuses on the generational discrepancy between Filipino students whose parents migrated in the late 1970s and the 1980s and those whose parents more recently immigrated.

Overall, I argue that while many Filipino Canadian UBC students are privileged with particular circumstances that have facilitated entry into university, their experiences still demonstrate elements of segmented isolation and discord. Further, I discuss students' positioning as unique to an institutionalized academic setting and factors that may allow them, but not others, to achieve success. In such positions, students are subordinate minorities to the greater whole, yet still educated elites in their communities, positions that are adjudicated and reconciled individually. This research bears witness to Filipino students for whom education has been an upward journey and their considerations for other Filipino Canadian students who may not always share the same fortune. It is my first hope that in sharing these narratives of Filipino

Canadian youth, I may enable a deeper understanding of this part of their community to emerge.

Filipino Canadian Students in Context

Schools become one of the first sites where immigrant children encounter and connect with their host culture (Hall 1997) because for many children, it is their first continued exposure to culture, practices, and education differing from their home. Educational outcomes for immigrants are less predictable for the current generation in comparison to those for previous generations of immigrants to Canada particularly because of their diversity and varying relationships to and reception by the host country (Davies and Guppy 2006). While immigrant education has been a continued focus of many scholars, little has documented Filipino Canadian students and their post-secondary educational attainment and experiences.

Forming one of Canada's largest ethnic-minority groups, over 230,000 immigrants identify as Filipino (Statistics Canada 2005). It is increasingly important to understand Filipino Canadian youth and their academic challenges. White and Kaufman (1997) examined the functions of ethnicity, generational status, duration in the United States, and language usage for high school completion. They concluded that recent immigrants had higher chances of dropping out than native-born, second-generation or immigrant students who had been in the United States for longer. Further, Feliciano (2005) argues that the selective nature of immigration coupled with pre-migration educational attainment in the home country affects the success of immigrant children. My study attempts to observe whether the analyses made by White and Kaufman and Feliciano apply and are significant for students in the Filipino Canadian context.

The diasporic impact of globalization and dislocation results in shaping the demographics of the Filipino Canadian community as many now migrate through temporary work arrangements such as the Live-In Caregiver Program. Further, transnational migration trends and the increasing need for low-skilled, low-paid workers in a globalized economy underscores the Filipino immigrant narrative. Extensive research has documented the Filipino diaspora, particularly in the Unites States (Espiritu 2003; Isaac 2006; Lott 2006), and Filipino migrant workers in Canada (Asis 2002; Pratt 2004; Stasiulis and Bakan 2005).

Existing research focuses on the effects of migration on the family unit as central to understanding transnational migration in the global North (Parreñas 2005; Yeoh et al. 2005).

In the Canadian context, such narratives recount the social consequences related to the precarious nature of the government-sanctioned Live-In Caregiver Program (LCP). However, researching the lives of Filipino youth in relation to their migrant parents and how reunification greatly affects parent-child relationships, acculturative stress, and educational outcomes still remains greatly underdeveloped. It is by analysing immigrant experiences and the factors that influence families once in Canada that we can understand educational attainment as cumulative, academic experiences that are structured by particular immigration trends specific to an ethnic community.

Further, I assess minority educational attainment in comparison with parental education status and influence. Researchers outline that parents with higher levels of education are more inclined to carry expectations for high academic performance in their children (Parcel and Dufur 2001; Hao and Bonstead-Bruns 1998). Kao and Tienda (1998) found that many parents expect completion of least a university degree, promoted by closely associating academic success to social mobility. By extension, Pong and Hao (2007) discuss how co-ethnic role models positively affect adolescent youth. In relation to the Filipino Canadian community, co-ethnic role models in positions of power are less pronounced.

This research sheds light on the formation of Filipino Canadian identities that influence how students view themselves within academe. Researchers have focused on the educational success of immigrant groups, particularly Asians (Kaufman 2004; Dinh and Nguyen 2006; Louie 2004). Song and Glick (2004) suggest that for Asian students, educational attainment, particularly in higher education, secures middle-class status and fulfils parental expectation. In contrast to Asian 'model-minority' perceptions and the Filipino Canadian experience, my research assumes that post-secondary attendance for each minority group is not homogeneous.

In her research on Filipino student experiences, Pratt (2003) draws upon Hirsh's work on 'post-memory' to study Filipino Canadian youth identity and their constructions of the Philippines as homeland. The concept suggests that children internalize the memories – often traumatic – of those closest to them and acknowledge them as though their own, thus influencing identity. Similarly, Diane Wolf (1997) uses the term 'emotional transnationalism' to describe the sentiments of students who negotiate their identities from the past and present, and between generations. I extend the understanding of post-memory and emotional transnationalism towards opinions of education, success, and memories of migration. My research draws upon Pratt's and Wolf's notions, outlining how such memories affect lived experiences through youth's interpretation of their migrant narrative (or that of their parents), and its incorporation into their identity and action as students.

Researching Filipino Students at the University of British Columbia

While Filipinos have one of the highest group rates of immigration in Canada, they are not as well represented in post-secondary education, particularly at UBC, an institution with a large international student enrolment and immigrant population. By focusing on university students, I sought not only to identify social determinants of Filipino Canadian educational achievement but also to see how they may inform the analysis of these students' presence in higher education institutions.

In February 2008, I interviewed eleven Filipino Canadian students, all but one of whom were from Kababayan, UBC's Filipino Students' Association. I asked questions regarding immigration histories, upbringing and expectations for education, and experiences in high school and at UBC. At the time, it was the club's first year as part of UBC's Alma Mater Society, after three years of being disbanded. The members of Kababayan used its first year as a renewed club to take strides in reaching out to each other and the UBC campus.[1] Boasting a large immigrant population, UBC prides itself on welcoming students from over 140 countries. In their Top Ten List of International Students, with the exception of the United States, within the top five there are four Asian countries: China, South Korea, Japan, and Hong Kong. However, only three international graduate and thirty-four undergraduate students (as of 2009)[2] were Filipino. Similar trends can be observed at neighbouring Simon Fraser University, which as of 2010 listed seventeen Filipino undergraduate international students and only one Filipino graduate student.

Admission to UBC is competitive, with entrance requirements of grade averages in the 'mid to high 80s' standard across all faculties, except for Forestry, which requires 'mid-high 70s.' For both immigrant and Canadian-born students, this grade average can be challenging. For newly arrived Filipinos, entrance to university may be difficult if they are first placed in ESL and then in classes in which university course requirements cannot be met. In contrast, local colleges have minimal requirements for enrolling students. For example, general admission to Langara College in Vancouver only requires legitimate citizenship status (Canadian or with valid study permit), completion of high school, proficiency in English through standardized testing, and an age requirement of nineteen years. Colleges also have university-transfer streams in addition to two-year diplomas where academic performance measures significantly.[3] It is perhaps for this reason that respondents claimed to have observed a larger Filipino Canadian student population in colleges than in universities.

The interview sample consisted of eight males and three females between their first and last year at UBC, varying in disciplines of study but mostly from the sciences and humanities. All but one were admitted as first-year students to UBC. One student had completed high school in the Philippines (but notably lived in Canada during elementary school years) and transferred from a local college after one year. All students had their education financed by parents or partially through student loans, but no one mentioned financial distress in paying for university or difficulty in accessing loans if necessary. Six were immigrants and were born in the Philippines, and five identified themselves as Filipino Canadians and were born in Canada. Of the six immigrants, two immigrated recently (within the last two years), while the remainder arrived during elementary school or younger. Second-generation Filipinos mentioned their parents immigrating between the late 1970s and the early 1980s, with some even meeting in Canada.[4] Often viewed as privileged in their respective Filipino communities, but part of a group still largely underrepresented at UBC, these students highlight the complexity of the migrant experience, and amplify the significance and effects of migration in higher education.

Filipino Students at UBC as Minority Elites?

Immigrant students' time of arrival ranged significantly from as recently as 2006 to as far back as 1991. The desire to enhance quality of life and economic factors were the two most common reasons given for their family's migration. Second-generation students' parents arrived in Canada during the 1970s and 1980s as working professionals and started their families with the same ideals of better economic opportunity and prosperity as the families of more newly arrived immigrant students. All applied as independent immigrants, with only one student's mother previously having a caregiver job in Spain before migrating to Vancouver in the 1970s.

Significantly, no immigrant student came here through the reunification process because a parent was a domestic worker in the LCP. All immigrant children arrived at the same time as their parents. While some families are separated as one parent remains in the Philippines, this is due to business commitments, not out of a lack of possible immigrant status or separation because of LCP regulations. This represents the main class differences between post-secondary students and recent immigrants that are separated by parents remaining in the Philippines due to economic disparity, not prosperity. UBC students demonstrate how class matters in the immigration experience by showing that educational attainment can be accessed by newly arrived immigrants whose parents, generally speaking, are more economically secure both in Canada and in the Philippines.

It is clear that reasons for and time of migration play a role in the educational success of UBC students. While not all parents maintained the high-skilled positions they held in the Philippines, for the most part parents met with employment success in Canada. All recent immigrants at UBC come from affluent backgrounds in the Philippines that can support Canadian education with their capital. Parents are generally highly educated and continue to work in better-remunerated, professional positions in Canada, compared to other recent immigrants.

All but one parent had received a university education in the Philippines prior to immigrating to Canada, many obtaining their degrees at some of the Philippines' top universities. One parent was even educated in the United States and came back to the Philippines to work. Pre-migration circumstances, including educational and economic success in the Philippines, varied. Several managed family businesses, while others had professional jobs as architects, civil engineers, and nurses. Many still maintain those jobs now, particularly those who migrated in the 1970s and 1980s, even if they temporarily accepted lower-skilled and lower-paid positions after arrival. Of the parents who continue to work and live in the Philippines, only one does so because of a lack of job qualifications in Canada.

All the students came from families who are very much established in Canada, having capital to finance their educations, including private school and university, though some students mentioned taking out small student loans. This class difference dichotomizes the Filipino population, and implies that certain Filipino youth are immunized from the vulnerability of dropping out of high school due to economic concerns while others are more at risk. How certain class structures within the Filipino community influence educational opportunities is at the centre of this discussion but still at the periphery of current research.

Further, the extent to which family values encourage education and affect students' performance and attitudes towards schooling became pronounced. Parental emphasis on educational attainment was evident, as all students felt pressures to do well in school. When asked about their parents' views on education, all students responded with the same answer: their parents valued education for the purposes of getting a good job, making good money, and forging a better life. Students mentioned that their parents believed that both education and career were synonymous with success:

> *They're super like, you need to get a college degree, and you need a good job ... it has a lot to do with the notion of the Philippines as somewhere where you don't have a lot of opportunities, and the only way you can move up is to be educated so they put a lot of emphasis on that.* (Joseph)

Educational expectation is directly linked to Canadian immigration, and the privileged act of giving their children a better education in Canada than they would have received in the Philippines. The pressure, students feel, comes from strong economic demands felt by their parents, transferred onto them. Some students expressed frustration in choosing their degrees, and how their decisions were sometimes looked down upon by their parents: *'My Dad values more university education ... There was a point where I wanted to stop university, and do something else, something artistic, but my dad wouldn't allow that'* (Pamela).

The interviews suggest that parental pressure and support had a positive effect on UBC Filipino students, developing the students' sense of the value of education in their formative, younger years. Children attribute successes to their parents' efforts, recognizing that while they may have been demanding, they can appreciate sacrifices made for education. While parental influences could be factors in preventing the failure of their children in high school, it would be inaccurate to say that parents of those who drop out do not also value education. It would also be inaccurate to imply that those more newly arrived, with parents in the LCP, have not sacrificed just as much, or in differing ways. However, what can be concluded is that for the majority of UBC

Filipino students, their particular socio-economic position gives them specific educational opportunities not afforded to the majority of youth in their community.

Attending Private vs Public Schools

Out of the eleven students interviewed, four went to public school, five attended a Catholic private school, and two went to private schools in the Philippines before UBC. Overall, while the difference between private and public school resonates in the findings, it is difficult to conclude if this is a defining rather than contributing factor for graduating from high school and moving on to university. Of those who attended public school, it is notable that none of those schools were in Vancouver but in surrounding suburbs in the Lower Mainland such as Burnaby, Richmond, Surrey, and Delta, areas with less – but increasing – recent immigrant concentration.

The private and public experience in high school, however, made a difference in the representation of other Filipino students in their classrooms. In British Columbia, private Catholic schools receive partial funding from the provincial government and offer religious curricula. Filipino parents perhaps choose to send their children to private schools because of the long-standing influence of private education in the Philippines as the desired option, in contrast to the stigma of underfunded public schools offering poor education for those that cannot afford otherwise. The belief that educational attainment is a social determinant of class is demonstrated in the actions of parents who decide – often at the expense of increasing their labour in Canada – to send their children to private schools even after immigration. Any positive knowledge of the quality of BC public schools is overridden by attachments to beliefs in the superiority of private education coupled with the desire to instil and maintain the Catholic faith for their children.

While private schools have a high representation of Filipinos (conservative student observations being at about 40 per cent, while in other schools representation is seen as about 60 per cent), public schools have much less representation, as most public school attendees indicated knowing only a handful of Filipinos in their graduating classes. Almost all of the respondents who attended public high schools did not know more than one or two Filipino students who did not graduate. Private school students, in contrast, reported 100 per cent graduation rates, as did those who attended high school in the Philippines. All but one student reported that all their friends attended some form of post-secondary institution, although not all of their friends attended university, instead choosing colleges, either because their grade averages were not high enough or because of high tuition costs. Finally, while high representations of Filipinos in private high schools were evident, the number of private school students enrolled at UBC in particular was not remotely as high. In other words, Filipino students from private schools were underrepresented in the university in comparison to their proportion in their respective schools.

Filipino Students at UBC as Marginalized Minority?

Feelings of marginalization varied, as some students, especially in private school, did not feel like minorities at all. Private school students mainly viewed their 'Asianness' among other students as beneficial, allowing them to group themselves with students that were considered smart, but at times still feeling different from other Asian groups. One student shared:

> *I didn't think I couldn't succeed because I was Filipino, I just thought I couldn't be at the top of the class, because usually those that are at the top of the class are Chinese and Koreans, really smart people.* (Lisa)

Comparing Filipino Canadian students to other Asian groups reflected how students defined their academic and social positions. Some felt no intrinsic difference, but those students came from schools with a very small Asian population and were grouped as simply Asian themselves, not Filipino. The majority, though, felt there was a great difference between Filipinos and other Asians, expressing the propensity for poorer academic performance:

> *I've been fortunate enough to be in a pretty good environment, but I think in general, most Filipinos are looked down upon by others. We're seen as a more inferior race compared to like, let's say, Chinese people or something.* (Johnny)

These sentiments reveal common experiences in identifying Filipino stereotypes. Students describe a lack of recognition of Filipino students, especially academically. Students compare themselves, to other Asian groups particularly, as less financially secure or successful academically.

Similarly, students felt themselves to be paradoxically both marginalized and privileged to be at UBC because they observed the absence of other Filipinos. While students interviewed are seen as successes, many are constantly reminded that they are only a select few on campus. Those who attended private school come to UBC shocked, finding that they are far less numerous than they were in their high schools. So while Filipino UBC students are increasingly becoming aware of their privileged position in higher education, they remain very isolated on campus.

What was most surprising to realize was how little students interact with or even meet other Filipino UBC students. Excluding Kababayan, most had only met two or three other Filipinos, at best, in their classes. Overall, they were concerned by the general lack of representation of Filipinos in the student body. All felt extremely underrepresented, and none hesitated to express their isolation and distinct awareness of their position as a minority:

Yes, [I feel] extremely underrepresented ... I go to an environment from seeing Filipinos every day, to here, where I could go weeks without seeing a Filipino I didn't know or wasn't already friends with. (Joseph)

When the students were asked why they felt their representation was low, they explained how more Filipino students were in local colleges, perhaps for financial and academic standard reasons, and all agreed that UBC had the least representation of Filipinos of all post-secondary options. A feeling of difference – an 'Otherness' – from other Asian groups was equally salient in post-secondary experiences. Students felt little, if any, representation in their curricula, noting how other Asian groups are studied in the classroom whereas Filipinos are not. This is exhibited by a lack of Philippine studies courses or Philippine content in existing course curricula, in contrast to the prevalence of Asian studies curricula that highlight Chinese, Japanese, Korean, and Southeast Asian languages and cultures. Overall, students felt that the UBC population is more informed about and exposed to other Asian groups, whose presence on campus is more unified as demonstrated by many cultural associations. The high school sentiment of being seen as smart by their peers because Filipinos are Asians largely disappeared in the comparisons at UBC, instead replaced by feelings of being marginalized and lacking in social cohesion: *'There are like a million Chinese clubs ... I thought it was kinda weird that there wasn't a Filipino club. I think it's just a lot of them don't care'* (Eli).

Clearly, underrepresentation leads to students' insecurities. The same way Filipino students do not see many other Filipino students, they see few successful Filipinos, even at UBC. When asked how they felt about the stereotype that Filipinos are only good in low-skilled, low-paid positions in janitorial, caregiving, or food services, all but one agreed that the negative stereotypes still heavily exist. Spending their time on campus, students observe that the service staff at UBC, particularly in the janitorial and food services, are Filipinos. Eli continues his observations: *'When I'm taking the [bus] to school . . . there would be four, five Filipino nannies . . . I'm the only one going to school . . . and the Filipinos I see here, generally, they work at Subway, Starbucks . . . There's a guy I see . . . that cleans all the time.'*

Others share similar sentiments, being concerned in their privileged positions as students yet conflicted in their fragmented identities, facing discord by trying to reconcile their privilege with their marginalization. Students reject the stereotypes ascribed to them, but still retain their social privilege. One student admits:

> *Being Filipino is something different. When we meet [as a club] it's cool to see and be Filipino . . . when I'm playing on the [team], it's almost uncomfortable being Filipino, because it's just so obvious . . . it's not that I want to get rid of my 'Filipinoness,' but it's just difficult for others to associate with me sometimes . . . when some of the Filipinos they've known have been nannies to them.* (Mark)

When the only representations students receive in their university environment or on their way to school are of other Filipinos in low-skilled, low-paid positions, it inherently expresses the vulnerability students' face. Those that move into higher education still face forms of the same educational barriers as in high school. Additionally, these findings give rise to examining how, given elite, educational opportunities, marginal status still contextualizes the isolation of students. How might students reconcile this positioning? Perhaps marginal status gives rise to a particular improvement in minority education, while still perpetuating a certain (in)visibility in Canadian educational institutions, one where only certain youth access higher education opportunities while most are denied. Further, is such marginalization indicative of the educational trajectory future post-secondary students face, and further still, is this marginalization only a mirror of the marginalization the community experiences as a whole? The implications for this population – a minority elite – should be assessed.

The presence of a minority elite suggests that the reproductive nature of class is salient in educational attainment. The current minority status of Filipino Canadian students in post-secondary education, while understudied, carries significance for the next generation as class reproduction and professionalization of a specific part of the population help to shape the greater standing of the Filipino community more generally. Acquired education speaks to a more complex narrative of both attainment and isolation, one where the trajectory of social or even professional mobility is inhibited by specific lived experiences.

Access to post-secondary education, if relegated to only a minority elite, creates certain assumptions about Filipino Canadian education and its limited accessibility. Does suggesting that education is a 'minority-elite' experience mean that certain ideas about Filipino Canadian youth become reified? Awareness of social structure should be made explicit, if only to recognize the privileging of education that occurs. Yet, this privileging bears social costs. The isolation resonates throughout academe, where structuring of educational fields is also at stake, as students feel they are directed toward professional occupations and away from more theoretical degrees, perhaps leading to an even greater absence of Filipino Canadian youth at the graduate and faculty levels in university.

Are such students simply role models, or are they markers of difference, the embodiments of success reminding others of their inability to have the same status? Some students must reconcile themselves with their differentiation from the majority in their community, as they must bear in mind their unique position. Does the educational attainment of Filipino Canadian youth better serve the community, or, much like their experience in school, will their professional lives similarly exhibit marginalization? These are important considerations to make when evaluating the structuring of education, not only during time spent at school, but after.

UBC Students: Awareness and Action

The Filipino Canadian community, as previous research highlights, continues to struggle with assimilation, integration, and settlement in Canada. With this struggle, the community has one of the highest drop-out rates in high schools across Canada, particularly in the largest metropolitan areas of Vancouver, Toronto, and Montreal (Pratt 2008). Given the status of students interviewed, it is crucial to compare and contextualize their experiences but also to acknowledge that studying students who have not witnessed or experienced prevalent educational failure affects the extent to which these problems can be analysed.

Overall, at least for those interviewed, there is no consensus regarding the barriers immigrants face in the school system. Partly due to feeling sheltered from the situation in private schools, but more generally because perceptions of the problem are mixed, some students believe that these barriers are not a problem endemic within Filipino communities, others point towards gang violence, while others still suggest that financial barriers remain detrimental to educational attainment. Few students articulated structural barriers such as struggles tied to family reunification with LCP caregiving parents, but responses described a non-inclusive environment, with little integration support. A lack of articulation suggests either that the problem was not present in the high schools these students went to – as demonstrated in private schools – or that their high school experiences were in some way immune to it. This results in the perpetuation of a small percentage of Filipino minorities in higher education. While the students' ambiguity could be because of a lack of general perception in the teen years, as expressed by certain students, it indicates a lack of awareness about the problems at hand, even within the Filipino community, in their high school years:

> *I didn't really think that Filipinos were anything special, like, academically. In high school . . . in public school, I guess, you didn't see too many Filipinos excelling or even, like, failing, but then again, I didn't know how I perceived being marginalized back then, in terms of education, or even being privileged.* (Mark)

The reasons for poor educational attainment that were given, however, were not usually specific to Filipino immigrants. Instead reasons that can be applied more generally to any new immigrants were listed, such as language barriers, lack of preparation for careers and information about higher education, and social barriers inhibiting intercultural communication with Canadian students. Further, a perceived lack of barriers, particularly concerning the influence of migratory factors, suggests that the knowledge of the Filipino migrant experience is not internalized explicitly by Filipino youth, and that drop-out trends in the Filipino community are not viewed as a communal concern. This is problematic, because, on the one hand, it suggests that students may have been exposed to more equitable school environments, ones in which they thrived and which fostered opportunities to come to university. However, on the other hand, segregation and immunization of privileged students from the problems perhaps does little to create awareness of or support for existing problems within the larger community.

When asked about community support and their thoughts on the Filipino community addressing educational problems, UBC students also had no consensus about what was being done and how, or even over what. One student lamented the Filipino community's failure to take joint action on issues that concern its people: *'I always thought it was weird compared to other cultures. Filipinos are the third largest minority, but there's no Filipino centre . . . My friend told me his theory . . . that the Filipino community is so divided . . . there's no unity . . . that's an interesting thought'* (Eli). Another student commented on the class division between newly arrived parents and the more successful immigrant families, capturing the nuanced class differences and interactions:

> *I don't think the Filipino community as a whole here in Vancouver . . . push educational initiatives . . . I think, still, there's really big division there . . . between those who come here and are able to get established, and send their kids to like, private school and all that . . . I don't think the people that are established are reaching out to newly arrived and helping them get established.* (Joseph)

When referring to community actions, students mentioned KAMP (Kababayan Academic Mentorship Program), a mentorship program developed by the Filipino Students Association beginning in early March 2008. KAMP's motivations encourage high school graduation and pursuing higher education. UBC students serve as a support system for high school students, encouraging improvement, while enacting the club mandate of community service. The club acknowledges the vulnerability attached to high drop-out rates, and sees KAMP as an opportunity to be a positive influence on newly arrived Filipino youth.

During the interviews, KAMP was in its initial planning stages. Students expressed excitement about the initiative because this gave them the opportunity to observe the struggles of Filipino youth and to positively influence younger students. Though I have been critical of the ambiguity of students in articulating the problems, their sense of excitement, despite admitting their lack of understanding, points towards a growing commitment and mobilization of students for other Filipino youth.

However, a prevalent issue arising throughout the interviews was the notion of a complex and fragmented Filipino identity, one that at times was rejected by students, and one that is hard for outsiders to understand. For some, it was a concern because they felt deeply attached to their Filipino heritage, troubled that their fellow youth are doing poorly in the same education system they excelled in. Others saw the issue more as a concern for education at large, and the poor economic conditions that can result in lower educational attainment:

> *It concerns me, yeah, 'cause I'm a Filipino. Being a member of this sort of culture in Canada … I don't wanna have this negative stigma about being a Filipino Canadian. You know, I'm Filipino Canadian and I don't want Filipino Canadians in general to be looked as as drop-out gangsters … I wanna address these sort of issues. (Jim)*

Besides their lack of first-hand exposure to barriers affecting educational attainment, most high school experiences for the students interviewed included periods where they chose to segregate or disassociate themselves from other newly arrived Filipinos. This disassociation is significant because it highlights the distinct isolation of newly arrived youth, not only by other ethnicities, but by other Filipinos. Most notably, these students disassociated with newly arrived Filipinos because of their perception of being more 'cool.' Even if their peer groups included other Filipinos, they were more 'white-washed' and identified more as being Canadian. While most at some point disassociated, they also recognized in themselves both a Canadian and a Filipino identity. In such moments of self-awareness, students exhibited the most capability in expressing not only the struggle between different groups of Filipino youth, but what is required to reconcile their differences:

> *All through elementary school … it was really white, fairly affluent … I was like, I'm not even Filipino, for the longest time. When I was younger, and I guess dumb, I would highlight the differences … I would bring attention to how I don't speak Tagalog … now, well my friends are like 'why are you so Filipino?' (Eli)*

It is apparent that there is a growing urgency among students to recognize the greater needs of their community and that these realizations are deeply personal. Students very much struggle with their identities as young, educated Filipino Canadians. In relation to post-memory theories, the interviews demonstrated internalized immigration narratives. While students could not fully articulate many structural problems, their responses carried an undertone of a co-opted, collective narrative of the migratory experience. This internalization underscores blurred identities, as students negotiate their transnational connections between Canada and the Philippines. Additionally, pressure to perform well in school was internalized by students from a young age, again through post-memory experiences of parents, who at times leveraged their experiences to remind their children about the lives left behind in the Philippines:

I really valued school, just because I understand my parents went through hard times in the Philippines, and they tried so hard to get out of Philippines . . . I never took advantage of that . . . I just always valued school just because I know if we were to stay in Philippines, our life could be worse. (Lisa)

The sympathies for the immigrant experience, although not completely iterated by all, imply a sense of acknowledgment of the sacrifices made for them, invoking the 'post-memories' of their parents' sacrifices and weaving them intricately into their own identities. Part of these students' concern for Filipino youth today is rooted in the experiences of their parents, as they listened to their parents' stories or observed the difficulties they faced in acculturating to a Canadian lifestyle with less economic success than perhaps in the Philippines. It brings into focus the consideration that the agency of students to understand their situated positions, either as second-generation Filipino Canadians or as immigrants, still relies heavily on their internalization of parental experience by relating to, or even sometimes temporarily rejecting, their histories. Filipino youth need only look to the struggles of their parents (or even themselves) to begin to piece together solutions to problems not only in schools, but in the greater Filipino community.

The aspect of parental memory and experience influencing student perspectives is unique to this research. By relating their academic performance to a sense of obligation in return for their parents' sacrifices, post-memories serve as homages to the youth's desire to fulfil the legacies their parents intended for them upon migration. These post-memory observations indicate the potency of parental narratives in shaping the sentiments of Filipino youth, and this is an area of research that can only be built upon in the future. Further, the abstraction of post-memory may not always be explicit to students, nor are these memories fully accepted into personal identities. Some students reject the educational trajectory and traditional careers that their parents desire, which parents believe can offer genuine settlement and financial security in Canada.

The Future of Filipino Canadians in Higher Education

These findings indicate that in the home, in high schools, and at UBC, Filipino students have support systems that have allowed them to excel in their education. Parents, teachers, and personal motivation all contributed to successful high school completion and facilitated entry into post-secondary institutions, a fact that respondents credited for their academic success. However, perhaps the qualitative findings of my research have captured the exception, and not the dominant experience, when related to the greater Filipino Canadian population. The risks of poor educational attainment are still understated within the community as minority representation and poor role model support still greatly carry on into higher education. Support systems in the form of positive peer groups, familial financial contributions, and physical presence, monitoring, and guidance through high school may not always be experienced by all students and, as such, not all are equipped with resources for post-secondary attendance at UBC.

This research indicated that feelings of being a minority – the educated elite – specifically in a school environment are deeply internalized, even for those who attend university. This realization only grows more pronounced when the students leave high school. The lack of visibility of Filipinos at UBC does trouble them, and is only negatively enforced when they observe more successful and cohesive Asian groups, as well as Filipinos in low-skilled support services on campus. This extends from high school impressions where students felt inferior, at least academically if not also socially, to other students. While some students came from high schools with large Filipino populations, education at UBC is remarkably different, as many meet almost no other Filipino students.

Being minorities remains central to the socialization of their educational experience, certainly in high school, during their post-secondary schooling, and perhaps into future vocations. While Filipinos are excluded from the stereotype of the successful Asian student – largely propagated in their high schools – the effects at the post-secondary level are largely underdeveloped in the research. The formation of an educational elite gives currency to the idea of an exclusive group who will be professionalized, acquiring and possessing certain social capital inaccessible by others in their community.

I conclude that support for students is as crucial to the problems as awareness, and that while the problems students face are still largely ambiguous, peer and family support, including pressure to a healthy degree, encourages and yields positive performance. Also, the findings suggest that the school itself is secondary to the family context, and that time and reasons for migration affect student performance as a whole, as they dictate parental capacity to establish the family. Finally, this research illuminates that the internalization of parental memories is salient in framing Filipino identity, for much of the students' understanding of Filipino issues is built upon their understanding of their parents' lives, albeit only through their memories and narratives. Overall, the success of Filipino students at UBC should be celebrated, as the value of their experiences, both in high school and at UBC, adds richness to research on Filipino immigrant education.

Attention is given to the failures of students, not so much their successes. Students were surprised at being research subjects, which indicates that in higher education, their efforts have been unacknowledged, presenting a gap in research that I have attempted to fill, albeit still limitedly. Profoundly, students regarded this research as an enriching experience and chance for self-reflection. Many felt as though they gained much from simply talking about their situations.

Do you feel this research is important? The simplicity of this question came to me at the end of the first interview, and I asked it at the end of all interviews. The responses affirmed the necessity of my research. In the words of one student:

> *Anything to do with figuring out why the Filipino community is the way it is, is definitely welcomed ... Filipinos really need to expand in terms of all aspects of society, especially academia. Filipinos in the academic world will really, really help other people to understand us, and ourselves understand us. So any academic work for Filipinos by other Filipinos is a good thing.* (Joseph)

The call for Filipino Canadian research done by those within the community stems from a greater call for mobilization as a whole. Efforts to share experiences with each other are unique to this research. The lack of research on Filipino students by other Filipino scholars demonstrates that marginalization in academe extends into the marginalization of the production of Filipino Canadian education scholarship. In the statement above, the student mandates a type of scholarship not only for knowledge production in academe, but also for an increasing awareness within the community in order to enrich its strengths, identify struggles, and unite for challenges we face as a community.

Understanding ourselves in academia as privileged, 'educated elite' has its own implications. Representation of Filipino Canadian students in post-secondary institutions determines representation as future scholars. Further, establishing the discipline of Filipino Canadian studies remains contingent upon the mobilization of these students coupled with support from current faculty members. Efforts to connect with one another to build upon Filipino Canadian scholarship can only be strengthened through increased representation and support for such knowledge production. Scholarship cannot be solely dictated by outside claims of the community, but also by the voices within the community, not just those in academe. It is in this area that the educated minority must continue to strive to ensure not only the survival and legitimation of, but also success in, a growing discipline.

It is evident that the classroom remains one site where both marginalization and privileging of Filipino Canadian students take place. These students are minorities not only in schools but also in relation to their communities and within their peer groups. Acquiring skills and credentials gives currency to the possibilities afforded after graduation, allowing students to maintain or even exceed the socio-economic status in which they grew up. This research is not only a testament to the success of Filipino Canadian students, but brings awareness of marginalization within higher education that may come with particular social costs. Student involvement within higher education is just one measure of integration into Canadian society. Therefore, further analysis of the community's greater integration into Canadian society should also be conducted.

Ultimately, the problems Filipinos face in high school as immigrants and second-generation Canadians are complex and in many ways unlike those faced by other immigrant minority groups, partly because of our unique immigration history in Canada. Clearly educational attainment is shaped culturally by family history and values, as well as by school support and community involvement. This research also observes that students are not passive pupils within an educational system, but develop and maintain their own efficacy and agency, despite barriers of being a minority as well as negative stereotypes that influence outside perception of Filipino students.

Further research is needed to shed light on the pursuits of Filipinos in higher education, including their experiences in high school that structured their entry to post-secondary institutions. Future investigation on the defining and varying experiences among first-generation, second-generation, and newly arrived students may carry insight into how differing experiences in programs, such as ESL, may impede or facilitate post-secondary studies. Deeper analysis into peer networks and family support can help to differentiate between experiences and highlight similarities in upbringing between students who attend universities and other post-secondary institutions, such as colleges and trade schools. Moving beyond qualitative case studies to improve the collection and analysis of aggregate data in post-secondary institutions outside of UBC will help to create a clearer picture of Filipino students and their educational attainment. Finally, continued research into the experiences of how second- and 1.5-generation Filipino Canadians who complete post-secondary degrees negotiate their positions as educated minorities may shed light on the capacity of the Filipino Canadian community to strengthen and grow as its members slowly become more diverse, participate in civic affairs, and attempt to find solid ground in search for settlement and integration in Canada in academia and beyond.

It is evident that barriers still permeate educational attainment for Filipinos in Canada. Despite such barriers, students in my research have demonstrated success in their own lives, and carry in them a hope to better the lives of other Filipino youth. It is in observing such evident fervour in the lives of eleven students that this research places and finds the most hope.

NOTES

1 Kababayan's mission statement mandates social, cultural, and community growth while exploring Filipino Canadian identity (http://www.ams.ubc.ca/clubs/kababayan/about.html).
2 Statistics found at http://www.pair.ubc.ca/statistics/students/students.htm.
3 Admission requirements found at http://www2.langara.bc.ca/university-career-studies/admission/index.html.
4 I have avoided visualizing demographics to comply with ethical standards so that respondents cannot be singled out or identified, given the small population size.

REFERENCES

Asis, Maruja. 2002. From the life stories of Filipino women: Personal and family agendas in migration. *Asian and Pacific Migration Journal* 11: 67–94.

Davies, Scott, and Neil Guppy. 2006. *The schooled society: An introduction to the sociology of education.* Oxford: Oxford University Press.

Dinh, Khanh T., and Huong H. Nguyen. 2006. The effects of acculturative variables on Asian American parent–child relationships. *Journal of Social and Personal Relationships* 23: 407–26.

Espiritu, Yen Le. 2003. *Home bound: Filipino American lives across cultures, communities, and countries.* Berkeley: University of California Press.

Feliciano, Cynthia. 2005. Does selective migration matter?: Explaining ethnic disparities in educational attainment among immigrants' children. *International Migration Review* 39: 841–71.

Hall, Peter M. 1997. The integration of restructuring and multicultural education as a policy for equity and diversity. In *Race, ethnicity and multiculturalism,* ed. Peter M. Hall, 203–19. New York: Garland.

Hao, Lingxin, and Melissa Bonstead-Bruns. 1998. Parent-child differences in educational expectations and the academic achievement of immigrant and native students. *Sociology of Education* 71: 175–98.

Isaac, Allan Punzalan. 2006. *American tropics: Articulating Filipino America.* Minneapolis: University of Minnesota Press.

Kao, Grace, and Marta Tienda. 1998. Educational aspirations of minority youth. *American Journal of Education* 106: 349–84.

Kaufman, Julia. 2004. The interplay between social and cultural determinants of school effort and success: An investigation of Chinese immigrant and second-generation Chinese students' perceptions toward school. *Social Science Quarterly* 85: 1275–98.

Lott, Juanita Tamayo. 2006. *Common destiny: Filipino American generations.* Lanham, MD: Rowman and Littlefield.

Louie, Vivian S. 2004. *Compelled to excel: Immigration, education and opportunity among Chinese Americans.* Palo Alto, CA: Stanford University Press.

Parcel, Toby L., and Mikaela J. Dufur. 2001. Capital at home and at school: Effects on student achievement. *Social Forces* 79: 881–912.

Parreñas, Rhacel Salazar. 2005. *Children of global migration.* Palo Alto, CA: Stanford University Press.

Pratt, Geraldine. 2004. *Working feminism.* Philadelphia: Temple University Press.

Pratt, Geraldine, in collaboration with Ugnayan ng Kabataang Pilipino sa Canada. 2003. Between homes: Displacement and belonging for second generation Filipino Canadian youth. *B.C. Studies* 139: 41–68.

Pratt, Geraldine, in collaboration with the Philippine Women Centre of BC and Ugnayan ng Kabataang Pilipino sa Canada. 2008. Deskilling across the generations: Reunification among transnational Filipino families in Vancouver. Working Paper Series, No. 08-06, Metropolis.

Pong, Suet-Line, and Lingxin Hao. 2007. Neighborhood and school factors in the school performance of immigrants' children. *International Migration Review* 41: 206–41.

Song, Chunyan, and Jennifer E. Glick. 2004. College attendance and choice of college majors among Asian-American students. *Social Science Quarterly* 85: 1401–21.

Stasiulis, Daiva, and Abigail Bakan. 2005. *Negotiating citizenship: Migrant women in Canada and the global system.* Toronto: University of Toronto Press.

Statistics Canada. 2005. *Population projections of visible minority groups, Canada, provinces and regions, 2001 to 2017* (91-541-XIE). Ottawa: Statistics Canada.

White, M., and Kaufman, G. 1997. Language usage, social capital, and school completion among immigrants and native-born ethnic groups. *Social Science Quarterly* 78: 385–98.

Wolf, Diane L. 1997. Family secrets: Transnational struggles among children of Filipino immigrants. *Sociological Perspectives* 40: 457–82.

Yeoh, Brenda, Shirlena Huang, and Theodora Lam. 2005. Transnationalizing the Asian family: Imaginaries, intimacies and strategic interests. *Global Networks* 5: 307–15.

Chapter 18

Mas Maputi Ako sa 'yo (I'm lighter than you): The Spatial Politics of Intraracial Colourism among Filipina/o Youth in the Greater Toronto Area

CONELY DE LEON

'You're so dark. Yaaack!' My cousin would say to me in disgust, as she would place her forearm beside mine to compare her light skin to my dark skin.

As early as the age of four, I was taught to feel ashamed of my complexion. I did not understand what was so shameful about being the particular shade of brown that I was. This moment was one of my earliest encounters with colourism, defined by Herring et al. as 'the discriminatory treatment of individuals falling within the same "racial" group on the basis of skin color' (2004, 3). Contemporary accounts of the significance of skin colour and social hierarchies based on skin complexion illustrate that 'darker-skinned individuals are viewed as less intelligent, trustworthy, and attractive than their lighter-skinned counterparts' (Nakano Glenn 2008, 281). Such factors have a significant impact on the social mobility and overall life chances of darker-skinned youth (Fergus 2004). These findings are disconcerting and warrant further investigation to determine their applicability within a Canadian context. With the exception of Sahay and Piran's research on skin colour preferences among South Asian students at the University of Toronto (1997) and Mahtani's work on racial performance among 'mixed race' women in Toronto (2009), there does not appear to be substantial research on the ways in which colourism operates among youth of colour in the Greater Toronto Area (GTA).

The following chapter considers the ways in which diasporic Filipina/o youth express colourism within the Greater Toronto Area. Specifically, I explore *spatial* articulations of intraracial colourism between and among self-identified light-skinned and dark-skinned

Filipina/o youth in the GTA. Engaging with concepts of space is particularly useful because it takes into account intersecting hierarchies of race, class, and gender in expansive and meaningful ways. As Sherene Razack argues, 'the lure of a spatial approach is precisely the possibility of charting the simultaneous operation of multiple systems of domination' (2002, 6). This chapter will also critically engage with notions of the *body*, the degenerate body, the bourgeois body, the ab/normal body *in space,* and dwell upon considerations of the spatiality of *skin* itself, as the place where identity can be 'formed and assigned,' as 'boundary and contact surface,' and as a 'place of encounter' (Benthien 1999, 1–2). Taking considerations of the spatiality of skin itself one step further, I draw on Ahmed and Stacey's challenge to think '*with* or *through* the skin' but in a way that fundamentally engages with the significance of skin *colour* (2001, 1). Hence, to think through spatial articulations of intraracial colourism in this chapter will inevitably mean thinking through the multitudinous ways in which *skins* are made intelligible, imbued with social meaning, enabling the production and re-production of subjectivities and identities, constantly read and re-read, produced and re-produced, written upon, managed, and controlled according to ever-shifting historical, social, and political moments.

Filipina/os in the Greater Toronto Area

In choosing to examine spatial expressions of intraracial colourism among Filipina/o youth, a key goal of this research is to dispel any notion of a presumed racial and ethnic homogeneity among these communities. This work further defies assumptions of a singular form of so-called Filipina/o solidarity. This is not to say that solidarity networks among Filipina/os do not exist. Indeed, solidarity and coalition building have been politically necessary in light of some of the challenges that Filipina/os, particularly Filipino women who have come to Canada under the Live-In Caregiver Program, have had to face (on solidarity and coalition building, see chapters by Tungohan, Davidson, and Eric in this volume; on coalition building involving Filipina/o youth, see chapters by Largo, Balmes, Catungal, and Mendoza in this volume). But Filipina/o communities in the GTA are strikingly diverse with different commitments, such as linguistic and regional affiliations, which have extended beyond first-generation Filipina/o im/migrants in Canada. Moreover, while Filipina/os have been identified as the fourth largest 'visible minority' group in Toronto (Statistics Canada 2007),

Filipina/o settlement patterns are not as highly concentrated as they are in Canadian cities like Montreal and Winnipeg, but more widely dispersed, thus having an impact on Filipina/o community formations. This chapter therefore serves as a self-reflexive investigation of some of the constructed spatial divisions within and among Filipina/o youth in different regions of the GTA today, and the messy and internal conflicts that have emerged as a result.

Methods

To understand how spatial expressions of intraracial colourism operate within and among Filipina/o youth in the GTA, I conducted focus groups on colourism in July and August of 2009 with Filipina/o youth in two major demographics within the GTA: Mississauga and Scarborough. The call-out for focus group participants was mass-distributed through the Sisters of Colour Collective (SOCC)[1] online network as part of our 'Colourism: Interrogating Shades of Difference' campaign to raise awareness around the issue. Focus group sessions were formed based on responses to the mass call-out. Follow-up calls were made to schedule and confirm the date, time, and place of each session. One session comprised four female and three male youth from the Mississauga region of Greater Toronto. This session took place in Mississauga in one female participant's home. The other session took place in a small coffee shop in downtown Toronto and consisted of three male youth from the Scarborough region of Greater Toronto. In total, ten focus group participants between the ages of twenty-one and twenty-six were interviewed. Each session was digitally recorded and lasted an average of two hours. All ten focus group participants identified themselves as Filipina/o. One male participant from the Mississauga focus group further acknowledged that he was 'mixed race,' identifying his mother as Filipina and his father as 'white.'[2] It is significant to note that the Filipina/o youth participants from Mississauga all identified as light-skinned, while Filipino youth participants from the Scarborough area all identified as dark-skinned. To be very clear, this is not to say that only light-skinned Filipina/os live in Mississauga and dark-skinned Filipina/os live in Scarborough. While my sample consists of a very small number of Filipina/o youth in the GTA, it is intended to present a more intimate and in-depth look at the ways in which some Filipina/o youth spatially express intraracial colourism in their lives. Pseudonyms are used throughout in order to protect the identities of all focus group participants.

Mississauga

Mississauga is a suburb that lies west of the GTA, located in the Regional Municipality of Peel. According to Statistics Canada's 'visible minority' population characteristics, following the categories of 'South Asian,' 'Chinese,' and 'Black,' 'Filipino[s]' were designated as the fourth largest ethnic group in Mississauga at 4.6 per cent, while those identified as 'white' constituted the majority of the total population at 50.6 per cent (2006). Mississauga is hailed as 'one of the largest corporate/financial districts in Canada [drawing in] major international companies such as *Hewlett-Packard*, *Microsoft*, *General Electric*, and *Wal-Mart Canada*, among many other *Fortune 500* companies' (Statistics Canada 2006). Aside from its reputation as an epicentre of corporate activity, Mississauga also advertises itself as 'the safest city in Canada 8 years in a row' (Heritage 2010). This image of a safe and thriving Canadian city is bolstered by what is purported to be a 'rich' history of nineteenth-century European settlement. Mississauga is thus constructed and perceived as a very particular space of privilege and power since it is recognized as a *valued* space of thriving Canadian commerce and wealth, but, more importantly, because it sustains the grand myths of Canadian 'nation-building' and European imperial grandeur.[3]

Scarborough

Scarborough is a suburb that lies within the Greater Toronto Area, on the eastern border of the city. Large-scale development along with the liberalization of Canadian immigration policies during the 1960s led to an 'overabundance' of low-income housing projects in affordable parts of Scarborough and an increase in new immigrants to the area (Teelucksingh 2007, 652). At this time, Scarborough became marked by economic decline, and limited job availability and social services. As a result, parts of Scarborough have been cited as areas in need of 'rehabilitation and socio-economic improvement' (Teelucksingh 2007, 652). Today, a significant portion of Scarborough's population is composed of immigrants and descendants of immigrants who have arrived in Canada in the last four decades. For example, Filipina/o residents in Scarborough made up 6.5 per cent of a total 'visible minority' population of 67.4 per cent, according to a 2006 City of Toronto Community Council Profile (Scarborough 2006). Based on a comprehensive youth safety study conducted by Williams and Clarke (2003), 'racial minorities are more likely to live in Scarborough than non-racial minorities.'

Teelucksingh confirms: 'As the proportion of immigrants and racial minorities has increased, Scarborough has become culturally and demographically identified with predominately marginalized lower-income and racialized residents' (2007, 652). In sharp contrast to Mississauga then, the Scarborough area is constructed as a space of low-income housing projects, of neglect and limited economic opportunity, of a significantly larger immigrant population, and concentrated racialized bodies in particular – a space that Razack might deem a space of perceived 'degeneracy' (2002, 102).

The Philippine-American War and the Language of Empire

Although there is no direct context in which the term 'intraracial colourism' is used in reference to the racializing discourse surrounding Spanish and American imperial expansion in the Philippines, some inferences may be drawn from the imperialist language that emerged from Philippine-American relations during the Philippine-American War. U.S. soldiers in occupied Manila 'commonly characterized Filipinos on the whole as filthy, diseased, lazy, and treacherous in their business dealings, sometimes applying the term "nigger" to them' (Kramer 2006, 102; for a discussion of the genealogical link between Native Americans and Filipina/os as colonized subjects, see McElhinny, this volume). Explicit racial reference to Filipina/os as 'niggers' is important to note here as it highlights the 'cyclic discourses that generate symbolic meanings which transpose and reinterpret earlier wars' such as the American Civil War (Balce 2006, 51–2). It further points to the United States' outright dismissal of 'the ethnic, socioeconomic, spiritual, regional, and linguistic heterogeneity' among Filipina/os, thereby functioning as an exclusionary technique to foreground a particular representation for imperialist purposes (Coloma 2009, 500). Such racial-imperialist techniques underline the changeability and reframing of racial terms, as well as the contingent and ever-shifting relations between Americans and Filipina/os in Occupied Manila at the time. Poignantly, on December 10, 1898, after Spain ceded the Philippines, along with Puerto Rico, Guam, and Cuba, to the United States with the signing of the Treaty of Paris, the racialization of Filipina/os as 'savage black bodies' became increasingly pronounced both on and off the ground (Balce 2006, 45). This is demonstrated in persistent racial terms: 'Being dark men, they are therefore "niggers," and entitled to all the contempt and harsh

treatment administered by white overlords to the most inferior races'
(Kramer 2006, 128). According to Kramer, such language exposed the
racial-imperialist logic that came to justify colonization of the entire
archipelago. Furthermore, this logic mutually relied on the racialization of Americans themselves as Anglo-Saxons, as part of a 'grand'
and 'glorious' tradition of empire-building constituted by the dual
histories of British and American imperial conquest (Kramer 2006,
90, 121). This marked control over Filipina/o peoples, lands, and
resources as simply inevitable – 'proof' of the Anglo-Saxon peoples'
'racial genius.'

In his analysis of 1903 census data, Vicente Rafael further illustrates
the ways in which Philippine history was explicitly racialized, framing
the land itself as empty, passively waiting to be 'settled by successive
waves of colonizers.' These 'waves of colonizers' signalled

> the inevitable retreat of darker-skinned, more savage inhabitants in the
> face of advancing groups of lighter-skinned, more civilized, and physi-
> cally superior conquerors . . . culminating, presumably, in the arrival of the
> strongest, most progressive, and lightest-skinned colonizer to date: whites
> from the United States. (Rafael 2000, 35–6)

The language Rafael uses here to mark these 'waves' is important, for
it draws out a language of imperialism that persists today in the evolu-
tionist language used to market skin-lightening products – 'the lighter,
the better.' Clearly, the ways in which skin colour is addressed in racial-
imperialist discourse demonstrates the complexities and contradictions
of forming classifications around 'colour.' Dehumanizing Filipina/os
by referring to them as 'dark savages' illustrates the necessity of such
terminology in justifying U.S. imperial expansion and control over
the Philippines as the 'Filipino' was visually and discursively constructed and tailored to a U.S public audience. Although 'colourism' is
not explicitly discussed as such here, references to skin colour and the
conflation of specific colonial subjects into visually recognizable stereotypes suggest evidence of skin colour hierarchies.

Impact of Racial-Imperialist Discourse on the Philippines Today

To understand the lasting impact of racial-imperialist discourse on contemporary perceptions of skin colour hierarchies in the Philippines,
it is worth briefly sketching out what can be referred to as 'light skin

aspirations' among Filipina/os today. This is perhaps best reflected in reported rates of skin-lightening product consumption. Indeed, Rondilla and Spickard (2007) offer some alarming statistics drawn from a 2003 report which states that 'over 2 million units of skin lightening soap are sold annually in the Philippines,' followed by a 2004 survey documenting skin-lightening usage in the Asia-Pacific region in which 'the Philippines reported the highest rate of usage, with 50 percent of the respondents stating that they currently use skin-lightening products' (63). Considering the widespread usage of skin-lightening products and historically overwhelming Western ideological and cultural influences rooted in the Philippines' colonial and imperial past, it is no wonder that Filipina/os have developed, to borrow Rondilla and Spickard's phrase, 'a color complex' (ibid.). Clearly, the complex workings of intraracial colourism warrant as much attention among diasporic Filipina/o populations, including those who have settled in Canada, as they do among Filipina/os currently living in the Philippines. However, it is worth noting that while the Filipina/o youth participants I spoke with engaged in discussions about intraracial colourism, they did not express a desire to purchase and use skin-lightening products. Rather, spatial expressions of intraracial colourism seemed to be adopted among focus group participants to denigrate other Filipina/o youth, reflecting conflict and tension between and among Filipina/o communities in the GTA.

Mississauga and Scarborough: Some Spatial Reflections on Colour and Class

In this section, I introduce spatial articulations of intraracial colourism as expressed by focus group participants from the Mississauga and Scarborough areas of Greater Toronto in order to map out some of the constructed spatial divisions within and among Filipina/o youth in different regions of the GTA today, and the messy internal conflicts around colour and class that have emerged as a result.

Understanding Mississauga as a particular site of white, middle-class respectability is important in understanding how intraracial colourism is expressed spatially as a marker of class. For example, when focus group participants from Mississauga were asked whether they perceived any notable differences between Filipina/os who live in Mississauga and Filipina/os who live in Scarborough, all participants responded in unison, 'Yes, absolutely.' The conviction displayed in this unanimous response is striking. When asked to elaborate on these differences, Grace, with her long, dark brown hair, almond-shaped hazel eyes, and olive complexion, insisted that Filipina/os from Scarborough are from the *'wrong side of the tracks.'* This statement presumes, then, that there is a 'right side of the tracks,' and that the right side is embodied in the west end suburb of Mississauga. These spatial conceptualizations of Mississauga and Scarborough are further reinforced when male participant Chris remarks, *'You're going from Mississauga to Scarborough, so just saying that alone, you're already going, "Scarborough = ghetto."'* This discursive movement from a discussion about Mississauga to Scarborough highlights the spatiality of discourse itself. The very words 'Mississauga' and 'Scarborough' already carry in them particular histories of spatialized class difference, hence the term 'Scarborough' becomes synonymous with the single-word definition 'ghetto' (read: poor, working class).

By contrast, during the focus group with male youth participants from the Scarborough area, two participants in particular defined themselves as exemplifying *'toughness and roughness,'* whereas they perceived Filipina/os from Mississauga to be *'soft'* and *'a bunch of wussies.'* Standing at about five feet and four inches, Scarborough participants Edgar and Rommel both identify as dark-skinned. For them, to perceive Filipino males from Mississauga as soft and effeminate can be understood as an opportunity to define themselves and Scarborough itself as hypermasculine, or as Rommel asserts, *'to show dominance.'* It is important to reiterate that the all-male participants from this Scarborough focus group tended to emphasize their heterosexuality and hypermasculinity, while female and male youth from the Mississauga focus group did not openly discuss their sexual orientation, which seemed to have an overall impact on the trajectory of the discussions and the Scarborough participants' preoccupation with particular understandings of Filipino masculinity. Edgar identified the act of Filipino male youth from Scarborough entering Mississauga and other spaces outside of Scarborough in the following way: *'Yo, I'm from the ghetto and we're coming here to terrorize you.'* Rather than rejecting existing stereotypes about racialized youth living in Scarborough, these participants chose to embrace the stereotype of the threatening, racialized male body from Scarborough and use it as a strategic positioning from which to take up space in other areas of the GTA. To borrow from Katherine McKittrick's theorizations on black counter-geographies, racialized bodies can also inhabit 'the crevices of power ... and from this location ... manipulate and recast the meanings' of dominant spaces, thus creating the possibility of an 'alterable terrain' (2006, xvii). Moreover, as Doreen Massey argues, a given place does not denote a 'seamless, coherent identity, a single sense of place which everyone shares' (1994, 153). Edgar's relationship to Mississauga is obviously different from the relationships Mississauga participants have to this area. This serves to highlight the 'open and porous networks of social relations' which constitute our social interactions with places and through which our identities can be multiply constituted (Massey 1994, 121).

Second Skin

Shirley Tate defines skin as 'a mark of ethnicity, status, identity, [and] self-hood' (2001, 209). Tate's definition of skin can be expanded to include the ways in which clothing can also be understood as a 'second skin' that marks bodies in rather similar ways, though of course we do not live *in* and *with* our clothing in precisely the same ways we live *in, with,* and *through* our skin. Understanding clothing as a second skin, and keeping in mind Ahmed and Stacey's understanding of skin itself as spatial, might allow us to understand the extent to which class differences between Filipina/os from Mississauga and Filipina/os from Scarborough are expressed. As Grace, dressed in Gucci flats and designer denim, articulates:

> *I think a lot of it has to do with class — the way they dress, the way we dress. Let's just put it this way, there's two of me, me who's dressed the way I do and the other me who's dressed in Nikes, really, really baggy pants, and jerseys. Which one are you gonna befriend first?*

Grace separates herself into two selves, one of middle-class status from Mississauga who can afford to purchase designer clothing and her other self of working-class status from Scarborough who wears baggy pants, jerseys, and Nikes. Here, Grace constructs her own assumptions about the social status of her Mississauga self and her Scarborough self. She perceives her Mississauga self as more capable of making friends while her Scarborough self is perceived as less capable of initiating and sustaining meaningful relationships. Grace's ability to make friends seems to rely heavily on her socio-economic status and, significantly, on her light skin. She shares, *'I think it was easier for me to make friends with everybody. I personally think it is because of my skin colour.'* Grace's statement not only highlights the ways in which space, skin colour, and clothing as a second skin intersect as symbolic markers of socio-economic status, but also points to a need for a more expansive definition of skin, which acknowledges the ways in which clothing as a second skin can further communicate aspects of our social identities to others. But Grace's statement articulates something more and that is her strategic ability to move between spaces and *perform* different roles which reflect varied aspects of her identity or multiple selves. It is not that her Scarborough self cannot make friends but that she deems her Mississauga self as the self with greater social capital, which, for Grace, translates into a greater ability to establish stronger social networks. This is complicated by Grace's physical appearance, which can be read as ambiguous – an ambiguity which she can utilize to her advantage depending on the spaces she moves through. As Mahtani suggests in her work on 'mixed race' women performing race, 'In some spaces, they might be seen as white; in others, they may be seen as people of colour, but often these readings of racialized bodies can be unstable and constantly changing' (2009, 170).

As with the focus group participants from Mississauga, the participants from Scarborough also identified the ways in which their 'second skin' proved to be a powerful identity marker carrying with it certain spatial connotations with respect to their sense of pride and allegiance to Scarborough. According to Edgar, being a straight, male youth from Scarborough meant dressing in a particular way, *'You go to Stitches[4] or buy yourself thirty dollar Timberland boots knockoff. Those are the clothes, gangster clothes, we can afford.'* The purchasing and wearing of affordable designer 'knockoffs' based on such trendy items as the Timberland boot were popularized by New York hip-hop artists like Wu Tang Clan, Boot Camp Clik, and Notorious B.I.G (see Klein 2002). Particular designer brands such as Timberland, Nike, and Tommy Hilfiger became synonymous with the construction of a particular identity, that of the 'gangster rapper,' which, for working-class youth of colour like Edgar, carried its own set of status markers negotiated by racialized male youth themselves. In this case, their *skins,* their skin colour *and* their clothing, together completed the hypermasculine image of a rough, tough 'gangster' from the Scarborough area, an image that for Edgar seemed to communicate a sense of pride and resilience, rather than shame or embarrassment as implied by some Mississauga youth participants. Edgar is well aware of how his identity is framed by others, but his response to such framings marks a spatially transgressive moment, transgressive in that Edgar insists on 'playing up' a specifically gendered and racialized image associated with the Scarborough area in order to actively communicate his self-pride and resilience in and through different spaces. Mahtani best articulates such performative acts in the following way:

> Choosing what performance depends upon a myriad of conditions – a complex exchange among a variety of characters, where everyday interactions occur across gendered and racialized terrains ... The ground upon which these performances are enacted is not permanent, fixed, nor stable. Rather, it is continually shifting and changing. (Mahtani 2009, 172)

But in an attempt to avoid naming and identifying subversive acts too quickly, it is best to take note that such acts can still contribute to the maintenance of certain racialized and gendered boundaries, while simultaneously transgressing others.

Perceptions of Light-Skinned Beauty and 'Ghetto Fabulosity'

Since the participants from the Mississauga focus group identified as light-skinned Filipina/os, this enabled them to identify and communicate with each other in particular ways, most notably in ways that constructed themselves as 'closer' to whiteness and its attendant privileges. As Maria, tall, slender, and pale, remarks, '*How many light-skinned Filipinos do you know in Scarborough? I can tell you – zero! Mississauga Filipinos are better looking, hands down.*' Here, light skin is directly associated with Maria's perception of beauty, but what is more intriguing are the ways in which light skin and beauty are imagined as spatially connected to a particular western region of the GTA. In other words, light skin and, therefore, beauty are seen as *belonging* to the respectable, white spaces of Mississauga, whereas dark skin and, therefore, ugliness are rejected and expelled from the spatial parameters of the Mississauga area and consigned to the dark, degenerate space of the eastern region of the GTA. This understanding of light-skinned beauty and privilege is reiterated in different ways throughout the focus group discussion. Building upon and reinforcing Chris's earlier reference to Scarborough as 'ghetto,' Grace later suggests that dark-skinned Filipinas from Scarborough are a lower-class *type* of beauty, which Grace describes as '*ghetto fabulous.*' Grace insists that this is '*how Scarborough girls present themselves.*' She seems to suggest that there exists an unattainable standard of beauty that the 'ghetto fabulous' cannot live up to. Presumably, how Filipina youth from Scarborough *present* themselves pushes them outside the parameters of light-skinned beauty. This issue of presentation is crucial because it highlights a contradiction in Grace's narrative. On the one hand, she seems to suggest that Filipinas from Scarborough simply cannot achieve this 'higher' standard of beauty because their lower-class status, imprinted on their very skins, serves as a barrier, preventing them from achieving the socio-spatial mobility that light skin affords middle-class Filipina/os. On the other hand, she seems to be implying that if Filipina youth living in the Scarborough area were to present themselves differently (by using skin lightening products or *appearing* as if they were of a higher-class status through such symbolic markers as designer clothes, for example) they might attain a supposed higher standard of beauty. Of course, Grace's and Maria's statements operate on the assumption that Filipina youth from the Scarborough area desire light skin and middle-class status. Unfortunately, there was no opportunity to challenge this assumption directly since the participants from the Scarborough focus group session all identified as straight, male youth.

Dark and Dirty

As I have mentioned, compared to the light-skinned focus group participants from Mississauga, focus group participants from the Scarborough area were of significantly darker skin tone. Thus participants' skin tones had a further impact on the trajectory of the focus group discussion. For example, Edgar recalls distinct memories of his family reprimanding him for being dark-skinned: *'"Come out of the sun." Your parents [and] your uncles will tell you, "You look dirty. Go clean yourself up. Next time, don't go into the sun too much."'* In response, another participant, Ritz, shares, *'Let's try to keep you inside so that you don't get darker.'* Studies on colourism confirm the ways in which dark skin has become a symbolic marker of one's status as a member of the labouring class: 'Immigrant generations have a particular idea of what success should look like. In the home country, success is defined by light skin because it illustrates that one is not part of the laboring class and does not have to work under the hot sun' (Rondilla and Spickard 2007, 67). While Edgar's point of reference is *leisure* rather than labour, what is interesting to note is the *possibility* of cleanliness expressed in the phrase 'Go clean yourself up.' In other words, it is *possible* to strive towards whiteness if one stays out of the sun. As Kalpana Seshadri-Crooks would argue, what is being made possible here is not simply the achievement of lighter skin but 'the fantasy of wholeness, of being,' that is, the fantasy of achieving the status of 'master signifier, of Whiteness' (2000, 5).

What is further intriguing about Edgar's statement are the spatial restrictions being placed on him by his family. He is unable to freely enjoy the sun and the heat for fear that he will get darker. This instilled fear of darkness and imposed desire for whiteness dictate when, where, and how Edgar takes up certain spaces. His mobility is restricted by the possibility of his skin becoming shades darker and consequently dirtier, effectively destroying his chances of upward social mobility, as implied by his elders. Radhika Mohanram better describes this concept of spatial immobility and mobility in terms of how 'whiteness has the ability to move [resulting] in the unmarking of the body [while] blackness is signified through a marking and is always static and immobilizing' (1999, 4).

Rommel frames other Filipina/os' valorization of whiteness in the form of a question when he asks, *'Why is lighter skin always exalted, idealized whereas the darker shades [are] associated with dirt and uncleanliness?'* Here, Rommel's sentiments seem to echo W.E.B. DuBois, who writes that 'everything great, good, efficient, fair and honorable is associated with whiteness, while everything mean, bad, blundering, cheating and dishonorable is "yellow"; a bad taste is "brown"; and the devil is "black"' (DuBois 1996, 60). Another participant, Ritz, articulates that it is like being *'born with a disease or a curse if you [have] darker skin.'* The fear and threat of dirt, disease, and curses incite frustration in the dark-skinned body. This fear and disgust of dark skin has, under Western eyes, been constituted alongside the contrasting idealization of light skin as bright, pure, clean, and good. Frantz Fanon is helpful in illustrating the corporeal encounters between differently racialized bodies in describing the existence of an 'epidermal hierarchy' that 'equates the racial body with a perceptible blackness' (1967, 112). Indeed, these participants can be seen as living the Fanonian 'racial epidermal schema.' As Mohanram aptly articulates, Fanon 'rages against the strictly epidermal identity bestowed upon blacks in colonized and metropolitan spaces which is different from the corporeal schema normally reserved for whites' (1999, 26). That corporeal difference is perceptible, tangible in the ways that whiteness is constructed as *dis*embodied, as transcendent, as the antithesis *to* colour as *non*-colour, invisible, and unmarked. Just as whiteness is seen as invisible, dark skin is seen as hypervisible, merely functioning 'to grant a perspective to the white man' (Mohanram 1999, 26–7). This issue of perspective is relevant insofar as it exposes the ways in which light-skinned focus group participants imposed their own imaginings of what dark-skinned Filipina/os from Scarborough represent to them. Through spatially discursive practices of Othering *other* Filipina/os from a distant, eastern region of the GTA, they came to know and understand themselves as superior. Poignantly, rather than expressing disappointment in being dark-skinned, the focus group participants from Scarborough dismissed the desire for light skin altogether as a preoccupation of Filipina/o youth who must struggle with sustaining higher class status and privilege:

> *I think the dark-skinned–light-skinned thing is prevalent as you go higher in social class. Especially when you go upwards in social status you tend to see that in order for you to stay on that level, like being with the Joneses, you have to assimilate with the Joneses.*

Here, Edgar underscores some of the ways in which a preoccupation with sustaining light-skinned privilege becomes an increasingly important aspect of one's social identity as one rises in class status, precisely because light-skinned privilege for Filipina/os is so *precarious,* merely granting them a 'toehold on respectability,' as Razack would argue (2002, 103). The imagined attainment of white, middle-class respectability is emphasized by perceptions of Mississauga as a particularly valued space of thriving Canadian commerce and wealth. Light-skinned Filipina/o youth who strive to conform to standards of white, middle-class respectability through the acquisition of social and symbolic capital can imagine themselves as part of this valued space. And yet, the promise of white, middle-class respectability and its attendant privileges are ultimately *illusory.* Illusory in that this promise is never fully and permanently attainable for either light-skinned, or dark-skinned bodies for that matter, living in the Greater Toronto Area. Illusory in that this promise is ultimately premised upon a false stabilization of racialized, gendered, and classed categories of being. To paraphrase Fanon, one can never be sure how close one is to disgrace (2000, 261). In other words, the ways in which light-skinned Filipina/o participants from Mississauga secure any notion of white, middle-class respectability is through the degradation of dark-skinned Filipina/o youth from the Scarborough area, signalling their own complicity in spatially sustaining dominant systems of racial oppression.

'Passing': Racialized Bodies Accessing Spaces of Light-Skinned Privilege

Bucholtz (1995) argues that 'passing is the active construction of how the self is perceived when one's ethnicity is ambiguous to others' (352). I want to draw attention to the agentive and performative character of 'passing,' while also keeping in mind the ways in which spatial boundaries are constructed and transgressed in, through, and around racialized bodies. Those able to 'pass' may 'patrol their own borders using the tools of language and self-presentation to determine how the boundaries of ethnic categories are drawn upon their own bodies' (ibid.). Here, I wish to highlight the narrative of Joseph, a light-skinned Filipino youth participant from Mississauga. He shares:

> *My girlfriend's eastern European and her Dad is really racist [but] he doesn't mind me. I think it's easier 'cause I don't look it to them. 'Cause if I did, it'd be a lot different. For them to accept me, it's easier 'cause I'm more Europeanized to them.* I don't look Filipino. (Emphasis added)

Joseph seems to pride himself on not looking Filipino, but on *passing* as white, which grants him access to certain spaces of privilege like his girlfriend's parents' home, a space that would be closed off to him if he were of notably darker skin. Joseph's ability to transgress certain social boundaries is conditional and dependent on a denial of that which would mark him as Filipino. Significantly, Joseph shares, *'This is what I never really got 'cause I was like, Asian too. [My friends] were really racist. It's almost like they didn't include me [as Asian] 'cause they didn't think I was a part of that.'* Although Joseph recognizes that he can pass as white, he still knows himself as 'Asian.' In the presence of friends whom he acknowledges as openly racist, he is never subject to threats of racism himself. This makes Joseph acutely aware of how others have chosen to perceive him and the ways in which the 'desire to pass offers itself as a temporary solution to racism and rejection' (Bucholtz 1995, 358). His inclusion in primarily white social networks grants him the ability not only to move in and through particular spaces of privilege but also to participate in racist acts based on an assumed membership. This is made all the more clear when Joseph shares the following story: *'I went to the convenience store and I was behind this white guy. And there was this Chinese guy taking really long. I guess he [the white guy] didn't know I was [not] white. And he's like, "C'mon, hurry up, ping pong." But he looked at me like I was a white guy.'*

Here, in the space of a Mississauga convenience store, Joseph is invited to participate in a racist act through a *look*. Significantly, Joseph does not respond to the invitation. It is this look that denotes a (mis)recognition of Joseph's racial and ethnic identity. Joseph goes on to say, *'I just always get the feeling that – not that they think that I'm white – but so much more* familiar, *really, just* normal. *It makes my life easier'* (emphasis added). The desire to have an easier life, to be more *familiar* and *normal* rather than *unfamiliar* and *abnormal,* shores up a 'fantasy of wholeness' which his strategic performance renders possible (Mercer 1999, 201). Joseph's ability to perform whiteness and perform it *well* at specific moments, then, enables him to freely move through privileged spaces and take up space as a presumably white body without the imminent danger or threat of being subject to racism and rejection. So long as Joseph denies any intelligible trace of an essential 'Filipino-ness,' he can live a life that, for him, maintains some semblance of 'normalcy,' but this begs the question – what *is* 'normal'? At the same time that whiteness is reinforced as normative and superior, it can also be disrupted, as denoted by Joseph's decision not to respond to the look. As Puwar points out, the white mask on non-white skins (whether perceptible to the naked eye or not) must be understood as being 'acquired slowly through time by moving through white "civilizing" spaces (educational, neighbourhoods, friends, and institutional positions)' (2004, 114).

Conclusion

What does it mean to expose the ways in which intraracial colourism is expressed spatially by Filipina/o youth in the GTA? What does it mean to focus specifically on such stark oppositions as west side versus east side; middle class versus working class; light-skinned versus dark-skinned? I chose to draw on these more extreme, and understandably problematic, dualities in order to draw out the class and colour tensions within and among Filipina/o communities, in order to expose the prejudices that are not spoken of yet which are spatially articulated in confrontations, in unspoken gestures, in the physical and psychological distancing from those Filipina/os considered too dark, too dirty, too inferior, or too unworthy to associate with. Placing the different focus group discussions in conversation with each other demonstrated how spaces can be unstable and negotiated, taken over and taken up for different purposes, even as the participants themselves may have perceived and imagined these spaces in particular, fixed ways. Significantly, how participants construed certain spaces in the Mississauga and Scarborough areas as white and privileged or degenerate and dirty exposes the associations made between skin, skin colour, and space. Moreover, recalling my challenge to think through skin *colour* and keep in mind the ways in which skin itself is spatial was critical in understanding how the participants' bodies and skins encountered each other in real and imagined ways, as well as how the meaning carried *within* light or dark skin created particular epidermal boundaries. Furthermore, investigating the ways in which these spatial expressions of intraracial colourism shaped the participants' identities underlines how these spatial expressions were charged with tension, reflecting conflict between and among Filipina/o youth from different regions of the Greater Toronto Area. In this chapter, the discussions that emerged out of each focus group were placed in conversation with each other so as to illustrate the very real and complicated debates that have been and still are causing divisiveness in our communities and simultaneously sustaining dominant systems of oppression. Understanding that intraracial colourism among Filipina/o youth is grounded in the Philippines' messy colonial and imperial history is one entry point for getting at the roots of such conflictual positionings; however, further analysis and, more importantly, *sustained* communication and conversation between and among Filipina/o communities in the Greater Toronto Area are needed to break down the real and imagined spatial divisions caused by intraracial colourism today. Being open to such dialogue can push against those dominant systems of racial oppression that our communities both knowingly and unknowingly sustain.

NOTES

1 Formed in early 2009, the Sisters of Colour Collective is a small, volunteer-based organization committed to raising critical awareness around issues of diversity, equity, and human rights through creative writing and performance art. The SOCC's mandate is to create a space where young women can speak openly and creatively about issues that concern themselves and their communities.

2 Far from being a fixed category, perceptions of whiteness have been multiple and complex, shifting according to a given historical moment and the prevailing racial discourse of the time. Some argue that the perceived 'whitening' of specific European immigrant groups and other racial and

ethnic groups was, in part, due to supposed levels of assimilability and upward social mobility (cf. Sacks 1997; Barrett and Roediger 1997).

3 Sherene Razack states that 'mythologies or national stories are about a nation's origins and history. They enable citizens to think of themselves as part of a community, defining who belongs and who does not belong to the nation ... a quintessential feature of white settler mythologies is, therefore, the disavowal of conquest, genocide, slavery, and the exploitation of the labour of peoples of colour' (2002, 2).

4 Stitches is a Canadian retail franchise that sells trendy and affordable clothing to young adults.

REFERENCES

2007. Community profile, City of Mississauga. *Statistics Canada*, 2006 census of population. Accessed December 8, 2006. http://www12.statcan.ca/english/census06/data/profiles/community/Details/Page.cfm?Lang=E&Geo1=CSD&Code1=3521005&Geo2=PR&Code2=35&Data=Count&SearchText=Mississauga&SearchType=Begins&SearchPR=01&B1=All&Custom=.

Ahmed, Sara, and Jackie Stacey, eds. 2001. *Thinking through the skin*. London: Routledge.

Balce, Nerissa S. 2006. Filipino bodies, lynching, and the language of empire. In *Positively no Filipinos allowed: Building communities and discourse*, ed. Antionio Tiongson, Jr, Edgardo V. Gutierrez, and Ricardo V. Gutierrez, 43–60. Philadelphia: Temple University Press.

Barrett, James R., and David Roediger. 1997. How white people became white. In *Critical white studies: Looking behind the mirror*, ed. Richard Delgado and Jean Stefancic, 402–6. Philadelphia: Temple University Press.

Benthien, Claudia. 1999. *Skin: On the cultural border between self and the world*. New York: Columbia University Press.

Bucholtz, Mary. 1995. From mulatta to mestiza: Passing and the linguistic reshaping of ethnic identity. In *Gender articulated: Language and the socially constructed self*, ed. Kira Hall and Mary Bucholtz, 351–74. New York and London: Routledge.

Coloma, Roland Sintos. 2009. 'Destiny has thrown the Negro and the Filipino under the tutelage of America': Race and curriculum in the age of empire. *Curriculum Inquiry* 39 (4): 495–519.

DuBois, W.E.B. 1996. *The Oxford W.E.B DuBois Reader*, ed. Eric J. Sundquist. New York: Oxford University Press. Quoted in Nerissa S. Balce, Filipino bodies, lynching and the language of empire. In *Positively no Filipinos allowed: Building communities and discourse*, ed. Antonio Tiongson, Jr,

Edgardo V. Gutierrez, and Ricardo V. Gutierrez, 60. Philadelphia: Temple University Press, 2006.

Fanon, Frantz. 1967. *Black skin, white masks.* New York: Grove.

– 2000. The fact of blackness. In *Theories of race and racism: A reader,* ed. Les Back and John Solomos, 258–65. London and New York: Routledge.

Fergus, Edward. 2004. *Skin color and identity formation: Perceptions of opportunity and academic orientation among Mexican and Puerto Rican youth.* New York: Routledge.

Heritage 2010. Mississauga. *Heritage.* Accessed April 21, 2010. http://www.mississauga.ca/portal/residents/heritage.

Herring, Cedric, Verna M. Keith, and Hayward Derrick. 2004. *Skin deep: How race and complexion matter in the 'color-blind' era.* Chicago: University of Illinois Press.

Klein, Naomi. 2002. *No logo.* New York: St Martin's.

Kramer, Paul A. 2006. *The blood of government: Race, empire, the United States, and the Philippines.* Chapel Hill: University of North Carolina Press.

Mahtani, Minelle. 2009. Tricking the border guards: Performing race. In *The politics of race in Canada: Readings in historical perspectives, contemporary realities, and future possibilities,* ed. Maria Wallis and Augie Fleras, 166–77. Oxford: Oxford University Press.

Massey, Doreen. 1994. *Space, place, and gender.* Minneapolis: University of Minnesota Press.

McKittrick, Katherine. 2006. *Demonic grounds: Black women and the cartographies of struggle.* Minneapolis: University of Minnesota Press.

Mercer, Kobena. 1999. Busy in the ruins of a wretched phantasia. In *Frantz Fanon: Critical perspectives,* ed. Anthony Alessandrini, 195–218. London and New York: Routledge.

Mohanram, Radhika. 1999. *Black body: Women, colonialism, and space.* Minneapolis: University of Minnesota Press.

Nakano Glenn, Evelyn. 2008. Yearning for lightness: Transnational circuits in the marketing and consumption of skin lighteners. *Gender and Society* 22 (3): 281–302.

Puwar, Nirmal. 2004. *Space invaders: Race, gender and bodies out of place.* Oxford: Berg.

Rafael, Vicente L. 2000. *White love and other events in Filipino history.* Durham, NC, and London: Duke University Press.

Razack, Sherene. 2002. *Race, space, and the law.* Toronto: Between the Lines.

Rondilla, Joanne L., and Paul Spickard. 2007. *Is lighter better?: Skin-tone discrimination among Asian Americans.* Lanham, MD: Rowman and Littlefield.

Sacks, Karen Brodkin. 1997. How did Jews become white folks? In *Critical white studies: Looking behind the mirror,* ed. Richard Delgado and Jean Stefancic, 395–401. Philadelphia: Temple University Press.

Sahay, Sarita, and Niva Piran. 1997. Skin-color preferences and body satisfaction among South-Asian-Canadian and European-Canadian female university students. *Journal of Social Psychology* 137 (2): 161–71.

Scarborough 2006. Scarborough. *City of Toronto community council profiles.* Accessed December 8, 2006. http://www.toronto.ca/committees/council_profiles/pdf/scarboro_2006_cc_profiles.pdf.

Seshadri-Crooks, Kalpana. 2000. *Desiring whiteness: A Lacanian analysis of race.* London and New York: Routledge.

Tate, Shirley. 2001. 'That is my Star of David': Skin, abjection and hybridity. In *Thinking through the Skin*, ed. Sara Ahmed and Jackie Stacey, 209–22. London: Routledge.

Teelucksingh, Cheryl. 2007. Environmental racialization: Linking racialization to the environment in Canada. *Local Environment* 12 (6): 645–66.

Williams, Chris, and Jennifer Clarke. 2003. Toronto community profile. *Racism, violence and health project.* Accessed December 8, 2006. http://rvh.socialwork.dal.ca/04%20Community%20Profiles/Toronto/profile2003to.html.

Chapter 19

The Social Construction of 'Filipina/o Studies': Youth Spaces and Subjectivities

JEFFREY P. AGUINALDO

Upon being invited by the editors to contribute to this volume, I was immediately forced to think (and theorize) 'why me?' I am Filipino. My parents are first-generation immigrants. My mother was selected to join one of the first cohorts recruited by the College of Nurses of Ontario in the mid-1960s to replenish the apparent shortage of healthcare professionals in Canada (see Damasco in this volume). Around the same time, my father, trained in the Philippines as a mechanical engineer, immigrated to Canada, and was obliged to retrain in order to qualify as a professional engineer in this country (see Kelly et al. in this volume). However, throughout my fourteen years of academic training, with its false starts, detours, and roadblocks, and another four or so years as a professor and health researcher, I have not so far identified my scholarship as in any way contributing to the field of 'Filipina/o studies.'

In coming to my own, academically and politically, I was first attracted to the panache of queer theory and the rage of lesbian feminism. These theories were a starting point in my work in gay men's health and offered me an analytic framework, a methodology, and most of all a politics from which I could identify and articulate the operation of heterosexism in the social exclusion of gay men from healthcare theory and practice. In Canada, gay men are barred as blood donors even to their partners, children, or other family members. Public health research on gay men has been used as a warrant for such policies, and continues to be used in Canada and elsewhere as justification for denying equality to gay men (Ellis and Kitzinger 2002). Inspired by queer and feminist theories, I pursued training as a public health scientist to produce research that would challenge public health's misrepresentations of gay men. Sexuality was the focus of my research wherein gay men were unified by a shared marginality through heterosexism (Aguinaldo 2008). But as others have aptly argued (e.g., Collins 1990; hooks 2000), the universal subject of gender and sexuality theorists has been primarily white and middle-class.

It was for this reason that I turned my attention to those that gender and sexuality theories often neglected: racially marginalized bodies. In this work, my scholarship focused on race and ethnicity as the basis for subordination. My scholarship in this area looked at the ways through which 'Asian cultures' have been represented in HIV prevention research. Gay Asian males are depicted as wholly ignorant of their sexual health, or in some cases, as well aware of their sexual health, but willingly placing themselves at risk for HIV or other sexually transmitted diseases to appease the demands of their white male sexual partners (e.g., Choi et al. 1995; Nemoto et al. 2003). In this literature, Asian cultures are constructed as intensely hetero/sexist and gender rigid (e.g., Choi et al. 2002), characteristics that are said to promote HIV risk among gay Asian men (e.g., Poon and Ho 2002). By implication, rejecting Asian culture and adopting 'less oppressive' white Western values are put forth implicitly as 'HIV prevention.'

In this work, my point of departure was 'Asian' and the tool I used to interrogate its position was, broadly speaking, anti-racist theory (e.g., Ahmad 1993; Stubbs 1993). However, I always had an ambivalent relationship with the term 'Asian.' It was certainly not something I felt adequately characterized who I think I am or how I necessarily identify myself. The term was, quite plainly, something I was called in census data, in surveys, and in racial slurs by white folks walking past me. As with the signifier 'person of colour,' the term 'Asian' erased the depth and specificity of my Filipino-ness if only to forge a coherent community. Despite my ambivalence, the term offered a rallying cry, a body of scholarship, and a critical analysis from which to start. Irrespective of whether or not I felt that the term 'Asian' spoke to my own sensibilities, it offered a readily available language to claim an experience and a politics. In other words, it gave me a position from which to demand social justice.

But presenting myself in this way comes with considerable costs. In order to gain access, I/we have had to represent ourselves by a monolithic 'Asian.' Through this term, we silence the specificity of our marginality and the conditions from which it manifests in order for 'us' to be seen. This leaves many to assume too much about who we are and what we experience. At its most banal, the erasure of Filipina/o-ness comes in the form of presupposing we know how to use chopsticks. At its worse, it is a complete and total amnesia of Filipina/o history. This realization came to me after a recent trip to the Philippines followed by a tour of China. My trip to Beijing turned out to be a lesson in 'Hollywood history' – history that you hear about in 'all the movies.' By contrast, my time in the Philippines was, for me, a lesson in 'small history' – no less important or meaningful, but a history that has been largely ignored by most of the world.

My goal, here, is not to present a grand narrative that I am heading towards some authentic Filipino identity. It is to flag, first, the construction of our social identities and, second, the ways this might bear on our scholarship. This collected volume is an indication, if not a representation, of the burgeoning field of Filipina/o studies from a specifically Canadian perspective. It articulates the experience of a Filipina/o diaspora as somehow distinct from other diasporas within Canada or from Filipina/o diasporas elsewhere. The chapters reviewed here specify the unique perspectives of Filipina/o youths. Taken together, these chapters represent Filipina/o studies as both an academic field and a real-world undertaking to improve the social conditions of Filipina/os.

On Social Constructionism

I write this chapter from an explicitly social constructionist perspective. First articulated by Berger and Luckmann's *The Social Construction of Reality* (1980), social constructionism emphasizes the constructive role of language in categorizing and dividing up the world. Gergen (1985) describes the constructionist inquiry as 'explicating the processes by which people come to describe, explain, or otherwise account for the world (including themselves) in which they live' (266). This type of social constructionism is primarily occupied with how the language we use and the categories we employ construct our experience in ways that are then reified as natural and normal (Burr 1995; Gergen 1999). Language, according to Edley (2001), does not provide a set collection of labels for objects and events assumed to exist out there in the world; rather, language constitutes those objects.

Social constructionists have developed powerful analytic tools to identify and understand power and oppression. I briefly mention two. First, social constructionism does not assume a unitary 'essential' person, but a fragmentary self (Kitzinger 1992). By this it is meant that there is no one coherent identity that one can claim, but a contested terrain of multiple selves or 'subjectivities' from which one can take up or be positioned. In contrast to standpoint epistemology that assumes our scholarship can speak from a single unitary Filipina/o position, social constructionism rejects the notion that there is such a perspective or an authentic Filipina/o voice with which we can speak. Such a commitment brings to the fore the 'realities' of multiple Filipina/o perspectives and voices.

Given its refusal of a unitary subject, social constructionism, secondly, allows for the possibilities of not only intersecting but also interlocking forms of social oppression. We are not only defined or categorizable by our race and ethnicity, but our class, sexuality, gender, and so on. According to Grillo (1995),

> At any one moment in time and in space, some of these categories are central to her being and her ability to act in the world. Others matter not at all . . . When something or someone highlights one of her categories and brings it to the fore, she may be a dominant person, an oppressor of others. Other times, even most of the time, she may be oppressed herself. (17)

An appreciation of intersecting systems of oppression forces us to think through just whose experience we purport to write about in our scholarship and to appreciate the unique experiences of women as distinct from those of men, queers from those of heterosexuals, disabled from those of able-bodied, *balikbayan* from those who stayed, and despite shared Filipina/o heritage.

An analysis of interlocking oppressions forces us to consider that multiple systems of oppression require and sustain one another for each to exist (Fellows and Razack 1998). It is not enough to single out and challenge one system of oppression in our scholarship; we must consider the multiple oppressions that converge on and constitute the range of experiences from which our scholarship claims to speak.

> The significance of seeing race, class, and gender as interlocking systems of oppression is that such an approach fosters a paradigmatic shift of thinking inclusively about other oppressions, such as age, sexual orientation, religion, and ethnicity. (Collins 1990, 225)

In sum, social constructionism brings us to an altogether different level of inquiry. While Filipina/o studies can (and should) examine the social conditions of Filipina/o lives, it should also articulate whose

Filipina/o lives *specifically* we write about in our scholarship and, more importantly, whose we might ignore. Put more concretely, I am Filipino, but I am also male, queer, middle class, a university professor, short, cynical, and many others. Formulating the context of my experience is equally complex. My experience is informed by colonialism, but also by heterosexism, patriarchy, and capitalism. If we do not address issues of ability, class, sexuality, and so on, insofar as these intersect and interlock with experiences as a Filipina/o, we simply produce a monolithic Filipina/o subject and the abject bodies it creates. In speaking of a shared colonial experience, social constructionism forces us to ask *whose* 'shared colonial experience' we are talking about and whose we are not. The language we use to represent ourselves in our scholarship and elsewhere always comes with particular political costs and benefits. We must always recognize what we let fall by the wayside in every moment of our representation, even if for the purposes of forming a coherent community for us to demand justice.

Scholarly Examples on Filipina/o Youth

In reading the chapters of this section, I constantly asked myself this simple question: What are the costs and benefits of defining and organizing ourselves as Filipina/o scholars in our academic work and our politics? The four chapters I am discussing place at the centre of their analysis Filipina/o identity and the legacy of its history on Filipina/o youth. These chapters are, as far as I am concerned, fine examples of the benefits of doing so.

Conely de Leon encapsulates the unique socio-political position of Filipina/os as a subordinate group. She is concerned with what others have called intraracial colourism among Filipina/o youths, and gives voice to a violence we sometimes willingly silence in the service of coalition building to challenge the broader experience of white supremacy. Intraracial colourism is 'the discriminatory treatment of individuals falling within the same "racial" group on the basis of skin color' (Herring, as cited in de Leon in this volume). Put simply, a distinction is made between so-called light-skinned and dark-skinned Filipina/os, and it is through this distinction that light-skinned Filipina/o youth attempt to distance themselves, spatially, psychologically, and socially, from dark-skinned Filipina/o youth.

Maureen Grace Mendoza is concerned with the factors that influence Filipina/o Canadian youth's experiences in post-secondary education, in particular their undergraduate experiences at the University of British Columbia. She attempts to come to some understanding of the 'deeply fragmented minority narratives' of Filipina/o Canadian students and the terrain through which they must negotiate to attain education. Through an analysis of retrospective accounts, Mendoza seeks to understand how racial marginalization both facilitates and impedes post-secondary education. More broadly, she documents the social determinants of Filipina/o Canadian educational achievement. Participants expressed that parents and the immigrant experiences, (high school) peer groups, and community support or lack thereof influence their education.

John Paul C. Catungal provides a critical analysis of media representations of slain Filipino Canadian youths and situates these killings within a broader social context. His point is, following Žižek (as cited in Catungal), to encourage 'us to look at individual incidents not as mere flashes in the pan but as "normal" incidences' of a particular racist social order. Just as patriarchy as an institution renders violence against women as 'the way things are,' so too does racism institutionalized in Canadian immigration policies frame the violence perpetrated against Filipino youths as mere aberrations of a seemingly just society. And as patriarchy attempts to conceal itself as the cause of violence against women, so too does racism conceal its harmful role in the lives of Filipino youths. According to Catungal, 'speaking truth to power would necessitate . . . calling into question the normalizing institutions that sustain social order itself.' For Catungal, the locus of intervention is not only on the individual lives and families of the victims of violence, but the national policies that can have negative long-term impact on Filipina/os.

Christine Balmes details one potential strategy to redress the types of problems identified by de Leon, Mendoza, and Catungal. The Kapisanan Philippine Centre for Arts and Culture, according to Balmes, formed under the initiative of Filipina artists Nadine Villasin and Caroline Mangosing. Their vision of Kapisanan is 'to respond to problems of the Filipino Canadian community such as racism, invisibility, cultural shame, lack of role models and leadership, and divisions between different generations and between newcomers and those integrated into mainstream society' (Balmes in this volume). Through artistic endeavours and cultural programs, Kapisanan members attempt to disseminate alternative visions of Filipina/o-ness, ones that challenge the colonial mentality and cultural shame that exacerbate the problems that de Leon, Mendoza, and Cantungal describe. Collectively,

Kapisanan's efforts have been to offer Filipina/o Canadian youths a counter-discourse 'providing examples of Filipino culture as young, "cool," and "hip"' (Balmes in this volume). The strategy is one that develops 'a strong sense of community, awareness, and empowerment' among Filipina/os, and asserts 'Filipino Canadian community' through 'the emergence of a "Filipino Canadian" cultural movement.'

In sum, the four chapters discussed here exemplify, for me, the potential for what I see as an emerging field of Filipina/o studies in Canada. Filipina/o studies is inherently political. Each of the chapters reviewed has as its goal to locate a specific marginality and to eliminate its effects on Filipina/o youths in Canada. However, having been asked by the editors to comment on the social construction of Filipina/o studies as an academic field more generally, I now take a reflexive moment to consider the costs of privileging Filipina/o identity in our scholarship. To do so, I address two fundamental questions – Who are 'we'? and How are we accomplishing what we want to do? – pertinent to the development of an academic field, and attempt to discern how they have been answered (to the extent that they have) within the confines of the preceding chapters.

Who Are 'We'?

I am centrally concerned with the production of 'the subject' in our analyses.[1] As much as we are Filipina/o, we are also a host of other things. When we foreground our shared cultural identity or a shared colonial experience in our scholarship even for strategic purposes, we must be mindful of the identities, politics, and epistemologies that we set aside. So for example, while de Leon's analysis foregrounds a form of oppression that we commit towards each other, she presumes a unitary experience of that oppression. I like her historicalization of intraracial colourism and her use of spatial theory. She articulates intraracial colourism not as an aberration of the present, but as an *enduring* consequence of imperialism that structures the psychic and physical lives of Filipina/o youths in Canada. However, her analysis implies that both dark-skinned males and females experience colourism equally, despite her disavowal of a 'singular form of so-called Filipina/o solidarity' among Filipina/o youths. To de Leon I ask, is there room for a feminist critique, one that distinguishes between the unique experiences of colourism of Filipinas and Filipinos? I imagine colourism places a powerful policing effect on the construction of normative femininity, as evidenced by the targeting of skin-lightening creams specifically to young Filipinas. This remains conspicuously silent among her focus group data or her analysis more generally.

The radical critique that Catungal develops (ultimately) targets Canada's contemporary labour and immigration policies that build and sustain Canadian nationhood, but simultaneously facilitate colonial violence towards Filipina/os. My question to Catungal is this: Is there room for a queer analysis? The 'divided family' for which he seeks unification reads vaguely heterosexual, if only because the immigration policies he challenges are typically heteronormative. It seems that a radical Filipina/o critique of Canadian immigration policies solely for their racist effects leaves standing the heterosexual family as the presumed norm. This necessarily ignores other forms of familial configurations. Whose Filipina/o families are we fighting to unify, and whose Filipina/o families do we ignore? Put in broader terms, in assailing the very structures that sustain violence against or among Filipina/os, is there a possibility of reproducing or ignoring other modes of violence?

In sum, I argue that Filipina/o studies should, by necessity, assert a Filipina/o identity in order for us to 'be seen.' It must, however, simultaneously interrogate the formation of that identity or risk the violent exclusion of those Filipina/os who do not conform to the normative assumptions (oftentimes heterosexual and able-bodied) of that identity.

How Do We Accomplish What We Want to Do?

The four chapters draw from a range of theoretical frameworks available to a critical project, though they vary in their explicitness. On the one hand, de Leon utilizes spatial theory as it has been developed by Razack, and Catungal draws on Foucault. These theoretical perspectives are, at least to some degree, congruous with my own social constructionist commitments from which I write this chapter. On the other hand, Mendoza undertakes what, in public health parlance, would be called a social determinants approach to the educational experiences of Filipina/o youths, and Balmes conducts an ethnographic study of Kapisanan. Such 'essentialist' or 'realist' approaches contrast with those of de Leon and Catungal (as well as my own) in their analytic assumptions.

The merits of social constructionism versus essentialism in achieving an emancipatory project have been thoroughly thrashed about, for instance within lesbian and gay, feminist, and anti-racist movements

(Fuss 1989; Kitzinger 1995; Razack 1998; Wilkinson 1997). Some scholars reject particular theories and methods on the grounds that they are deemed antithetical to the critical project ('the master's tools will never dismantle the master's house'). Social constructionism, postmodernism, and other 'post-' frameworks are often the targets of such critiques. On postmodernism, feminist psychologist Naomi Weisstein (1993, 243–4) writes,

> *Of course*, there is paralysis: once knowledge is reduced to insurmountable personal subjectivity, there is no place to go; we are in a swamp of self-referential passivity. Sometimes I think that, when the fashion passes, we will find many bodies, drowned in their own wordy words, like the Druids in the bogs. Meanwhile, the patriarchy continues to prosper. (Emphasis in original)

For Weisstein, postmodernism offers nothing to a critical project and should be rejected outright.

I am at odds with those who suggest that there is one theoretical perspective better suited to achieve Filipina/o liberatory politics. As de Leon and Catungal demonstrate, social constructionist approaches are uniquely fitted to expose how power and oppression operate where they are believed not to operate. Such an approach stands in stark contrast to realist approaches, exemplified by Mendoza, that nonetheless offer 'empirical evidence' that is rhetorically persuasive to decision makers who could change policies, laws, or curriculum. Balmes in particular adopts a ruthlessly essentialist perspective. Her yearning for a Filipina/o community with which she could identify and to define 'the parameters for a Filipino Canadian identity' presumes a unitary 'Filipino-centred consciousness' and a singular 'Philippine-inspired viewpoint' in Canada.

I am careful to note that while Balmes's essentialism may be antithetical to my own social constructionist commitments, it does not negate political efficacy. Political acts of resistance, such as those produced by Kapisanan, must make concrete decisions and at times forego a sustained theoretical analysis to affect real-world changes in the 'here and now.' Of course, such decisions render that very intervention open to attack from a bewildering array of academic perspectives and political persuasions. Chastising Balmes or Kapisanan members for failing to conform to the interlocutor's theory of choice or for having fallen short of some illusory position of 'absolute resistance' does nothing but limit and stifle social action. We should evaluate any political act of resistance for its social and political costs and benefits in advancing a way forward, while we simultaneously acknowledge where it has failed. My point is simply that our theories should be chosen (as Kapisanan has been) for their political expediency and their capacity to produce social change, and not to claim theoretical superiority.

Clearly, the chapters reviewed here collectively demonstrate that both social constructionist and essentialist theories can be harnessed to achieve Filipina/o emancipation. While I readily admit that social constructionism has been used for oppressive ends (e.g., to claim that race is a social construction and racism is therefore imagined), so too have essentialist or realist approaches. Wholesale rejection of any one perspective simply limits the analytic tools we can use to challenge oppression. I would urge Filipina/o activists and scholars not to dismiss any particular theoretical perspective if for no other reason than they risk delegitimizing work that has productively utilized that very perspective in ways that affect (Filipina/o) emancipation.

In sum, the chapters in this section partake in the constitution of Filipina/o studies. As this field develops and no doubt flourishes, I ask that we attend to the omissions, the blind spots, and the elisions. We can learn from the lessons of other academic fields. This means, as Kitzinger and Wilkinson (1994) argue in the context of the feminist movement, that we avoid 'constantly having to go over the same ground, the same debates, the same dead ends – continually reinventing the wheel, instead of being able to move forward, learning from the past and developing theory accordingly' (331). I say this not to indict any individual failings of the preceding chapters, or to undermine their political projects. It is to further articulate what those projects are and how they contribute, define, and demarcate the field of Filipina/o studies and the subjects of that scholarship. It is in the doing of this articulation and the attention we give to our exclusions that each and every one of us can say, this is 'why me.'

NOTES

1 There is, of course, a related question of who are the 'we' that can 'do' Filipina/o studies. The vast majority of the authors in this edited volume are those who are of Philippine heritage and whose work is primarily focused on the subject of Filipina/os. By contrast, there are those who are of Philippine heritage, but whose scholarship does not primarily focus on the subject of Filipina/os (e.g., me). Still further, there are those authors who

are not of Philippine heritage but whose work primarily focuses on the subject of Filipina/os (e.g., Pratt, Kelly, and McElhinny). I do not intend to take up this issue here, but such discussions may be productively informed by those debates that have taken place within, for example, black feminism (hooks 2000).

REFERENCES

Aguinaldo, Jeffrey P. 2008. The social construction of gay oppression as a determinant of gay men's health. *Critical Public Health* 18 (1): 87–96.

Ahmad, Wagar Irsan-Ullah. 1993. Making black people sick: 'Race', ideology and health research. In *'Race' and health in contemporary Britain,* ed. Wagar Irsan-Ullah Ahmad, 11–33. Buckingham, UK: Open University Press.

Berger, Peter L., and Thomas Luckmann. 1980. *The social construction of reality: A treatise in the sociology of knowledge.* New York: Irvington.

Burr, Vivien. 1995. *An introduction to social constructionism.* New York: Routledge.

Choi, Kyung-Hee, Thomas J. Coates, Joseph A. Catania, Steve Lew, and Prescott Chow. 1995. High HIV risk among gay Asian and Pacific Islander men in San Francisco. *AIDS* 9 (3): 306–8.

Choi, Kyung-Hee, Chong-Suk Han, Esther Sid Hudes, and Susan Kegeles. 2002. Unprotected sex and associated risk factors among young Asian and Pacific Islander men who have sex with men. *AIDS Education and Prevention* 14 (6): 472–81.

Collins, Patricia Hill. 1990. *Black feminist thought: Knowledge, consciousness, and the politics of empowerment.* New York: Routledge.

Edley, Nigel. 2001. Unravelling social constructionism. *Theory and Psychology* 11 (3): 433–41.

Ellis, Sonja J., and Celia Kitzinger. 2002. Denying equality: An analysis of arguments against lowering the age of consent for sex between men. *Journal of Community and Applied Social Psychology* 12 (3): 167–80.

Fellows, Mary Louise, and Sherene Razack. 1998. The race to innocence: Confronting hierarchical relations among women. *Journal of Gender, Race and Justice* 1 (2): 335–52.

Fuss, Diana. 1989. *Essentially speaking: Feminism, nature and difference.* New York: Routledge.

Gergen, Kenneth J. 1985. The social constructionist movement in modern psychology. *American Psychologist* 40 (3): 266–75.

– 1999. *An invitation to social construction.* London: Sage.

Grillo, Trina. 1995. Anti-essentialism and intersectionality: Tools to dismantle the master's house. *Berkeley Women's Law Journal* 1995 (10): 16–30.

hooks, bell. 2000. *Feminist theory: From margin to center.* Cambridge, MA: South End.

Kitzinger, Celia. 1992. The individuated self concept: A critical analysis of social-constructionist writing on individualism. In *Social psychology of identity and the self concept,* ed. Glynis M. Breakwell, 221–50. London: Surrey University Press.

– 1995. Social constructionism: Implications for lesbian and gay psychology. In *Lesbian, gay, and bisexual identities over the lifespan: Psychological perspectives,* ed. Charlotte Patterson and Anthony R. D'Augelli, 136–61. New York: Oxford University Press.

Kitzinger, Celia, and Sue Wilkinson. 1994. Re-viewing heterosexuality. *Feminism and Psychology* 4 (2): 330–6.

Nemoto, Tooru, Don Operario, Toho Soma, Daniel Bao, Alberto Vajrabukka, and Vincent Crisostomo. 2003. HIV risk and prevention among Asian/ Pacific Islander men who have sex with men: Listen to our stories. *AIDS Education and Prevention* 15 (Supplemental A): 7–20.

Poon, Maurice K., and Peter T. Ho. 2002. A qualitative analysis of cultural and social vulnerabilities to HIV infection among gay, lesbian, and bisexual Asian youth. *Journal of Lesbian and Gay Social Services* 14 (3): 43–78.

Razack, Sherene. 1998. *Looking white people in the eye: Gender, race, and culture in courtrooms and classrooms.* Toronto: University of Toronto Press.

Stubbs, Paul. 1993. 'Ethnically sensitive' or 'anti-racist'?: Models for health research and service delivery. In *'Race' and health in contemporary Britain,* ed. Wagar Irsan-Ullah Ahmad, 34–47. Buckingham, UK: Open University Press.

Weisstein, Naomi. 1993. Power, resistance, and science: A call for a revitalized feminist psychology. *Feminism and Psychology* 3 (2): 239–45.

Wilkinson, Sue. 1997. Prioritizing the political: Feminist psychology. In *Critical social psychology,* ed. Thomas Ibáñez and Lupicinio Íñiguez 178–94. Thousand Oaks, CA: Sage.

PART FIVE

Afterword

Chapter 20

Contemplating New Spaces in Canadian Studies

MINELLE MAHTANI AND DAVID ROBERTS

Filipinos in Canada: Disturbing Invisibility is a wide-ranging collection that poses provocative questions for the future of Filipina/o Canadian studies and Canadian studies more broadly. In a volume that brings together disparate yet interconnected themes including, but not limited to, issues of difference, recognition, gender, labour, representation, and youth subjectivities, *Filipinos in Canada* provides a contemporary snapshot of the many varied ways that Filipina/o Canadians challenge and contest the quintessentially myopic mythology of the Canadian nation-state.

Particularly exciting to us are the contributions from up-and-coming graduate students who represent the next generation of scholars concerned with situating a decidedly Filipina/o Canadian perspective into existing debates about racialized lives in a Canadian context. The book is also marked by an innovative structure. In its efforts to include art, along with poignant artist statements, and accompanying commentaries from key figures in the Filipina/o Canadian academic arena conversing with various chapters of the book, *Filipinos in Canada* offers a dynamic investigation into what it means to be Filipina/o Canadian in the contemporary Canadian nation-state.

The volume also represents a 'coming of age' of Filipina/o Canadian studies in some respects, as it is the first time that we have seen so many chapters dealing squarely with the lives of Filipina/o Canadians within one book. This holds the possibility of informing a transformative politics for Canadian studies. In this Afterword, we offer a brief meta-commentary on the volume without speaking to each and every one of the chapters, as that would be virtually impossible.

Instead, we gesture to the intellectual and political interventions that the contributors make across various fields, especially pertaining to Canadian studies. We suggest that the book marks an important intervention for this growing subdiscipline. Drawing from a critique of a *Globe and Mail* article, we will point to future directions that this book illuminates for a politically progressive Canadian studies epistemology.

Mediating Representations of Filipina/o Canadian Identity: No Surprise

To begin, we want to juxtapose this volume with an article that appeared in the *Globe and Mail,* one of Canada's largest national newspapers, on immigration and multiculturalism on October 6, 2010. The article challenged readers to choose an immigrant for Canada based on fictional profiles of prospective immigrants. Each profile was accompanied by an assessment by two 'experts' on whether the prospective immigrant was a 'good choice' for Canada.

One of the five potential immigrant stories included was that of Maricel, a forty-year-old woman from the Philippines. Readers were given the following scant description to determine if she would be an immigrant 'good enough' for Canada:

> Maricel has an offer to work as a live-in nanny for an Anglophone family in Montreal. Working abroad is her only option for lifting her own family out of poverty: Her husband has been unemployed for the past year and their two children's education is suffering. But Maricel is worried about the toll the separation would take on her family. After two years in Canada, she would start the process of bringing over her husband and kids. Maricel speaks fluent English and is a nurse. Deeply Catholic, she hopes to find a church and make new friends. (Mahoney 2010b, A17)

Based on this coarse excerpt, readers were invited to judge if Maricel was a worthy candidate for potential Canadian citizenship in their eyes. Within the context of this book, it will probably come as no surprise that the *Globe and Mail* made the decision to include a Filipina/o nanny as a prospective immigrant in their series, nor will it be shocking to discover that they asked readers to rely on only a sparse account of her life in order to make a call as to whether she was worthy of a Canadian passport.

While some of us may not be surprised by the tacit way that the *Globe* continues to promote dangerous tropes about Filipina Canadians, what is surprising is that this kind of representation, both in the *Globe and Mail* and in Canadian society more broadly, continues to be tolerated. However, Katherine McKittrick (2006), in her book *Demonic Grounds: Black Women and the Cartographies of Struggle,* offers insight into the ways we make sense of the idea of surprise in the Canadian context. McKittrick encourages us consider how the element of surprise can be understood as materially manifest within a social and political landscape of Canada that 'presumes – and fundamentally requires – that subaltern populations have no relations to the production of space' (92). She claims, 'these people, places, events and activities are not "Canada," and contradict Canada: they are *surprises,* unexpected and concealed' (ibid., emphasis added). Within the discursive strategy of the *Globe and Mail*'s series, the Filipina experiences a socio-spatial exclusion and objectification within the pages of the newspaper and is narrowly positioned as outside of the nation-state in this very short excerpt; such representations work to sustain a particular kind of geographic marginalization.

As many of the chapters point out in this volume, the dominant popular depiction of Filipina/os in Canada is as live-in caregivers – a depiction that has wide-ranging implications for understanding Filipina/o connections to Canada, as well as its economy and politics. This narrow representation of Filipina/os in Canada as nannies or other caregivers – a common portrayal not only in the media but also in the preponderance of academic writing on Filipina/os in Canada – ignores the complexity of Filipina/o identities within Canada. In the process, it makes other identities, such as entrepreneurs of ethnic businesses, invisible or excluded from conversations, political organizing, academic discussions, and recognition as possible components of the Canadian state. What this depiction does is effectively portray Filipina/os (and other racialized groups) as always already 'not quite Canadian.' This is the discursive terrain against which the contributors are writing.

It is also not surprising that the *Globe and Mail* takes a decidedly neoliberal approach by focusing on the supposed 'value' of the immigrant. In a study that we conducted (Roberts and Mahtani 2010), we looked at the discourses on immigrants and immigration found in the pages of the *Globe and Mail* from October 1, 2002 to September 30, 2006 to analyse how the paper discussed immigration within contemporary Canada. We concluded that 'despite the calls to embrace immigrants because of their contribution to Canada's well being, beneath the surface lies a much more pernicious level of discourse that persistently racializes immigrants as not-quite-Canadian' (252). We argue that despite the idealized notion that neoliberal approaches to immigration, such as those codified in the immigrant point system, allow for an even playing field where one's position in society is correlated to one's contribution, neoliberalism in Canada is thoroughly imbued with race. Yet, 'neoliberalism effectively masks racism through its value-laden moral project: camouflaging practices anchored in an apparent meritocracy, making possible a utopic vision of society that is non-racialized' (253). What is clear from this volume is that the racialization of Filipina/os in Canada continues to operate to depict Filipina/os as not-quite-Canadian. This 'constituting the immigrant as not-quite-Canadian allows for the continued disconnect between their ability to play the neoliberal game and the rewards that they receive for successful play' (ibid.).

In his book *Multicultiphobia,* Phil Ryan (2010) forcefully states that 'multiculturalism should *not* be a state of affairs in which some groups of citizens enjoy the psychic certainty that Canada is *theirs* in some special way, that they constitute the "mainstream," that those without the "ideal Canadian face," or who speak with a different accent, or who practice a different religion, are part of some different "stream" that moves alongside the mainstream' (215). In a sense, the *Globe and Mail*'s call to readers to choose an immigrant for Canada plays right into this conception that immigrants are travelling in this different stream. Filipina/o Canadians are not seen as fitting into the Canadian aesthetic, nor are they envisioned as complex individuals who contribute in fundamental ways to shaping the Canadian nation on their own terms. The authors in this volume challenge the notion that there is one way (generally as an agent of the economy) of understanding Maricel or any other Filipina/o live-in caregiver. Through providing a complex account of the nature of Filipino life in multicultural Canada, they provide insights generally unseen in media depictions.

The *Globe and Mail* combined its fictitious profiles of potential immigrants with a short editorial asking 'is immigration about the economy or nation building?' (Mahoney 2010a, A17). In this piece, Mahoney asks many questions about how immigration ought to be used in Canada: 'Is immigration about the economy or nation building? What kinds of people should we be selecting? Do we want immigrants who espouse Canadian ideals or do we tolerate them holding tight to conflicting values from back home? How will newcomers adjust to the demands of a different culture? Do they have the commitment to learn a new language or two? Does that even matter?' And, finally, 'Who would you choose?' (ibid.). Readers are left with the notion that choosing the 'right' immigrant is the key to a strong economy and to nation building, not an indication of institutional racism or prejudices for certain types of immigrants. The act of choosing the 'right' immigrant is also significantly one-sided and ignores the needs, desires, and wants of those coming to Canada. As a consequence, for many, the transition into life in Canada is far from a smooth one and often characterized by downward socio-economic mobility.

Solidarity in the Struggle?

Unfortunately the downward mobility that is highlighted by Philip Kelly and his co-authors in this volume is not unique to the experience of Filipina/o migrants to Canada. In 2007, the Colour of Justice Campaign launched the Colour of Poverty Campaign to raise public awareness of the intimate and pervasive connection between poverty and racialization in the province of Ontario, Canada. Sponsored by the Department of Canadian Heritage, the campaign brought together many key organizations serving immigrant and racialized communities in Toronto and the province of Ontario more broadly. Among the key findings of the campaign is that 'between 1980 and 2000 in Toronto, the poverty rate for the non-racialized population fell by 28%, but poverty among racialized families rose by 361%' (United Way of Greater Toronto 2004). Moreover, 'almost 3/4 of immigrants to Ontario have a university education. Many find that their training and work experience from other countries are not recognized or undervalued in Canada' (Colour of Poverty: Employment 2007). Systemically, the lack of recognition of foreign-earned degrees and other credentials, the racialization of the workforce, and other aspects of formal and informal economic policies and practices in Ontario work to de-skill immigrant workers and pigeonhole them into certain sectors of employment. For Filipina/os this process has largely directed them into caregiving fields, but the de-skilling and pigeonholing is experienced in many racialized communities in Canada. We state this not to diminish the importance of research that explores the unique and varied experiences of the Filipina/o community in Canada, but rather to point to the places where the struggle is one that is shared by many racialized immigrant groups in Canada. An understanding of a shared struggle against a common set of experiences could strategically enhance the activism at the centre of several of the chapters in this volume. While certainly the options for activism for live-in caregivers are circumscribed by the particularities of their status or lack of status in Canada, Tungohan's analysis of Filipina migrant activism in Canada provided a refreshing and needed exploration of how, despite the challenges to activism, Filipinas have fought for better working conditions and changes to policies that govern many of their experiences in Canada. Solidarity with other immigrant and racialized groups, in areas where there are overlapping struggles, could add considerable strength in the collective fight for social justice.

Whither Canadian Studies?

This volume also holds significant implications for the future of Canadian studies more broadly. Canadian studies emerged as a disciplinary field more than thirty years ago, with more than ten Canadian universities now offering undergraduate degrees in it. With partial support from the Canadian government, Canadian studies centres or programs have also been set up around the world, for instance, in Argentina, the Netherlands, South Korea, and India. There are also many institutions related to Canadian studies, including the International Council for Canadian Studies (founded in 1971), the Association for Canadian Studies (founded in 1973), the British Association for Canadian Studies (founded in 1975), and the Australia-Canadian Studies (founded in 1982).

Since its inception, however, it remains an open question what scholarship is considered part of the Canadian studies canon. Although some insist that Canadian identity remains nebulous and opaque, Canadian studies has been critiqued for its tendency to valorize particular historical repertoires that are marked by whiteness (Walcott 2000), especially related to the literary scene. This critique is well founded: one needs only to look at readings required in a 'Canadian Studies 101' course to recognize that, despite a few exotic add-ons, the majority of (especially literary) sources and authors remain white (and here we are thinking of authors like Margaret Atwood, Alice Munro, and Farley Mowat, among others). If writers of colour are invoked at all, they are often positioned on the outskirts of Canadian studies and employed to provide a surface commentary about processes of integration and social cohesion, both contentious terms for scholars working on issues of anti-racism and anti-colonialism in the Canadian context.

In his important analysis of Canadian studies, Rinaldo Walcott (2000) pushes the discipline to think beyond its racially defined borders. Although Walcott is referring here to the important contributions that blackness can make to redefine Canadian studies, what his critique does effectively is to show how Canadian studies as a disciplinary space needs to be opened up, rethought, redeveloped, and re-examined to include the perspectives of those who are positioned outside of the traditional national Canadian narrative. This volume contributes to that task, urging Canadian studies to recognize its previously delineated limitations and to move towards a new project that includes a commitment to valuing the voices of Filipina/o Canadians in their own right.

In our view, Canadian studies has experienced a form of Orientalism. Filipina/o Canadian voices have become subsumed under the rubric of Asian Canadian studies as if these voices are all one and the same. While Filipina/o Canadian voices can indeed be envisioned as part of Asian Canadian studies, and we appreciate the value of employing the label of Asian Canadian from which to speak to and about various solidarity struggles, it can also be highly problematic. Indeed, in this volume Jeffrey Aguinaldo explains that 'the term "Asian" erased the depth and specificity of [his] Filipino-ness if only to forge a coherent community.' What this book does is offer a way for Filipina/o Canadian studies to situate itself within the Canadian studies canon beyond its place in Asian Canadian studies.

In this volume, Nora Angeles asks an important reflexive question. She asks us to consider how it is that the very diasporic identities who speak here influence new and emerging scholarship, and then in turn, how this scholarship influences and shifts diasporic identities, commitments, and loyalties. Indeed, every single one of the contributions in this volume could also be located within other disciplinary spheres, including political science, sociology, and geography, as well as Filipina/o Canadian studies. But it is precisely that doubled location that is of value. These chapters do more than simply contribute to diaspora studies, transnational studies, or even Canadian studies separately.

We are also impressed with the generational impact of this volume – including established scholars who have worked on issues of race and racialization for decades, in conversation with other junior scholars. It provides a particularly potent space for cross-pollination and a remapping of Filipina/o Canadian studies beyond historically defined understandings of 'Philippine studies' (see Angeles in this volume) in the Canadian context.

This book forces Canadian studies to imagine itself beyond its continuing parochial whiteness. For Canadian studies to remain current, it must move from compartmentalizing and conflating the voices of marginalized racialized individuals towards placing differently positioned racialized voices front and centre within its analysis of the nation-state. Canadian studies would greatly benefit from opening itself up to recognize the way it has actively omitted Filipina/o Canadians. Attention to these stories would allow us to critically reconsider the contours of Canadian studies. This process can perhaps be informed by the ways that American studies is currently undergoing revitalization, working to include racialized voices towards a more politically progressive epistemological landscape.

Future Directions

While we appreciate the contribution of this volume to the conversations around immigrant justice, multiculturalism in Canada, and representations of Filipina/os in the media and scholarship, we want to point out some future directions for work in Filipina/o Canadian studies. We look forward to seeing authors in this field continue to connect the experiences that Filipina/os face in Canada to the broader context of the embeddedness of race and racialization in Canadian culture and institutions or what Goldberg (1993) refers to as the 'terrains of racialized expression, their means and modes of discursive articulation, and the exclusions they license with the view to contending and countering them' (9).

Although it is true that several of the chapters worked to provide a larger context to the experiences of Filipina/os in Canada by including analysis on the role of race within the Canadian nation-state and economy, we felt that this contextualization was done unevenly throughout the book. Policies like the Live-In Caregiver Program and other similar ones, such as the farm worker program, produce secondary classes of people with little ability to lay claim to the Canadian nation. These policies do not just complicate Filipina/o lives in Canada. They are also instrumental to the production and maintenance of an immigrant class in the service of a racialized Canadian state. Connecting the specifics of the Filipina/o Canadian experience to these broader processes of racialization and racialized dynamics of power at work in Canada would provide a fruitful basis for further analysis of the 'terrains of racialized expression' while also establishing the foundation for solidarity work with other groups that are similarly situated.

Second, we were hoping for a more concrete articulation of how to move forward armed with our much more complex understanding of the Filipina/o lives in Canada. While many of the chapters' topics require accountability and make demands on the state and civil society, some of which are presumably normative in nature, there is a paucity of concrete ideas on how this might happen or what this accountability could look like. This absence seemed especially noticeable in the sections that dealt specifically with Canadian policy, such as the Live-In Caregiver Program, where authors seemed timid about providing concrete policy recommendations, instead focusing more squarely on policy critique and analysis of the complex ways that negotiating within a particular framework affected Filipina/o lives. We understand that this was largely a conscious decision, given the complexity of political differences among Filipina/os, even those who were a part of the collective that organized this volume, as discussed in the book's first chapter. Yet, the lack of some theorization or recommendation on how to move forward, even if it is not unanimously held by Filipina/o Canadians – or even among the scholars whose thoughts and ideas are documented in this text – was a rather glaring absence given the topics tackled by the authors.

Finally, perhaps the biggest elephant in the room is that this work is written against and within the context of the present and ongoing colonialism of Canada as a white settler society. What might be Filipina/o Canadians' roles in dismantling ongoing racial violence in the lives of Aboriginal peoples in Canada? How can Filipina/o Canadians, given their complex transnational role and relationships with other colonizing societies, such as Spain and the United States, understand and consider their relationship with Canadian First Nations? How might this complicate the types of activism and thinking around social justice that would likely form the basis of a way forward or a next step with this analysis? How can Filipina/o Canadians integrate understandings of the Canadian state as a white settler nation into their conceptions of identity? These questions are at the very root of a collective struggle for social justice in Canada and will lead us into new collective spaces for a progressive politics in Filipina/o Canadian studies.

REFERENCES

Colour of Poverty Fact Sheets: Employment. 2007. September 4. Retrieved January 24, 2011 from http://cop.openconcept.ca/sites/colourofpoverty.ca/files/FactSheet_5_Employment.pdf.

Goldberg, David Theo. 1993. *Racist culture: Philosophy and the politics of meaning*. Oxford: Blackwell.

Mahoney, Jill. 2010a. Is immigration about the economy or nation building? *Globe and Mail*, 6 October, A17.

– 2010b. Which immigrant would you choose for Canada? *Globe and Mail*, 6 October, A17.

McKittrick, Katherine. 2006. *Demonic grounds: Black women and the cartographies of struggle* Minneapolis: University of Minnesota Press.

Roberts, David, and Minelle Mahtani. 2010. Neoliberalizing race, racing neoliberalism: Placing 'race' in neoliberal discourses. *Antipode* 42 (2): 248–57.

Ryan, Phil. 2010. *Multicultiphobia*. Toronto: University of Toronto Press.

United Way of Greater Toronto. 2004. *Poverty by postal code: The geography of neighbourhood poverty, 1981–2001*. Toronto: UWGT/CCSD.

Walcott, Rinaldo, ed. 2000. *Rude: Contemporary Black Canadian cultural criticism*. Toronto: Insomniac.

Contributors

Jeffrey P. Aguinaldo is Assistant Professor of Sociology at Wilfrid Laurier University. After receiving his PhD in Public Health, he served as a research officer at the University of Toronto's Dalla Lana School of Public Health. He pursues research in conversation analysis, critical public health, and gay men's health. His contribution to this edition was written while he was a visiting professor in the Department of Sociology, University of California at Santa Barbara.

Leonora C. Angeles is Associate Professor at the School of Community and Regional Planning and the Women's and Gender Studies Undergraduate Program at the University of British Columbia. She is also faculty research associate at the UBC Centre for Human Settlements, where she has been involved in a number of applied research and capacity-building research projects in Brazil, and in Vietnam and other Southeast Asian countries.

Mila Astorga-Garcia is Research Co-ordinator of the Community Alliance for Social Justice and Managing Editor of the *Philippine Reporter*. Her community-based research has focused on social justice and human rights issues in the Filipino community, particularly on youth-policing issues; the Live-In Caregiver Program; and access to trades and professions. Her broader policy research encompasses current social development issues and strategic policy approaches applicable to large urban municipalities.

Christine Balmes was born in Quezon City, Philippines, and moved to Canada with her family in 1998. She is currently a member of the performance collective Santa Guerrilla. She is pursuing her master's degree in Adult Education and Community Development at OISE University of Toronto. She received her Bachelor of Arts (Honours) in Asian Studies at the University of Michigan.

John Paul C. Catungal was born in Manila, Philippines, and raised in Greater Vancouver. He received his BA (Honours) from Simon Fraser University and an MA from the University of Toronto, and he is currently a PhD candidate in Geography and Planning at the University of Toronto. His dissertation research on the nexus of racial, sexual, and health politics investigates how place, difference, and community are negotiated in and through the work of Toronto-based ethno-specific HIV/AIDS service organizations.

Roland Sintos Coloma is Associate Professor in the Department of Humanities, Social Sciences and Social Justice Education and Co-Director of the Centre for Integrative Anti-Racism Studies at OISE University of Toronto. His research and teaching focus on history, cultural studies, and social theory; race, gender, and sexuality; transnationalism, empire, and diaspora. The editor of *Postcolonial Challenges in Education* (2009), he is working on a book manuscript entitled *Empire and Education: Schooling Subjects in American Philippines.*

The **Community Alliance for Social Justice,** established in 2004, is a Toronto-based organization of Filipino community groups and individuals dedicated to advancing social justice through research, advocacy, education, and community action.

Celia Correa is a Filipina visual artist living and working in Toronto. She is currently a staff member at OISE University of Toronto. She has joined group exhibits in Toronto since 2006 and had her first solo exhibit Mga Pinay sa Diaspora (Filipinas in the Diaspora) in 2009 at Nineveh Artspace in the Philippines. In her figurative paintings she explores issues of migration, marginality, estrangement, and dislocation, as well as the triviality/strength of the ordinary in any location.

Jean Marc Daga, also known as Tha Dagamuffin or Dags, is a community organizer and spoken word rap artist. He is a member of SIKLAB Ontario (Advance and Uphold the Struggle of Filipino Canadian Workers), one of the organizations housed under the Magkaisa Centre in Toronto, and is a member of the Congress of Progressive Filipino Canadians. Through his music and poetry, he aims to empower people and bring about social change.

Valerie G. Damasco is a PhD candidate in the Adult Education and Community Development Program at the University of Toronto. Her PhD research builds on her master's research on Filipino nurses, including her aunt, who migrated to Toronto in the early 1960s. Her doctoral research is funded by the Social Sciences and Humanities Research Council. The daughter of Filipino immigrants, Valerie was born in Toronto in 1981 and brings to bear her grounded experiences in conducting this research.

Lisa M. Davidson is a PhD candidate in the Department of Anthropology at the University of Toronto. She completed her BA (Honours) at the University of British Columbia and master's degree at the University of Toronto. Her PhD dissertation research considers the relationship between Christian (multi)ethnic churches and the production of multi-cultural ethics among and between racial communities in Ontario.

Conely de Leon is a PhD candidate in the School of Women's Studies at York University. She received her Master of Arts in Sociology and Equity Studies in Education and Women and Gender Studies at the University of Toronto, and her Bachelor of Arts (Honours) in Women's Studies and English Language and Literature at Queen's University. Her research interests focus on critical race theory, transnational femi-nist praxis, gender and migration, and the development of Critical Filipina/o Studies in Canada.

Josephine Eric is the Executive Director of the Migrant Workers Family Resource Centre in Hamilton, Ontario, a centre created through the efforts of Filipino caregivers to provide a safe space for vulnerable groups of newcomers. She came to Canada as a nanny. She obtained her BA in Social Anthropology from the University of Calgary in Alberta in 2001. She completed her first MA in Labour Studies from McMaster University in 2007 and her second MA in Anthropology from the University of Toronto in 2011.

Enrico F. Esguerra is Vice-President for Education, Community Alliance for Social Justice, and sits on the Board of the Kababayan Community Centre. He has done research and popular education with non-government organizations and Canadian churches focused on international debt, Canadian aid to the Philippines, and migrant workers. Before coming to Canada, he taught Political Science at the University of the Philippines, where he was Senior Research Assistant at the Third World Studies Centre.

Philip F. Kelly is Associate Professor in the Department of Geography at York University. He is the Principal Investigator of the Toronto Immigrant Employment Data Initiative, and of the Filipino Youth Transitions in Canada project, both funded by SSHRC. He is author of *Landscapes of Globalization: Human Geographies of Economic Change in the Philippines* (Routledge, 2000) and co-author (with Neil Coe and Henry Yeung) of *Economic Geography: A Contemporary Introduction* (Blackwell, 2007).

Marissa Largo is a Toronto-based artist, educator, and researcher. She is a graduate of York University's Fine Arts and Education programs, has a master's degree in Art Education from Concordia University, and is currently a PhD student in the Adult Education and Community Development program at OISE University of Toronto. Her art practice, community organizing, and academic research focus on community art education, anti-racism, and arts-based research with Filipino Canadian organizations.

Minelle Mahtani is Associate Professor of Geography and Planning, and in the Program in Journalism, as well as a Senior Massey Fellow, at the University of Toronto. She is also president of the Association of Canadian Studies and a Fellow of the Royal Canadian Geography Society. Dr Mahtani's research interests include 'mixed race' identity, media and minority representation, critical journalism, and women of colour in geography.

Bonnie McElhinny is Director of the Women and Gender Studies Institute, and Associate Professor of Anthropology and Women and Gender Studies, at the University of Toronto. She is founding co-editor of the journal *Gender and Language*. Recent publications include *Words, Worlds, Material Girls: Language and Gender in a Global Economy* and articles in *American Anthropologist, Philippine Studies,* and the *Annual Review of Anthropology.* Her SSHRC-funded research focuses on historical and contemporary investigations of North American interventions into Filipino healthcare and childcare practices, and reactions and resistance to these interventions.

Maureen Grace Mendoza received her BA (Honours) in Sociology and English Literature from the University of British Columbia and her MA in Sociology from the University of Toronto. She considers her research with Filipino/a Canadian university students her most fulfilling experience relating to her community, both academically and personally. She believes that the future of Filipino/a Canadian scholarship continues to be shaped by those who bridge academe and the community, acknowledging and acting upon the community's struggles and its hopes.

Cesar Polvorosa, Jr is Professor of world geography and economics at Humber Business School and sessional faculty teaching international business at Algoma University Brampton. He is a writer, a strategic planning and socio-economic consultant, the editor of the *Canadian Business Strategist* magazine, and an advisory member of the Canadian Business Strategy Association. He was a 2008 Diaspora Dialogues' Emerging Writer for short stories. He garnered his BA (cum laude) from the University of the Philippines and his MA from the National Graduate Institute for Policy Studies in Japan. He is a PhD candidate in Geography at York University with a research focus on ethnic entrepreneurship.

Geraldine Pratt is Professor of Geography at the University of British Columbia. She has collaborated with the Philippine Women Centre of BC for the last seventeen years, researching various aspects of Canada's temporary foreign domestic worker program, including the marginalization of Filipino youth. She is author of *Working Feminism* (2004) and *Families Apart: Migrant Mothers and the Conflicts of Labor and Love* (2012), co-author of *Gender, Work and Space* (1995), and co-editor of *The Global and the Intimate: Feminism in Our Time* (2012). She co-authored *Nanay*, a testimonial play which was staged in Vancouver in February 2009 and Berlin in June 2009, and partially restaged in Edinburgh in 2012.

David Roberts is a post-doctoral fellow in the Department of Geography and Planning at the University of Toronto. His dissertation research focused on the social implications of the intense securitization of public space during the 2010 South African World Cup for marginalized members of South African society. For his master's thesis, he analysed discourses on immigration in the pages of the *Globe and Mail.*

Reuben Sarumugam is a graduate of York University with a BA (Honours) in Art History. Born in Toronto, Ontario, he was raised by his mother, who came to Canada through family sponsorship from the Philippines in the late 1970s. A member of the Magkaisa Centre since 2008, he has assisted in planning and co-ordinating countless activities and projects, including the Anti-Racism Education Research Project, Maleta (Suitcase) Project, and Roots, Rhymes and Resistance (2009 and 2010).

Carlo Sayo was thirteen when he started volunteering with the Vancouver-based Ugnayan ng Kabataang Pilipino sa Canada (Filipino Canadian Youth Alliance). A graduate of Emily Carr Institute, Sayo noted that the arts is a powerful medium for activists. A graphic designer and a poet, he is also a founding member of the Sinag Bayan (Light of the Nation) Cultural Arts Collective, a Filipino Canadian group that combines performance, theatre, song, spoken word, and visual arts to promote empowerment.

Bryan Taguba was born in the Philippines in 1986, and was sponsored into Canada along with his two brothers by their mother in 1995. The son of a domestic worker, he is interested in community-based research conducted by PWC-ON and SIKLAB-ON looking into the ways in which people immigrate into Canada and how policies affect their lives. Because of his involvement with UKPC/FCYA-ON and SIKLAB-ON since 2007, he aspires to utilize his artistic training through York University's Fine Arts program as a tool for social change and community empowerment.

Eric B. Tigley is a digital media artist and visual arts teacher, who co-founded Youth Education through Interactive Arts, a non-profit organization committed to channelling children's creative energy through contemporary and traditional art techniques. He received his Bachelor of Education from OISE University of Toronto, and his Bachelor of Fine Arts from York University. He also holds a diploma in Digital Media Arts from Seneca College. Born and raised in the Jane and Finch area of Toronto, Tigley has also worked extensively on various community art projects with the Black Creek Community Health Centre and the Jane and Finch Boys and Girls Club.

Vernon R. Totanes received his PhD in the Faculty of Information, University of Toronto, where he wrote a thesis on the history of the Filipino history book as part of the Collaborative Program in Book History and Print Culture. He is a licensed librarian with a master's degree in Library and Information Science from the University of the Philippines, and a bachelor's degree in management engineering from the Ateneo de Manila University.

Ethel Tungohan is a PhD candidate in Political Science and Women and Gender Studies at the University of Toronto. Her research interests include transnationalism, social movements, migration, and development. She previously worked as a gender, migration, and development consultant for the United Nations.

Eleanor Ty is Professor of English and Film Studies at Wilfrid Laurier University. She has published on Asian North American and on eighteenth-century literature. She is the author of *Unfastened: Globality and Asian North American Narratives* (2010), *The Politics of the Visible in Asian North American Narratives* (2004), *Empowering the Feminine: The Narratives of Mary Robinson, Jane West, and Amelia Opie, 1796–1812* (1998), and *Unsex'd Revolutionaries: Five Women Novelists of the 1790s* (1993). She co-edited, with Christl Verduyn, *Asian Canadian Writing beyond Autoethnography* (2008), and, with Donald Goellnicht, *Asian North American Identities beyond the Hyphen* (2004). She was born in Manila and moved to Canada in her teens.

Index